The Indigenous Music of Australia, Book 2

For the sake of a song

WANGGA SONGMEN AND THEIR REPERTORIES

Allan Marett
Linda Barwick
Lysbeth Ford

SYDNEY UNIVERSITY PRESS

Published 2013 by SYDNEY UNIVERSITY PRESS

©Allan Marett, Linda Barwick and Lysbeth Ford 2013

© Sydney University Press 2013

Reproduction and Communication for other purposes

Except as permitted under the Act, no part of this edition may be reproduced, stored in a retrieval system, or communicated in any form or by any means without prior written permission. All requests for reproduction or communication should be made to Sydney University Press at the address below:

Sydney University Press

Fisher Library F03, University of Sydney NSW 2006 AUSTRALIA

Email: sup.info@sydney.edu.au

National Library of Australia Cataloguing-in-Publication entry

Author:	Marett, Allan, author.
Title:	For the sake of a song: Wangga songmen and their repertories / Allan Marett, Linda Barwick and Lysbeth Ford.
ISBN:	9781920899752 (pbk.)
Series:	Indigenous music of Australia; volume 2.
Notes:	Includes bibliographical references and index.
Subjects:	Wangga--Northern Territory--Daly.
	Aboriginal Australians--Northern Territory--Daly--Music.
Other Authors/Contributors:	
	Barwick, Linda, author.
	Ford, Lysbeth Julie, author.
Dewey Number:	781.629915094295

Cover design by Miguel Yamin.

Front cover: Wagon Dumoo, composer of 'Kubuwemi', sings at a circumcision ceremony in Wadeye in 1988. Photograph by Mark Crocombe, reproduced with the permission of the Dumoo family.

Back cover: Portrait of Tommy Barrtjap (Burrenjuck), photograph by Alice Moyle, Delissaville (Belyuen), 1976. Photograph by Alice Moyle, courtesy of Alice Moyle family and AIATSIS (Moyle. A3.Cs - 6412), reproduced with the permission of Belyuen community.

for wangga *songmen*
past, present and future,
and to Frank Dumoo,
leader, mentor and friend

CONTENTS

Wangga songmen and their repertories	1
List of figures	7
List of tables	11
Preface	13
Acknowledgements	15
A note on orthography	16
How to read Marri Tjavin/Marri Ammu words	17
How to read Batjamalh words	18
How to read Emmi-Mendhe words	19
Abbreviations in morpheme-by-morpheme glosses to song-texts	20
A note on the sound recordings	21
1. A SOCIAL HISTORY OF *WANGGA*	23
2. THE MUSIC AND DANCE CONVENTIONS OF *WANGGA*	45
3. THE LANGUAGE OF *WANGGA*	65
4. BARRTJAP'S REPERTORY	93
5. MULUK'S REPERTORY	155
6. MANDJI'S REPERTORY	219
7. LAMBUDJU'S REPERTORY	239
8. THE WALAKANDHA *WANGGA* REPERTORY	281
9. THE MA-YAWA *WANGGA* REPERTORY	355
References	409
Appendix 1: Characteristics of the rhythmic modes	413
Appendix 2: List of recordings	417
About the authors	419
List of CD tracks	421

LIST OF FIGURES

Figure 1.1 Map of northwestern Australia.	24
Figure 1.2 Philip Mullumbuk and Les Kundjil sing *wangga* at Wadeye, early 1990s.	24
Figure 1.3 Dancers at a Belyuen *kapuk*.	27
Figure 1.4 Ritual washing by mourners.	28
Figure 1.5 Circumcision ceremony at Wadeye, 1988.	28
Figure 1.6 'Corroboree group' at Mandorah, 1968.	31
Figure 1.7 Charles Kungiung and Les Kundjil singing *wangga* at the funeral for Cyril Ninnal, Wadeye, 1999.	41
Figure 1.8 *Wangga* dancers painting up at Peppimenarti, 1998.	43
Figure 2.1 Summary of musical and textual structure of 'Tjerri'.	46
Figure 2.2 Unknown dance at the tourist corroboree, Mica Beach, September 1972.	47
Figure 2.3 Men and boys at Belyuen dancing at the launch of Allan Marett's book *Songs, dreamings and ghosts*, Belyuen, 2006.	51
Figure 2.4 A line of women dancing *wangga* at a circumcision ceremony in Wadeye, 1988.	50
Figure 2.5 Frank Dumoo dancing *wangga* at a Wadeye circumcision ceremony.	51
Figure 2.6 Ambrose Piarlum dancing *wangga* at a Wadeye circumcision ceremony, 1992.	51
Figure 2.7 Musical transcription of 'Tjerri'.	52
Figure 2.8 Maurice Ngulkur performing Ma-yawa *wangga* at Peppimenarti, 7 October 1998.	53
Figure 3.1 Lysbeth Ford and Kenny Burrenjuck working on Jimmy Muluk song texts, Mandorah, 1997.	66
Figure 4.1 Portrait of Tommy Barrtjap (Burrenjuck).	92
Figure 4.2 Tommy Barrtjap (seated) singing for a group of dancers at Belyuen, 1952.	95
Figure 4.3 Tommy Barrtjap standing and singing.	95
Figure 4.4 Jimmy Bandak singing at a *burnim-rag* ceremony at Bagot, 1953.	130
Figure 4.5 Kenny Burrenjuck singing for the launch of Lysbeth Ford's Batjamalh dictionary, Belyuen, 1997.	145
Figure 5.1 Jimmy Muluk performing for tourists at Mica Beach, early 1970s.	155
Figure 5.2 Jimmy Muluk playing with Johnny Singh's band at Mica Beach, early 1970s.	156
Figure 5.3 Buffalo dance at the tourist corroboree, Mica Beach, September 1972.	158
Figure 5.4 The 'Buffalo' chases a dancer up a tree at the tourist corroboree, Mica Beach, September 1972.	158
Figure 5.5 Numbali, dancing at the tourist corroboree, Mica Beach, September 1972.	175
Figure 5.6 Henry Jorrock performing a standing version of the number four leg pose, Belyuen, 1997.	179

Figure 5.7 This picture from a tourist corroboree, Mica Beach, September 1972, may show the dance for 'Lame Fella'. 192

Figure 6.1 Tourist corroboree group at Mandorah, 1968. 218

Figure 6.2 Billy Mandji's daughter, Marjorie Bilbil, helps Allan Marett and Lysbeth Ford to write down texts of Billy Mandji songs, Mandorah, 1997. 218

Figure 6.3 Les Kundjil (pictured here in Wadeye, 1999). 220

Figure 6.4 Colin Worumbu, son of Billy Mandji, teaches Allan Marett to sing one of his songs, at AIATSIS conference, Canberra, 2001. 220

Figure 6.5 Billy Mandji's grandson Ian Bilbil plays kenbi (didjeridu) for Kenny Burrenjuck at Belyuen, 2006. 224

Figure 7.1 Bobby Lambudju Lane at Indian Island, 1989. 239

Figure 7.2 Tourist corroboree performers at Mandorah, 1987. 240

Figure 7.3 Colin Worumbu singing 'Rak Badjalarr' at Mandorah, 1997. 248

Figure 7.4 Women at Belyuen, including Lambudju's daughters, dancing at the launch of Allan Marett's book, Belyuen, 2006. 265

Figure 7.5 Roger Yarrowin leads the dancing at Belyuen to celebrate the 2006 launch of Allan Marett's book *Songs, dreamings and ghosts*. 273

Figure 7.6 Bobby Lane and Benmele Rusty Benmele Moreen singing *wangga* at Belyuen in 1979. 275

Figure 8.1 Large group of Walakandha *wangga* dancers including Les Kundjil, Maurice Ngulkur Warrigal Kungiung and Philip Mullumbuk. 281

Figure 8.2 Edward Nemarluk, Tommy Moyle and John Chula dancing, Wadeye, 1988. 288

Figure 8.3 Some of the main contributors to the 'golden age' of the Walakanda *wangga*. 302

Figure 8.4 Wagon Dumoo, composer of 'Kubuwemi', sings at a circumcision ceremony in Wadeye in 1988. 303

Figure 8.5 Philip Mullumbuk, Les Kundjil and Colin Worumbu sing Walakandha *wangga* for a circumcision ceremony at Wadeye, 1997. 324

Figure 8.6 Charles Kungiung, Wadeye, 1999. 325

Figure 8.7 Les Kundjil singing Walakandha *wangga* for Allan Marett, Wadeye, 1998. 327

Figure 8.8 Philip Mullumbuk singing his *wangga* for Allan Marett, Wadeye, 1999. 328

Figure 8.9 Ambrose Piarlum singing 'Tjinmel' for Allan Marett, Wadeye, 1998. 343

Figure 9.1 The originator of the Ma-yawa *wangga* repertory, Charlie Niwilhi Brinken at Wadeye, 1988. 355

Figure 9.2 A bark painting by Charlie Niwilhi Brinken, showing Ma-yawa dancing in ceremony. 356

Figure 9.3 Maurice Tjakurl Ngulkur taking a break from performing *wangga* for Allan Marett, Wadeye, 1999. 357

Figure 9.4 Maurice Tjakurl Ngulkur dances to the Walakandha *wangga* at a circumcision ceremony in Wadeye in 1988. 361

Figure 9.5 A bark painting by Charlie Niwilhi Brinken, depicting a Ma-yawa ancestor. 364

Figure 9.6 The cliffs at Karri-ngindji. 389

Figure 9.7 Maurice Ngulkur points out Na-Pebel to Allan Marett, 1999. 396

Figure 9.8 Maurice Ngulkur shows Allan Marett a dilly bag, *pebel*. 398

Figure 9.9 A bark painting by Charlie Niwilhi Brinken. 402

LIST OF TABLES

Table 1.1 Main recordings of Belyuen singers, by repertory, 1948–2008.	34
Table 1.2 Main recordings of Wadeye *wangga* singers, by repertory, 1954–2009.	40
Table 2.1 Summary of rhythmic mode terminology, showing associated features of tempo and clapstick beating patterns.	48
Table 2.2 Measured rhythmic modes by tempo band and clapstick beating style.	48
Table 2.3 Text of 'Tjerri' as performed by Ngulkur in chapter 9, track 13.	53
Table 2.4 Distribution of melodic mode across the six repertories.	58
Table 2.5 Tempo bands by repertory.	59
Table 2.6 Proportional use of the various tempo bands across repertories.	59
Table 2.7 Proportional use of the various clapstick patterns across repertories.	60
Table 3.1 Batjamalh consonant phonemes.	70
Table 3.2 Batjamalh vowel phonemes.	70
Table 3.3 Emmi-Mendhe consonant phonemes	78
Table 3.4 Emmi-Mendhe vowel phonemes.	78
Table 3.5 Lexical variants between Emmi and Mendhe.	79
Table 3.6 Marri Tjavin-Marri Ammu consonant phonemes.	84
Table 3.7 Marri Tjavin-Marri Ammu vowel phonemes.	84
Table 3.8 Lexical variants between Marri Ammu and Marri Tjavin.	84
Table 4.1 Songs from the Barrtjap repertory discussed in this chapter.	94
Table 4.2 Rhythmic modes used in Barrtjap's repertory.	150
Table 5.1 Songs from Jimmy Muluk's repertory discussed in this chapter.	157
Table 5.2 Rhythmic modes used in Jimmy Muluk's repertory.	211
Table 5.3 Rhythmic modes in Jimmy Muluk's performance of 'Puliki' (track 1).	215
Table 5.4 Rhythmic mode use within vocal sections of all five items of 'Piyamen.ga'.	217
Table 6.1 Songs from Billy Mandji's repertory discussed in this chapter.	221
Table 6.2 Rhythmic modes in Billy Mandji's repertory.	235
Table 7.1 Songs from Lambudju's repertory discussed in this chapter.	241
Table 7.2 Rhythmicmodes performed by Lambudju.	277
Table 7.3 Melodic modes and attributions of songs	278
Table 7.4 Rhythmic mode in six versions of Lambudju's song 'Rak Badjalarr'.	279
Table 7.5 Rhythmic mode in four modern performances of Lambudju's songs.	280
Table 8.1 Songs from the Walakandha *wangga* repertory discussed in chapter 8.	284

Table 8.2 The Walakandha *wangga* repertory subdivided on the basis of text structure. 347

Table 8.3 Rhythmic modes in the early and transitional period Walakandha *wangga*. 347

Table 8.4 Rhythmic modes used in the later Walakandha *wangga* (1986–2000). 349

Table 8.5 Melodies and modal series used in the vocal sections of Walakandha *wangga*. 350

Table 9.1 Songs from the Ma-yawa *wangga* repertory discussed in chapter 9. 358

Table 9.2 Rhythmic modes used in the Ma-yawa *wangga*. 405

Table 9.3 The melodies of the Ma-yawa *wangga*. 407

PREFACE

Why, a reader might ask, do we need another book on *wangga*? Surely Marett's volume *Songs, dreamings and ghosts* published in 2005 has already covered this topic fairly exhaustively. The answer is that the present volume, *For the sake of a song: wangga songmen and their repertories,* is a quite different type of book. *Songs, dreamings and ghosts* focused on showing how, in specific performative moments, performances of *wangga* enact important cosmological, political and personal themes. Insight into these enactments and articulations was sought, through analysis, in the very fabric of the music and dance. Marett showed precisely how singers manipulate performative conventions in order to enact a variety of ontological and cosmological themes, and in order to respond to the personal and political exigencies of the moment. For this reason *Songs, dreamings and ghosts* dealt with only a relatively small number of performances—around twenty—albeit in exhaustive detail. The interpretation of these rested, however, on an understanding of the conventions of music and dance, which in turn rested on the analysis of a much greater body of songs. The vast majority of this larger body of *wangga* songs never made its way into *Songs, dreamings and ghosts*.

By contrast, *For the sake of a song* presents this larger body of material—more than 100 songs, recordings, transcription of texts, linguistic glosses, translation of texts and exegesis. The result of twenty years' work by Marett, Barwick and Ford, it does not attempt the detailed musical analysis undertaken in *Songs, dreaming and ghosts* but rather presents at least one example of almost every *wangga* song recorded in the Daly region over the past 35 years or so and locates each within the broad context of *wangga* musical style.[1]

In addition, the repertories of two important singers, Jimmy Muluk and Billy Mandji, neither of whom were included in *Songs, dreamings and ghosts,* are examined here. On the other hand, recordings of *wangga* composed outside the Daly region—songs from the Beswick/Barunga area or the Kimberley—are not included here. These more marginal songs that were composed in the wider diaspora were dealt with in some detail in *Songs, dreamings and ghosts*.

The recordings, texts, glosses and translations in *For the sake of a song* form the core of the volume. They are preceded by an outline of the broader historical and ceremonial contexts of *wangga* and a summary of its main musical and linguistic characteristics.

In the years since the publication of *Songs, dreamings and ghosts*, Marett's relationship with the *wangga* tradition has changed in significant ways. Up until 2005, he had been invited to perform as a singer only in informal contexts and in minor celebrations such as CD launches or the opening of the Belyuen sound archive. This changed in 2007 when he was invited by Kenny Burrenjuck to join him as the second singer at the funeral service for an important Marranungu elder, and two years later he was invited by the family to perform at her final rites with singers of the Walakandha *wangga* repertory. After only a year singing with Burrenjuck, Marett found himself performing and at times leading the singing for the final mortuary rites (*kapuk* or *burnim-rag* ceremony) for Kenny Burrenjuck himself, who had tragically passed away during the previous year (Barwick & Marett, 2011; Marett, 2010). This experience of performing, rather than writing about, the ritual in which songs given by the dead are sung by the living in order to send the deceased into the company of the ancestors, was profound, and represents a major realignment with the tradition. While he has chosen not to write

---

1 Apart from a few rare exceptions, songs from earlier recordings, for example those made at Belyuen by Hemery (1942) Simpson (1948) and Elkin (1948–52) as well as those made by Stanner at Port Keats in 1954, have not been included, largely because of the difficulties of documenting the songs so long after the event. *Wangga* is a dynamic tradition in which few songs survive beyond a couple of generations.

about this experience in any detail in the present volume, something of this experience will inevitably have flowed into these pages.

The loss of Kenny Burrenjuck in his late 50s underscores yet again the fragility of traditions such as *wangga* and the urgency of not only documenting them for future generations of both Aboriginal and non-Aboriginal Australians, but also positioning them as integral, but as yet unrecognised, treasures of the world's intangible cultural heritage. Everything we know about the history of *wangga* suggests that it was always a tradition in which new songs were dreamt as others became forgotten; but in recent decades, songs that are lost are not replaced at anything like the same rate, so that over the period covered by this book whole repertoires have been lost. But the loss of songs and dances, of repertoires and ceremonies, is more than just a cultural loss. It has practical implications for the health outcomes of Indigenous Australians and for closing the gap in life expectancy between the indigenous and non-indigenous population. Tragically, almost every voice that you will hear in this book is that of a ghost. These ghostly voices call on us to do whatever is necessary to ensure that the extraordinarily powerful and beautiful, but frighteningly endangered, traditions of Aboriginal song and dance are not lost to future generations. The title of the volume, *For the sake of a song*—an English translation of the Batjamalh term *bangany-nyung* which occurs in the songs of both Barrtjap (chapter 4, track 3) and Lambudju (chapter 7, track 1)—expresses the commitment of the *wangga* songmen, their families and communities, and the authors, to upholding the knowledge, skills and values embodied in the these repertoires. It is in this spirit that we dedicate our book, the second volume in the National Recording Project's series, *The Indigenous music of Australia*, to the *wangga* songmen, of the past, present and future, and to the great late Marri Tjavin ceremonial leader, Frank Dumoo, who has inspired, encouraged and guided our work over several decades.

ACKNOWLEDGEMENTS

Our greatest debt of gratitude is to the *wangga* songmen and to Frank Dumoo, who, as the senior ritual leader for *wangga*, has generously guided our work over several decades. At Belyuen, we thank Tommy Barrtjap, Billy Mandji, Bobby Lambudju Lane, Kenny Burrenjuck, Timothy Burrenjuck, Roger Yarrowin, Simon Moreen; and at Wadeye and Peppimenarti, Thomas Kungiung, Maurice Ngulkur, Les Kundji, Philip Mullumbuk, Charles Kungiung, Ambrose Piarlum (all of Wadeye), Colin Worumbu Ferguson (Belyuen and Wadeye) and Martin Warrigal Kungiung (Peppimenarti). We would also like to thank the didjeridu players, Robert Daly (Peppimenarti), Nicky Jorrock, Ian Bilbil and Peter Chainsaw (Belyuen), and at Wadeye Gerald Longmair and Columbanus Warnir.

At Belyuen, Esther Burrenjuck, Alice Jorrock, Marjory Bilbil, Agnes Lippo, Audrey Lippo, Ruby Yarrowin and Theresa Timber have assisted in the translation, explication of text and in innumerable other ways. Without their ongoing support and support from the families of singers, our task would have been impossible. Particular thanks are due to Daniel and Lorraine Lane, and to Cathy Winsley.

At Wadeye, Marie Long, Jennie Jongmin, Mary Jongmin, Ruth Parmbuk, Patrick Nudjulu, John Chula, Laurence Kolumboort, Elizabeth Cumaiyi, Mary Magdalene (Manman) Birrarri, Rita Tharwul, Gypsy Jinjair, John Nummar, Pius Luckan, Clement Tchiburur, Benedict Tchinburur, Leo Melpi, Leon Melpi, Mercy Melpi, Martin Mullumbuk and Mary and Felix Bunduck all assisted our research and provided ongoing encouragement and support. Also at Wadeye, Mark Crocombe, Director of the Wadeye Aboriginal Language Centre and Curator of the Yile Kanamgek Museum, has provided ongoing support and advice over many years.

We are grateful to all the recordists and photographers and their families who have given us permission to reproduce the sound recording that are so integral to this publication. These are acknowledged individually in the text where relevant. We are particularly grateful to the family of Alice Moyle, and in particular her daughter, Carolyn Lowry, for granting us permission to publish, without fees, Moyle's invaluable body of *wangga* recordings. We are also grateful to Mrs Patricia Stanner for permission to publish excerpts from the field notebooks of her late husband, W.E.H Stanner.

We are grateful for to the Australian Institute of Aboriginal and Torres Strait Islander Studies for waiving publication fees for recordings and photographs reproduced in this volume. Particular thanks go to Russ Taylor, Grace Koch, Alana Harris and Luke Taylor. We are also grateful to Sotheby's for permission to publish reproductions of Charlie Niwilhi Brinken's paintings. Our friend and colleague Dr Payi Linda Ford has provided valuable feedback on our manuscript at various stages.

Thanks to the editorial and production staff at PARADISEC: Amanda Harris, Diego Mora, and Frank Davey; and in earlier years, sound engineering provided by Jim Franklin.

We're deeply grateful to Ross Coleman, Susan Murray-Smith and Sten Christensen at Sydney University Press for responding so enthusiastically when this publication project was first mooted. From them, and also from Agata Mrva-Montoya (our editor) and Gary Browne (our web designer) we have received unfailing support and endless patience throughout the gestation of this long and technically challenging book.

The work presented here has been supported over the years by a series of grants from the Australian Research Council, the Australian Institute of Aboriginal and Torres Strait Islanders Studies, the Hong Kong Research Grants Committee, the Hans Rausing Endangered Languages Project, and the University of Sydney.

A NOTE ON ORTHOGRAPHY

The spelling system for Marri Tjavin and Marri Ammu, which are closely related dialects of the same language, has been developed by Lysbeth Ford in consultation with the staff of the Wadeye Language Centre and the teacher aides at the Wadeye school. The spelling system for Emmi and Mendhe, which are closely related dialects of the same language, and for Batjamalh were also developed by Lysbeth Ford in consultation with fluent speakers at Belyuen.

HOW TO READ MARRI TJAVIN-MARRI AMMU WORDS

Vowel	Marri Tjavin-Marri Ammu	English (Standard Australian unless otherwise stated)
middle **i**	n**i**din (country)	b**i**t
end **i**	wud**i** (water)	sk**i**
u	k**u**wa (he/she stands)	p**u**t
a	m**a**-yawa (Marri Ammu ancestor)	b**u**t
e	y**e**ndili (place name)	b**e**t
Consonant		
t	**t**itil (clapstick)	**t**ar
d	ni**d**in (country)	hi**d**
rt	**rt**adi (back, on top)	American English "pa**rt**"
th	**th**anggurralh (Marri Ammu and Marri Tjavin people)	Not in English but as in Italian "**t**u"
dh	walakan**dh**a (Marri Tjavin ancestor)	an**d th**is
tj	**tj**iwilirr (Hairy Cheeky Yam)	**ch**at
dj	**dj**in**dj**a (here)	**g**inger
p	**p**urangang (salt water)	**p**ut
b	**b**ugim (white)	**b**ut
k	**k**uwa (he/she stands)	**c**ut
g	**g**apil (big)	**g**ut
rz	**rz**amu (sea turtle)	Dr. **Zh**ivago
sj	gi**sj**i (like this)	fu**s**ion
v	**v**erri (foot)	**v**ery
n	**n**idin (country)	**n**ut
ny	pumini**ny** (spring)	o**ni**on
m	**m**ana (brother)	**m**ud
ng	**ng**ata (house)	si**ng**
l	wu**l**umen (old man)	ho**l**y
lh	kavu**lh** (he/she lies down)	stea**lth**
rr	ve**rr**i (foot)	trilled *r* as in Scottish "spo**rr**an"
r	ye**r**i (child)	ve**r**y
y	**y**eri (child)	**y**es
w	**w**udi (fresh water)	**w**et

HOW TO READ BATJAMALH WORDS

Vowel	Batjamlh	English (Standard Australian unless otherwise stated
middle **i**	y**i**ne (what?)	b**i**t
end **i**	nga-m**i** (I sit)	sk**i**
u	nya-m**u** (sit!)	p**u**t
a	y**a**garra (Oh no!)	b**u**t
e	w**e**rret (quick)	b**e**t
ü	tj**ü**t (foot)	f**ew**
Consonant		
t	**t**jüt (foot)	cu**t**
d	**d**awarra (belly)	**d**ot
tj	ba**tj**amalh (language)	ba**tch**
dj	ba**dj**alarr (place)	ba**dge**
p	nga-**p**-**p**indja-ng	ha**pp**y
b	**b**angany (song)	**b**ut
k	ma**k**a (for; perfective marker)	la**cqu**er
g	ya**g**arra (Oh no!)	bu**gg**er
v	nga-**v**e (I go)	ha**v**ing
n	**n**üng (him)	**n**ut
ny	**ny**ung (for)	o**ni**on
m	**m**aka (for; perfective marker)	**m**ud
ng	**ng**a-mi (I sit)	si**ng**
l	badja**l**arr (place)	ho**l**y
lh	batjama**lh** (language)	stea**lth**
rr	badjala**rr** (place)	trilled *r* as in Scottish "spo**rr**an"
r	**r**ak (patri-country)	ve**r**y
y	**y**agarra (Oh no!)	**y**es
w	**w**erret (quick)	**w**et

HOW TO READ EMMI-MENDHE WORDS

Vowel	Emmi-Mendhe	English (Standard Australian unless otherwise stated)
middle **i**	-p**i**t (clean)	b**i**t
end **i**	endhen**i** (now)	sk**i**
u	g**u**mbu (foot)	p**u**t
ö	m**ö**rö (buttock)	w**o**rd
a	m**a**ndha (throat/ song)	b**a**t
e	d**e**rr (native bee; policeman)	b**e**t
Consonant		
t	-**t**it (bend)	**t**ar
d	**d**örr (ground)	hi**d**
rt	**rt**edi (back, on top)	American English "pa**rt**"
th	**th**awara (mangrove)	Not in English but as in Italian "**tu**"
dh	**dh**err (cheek)	and **th**is
tj	**tj**elmundak (garfish)	**ch**at
dj	**dj**e**dj**et (sit down)	**g**inger
p	**p**öndör (elbow)	**p**ut
b	-**b**et (open)	**b**ut
k	**k**uman (he/she pokes)	**c**ut
g	**g**ulukguluk (cough)	**g**ut
rz	-we**rz**ame (shriek)	Dr. **Zh**ivago
sj	mu**sj**ulng (swag)	fu**s**ion
v	**v**iye (head)	**v**ery
n	**n**a (he/him)	**n**ut
ny	-gurri**ny** (belonging to)	o**ni**on
m	**m**ana (older brother (M))	**m**ud
ng	**ng**any (I/me)	si**ng**
l	me**l**e (older brother (E))	ho**l**y
lh	**lh**umbu (leg)	stea**lth**
rr	-wu**rr**i (to speaker)	trilled *r* as in Scottish "spo**rr**an"
r	ma**r**i (belly)	ve**r**y
y	**y**aya (s/he lies down)	**y**es
w	**w**öröör (mudcrab (M))	**w**et

ABBREVIATIONS IN MORPHEME-BY-MORPHEME GLOSSES TO SONG-TEXTS

Each of the following abbreviations represents a morpheme (chunk of meaning). The morpheme-by-morpheme glosses consist of ordered strings of morphemes, each separated by a period; some morphemes are bundles of more than one chunk of meaning. For definitions of terms, see chapter 3.

Ø	Zero	NC	Noun Classifier
1	First person	O	Direct Object
1/2	First person inclusive of addressee	PERF	Perfective
2	Second person	POSS	Possessive
3	Third person	PRES	Present Tense
AUG	Augmented	PRO	Pronoun
A	Agent of transitive verb	PURP	Purposive
ABL	Ablative case marker	R	Realis
ADVERS	Adversative	REDUP	Reduplicated
ANAPH	Anaphoric	REFL	Reflexive
BEN	Benefactive	S	Subject of intransitive verb
CAUS	Causative	S/A	Form is identical for Subject or Agent
CONT	Continuant	SIM	Simultaneous
DAT	Dative	SW	Song word
DEIC	Deictic	TOP	Topic
DTOP	Different topic	UAUG	Augmented by one
EXCL	Exclusive of addressee		
F	Female		
FUL	Full of		
INC	Inclusive of addressee		
IO	Indirect Object		
IR	Irrealis		
LOC	Locative		
M	Masculine		
MIN	Minimal		
NEG	Negator		

A NOTE ON THE SOUND RECORDINGS

This book is intended to be read in conjunction with the relevant sound recordings, which are available online as virtual CDs via the website wangga.library.usyd.edu.au, as well as in a separately issued set of seven CDs (see the 'List of CD tracks' at the end of this volume). The song structure summaries in chapters 4 to 9 are intended to be read while listening to the relevant tracks.

Chapter 1
A SOCIAL HISTORY OF *WANGGA*

Wangga is a genre of public dance-song from the Daly region of northwest Australia; the country that lies to the north and south of the mouth of the Daly River (see figure 1.1). This book focuses on the songmen (*medjakarr* in Batjamalh; *ngalinangga* in Marri Tjavin) who have composed and performed *wangga* in the Daly region in the last fifty years.[1] Many of these singers are now deceased, though their descendants and heirs continue to perform the songs in ceremonies and various public events. At the core of the book is a corpus of some 150 *wangga* song texts, organised into six repertories: four from the Belyuen-based songmen Barrtjap, Muluk, Mandji and Lambudju, and two from the Wadeye-based Walakandha and Ma-yawa *wangga* groups, which are named after the ancestral song-giving ghosts of the Marri Tjavin and Marri Ammu people respectively. In this chapter we provide an introduction to *wangga* and its performance contexts, before presenting a social history for each of the main communities (Belyuen and Wadeye), and tracing the performance lineages of the repertories presented here.

In recent times *wangga* has been composed and performed primarily by people from five main language groups. Three language groups—the Wadjiginy (who speak Batjamalh), Emmiyangal (who speak Emmi) and Mendheyangal (who speak Mendhe)—live mostly at the community of Belyuen (formerly Delissaville) near Darwin, while the Marri Tjavin and Marri Ammu language groups live mainly in and around the township of Wadeye (formerly and still commonly known as Port Keats). Members of other Daly language groups—such as the Kiyuk, Marranunggu, Malak Malak, Ngen'giwumirri, Ngan'gikurunggurr, Marrithiyel, and Matige—also identify with and perform *wangga*, primarily as dancers and ceremonial participants. None of this last group of languages has, however, produced a composer or songman within the past 50 years or so.[2]

In the past, members of other language groups such as the Murriny Patha and Marri Ngarr have also performed *wangga*, but at present these groups own and perform their own genres of song and dance, primarily *djanba* and *lirrga* respectively.[3] *Wangga* has also spread beyond the Daly into areas such as the Kimberley, where it may also be referred to as *lirrga*, to southern Arnhem Land, where it is called *walaka*, and to Western Arnhem Land, where it is called *djunggurinj* (Marett, 2005, chapter 10, p 211).

---

1 There are a small number of *wangga* songmen from non-Daly language groups, who became proficient in this genre as a result of its popularity spreading beyond the Daly. Among these were Alan Maralung of Barunga and Philip Pannikin of Kununurra. Their songs are not included in this study (for further detail of *wangga* in the wider diaspora see Marett, 2005, chapter 10).

2 Marett lists a number of defunct but still remembered *wangga* repertories for groups other than the five dealt with in this book, including *wangga ma-warrgat* (Marrithiyel), *wangga ma-merren* (Ngen'giwumirri, Ngan'gikurunggurr, Marri Dan, Marri Ngarr), *wangga ma-yirri* (Matige at Yederr), *wangga ma-kinwurri* (Matige at Kuy), and *wangga kardu kunybinyi* (Murriny Patha). Information about these defunct repertories was elicited from elderly people, in many cases using archival recordings from the 1950s (Marett, 2005, p 24).

3 For further information on *djanba* see various publications by Barwick and others (Barwick, 2011; Barwick, Marett, Blythe, & Walsh, 2007; Barwick, Marett, Walsh, Reid, & Ford, 2005); and for *lirrga* see works by Barwick and Ford (Barwick, 2006; Ford, 2006).

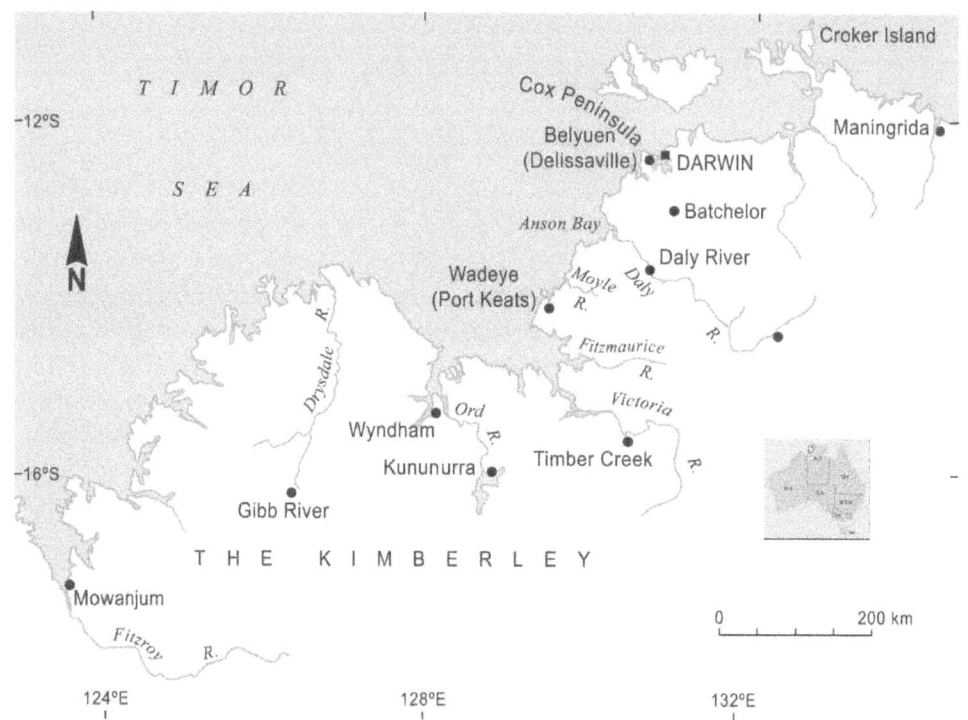

Figure 1.1 Map of northwestern Australia, showing some of the principal places where *wangga* is performed.

Figure 1.2 Philip Mullumbuk and Les Kundjil sing *wangga*, accompanied by didjeridu player Leo Melpi, during a circumcision ceremony at Wadeye, early 1990s. Photograph by Mark Crocombe, reproduced with the permission of Wadeye community.

Wangga songs are usually performed by two or more male singers who accompany themselves with clapsticks and are accompanied by another male playing didjeridu (*kenbi,* in Batjamalh and several other languages of the Daly region). Performances by a single singer are possible but not standard, because strong unisonal singing is the aesthetic ideal. Furthermore, some clapstick-beating patterns require two performers for interlocking beating patterns. The primary purpose of *wangga* is to accompany dance in ceremony, and there is a close relationship between the forms of dance and the musical form of songs. Not all performances, however, accompany dance. Singing can also accompany other ceremonial activities such as 'painting up' (the application of body paint), as well as being performed purely for entertainment.

The two principal performance occasions for *wangga* are the final mortuary rites known in Aboriginal English as *burnim-rag* and the rites by which boys are made into men by circumcising them. In the former the belongings (rags) of a deceased person are destroyed by fire and the spirit of the deceased is conducted away from the society of the living and into the society of the dead (see further below for detailed discussion of the significance of these two ceremonies). *Wangga* songs and dances are also used in a variety of other occasions such as funerals (conducted within days of a person dying, usually Christian ceremonies to which traditional elements are added), ceremonies of purification through smoking, graduation ceremonies, ceremonies for the opening of buildings, bravery awards and other occasions that require ceremonial enhancement. In addition, people perform *wangga* and listen to recordings of *wangga* purely for pleasure. It is rare in these days of television and hi-fi to hear corroborees being performed around the campfire at night, but it is common to encounter people listening to recordings of *wangga* in the home, when travelling by car, or in institutions such as pensioners' centres. Today, recordings are available in Wadeye though the Northern Territory Library and Knowledge Centre, and in Belyuen through the Belyuen Bangany *Wangga* digital archive established in 2002.

Wangga songs are given to songmen in dreams by the dead. In most cases the song-giving agents are deceased relatives of the songman (little distinction appears to be made between the transmission that occurs between a living songman and his apprentice, and between a deceased songman and a living songman). On occasion, women may dream a song, but in such cases the song will be passed to a male songman. Most *wangga* song texts are the words of the song-giving ghosts, which are initially sung to the living songman in the language of the dead, which differs from the everyday language spoken by the living. Part of the work that a living songman does is to render what he receives from the realm of the dead into a form fit for living humans. This involves translating the language of the dead into a living language such as Batjamalh or Marri Tjavin (though to varying degrees songmen may leave some text in the language of the dead, heard by the living as unintelligible vocables). The songman also shapes the musical structure into one of the forms conventionally used to accompany dance. The degree to which a song comes perfectly formed or in fragments appears to differ from songman to songman, and perhaps from one song-giving occasion to another. The fact that songmen sing the words of the dead, sometimes using the voice of a dead relative, underpins the transformative power of both mortuary and circumcision ceremonies.

Properly speaking, a singer does not become a *medjakarr* (Batjamalh for 'songman') or *ngalinangga* (Marri Tjavin) until he has composed songs of his own. Because the songs are his individual property, rights to them are inherited by his relatives (ideally, his sons). He also has the right to give or sell songs to another. For example, Lambudju gave his song 'Mubagandi' to Roger Yarrowin on the occasion of the death of Yarrowin's father (see notes to chapter 7, track 25).

Typically, *wangga* songs consist of bursts of singing (which we term 'vocal sections'), which are separated from one another by 'instrumental sections' performed by clapsticks and didjeridu. Vocal sections are accompanied by didjeridu, but not always by clapsticks. 'Unmeasured' vocal sections are accompanied only by didjeridu, while 'measured' vocal sections are accompanied by didjeridu and clapsticks. The latter are performed in a variety of tempo bands and with different beating patterns. Instrumental sections are also performed with a range of different tempi and beating patterns. The combination of tempo and beating pattern constitutes a system of rhythmic modes that correlate with different dancing styles. For a full description of overall form and the analytical terms used in this book, see chapter 2.

In chapter 3, Lysbeth Ford gives a detailed description of the five language varieties used in *wangga*: Batjamalh, Emmi, Mendhe, Marri Tjavin and Marri Ammu. All of these languages are now severely endangered. None has more than a dozen fluent speakers, and most current songmen have only imperfect command of their language. If the five languages are severely endangered then the songs in those languages are even more so. This *wangga* corpus represents an extremely valuable and fragile aspect of the Australian national heritage, and yet it constitutes only one of many highly endangered indigenous musical (and linguistic) genres nationwide (Marett, 2010; Marett & Barwick, 2003). Efforts to preserve and document this heritage before it is lost have become urgent. This book is part of a series that aims to raise the profile of the major indigenous musical traditions of northern Australia (Marett, et al., 2006).

The corpus is based on audio recordings (made mostly by Marett over a twenty-two-year period between 1986 and 2008, and supplemented by older archival recordings), all of which we have documented in collaboration with relatives of the singers. Audio examples are provided for every song text in chapters 4–9, which cover the six repertories (see p 23). Songmen for Belyuen (Delissaville) included: Tommy Barrtjap (Wadjiginy, who composed and sang in Batjamalh language), his father Jimmy Bandak and his son Kenny Burrenjuck[4] (see chapter 4); Jimmy Muluk (who composed and sang in Mendhe) (see chapter 5); Billy Mandji (Emmi and some Marri Tjavin, his ancestral language) (see chapter 6); and Bobby Lambudju Lane and Rusty Benmele Moreen (Batjamalh and some Emmi) (see chapter 7). In Wadeye (Port Keats) composers of songs in Marri Tjavin (the so-called Walakandha *wangga*) were Stan Mullumbuk, Thomas Kungiung, Wagon Dumoo, Martin Warrigal Kungiung, Les Kundjil and Philip Mullumbuk[5] (see chapter 8); and for Marri Ammu (the Ma-yawa *wangga*), Maurice Ngulkur[6] (see chapter 9). The singers alive and active today include (for Belyuen) Colin Worumbu Ferguson (Marri Tjavin, who also sings songs in Emmi, Batjamalh and Marri Ammu), Roger Yarrowin (Emmi and to a lesser extent Batjamalh) and Robert Gordon (Mendhe). Charles Kungiung (Marri Tjavin, but also sings in Marri Ammu) is now the main *wangga* singer for Wadeye.

Performance contexts for *wangga*

The principal performance context for *wangga* is the ceremony known in Aboriginal English as *burnim-rag*. This ceremony, which normally occurs in the country of the deceased between a year and two years after he or she has died, has a dual function: to release the 'sweat' or essence of a deceased person into his or her country, and to purify the environment of his or her surviving relatives. It is believed that after death the 'sweat' of the deceased remains in things that he or she had used habitually in life—bedding, clothing, treasured objects such as hunting implements, woven baskets, weapons and so on. By burning

---

4   Barrtjap's second son, Timothy Burrenjuck, also learnt this repertory and leads ceremonial performances, but has not, so far as we are aware, composed any songs of his own.

5   Wadeye resident Charles Kungiung, son of Thomas Kungiung, has recently composed songs of his own to add to this repertory, so is to be counted a composer and songman. We have not been able to work with him to document these songs, however, so they are not included in this volume.

6   Most of the Ma-yawa *wangga* repertory was composed by Charlie Niwilhi Brinken, but to our knowledge he was never recorded singing his songs. His relative Maurice Ngulkur inherited Brinken's songs and added to the repertory.

Figure 1.3 Dancers at a Belyuen *kapuk* (*burnim-rag* ceremony) for Agnes Lippo, July 1995. Photograph by Linda Barwick, reproduced with the permission of Belyuen community.

these chattels, the spirit of the deceased is forced out into the open, whence it can be coaxed, through the performance of appropriate songs and dances, to leave the society of the living and join the society of the dead. *Wangga* songs, like other genres used in *burnim-rag* ceremonies—*lirrga* and *djanba* in the case of Wadeye—play a major role in this process. Because *wangga* songs are given to humans by the ghosts of deceased relatives, and because their texts convey the utterances of the dead—either in the incomprehensible language of the dead, or in the human language of the songman—the songs reassure both the deceased and all ceremonial participants of the closeness of the world of the dead and the world of the living.

Song, dance and overall ceremonial form emulate ceremonies performed by the dead, and their enactment in ceremony has the power to temporarily close the gap between the world of the living and the dead. Thus, the singer sings as if one of the dead, using the words, melodies, rhythms and even, in some cases, the voices of song-giving ghosts. Dancers dance the dances of the dead and mingle with them in ceremony—people speak of the dead, joining the throng of dancers and dancing alongside or behind their living descendants, the footsteps of dead and living alike synchronised by the songman's clapsticks. Within this liminal space, that is both of the living and of the dead, but also of neither, the deceased is able to go and join his or her ancestors in the world of the dead and to leave human relatives in peace. At Belyuen, the ceremony is concluded by the ritual washing (*ka-puk*, literally, 'it washes') that gives the ceremony its name in that part of the world, but in other places, such as Wadeye, it concludes with purification by smoke. Once the ceremony has been completed the relatives express palpable relief that their lives and their country are no longer disturbed by the potentially troublesome and dangerous presence of a being who is between worlds and unable to complete its spiritual journey back to the totemic site from which it first emerged and to which it must return. It is after this ceremony that the name of the deceased person, which is placed under taboo after death, can again be uttered, since it no longer has the power to call the potentially dangerous spirit back into the world of the living.

Because of this strong association with death, the texts of *wangga* songs are saturated with associations with death: they are the utterances of the dead, they use the language of the dead, and

Figure 1.4 Ritual washing by mourners at the end of the *kapuk* ceremony, Belyuen, July 1995. Photograph by Linda Barwick, reproduced with the permission of Belyuen community.

Figure 1.5 Les Kundil, Thomas Kungiung, Martin Warrigal Kungiung, Maurice Ngulkur, Ambrose Piarlum (didjeridu) bringing up a boy, circumcision ceremony at Wadeye, 1988. Photograph by Mark Crocombe, reproduced with the permission of Wadeye community.

they contain metaphors referring to death, such as the going out of the tide in the Walakandha *wangga* (see chapter 8); or the intermingling of salt and fresh water in the Ma-yawa *wangga* (see chapter 9). They also contain reference to things that the living and dead share, like a deep attachment to country, and a distrust of outsiders.

At Belyuen, *wangga* is always performed for *kapuk* ceremonies, the songs usually being those from the family lineage to which the deceased belongs. Thus both the deceased and their relatives hear the voices of their ghostly ancestors emanating from the bodies of their living songmen. The names of people and places in the songs are ones with which both ceremonial participants and the deceased are intimate. The themes and underlying stories associated with the songs are theirs.

For historical reasons that will be addressed in more detail below, in Wadeye the situation is markedly different. Here themes of reciprocity between groups override those of familial intimacy. For a deceased person from the *wangga* group, it is not *wangga* songs that are sung and danced to, but rather the songs of either *lirrga*- or *djanba*-owning groups (for further information see historical discussion below). Here it is the *principle* of the human relationship to country, ancestors and totems that comes to be celebrated, rather than the specific country, ancestors and totems of the deceased.

The ceremony for making boys into men by circumcising them is the other major context in which *wangga* is performed both at Belyuen and at Wadeye.[7] The songs sung in this context are the same as those sung in the mortuary rites (Marett, 2005, p 4). The suffusion of the texts with references to death is entirely appropriate, because in this context an initiand is seen to die to his childhood and to be reborn as a man. The expression of grief, particularly from the mothers, is as dramatic and heartfelt as any encountered at mortuary ceremonies.[8]

Colin Simpson's book *Adam in Ochre* contains a vivid account of a *kapuk* mortuary ceremony that he witnessed at Belyuen (then known as Delissaville) in 1948 (Simpson, 1951). Simpson also put together an ABC radio program in which one can hear all the drama of the occasion (Simpson, 1948), which Barwick and Marett have related to another *kapuk* ceremony performed by members of the same families in 2008 (Barwick & Marett, 2011). Marett has also described in some detail a *kapuk* that he witnessed in Belyuen in 1995 (Marett, 2005, pp 68–69) as well as a *burnim-rag* ceremony that he attended at the small outstation of Nadirri in 1988 (Marett, 2005, pp 63–66). Vivid and enlightening accounts of circumcision ceremonies may be read in Furlan (Furlan, 2005), in Elkin (Elkin & Jones, 1958, pp 145–46), and in Stanner's *On Aboriginal Religion* (Stanner, 1989 [1963], pp 110–17). An abridged summary of Stanner's account occurs in *Songs, dreamings and ghosts* alongside Marett's account of the large 1988 ceremony that he attended at Wadeye (Marett, 2005, pp 72–74). Rather than reproduce these accounts here, we refer the reader to these publications.

History of *wangga*

We will now discuss the social history and main repertories of *wangga* in more detail. The two principal centres of *wangga* performance—Belyuen and Wadeye—will be treated separately because of their different histories and significant divergence within the principal rituals associated with *wangga*.

---

7   At circumcision ceremonies at Wadeye, but not Belyuen, the sister genres *lirrga* and *djanba* are performed alongside *wangga*.

8   Stanner's account of ceremonial life at Wadeye (Stanner 1989 [1963]) appears to foreground circumcision as the primary ritual context for *wangga*, but as Marett has argued elsewhere, Stanner did not actually witness any mortuary rituals, but rather compiled his account from fragmentary second-hand reports (Marett, 2005, p 60).

Social history of *wangga* at Belyuen (Delissaville) and surrounding areas

It seems likely that *wangga* has been practised in the Darwin area for a long time, if we accept that in this region the presence of didjeridu is indicative of the genre. Darwin (initially known as Palmerston) was established in 1869. Both Darwin and the Cox Peninsula, where Belyuen is located, belong to the traditional country of the Larrakiya. Etheridge cites Coppinger (1883, p 204) in reporting: 'Dr Coppinger … saw at a camp of the Larikia tribe, in the vicinity of Port Darwin, pieces of "hollow reed", about 4 feet long, that were blown "like cow horns," and produced "a rude burlesque of music"' (Etheridge, 1894, p 322).

Groups from neighbouring areas that began to gravitate towards the new settlement included the 'Waggite', who came from the coastal areas of the Daly region to the south of Darwin (the name of the group derives from the word *wagatj*, which means 'beach' in various coastal languages of the Daly region, including Batjamalh, Emmi and Mendhe). The earliest written reference to this group in the Darwin area is a report by Wildey, which records that according to the surveyors exploring the hinterland of Darwin for the overland telegraph line in 1874, 'the Waggites are located to the westward about Anson's Bay [sic]' (Ford, 1990, p 3; Wildey, 1876, p 115). Anson Bay is formed by the mouth of the Daly River and its shores include the traditional country of the Wadjiginy, Emmiyangal and Mendheyangal (speakers of Batjamalh, Emmi and Mendhe languages respectively). By 1879 there is a reference in the *Northern Territory Times and Gazette* of 3 May 1879 to a reception held by the 'Larrakeyahs' in Palmerston (Darwin), for 'their brethren from the Peninsula—the Waggites', which involved singing and dancing on the oval (Anonymous, 1879; Povinelli, 1993, p 71). Ford notes that the presence of the 'Waggites' at Point Charles on the west coast of Darwin Harbour was recorded in 1885 (1990, p 3).

In 1937, the Wadjiginy and their relations, including the Emmiyangal and Mendheyangal, were moved to the government settlement of Delissaville (now known as Belyuen), located on the Cox Peninsula on the site of a sugar plantation first established in the 1880s. By the middle of the twentieth century, the traditional country on Anson Bay was virtually depopulated. Even today, Belyuen people visit their traditional country only rarely, although a semi-permanent outstation has been established at Balgal in Wadjiginy country to the north of the Daly River, opposite Peron Island. The effect of this migration from their traditional country in the Anson Bay area has had profound effects on *wangga*: the way that songs are received, the way it forges links between people and country and the way it works in ceremony. All these in turn affect the texts and other formal elements of *wangga* at Belyuen. This matter is discussed in considerable detail in *Songs, dreamings and ghosts* (Marett, 2005, pp 32–36, 66–69, 74–75 passim).

The works of Basedow (1907), Spencer (1914), and Elkin and Jones (1958, pp 151–52) show that from very early on the Wadjiginy, Emmiyangal and Mendheyangal performed alongside the Larrakiya (traditional owners of the Cox Peninsula, where Belyuen stands) in ceremonies such as the final *kapuk* mortuary rites, as well as in male and female puberty rites, and other public occasions. Because of the settlement's proximity to Darwin, being located on the southern shore of Darwin Harbour, performers from Delissaville (Belyuen) often performed for non-Aboriginal audiences. Tourist corroborees were staged in Darwin for visiting dignitaries and cruise ships from as early as 1882 (Anonymous, 1882) and have continued since then, with the Delissaville (Belyuen) people often taking a leading role. According to Mountford's diary from 1948, the government superintendent Tom Wake encouraged performances by Delissaville people:

> Wake announced that the men were going to perform a dance for our benefit. Wake has stimulated the ceremonial life of his people, suggested that they dance [whenever] they want to, even allows them a week off from work when the initiation rituals are being carried out, and then [looks] after the circumcised boys, so that the convalescent period is much shortened.

Figure 1.6 'Corroboree group' at Mandorah, 1968, photographer unknown. Jimmy Muluk is the bearded man in the centre of the photograph. Northern Territory Library, Evan Luly collection, photo PH0784/0099, reproduced with the permission of Belyuen community.

> Although the aborigines were dancing in the first place to please Wake, it was not long before they were doing it for their own satisfaction. The performance, like every other aboriginal ceremony I have seen, was carried out with a great deal of real enthusiasm and enjoyment. (Mountford, 1948, pp 77–79)

In 1951 Aboriginal people refused the Northern Territory Administration's request to stage a corroboree in Darwin for visiting American tourists. This strike was in solidarity with the Larrikiya activist Fred Waters, who had been exiled to Central Australia for leading strikes by Aboriginal people in Darwin in support of better pay and conditions (Anonymous, 1951). But today the Kenbi Dancers, a Belyuen-based group led by Colin Worumbu Ferguson and Roger (Rossie) Yarrowin continue the tradition of performing for tourists, festivals and other public events.

When it became impossible for the Larrakiya members of the Delissaville (Belyuen) community to continue to exercise primary responsibility for ceremonies for the Cox Peninsula, this responsibility was passed on to non-Larrakiya groups there. The last Larrakiya songman, George King, is said to have died at Katherine during the Second World War.[9] Subsequently 'rights to sing some clan songs and to make songs' for the country around Belyuen were formally passed to the Wadjiginy songman Tommy Barrtjap by the Larrakiya elder, Tommy Imabulk Lyons (Brandl, Walsh, Haritos, & Northern Land Council, 1979, pp 27, 171). George King's son, Prince of Wales, was brought up by his Wadjiginy relations at Delissaville, and contemporary newspaper reports show he took an active part in ceremonial and tourist performances in the postwar period (Anonymous, 1948). In 1979 the Northern Land Council filed a land claim under the Northern Territory Land Rights Act over the Cox Peninsula, on

---

9   A recording of George King made by Peter Hemery for the ABC on 18 June 1942, probably at Delissaville, contains a number of didjeridu-accompanied songs that are clearly of the *wangga* type (Hemery, 1942). This performance reportedly occurred in front of over two hundred interested Aboriginal spectators (AM Moyle, 1966, pp 26–27). The title given for one of these songs, *Del nuk kuna*, glossed by Hemery as 'Dance of the lame man', is probably in Batjamalh: *del* is Batjamalh for 'spear', and *nguk* is 'knee'.

A social history of *wangga* • 31

which Belyuen stands, on behalf of its traditional owners, the Larrakiya people. Destined to become the longest running land rights case in Australian history, the case was finally resolved in 2000 when the Land Commissioner Justice Gray recommended that the majority of the land under claim be handed back to the traditional owners. Importantly, the judgement protected the rights of the Wadjiginy and other groups with traditional links to the Anson Bay area to remain at Belyuen.

History of the Belyuen song repertories

Four distinct song repertories or lineages[10] can be traced at Belyuen over the past five decades, two in Batjamalh, one in Mendhe, and one mainly in Emmi (with some Marri Tjavin). In the last decade, as the traditional languages have weakened and the lines of inheritance and transmission have converged, the distinctions between these repertories have been progressively eroded (Marett, 2005, pp 49–53).

Chapter 4 covers repertory 1, associated with the Wadjiginy songman, Tommy Barrtjap. While Barrtjap received some songs from his father's brother, Jimmy Bandak, and inherited others from the Kiyuk performer and composer Mosek (from the neighbouring Kiyuk language group), most of the recorded corpus was composed by Barrtjap, with the assistance of *wunymalang* ghosts, including the ghost of Jimmy Bandak. These he passed on to his own sons Kenny and Timothy Burrenjuck.

Repertory 2 (chapter 7) is associated with the Wadjiginy singer Bobby Lambudju Lane. Transmission within this repertory is, compared to the straightforward generation-to-generation transmission of repertory 1, somewhat complicated, and this is reflected in the songs themselves, which are far less homogenous than those of repertory 1. Lambudju's songs have now passed to Colin Worumbu Ferguson (Marri Tjavin), who was brought up with Lambudju, and to Lambudju's brother-in-law Roger (Rossie) Yarrowin (Emmiyangal), both of whom continue to perform some of his songs today.

Repertory 3 (chapter 5) stems from the Mendheyangal songman, Jimmy Muluk, who was immensely successful in the 1960s, when he was recorded by Alice Moyle, but was no longer alive when Marett first visited Belyuen in 1986. Some of Muluk's songs continue to be sung by Worumbu, who spent part of his childhood in Muluk's household. Muluk's grandson, Kenny Burrenjuck, also sang a few of these songs. The surviving repertory of Muluk's songs is only a fraction of the original, perhaps because neither Ferguson nor Burrenjuck were fluent Mendhe speakers. Because of the lack of recent recordings of Muluk's repertory, it was not discussed in detail in *Songs, dreamings and ghosts,* but we have come to realise that it is immensely significant for the history of *wangga* (Marett, 2007). The significance of this repertory lies not just in its widespread popularity (Muluk's songs have been recorded as far away as Derby in Western Australia), but also because it served as a model for the first songs of the Walakandha *wangga* (chapter 8) when it was being established at Wadeye in the 1960s and 1970s (Marett, 2007). Furthermore, Muluk's songs are, as we shall see in chapters 2 and 5, among the most complex and formally flexible examples of *wangga* that we have.

Repertory 4 (chapter 6), associated with the Marri Tjavin singer Billy Mandji, was also not discussed in detail in *Songs, dreamings and ghosts*. Mandji and his brother Harry Ferguson (father of Colin Worumbu Ferguson) migrated to Belyuen in the 1940s. A third brother, Ngundurl, remained in the southern Daly and his family eventually settled in Wadeye. The sons of these brothers, Ngundurl's son Les Kundjil and Harry Ferguson's son Colin Worumbu Ferguson, inherited rights to sing Mandji's songs.[11] Colin's sister Marjorie Bilbil, another Belyuen resident, assisted us with documenting Mandji's songs and in 2006 she too made a brief recording of a Mandji song. Most of Mandji's songs are in a

---

10 We maintain the numbering of repertories 1-4 as set out by Marett in *Songs, dreamings and ghosts* for lineages 1–4, while noting that the chapters in this volume are ordered chronologically according to the era of ascendancy of the relevant repertory, so that Muluk (chapter 5, repertory 3) and Mandji (chapter 6, repertory 4) appear before Lambudju (chapter 7, repertory 2).

11 Being Marri Tjavin, both Ferguson and Kundjil also had rights to sing the Walakandha *wangga* repertory.

Belyuen language, Emmi, with only a portion of one song being in his ancestral language, Marri Tjavin. Billy Mandji was involved in the pastoral industry, and for this reason recordings of him and his songs turn up over a widespread area. The recordings presented in chapter 6 by no means exhaust the corpus of recordings and it is expected that additional recordings may be discovered in the future.

Table 1.1 summarises the main recordings of the four Belyuen repertories over the past 60 years (1948–2008). Although *wangga* has always been the major public genre in Belyuen, it has by no means been the only music performed there. Both Mountford and Simpson recorded a wealth of other song genres during their separate 1948 visits to Delissaville, including *balga*, *tjarrarta* and *mindirrini* (Barwick & Marett, 2011). In the 1940s, other *wangga* repertories were also performed at Belyuen, including the songs of George King (Larrakiya) (Hemery, 1942), and George Ahmat (Emmiyangal) (Elkin & Jones, 1958, pp 149–50). By the early 1950s, however, the Wadjiginy songs of repertory 1 were well established, and the older repertories fell out of use with the deaths of their main composers and performers. Lambudju (repertory 2) and Mandji (repertory 4) were recorded as young men by Alice Moyle at Bagot in Darwin in 1959.

The 1960s were a time of considerable mobility, with many workers from the Daly region finding work in the pastoral industry, especially in the eastern Kimberley (Jebb, 2002). In 1961, Lamont West recorded Lambudju's adoptive brother Rusty Benmele Moreen (Emmiyangal) together with Larrakiya/Wadjiginy man Lawrence Wurrpen singing songs of repertory 2 in Beswick Creek government settlement, which had links with the nearby Beswick cattle station. West also recorded another Belyuen singer named 'Billy Brab'. It is possible that Muluk (repertory 3) was resident in the Kimberley during the 1950s (he doesn't appear in Delissaville records of this period),[12] but by 1962 he was very active back in the Darwin area, where Alice Moyle recorded him leading a *burnim-rag* ceremony at the Bagot community. He took an active part in tourist corroborees as well as in the Darwin eisteddfod, where Moyle recorded him in 1962 and 1964, along with three young boys he had trained to sing his songs, including a young Colin Worumbu Ferguson, and the Mendheyangal brothers Robert and Thomas Gordon. Mandji (repertory 4) was again recorded by Alice Moyle in 1962, singing *djanba* songs from Wadeye (Port Keats) with another singer Philip Mileru, whom he had perhaps met during his time on cattle stations in the southern Daly or the Kimberley. In 1964 Wurrpen was still in the Katherine area, this time singing songs of repertory 1, recorded by the anthropologist Ken Maddock. In 1966 we find Billy Mandji (or perhaps the Jaminjung singer Major Raymond) recorded by linguist John Cleverly in Timber Creek in the eastern Kimberley singing both Mandji songs (repertory 4) and some of those of Jimmy Muluk (repertory 3), but by mid-1968 Mandji was back in Delissaville, where Alice Moyle recorded him singing both alone and with Jimmy Muluk at a tourist corroboree. Later in the year, his songs were recorded by Moyle from the Jaminjung singer Major Raymond in Kununurra (WA).

	Repertory 1	Repertory 2	Repertory 3	Repertory 4
Mountford 1948, Delissaville	Mosek Nilku			
Simpson 1948, Delissaville	Mosek Nilku Bandak			
Elkin 1952, Delissaville	Bandak Barrtjap			

---

12 Muluk's relatives today state that he lived in the Kimberley, but cannot say exactly when.

	Repertory 1	Repertory 2	Repertory 3	Repertory 4
Elkin 1953, Bagot	Bandak			
Moyle 1959, Bagot		Lambudju		Mandji
West 1961, Beswick		Moreen Wurrpen		Mandji?
Moyle 1962, Bagot, Darwin			Muluk	Mandji
Moyle 1964, Darwin			Muluk, Mandji, Worumbu, R. Gordon, T. Gordon	
Maddock 1964, Katherine	Wurrpen			
Cleverly 1966, Timber Creek			Mandji (or Raymond)	Mandji (or Raymond)
Moyle 1968, Mandorah, Delissaville, Kununurra	Barrtjap		Muluk Mandji	Mandji Raymond
Marett 1986, Mandorah, Belyuen	Barrtjap	Lambudju	Barrtjap	
Marett 1988, Belyuen, Batchelor	Barrtjap (Lambudju)			Mandji
Marett 1991, Belyuen		Lambudju		
Marett 1995, Belyuen	T. Burrenjuck			
Marett and Barwick 1997, Belyuen, Wooliana	K. Burrenjuck	Worumbu Yarrowin	R. Gordon, T. Gordon, K. Burrenjuck, Worumbu	Worumbu
Marett 1998, Wadeye			Kundjil	Kundjil
Furlan 2002, Belyuen	K. Burrenjuck		Worumbu, K. Burrenjuck	
Marett 2006, Belyuen, Mandorah			Worumbu, R. Gordon	
Barwick 2006, Belyuen				
Barwick 2008, Fifteen-Mile	T. Burrenjuck (Marett)			
Treloyn 2008, East Point (Darwin)	Worumbu (Yarrowin)	Worumbu (Yarrowin)	Worumbu (Yarrowin)	Worumbu (Yarrowin)
Barwick 2008, CDU	Worumbu (Yarrowin)	Yarrowin (Worumbu)	Worumbu (Yarrowin)	Worumbu (Yarrowin)

Table 1.1 Main recordings of Belyuen singers, by repertory, 1948–2008. The use of brackets denotes a secondary 'backup' singer role, assisting the main songman. See chapters 4–7 for full details of the relevant recordings.

No substantial recordings of Belyuen *wangga* were made in the 1970s, though there is ample evidence of the continuation of the tourist corroborees at various locations in Darwin Harbour[13] as well as in

---

13 See, for example, various photographs of tourist performances at Talc Head and Mandorah included in the Pic-

ceremonial activities throughout the region (Brandl, et al., 1979). In 1986 Marett made the first of many visits to Belyuen, where he recorded the tourist corroboree at Mandorah, where Barrtjap performed his own songs as well as some of Jimmy Muluk's (Muluk was by then deceased). Later in the trip he elicited recordings of both Barrtjap and Lambudju singing their own repertories. In subsequent visits Marett re-recorded the repertories of Barrtjap (1988) (with Lambudju acting as second singer for Barrtjap) and Lambudju (1991) in elicited performances at Belyuen, as well as recording Billy Mandji performing in a *burnim-rag* ceremony at Batchelor. By 1995 all three of these songmen had died, and the younger generation of singers had started to emerge.

It is evident from the post-1990 recordings by Marett, Barwick and their collaborators Furlan and Treloyn listed in table 1.1 that the younger generation of singers have tended to mix songs from a number of repertories. Barrtjap, Lambudju, Muluk and Mandji usually sang only songs that they had composed themselves or inherited from relatives in a higher generation. The only exceptions were where singers collaborated for a particular purpose (for example, we have recordings of Billy Mandji and Tommy Barrtjap singing Jimmy Muluk's songs at tourist corroborees to accompany ensemble dance pieces) or where a singer supported another as the second singer, as when Lambudju assisted Barrtjap in Marett's 1988 recordings of Barrtjap (see chapter 4, tracks 11–15). Kenny Burrenjuck, who passed away in 2008, was probably the last singer who predominantly sang a single repertory—that of his father Tommy Barrtjap (repertory 1), to which he added a few of his own songs. Kenny also had rights to sing the songs of his maternal grandfather, Jimmy Muluk, which he included relatively rarely, and usually in non-ceremonial performance contexts. Kenny's brother, Timothy Burrenjuck, was also trained by their father, but is a rather reluctant singer these days, who performs songs from repertory 1 only when no other singer can be found.

Colin Worumbu Ferguson is arguably the leading Belyuen *wangga* songman today, and has inherited rights to almost all the repertories by one means or another: through direct inheritance in the case of Billy Mandji (repertory 4) and the Walakandha *wangga* (chapter 8); through spending large amounts of time as a child with the families of Bobby Lambudju Lane (repertory 2) and Jimmy Muluk (repertory 3); and, since the death of Kenny Burrenjuck, through a broadening of perceptions of community rather than family ownership of the various repertories, including those of repertory 1. While tending to favour songs he inherited (entirely conventionally) from his father's brother, Billy Mandji, Ferguson now includes songs from all four Belyuen repertories in his performances, as well as both Wadeye *wangga* repertories (Walakandha *wangga* and Ma-yawa *wangga*). Nevertheless, as far as we are aware, he has yet to compose any songs of his own and hence would not, at least under the old conventions, be counted as a fully-fledged songman. This lack of songs of his own may be related to the fact that he is not a native speaker of most of the languages in which he sings. Even in the case of Marri Tjavin, his ancestral language, he is of a generation that no longer regularly speaks this highly endangered language. The other active Belyuen songman, Roger (Rossie) Yarrowin, is from one of the prominent Emmiyangal families at Belyuen, and his father was a noted didjeridu player and dancer. Yarrowin received rights to sing some of Lambudju's songs via Lambudju's marriage to his sister, but like Ferguson he has a limited command of Batjamalh (the language of the songs) and, as far as we are aware, has not composed any songs of his own.[14] He often acts as backup singer to Ferguson, though on occasion he performs solo with the Kenbi dance group, whose resources now include songs from all four repertories.

---

tureNT collection of the Northern Territory Library such as www.territorystories.nt.gov.au/handle/10070/7964 (figure 1.6), which shows a group of performers from Belyuen painted up at a tourist corroboree (Evan Luly collection, 1968), and hdl.handle.net/10070/33438 (Mike Foley collection, 1970s) (figure 5.1), which bears the annotation 'This group of Aboriginals performed for tourists at Mica Beach resort on Cox Peninsula from 1969 to 1974'.

14 There is some suggestion that he may have received the song 'Mubagandi' from the ghost of Lambudju, but Yarrowin

Ferguson sometimes relies on recordings of earlier singers to learn songs, and in this he has been assisted by Marett and by the establishment of local repositories of archival recordings in Belyuen and Wadeye (Ferguson spends periods of time in both communities) (Barwick, et al., 2005; Marett, et al., 2006). This method of learning from recordings is not as unusual as it may at first sound. For decades singers in the Northern Territory have relied on recordings to support traditions—listening to cassettes of earlier performances by an earlier generation prior to singing in a ceremony, for example (Marett, 2010). Moreover, recorded voices belong to the same category (*maruy* in Batjamalh, *merimen.gu* in Marri languages) as the ghostly voices of ancestors singing in dreams, and hence modern transmission methods are closely related to the traditional method of receiving songs (Marett, 2003). Despite an ongoing transformation of the tradition, *wangga* performances remain viable at Belyuen, as evidenced by the number of recent recordings included in chapters 4–9. Nonetheless, we should never underestimate its intrinsic fragility: the loss of one or two key singers could, at any time, signal the end.

Social history of *wangga* at Wadeye (Port Keats) and surrounding areas

The history of *wangga* at Wadeye (Port Keats) is affected by the location of the community at the junction point of the *mayern kulu* traditional trade route (extending northwards to Darwin and southwards to the Kimberley) with the *mayern nonga-mandjikat*[15] trade route extending eastwards towards the Katherine region and beyond into southern Arnhem Land (Falkenberg, 1962, p 143; Stanner, 1989 [1963]). At Belyuen nearly all families had migrated north from the *wangga*-owning Daly region around Anson Bay. The settlement at Wadeye (Port Keats) included not only *wangga*-owning clans who had come into the area from the north (including speakers of Marri Ammu and Marri Tjavin), but also clans from the east (including speakers of Marri Ngarr) and south (including Jaminjung speakers). *Wangga* (associated with the northerly direction on the *mayern kulu*) thus co-exists in public ceremonies with other song genres deriving from the east and south.

One of the earliest references to *wangga* in the Daly region appears in a list of song types in Stanner's fieldnotes for September 1932, when he was at the Daly River. On 17 June of the same year, he recorded that a source had told him that most of the songs sung by the Madngella and Mulluk Mulluk were of Larrakia (Larrakiya) or Wogait (Wadjiginy) origin (in other words, composed by singers then mostly resident in the Darwin area)[16] and had been introduced to the Daly by visitors from these tribes or had been learned by Daly tribesmen on visits to these tribes. (At this early point in his fieldwork he seems to have been unaware that the Wogait were originally from the Daly.) Stanner was in no doubt that the Darwin compound acted as a distribution centre for songs.

In 1935 Stanner travelled to Port Keats with Father Richard Docherty, at the time of the founding of the Port Keats mission. In his later published discussion of Murinbata (Murriny Patha) circumcision, Stanner lists the following three types of song used for initiation (circumcision), 'determined by the region to which [the boy] was taken for isolation during the preliminary phase of the rite':

- *wangga* (to the north, the name having no discernible meaning in Murriny Patha, but being associated with the Daly River region)
- *manbanggoi* (to the east or north-east, being derived from the Murriny Patha *mayern pangguy* 'long road'), using the song and dance form *lirga [lirrga]* that originated in the Beswick area of southwestern Arnhem Land[17]

---

himself insisted that he had been given the song by Lambudju while he was still alive (Marett and Barwick DAT97/10 (AIATSIS A16966), recorded 1 August 1997).

15 Probably Murriny Patha *ngunga* 'sun' (by extension, 'east'), *mandjigat* 'varied lorikeet'.

16 This was before the establishment of Delissaville settlement in 1937.

17 The name of this dance-song form from the Beswick area was later adopted by the Marri Ngarr at Wadeye for their

- *naitpan* (to the south or south-east, derived from the Murriny Patha *ngatjparr* 'distant'), using the *mindirrini* dance form, identical with the *dingiri [dinggirri]* of the Ngan'giwumirri and the *kudjingga* of the Jaminjung. (summarised from Stanner, 1989 [1963], p 108)[18]

The links established between the boys and the distant people and countries to which they were introduced during the preliminary visit were reinforced by the music and dance performances during their circumcision. Afterwards, the boys were known by the name of the ceremony that had accompanied their circumcision, a practice that continues today. Marett states that links established in this way acted to the social advantage of the young man and his kin (Marett, 2005, p 71).

During his first visit to Port Keats in 1935, Stanner took some telegraphic, but nonetheless revealing notes on the use of *wangga* at a circumcision ceremony:

> Dance *wangga* repeatedly. This dance simple principles. Drone pipe, tapping sticks, singing men and leader, three or four dancers in semi circle formed by massed associates, First steps like rhythmic jog trot to breathed song (ye, ye, ye, ye); then dance begins. Only one leg used (in this case right). Much posturing, shaking of shoulders … Dance for several minutes near semi-circle. *Wangga* all the time. Then retreat to the other end of beach. (Stanner, 1992, fieldnotes for 3 July 1935)

Despite its telegraphic nature—Stanner was clearly jotting down observations of the performance as it occurred—this description is in accordance with how *wangga* is performed today.[19] It is clear from this, and other evidence, that *wangga* was already well established in the area. Indeed people at Wadeye today say that *wangga* has always existed in the Daly region.

According to Falkenberg, Father Docherty, the first priest at the Port Keats Mission, initially allowed the performance of corroborees at the mission station for the purpose of convincing people that the mission did not disapprove of their culture (Falkenberg, 1962, p 19). From the mid-1940s, however, circumcision ceremonies were prohibited at the mission. Stanner reports that:

> the local missionary, alarmed by a supposed risk to life or well-being from loss of blood and septicaemia, persuaded the elders to let him perform the operation on several boys. Soon afterwards, a hospital was established at the mission. It then became customary to have infant males circumcised by a trained sister. The traditional institution lapsed. The elders put up little resistance and the youths, one need scarcely add, were in favour of the change. (Stanner, 1989 [1963], p 109)

Stanner adds that at the time of his later fieldwork in the 1950s, it was felt by older men that the discontinuation of the ceremonies had had an adverse effect on the social behaviour of young men, but all attempts to start the ceremonies again foundered on the fact that there were no uncircumcised boys (Stanner, 1989 [1963], p 109). It is unclear precisely when circumcision ceremonies began again at Wadeye. According to Frank Dumoo, it was 'after the war' (Marett, 2005, p 70). It seems likely that the *wangga kardu kunybinyi* (*wangga* for the people of Kunybinyi[20]) of Joe Malakunda Birrarri and the Ma-yawa *wangga* (see chapter 9) were composed during this period, perhaps to provide songs for the

---

own newly composed genre.

18 We have maintained Stanner's original orthography for the names of the ceremonial styles, but use contemporary orthography for Murriny Patha and other language terms.

19 Perhaps to differentiate themselves from dancers of the *muyil lirrga*, composed locally in the 1960s and performed in Wadeye using a one-legged stamping action, *wangga* dancers today tend to use predominantly double-legged stamping.

20 Kunybinyi is the name of an area near Wadeye belonging to the Dimirnin clan, in whose traditional country the township lies. It is frequently mentioned in *djanba* songs.

newly resurrected circumcision ceremonies (Marett, 2007, p 66). According to Frank Dumoo, these local *wangga* traditions were supplemented by performances by Belyuen singers such as Jimmy Muluk and Tommy Barrtjap, who were brought in from Belyuen. As we shall see in chapter 2, it was these Belyuen songs that provided the strongest musical model for the new composition of the Walakandha *wangga* tradition in the late 1960s and early 1970s.

In the first decades of its existence, the mission had been unable to support its entire population, so a roster system was established whereby for one fortnight half the population worked in the community while the other half went bush. In the following fortnight, the positions were reversed. By the 1950s, the resources of the mission had become sufficient to support the population full-time. In the meantime, groups traditionally hostile to the Murriny Patha traditional owners of Port Keats had come into the mission, resulting in serious social conflict.[21] To provide a greater degree of social cohesion, elders from the competing groups developed a tripartite reciprocal ceremonial system whereby the three principal factions took on the obligations of providing ceremony for each other in the two main public ceremonial arenas, namely the final mortuary rites, known in Aboriginal English as *burnim-rag*, and circumcision ceremonies. For this purpose, three new repertoires were composed.

These were the Walakandha *wangga* (composed and performed mainly by Wadeye-based Marri Tjavin men, representing coastal clans whose traditional country lay to the north of Wadeye) (see chapter 8), the *muyil lirrga* (composed and performed by Wadeye-based Marri Ngarr men, representing those people whose traditional country lay to the east of Wadeye) (Barwick, 2006; Ford, 2006), and *djanba* (composed and performed by the Kardu Dimirnin, the Murriny Patha clan group on whose traditional country the township of Wadeye stands, as well as people from Yek Nangu, another Murriny Patha clan whose traditional country lies to the south of Wadeye[22]) (Barwick, 2011; Barwick, et al., 2010; Barwick, et al., 2007; Barwick, et al., 2005). Each of these new repertoires drew on the musical and dance characteristics of the three distant repertoires described by Stanner that were formerly used for circumcision (and perhaps mortuary rites), that is *wangga* from the Daly region to the north, *lirrga* from the Beswick region to the east, and *naitpan* (and according to our Wadeye informants, various repertoires of *balga*) from the south and ultimately the Kimberley, which had been traded along the old trade routes or brought into Wadeye by visiting groups from these areas.

The composition of these new local repertoires meant that it was no longer necessary to import singing groups from outside the community (although this practice has continued on occasion), because people from the relevant clans were already resident in Wadeye. Because all the songs were in a local comprehensible language (Marri Tjavin, Marri Ngarr or Murriny Patha) and about known places, it was now possible for everyone participating to have access to the content of the songs.[23] The new tripartite system of ceremonial reciprocity dictated that if a member of one group needed a ceremony to be performed as the final rites of one of their deceased, or for the circumcision of one of their sons, they should call on one of the other two groups to perform the ceremony. Thus, if a member of a Murriny Patha clan required ceremony, he or she could either ask the Marri Tjavin, together with other *wangga*-owning groups such as the Marri Ammu and Matige, to perform Walakandha *wangga*, or the Marri Ngarr group to perform *lirrga*. If, on the other hand it was a member of a Marri Tjavin, Marri

---

21 Indeed, these historical conflicts may form at least part of the root of the gang warfare that continues to plague Wadeye today.

22 Strictly *djanba* belongs to the Dimirnin clan, on whose land Wadeye is situated, while the clan associated with Nangu had a much older repertory *wurltjirri*, which is sometimes performed in place of or alongside *djanba*. A third Murriny Patha repertory, *malgarrin*, has become largely associated with the church.

23 This was in contrast to the previous situation, when the imported songs' use of distant languages and references to distant places (or untranslatable spirit languages) meant that few if any in Wadeye could understand the references.

Ammu or Matige clan that needed ceremony, he or she could call on the Murriny Patha to perform their *djanba* or the Marri Ngarr to perform *lirrga,* and so on.

This has important implications for the dynamics of ceremony, since it is the country, ancestors and totems of the group that provides the ceremony, rather than those of the deceased or the boy to be circumcised, that are sung. For example, singers of *djanba* perform songs about their own Murriny Patha country at Kunybinyi, their own *djanba* ancestors and their own totems, honey and black cockatoo, rather than, say, the deceased's Marri Tjavin country at Yendili with the Walakandha ancestors and totems of the Marri Tjavin. Clearly, despite this disjuncture, the songs of the 'other' group still have symbolic power to create a liminal space between the world of the living and that of the dead, and thus to effect the required transition from child to man, or from living person to ancestor.

The new tripartite system had significant continuities with the previous practice of using distant ceremonies in that it emphasised the building of social networks, here focused within the growing community. At the same time as celebrating the individual differences between the three groups, the new repertoires also stressed the fundamental principle, shared by all groups, of the quality and strength of an individual's personal attachment to his or her own clan country, ancestors and totems.

The circumcision ceremonies that Marett witnessed at Wadeye in the 1980s were very different from those Stanner wrote about from the 1930s. In the 1930s the ceremonies were much smaller, family affairs, which usually focused on one boy and lasted one day (excluding ceremonies associated with the seclusion of the boy prior to initiation). By the 1980s the ceremonies had become much larger and wide-ranging. Over three days in 1988, a large number of boys were circumcised. Singers and dancers from all three traditions performed in turn, according to the genre that had been chosen for a particular boy's circumcision.[24] Following this ceremony, however, there were expressions of dissatisfaction: the ceremony was so large partly because the responsibility to circumcise had been lax in preceding years, leading to a backlog of boys in need of ceremonial attention. Singers and dancers complained about being exhausted by the rigours of performing highly energetic forms that were designed for much shorter time frames. In the following years, attempts were made to redress these complaints by holding the ceremonies more frequently (and hence with fewer boys to circumcise). In 2003, in an attempt to recreate circumcision ceremonies in the form in which they had existed prior to the creation of the mission in 1935, elders went back to Stanner's accounts of circumcision in the 1930s and attempted to resurrect the smaller, family-based rituals of old (Furlan, 2005, pp 271–92 contains a detailed account of this ceremony).

Mortuary ceremonies, too, had changed. Stanner's 1963 account (based on fieldwork in the 1950s) suggested that Christian burial had by then largely supplanted the full-scale, six-stage mortuary rites described by Stanner's informants as having lapsed prior to the Second World War. Stanner himself never witnessed any mortuary ceremonies, and suggested that 'only fragments of the traditional rite now survive' (Stanner, 1989 [1963], p 118). Belying Stanner's pessimistic outlook for the future of mortuary rites, at the time of our fieldwork in the 1990s it was clear that *wangga* and its sister genres *djanba* and *lirrga* were still in regular use throughout the Daly region, including at Wadeye, to accompany *burnim-rag* ceremonies, which, while somewhat simplified from the full rites described by Stanner, nevertheless contained many of the same elements. Unlike the large-scale circumcision ceremonies, however, mortuary ceremonies continued to be performed within smaller family groups, usually on the country of the deceased when it was accessible from Wadeye. While most funerals included some traditional singing within the Christian liturgical framework (usually during the mass or to accompany the procession of the coffin into the church and to the graveyard), the *burnim-rag* ceremonies, which took place a year or two after death, were not mounted for every deceased individual. Rather, the holding

---

24 As previously mentioned, boys are nearly always circumcised to a tradition other than that to which they belong.

of a ceremony depended on the means and commitment of the family of the deceased to organise and fund the event and its associated logistics.

History of Wadeye *wangga* repertories

Turning now to focus on *wangga*, we have already mentioned the three local repertories of *wangga* originating at Wadeye (Port Keats): the *wangga kardu kunybinyi* of Joe Birrarri, the Ma-yawa *wangga* (see chapter 9) and the Walakandha *wangga* (see chapter 8). Table 1.2 presents a summary of the known recordings of these three repertories over the course of 55 years (1954-2009).

	Wangga kardu kunybinyi	Ma-yawa wangga	Walakandha wangga
Stanner 1954 (? Daly River)	Joe Birrarri		
Walsh, 1972-1974, Wadeye	Joe Birrarri		Stan Mullumbuk, Thomas Kungiung Ambrose Piarlum
Reilly, 1974-1976, Wadeye	Joe Birrarri		Stan Mullumbuk
?Hoddinott, c. 1982			Thomas Kungiung
Frances Kofod, 1986, Wadeye			Thomas Kungiung
Marett, 1988, Wadeye, Peppimenarti, Barunga, Batchelor, Nadirri			Thomas Kungiung, Martin Warrigal Kungiung, Wagon Dumoo
Enilane, 1992, Wadeye			Thomas Kungiung, Wagon Dumoo, Colin Worumbu Ferguson, Les Kundjil
Marett 1998, Peppimenarti, Merrepen, Kununurra, Wadeye		Maurice Ngulkur	Les Kundjil Ambrose Piarlum
Marett 1999, Wadeye		Maurice Ngulkur	Les Kundjil Philip Mullumbuk
Crocombe 2000, Wadeye		Maurice Ngulkur	
Crocombe 2004, Wadeye			Philip Mullumbuk
Treloyn 2008, Darwin		Frank Dumoo Colin Worumbu Ferguson	Frank Dumoo Colin Worumbu Ferguson
Treloyn and Barwick 2009, Batchelor		Charles Kungiung (Marett)	Charles Kungiung (Marett)

Table 1.2 Main recordings of Wadeye *wangga* singers, by repertory, 1954–2009. The use of brackets denotes a secondary 'backup' singer role, assisting the main songman. See chapters 8–9 for full details of the relevant recordings.[25]

Although several recordings exist of Joe Malakunda Birrarri's *wangga kardu kunybinyi*, the texts are in an untranslatable spirit language.[26] Because of the difficulty of transcribing texts made up entirely of

---

25 The 2009 recording of Charles Kungiung singing *wangga* at a *burnim-rag* ceremony at Batchelor is not included in this volume because we have not yet had the chance to work with him on the songs.

26 This was also the case with two other repertories recorded by Stanner in 1954, namely the Marrithiyel *wangga ma-*

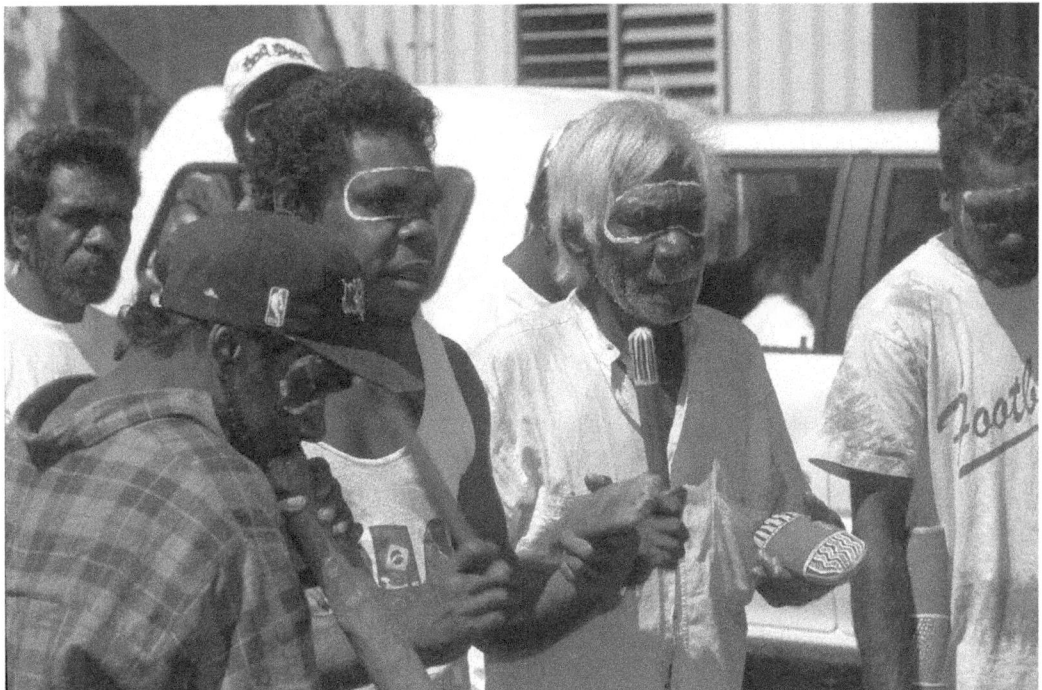

Figure 1.7 Charles Kungiung and Les Kundjil singing *wangga* at the funeral for Cyril Ninnal, accompanied by didjeridu player Basil Dumoo, Wadeye, 1999. Photograph by Mark Crocombe, reproduced with the permission of Wadeye community.

vocables once the singers have passed away (see Ford's comments in chapter 3), these songs have not been included in the present collection. The texts of the *wangga kardu kunybinyi* were entirely in spirit language because Joe Birrarri was not of the same language group as the beings that gave him the song, and hence could not translate their texts into human language (Marett, 2005, p 43). As Barwick and others have observed with reference to Western Arnhem Land, incomprehensible texts have certain advantages when ceremonies are performed for multilingual audiences, insofar as the texts are equally incomprehensible to all in the audience (Manmurulu, Apted, & Barwick, 2008). Malakunda's *wangga* songs have not been performed since his death in the mid-1970s.

The Ma-yawa *wangga* repertory (chapter 9) is the older of the two Wadeye *wangga* repertories (Ma-yawa *wangga* and Walakandha *wangga*) presented in this book. The texts of the Ma-yawa *wangga* are in human (Marri Ammu) language, and in this, they perhaps foreshadow the creation of the three new repertories created later (Walakandha *wangga*, the *muyil lirrga* and *djanba*) all of which use normal human language. All but one song was composed by the Marri Ammu songman, Charlie Niwilhi Brinken, but he was never recorded. The performances presented in chapter 9 were all elicited in the 1990s from his relative Maurice Tjakurl Ngulkur (who also added his own song to the set), sometimes backed up by the Marri Tjavin singers Ambrose Piarlum and Les Kundjil. The recordings exhibit a higher degree of variability than most other *wangga* in the corpus, perhaps reflecting the fact that by the 1990s the Ma-yawa *wangga* was rarely performed ceremonially. At the time of writing, the repertory seems effectively defunct, though two Marri Tjavin singers, Colin Worumbu Ferguson and Charles Kungiung, have recently been learning some of the songs from CDs. In 2008 Treloyn recorded Marri Tjavin elder Frank Dumoo backed up by Worumbu singing one Ma-yawa song in an elicited performance, and

---

warrgat and the Ngan'gityemerri *wangga ma-merren* (Marett, 2005, p 24).

Kungiung was heard to perform the same song, along with his own Walakandha *wangga* songs, in a *burnim-rag* ceremony directed by Dumoo in 2009. What will become of the remaining songs in this tradition is presently unclear.

The first Walakandha *wangga* songs were composed by Stan Mullumbuk[27] in the mid-to-late 1960s (according to Dumoo, this was the last of the three new repertories to be composed). Mullumbuk also composed a number of *wangga* songs with Christian themes, which were apparently performed in various church contexts in the 1970s but which have not been performed since his death in the late 1970s or early 1980s. His Walakandha *wangga* repertory, however, was taken over by a new group of singers, principally Thomas Kungiung and Wagon Dumoo.[28] When Marett arrived in Wadeye in 1988, the Walakandha *wangga* was at its height. While the majority of songs performed at that time had been composed by Kungiung and Wagon Dumoo, other singers, such as Kungiung's brother Martin Warrigal Kungiung and Les Kundjil, were also active both as composers and singers. Songs by Stan Mullumbuk were now rarely, if ever, performed. The more recently composed songs by Kungiung, Dumoo et al were regularly performed both in major ceremonial contexts and in less important ceremonies and in festivals. By this time, the repertory had also been adopted by the Peppimenarti community, and in 1988 an impressive body of men from both Wadeye and Peppimenarti danced together *en masse* at the Barunga Festival. By the second half of the 1990s, however, all the songmen who had been active in the previous decade, with the exception of Les Kundjil, had passed away.

In the 1990s and early 2000, the rising star was Stan Mullumbuk's much younger brother, Philip. Philip's songs are brilliant and complex, so complex in fact, that he was the only person who could perform them. This led to the slightly anomalous and less than ideal situation that *wangga* performances regularly had one rather than the requisite two or more singers. Tragically, Philip himself passed away in 2006. All hopes now rest on Thomas Kungiung's son Charles and on Colin Worumbu Ferguson. Marett, Barwick and Ford participated in a *burnim-rag* ceremony in 2009 at which Charles Kungiung performed numerous Walakandha *wangga* songs as well as one Ma-yawa *wangga* song. On this occasion he performed several of his own songs, and can thus be counted as perhaps the only fully-fledged songman of the younger generations.[29]

As with all traditions of Aboriginal music in northern Australia, the future of the Walakandha *wangga*, which flourished so vigorously in the 1980s, is now in doubt. As in Belyuen, we can observe in modern performances a movement towards coalescence of formerly distinct traditional repertories (in this case, the Ma-yawa and Walakandha *wangga*). Amongst the younger generations, there is strong support for the recording and documentation of the tradition, and for making available in the community knowledge centre the performances of the masters of old.

---

27 In a recent article, Marett speculated that the dedicatee of Sansom's book *The camp at Wallaby Cross* (Sansom, 1980), 'the Walakunda Singing Man now dead', was Stan Mullumbuk (Marett, 2007, p 73, footnote 6). More recent discussions with Frank Dumoo suggest, however, that this was not the case.

28 Together, the Mullumbuk, Kungiung and Dumoo families represent the three lineages of the Walakandha *wangga* (see further in Marett, 2005, pp 46-49).

29 We have not yet been able to discuss and translate the new song texts with Kungiung in person, so we are unable to include these newly composed songs in this volume.

Figure 1.8 *Wangga* dancers painting up at Peppimenarti, 1998. Photograph by Allan Marett, reproduced with the permission of Wadeye community.

Chapter 2
THE MUSIC AND DANCE CONVENTIONS OF *WANGGA*

This chapter provides a framework for understanding the musical and dance conventions of the six *wangga* repertories presented in full in chapters 4–9. While each composer and performer has his own preferred style or combination of features, variability and innovation is constrained by the ceremonial functions of *wangga*, including its symbolic significance (discussed in chapter 1) and its role in coordinating group action (especially ritual actions by dancers and others).

The conventions adopted in four of these repertories—Barrtjap (chapter 4), Lambudju (chapter 7), Walakandha *wangga* (chapter 8) and Ma-yawa *wangga* (chapter 9)—were previously treated in some detail in *Songs, dreamings and ghosts* (Marett, 2005, p 68), which explored how *wangga* performances enact broader social themes. In this volume we bring together a broader range of data, including two repertories never previously analysed, (belonging to the Belyuen singers Jimmy Muluk and Billy Mandji, presented in chapters 5 and 6), and in chapter 8 extra data on the early Walakandha *wangga* songs composed by Stan Mullumbuk (Marett, 2007). Readers interested in acquiring further understandings of the conventions of *wangga* are referred to *Songs, dreamings and ghosts* and to Marett's 2007 paper, 'Simplifying musical practice in order to enhance local identity: The case of rhythmic modes in the Walakandha *wangga* (Wadeye, Northern Territory)' (Marett, 2007).

This book documents the repertories by providing systematic detail on each song, to be read in conjunction with the primary data contained in the corpus of audio recordings.[1] Each of the chapters 4–9 contains an introduction to the relevant repertory, its performers and the recordings, a track-by-track discussion of each recorded performance (including a song structure summary for each track), and a music analysis section summarising and discussing the main musical features of the repertory. The data presented in this chapter draw together these repertory-specific analyses within the broader framework of structural conventions used for the whole *wangga* corpus. We begin with a summary of the main formal conventions of the music, which we explore in some detail through discussion of a single song performance.

Summary of musical forms used in *wangga*

Overall form and terminology

Wangga song items always begin with an instrumental introduction, which is followed by a number of vocal sections, which in most, but not all, cases are separated from one another by instrumental sections. Song items conclude either with a final instrumental section, or (in the case of Barrtjap alone—see further below) a coda. *Wangga* song items typically have two or three vocal and instrumental sections, but in some cases, particularly when there is dance, additional vocal sections can be added. At the end of each song item, it is the didjeridu player who finishes first (though the signal to finish comes from the singer, who will normally cue his didjeridu player by raising the clapsticks, or giving him a glance). As soon as the didjeridu player stops, the singer beats out the final terminating patterns and the song item comes to an end. The basic form of a song item is summarised in figure 2.1, based on a performance of Maurice Ngulkur's song 'Tjerri' (chapter 9, track 13), which will be discussed more fully below.

---

[1] These are available online at wangga.library.usyd.edu.au as well as in a seperately issued set of CDs available from Sydney University Press.

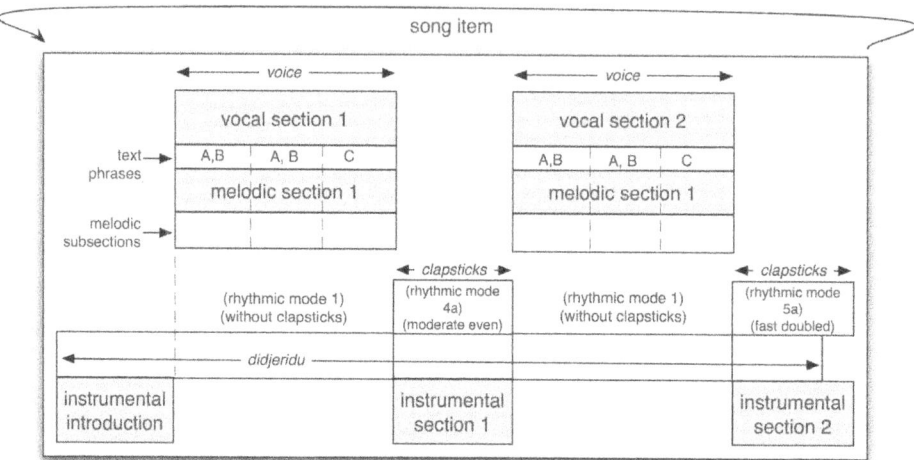

Figure 2.1 Summary of musical and textual structure of 'Tjerri' as performed by Ngulkur (chapter 9, track 13), illustrating the terminology used throughout this volume.

All *wangga* songs conform, in general terms, to this format of alternating vocal and instrumental sections, with successive vocal sections typically repeating the text and melody of the first.[2] Vocal and instrumental sections, melodic sections, text phrases and their corresponding rhythmic modes (see further below) are marked in the song structure summaries that are placed after the notes for each track in chapters 4–9.[3]

The length and complexity of each section (whether vocal or instrumental) varies from song to song and even from performance to performance of the same song. For example, the length of instrumental introductions is usually determined by the amount of time the songman needs before he is ready to begin the vocal section, and this in turn may rest on any number of extra-musical factors: the dancers may not be ready, the singer may be finishing a cigarette or a conversation, or he may want to settle a performance down by having a long instrumental introduction. At the height of a ceremony he may choose to move quickly from vocal section to vocal section and begin each song with only the shortest of instrumental introductions. Instrumental sections and codas also vary in length according to a number of factors: whether there is dancing or not (un-danced versions tend to be shorter), and, if danced, the level of energy of the dancers and the overall excitement of the performance (when the dancing is going well the instrumental sections tend to be longer).

Certain songmen tend to compose particularly long complex vocal sections while others prefer them to be shorter and less complex. Jimmy Muluk and Tommy Barrtjap, for example, liked to compose complex vocal sections, while Maurice Ngulkur preferred shorter ones. Even within the repertory of individual songmen, some songs have relatively short vocal sections and others longer; and in some cases the length of vocal sections might vary even within the same song item.[4] In this situation, an experienced ceremonial song leader (such as Jimmy Muluk) keeps other musicians and dancers in synch with him by visual and aural cues such as raising the clapsticks or vocalisations to signal the

---

2 An exception is Philip Mullumbuk's song, 'Wedjiwurang' (chapter 8, track 38). There is some dispute, however, whether this song is technically a *wangga* at all (see notes to track 38, chapter 8).

3 We do not include instrumental introductions in the song structure summaries in chapters 4-9; their rhythmic mode is always the same as that of the following vocal section 1.

4 For example, in Jimmy Muluk's performance of the first item of 'Piyamen.ga' (chapter 5, track 10), he sings the three text phrases in vocal section 1 twice, but then presents them only once in the following two vocal sections.

Figure 2.2 **Unknown dance at the tourist corroboree, Mica Beach, September 1972. Photograph by Allan Laurence, reproduced with the permission of Belyuen community.**

impending end of an item. Textual instability of the type that results from a song not being regularly performed in ceremony may also affect the length of a vocal section.

In general, performances that include dancing tend to have longer items, which are extended by increasing the number of vocal sections. From the evidence of Barrtjap's performances (Marett, 2005, p 88), as well as those of Mandji and Muluk analysed in chapters 5 and 6, it is clear that tourist corroborees provide the context in which the longest *wangga* items occur (up to 17 vocal sections occur in one performance of 'Puliki' by Mandji). Perhaps western audiences have difficulty in engaging with conventional *wangga* performances that are over almost before they start. It may have been in response to such reactions that the Belyuen performance groups developed a number of relatively lengthy dance dramas to use in tourist corroborees, which often had little or no relationship with the accompanying sung text. At tourist corroborees dancers enjoy engaging with the audience—joking and playing up to audience expectations—and since this type of interaction seems to be what particularly pleases tourist audiences, it is in the interest of the group, which has after all been engaged for a paying gig, that they are prolonged for as long as possible.

Rhythmic mode

Throughout this chapter we will pay particular attention to rhythmic mode, which is one of the main musical features used by songmen to differentiate their repertory from others. We have already mentioned the important topic of rhythmic mode, without yet fully setting out the rhythmic modal system. While the system of rhythmic modes is best appreciated with reference to individual repertories,[5] the principles shared by all repertories are basically as follows. Rhythmic modes are defined primarily by the combination of tempo (that is, the speed of the clapstick beating) with the patterns articulated by the clapsticks, which may be even or in a variety of uneven (gapped) patterns (see table 2.1).

---

5 Detailed discussion of rhythmic modal use in each repertory is contained in the music analysis section at the end of the relevant chapters.

Rhythmic mode	Tempo	Clapsticks
Rhythmic mode 1	None (unmeasured)	None
Rhythmic mode 2a†	Slow	Even
Rhythmic mode 2b	Slow	Suspended
Rhythmic mode 3a	Slow moderate	Even
Rhythmic mode 3b	Slow moderate	Uneven (triple) [xxo]
Rhythmic mode 4a	Moderate	Even
Rhythmic mode 4a (var)	Moderate	Even, suspended
Rhythmic mode 4b	Moderate	Uneven (quadruple) [xxxo]
Rhythmic mode 4b (var)	Moderate	Uneven (quadruple), suspended
Rhythmic mode 4c	Moderate	Uneven (triple)
Rhythmic mode 4d	Moderate	Uneven (quintuple) [xxoxo]
Rhythmic mode 4e	Moderate	Doubled
Rhythmic mode 4*	Moderate	Doubled, followed by even
Rhythmic mode 5a	Fast	Even
Rhythmic mode 5a (var)	Fast	Even, suspended
Rhythmic mode 5b	Fast	Doubled
Rhythmic mode 5c	Fast	Uneven (quadruple)
Rhythmic mode 5d	Fast	Uneven (triple)
Rhythmic mode 5e	Fast	Uneven (sextuple) [xxxxxo]
Rhythmic mode 5*	Fast	Doubled, followed by even

† In the song structure summaries, slow even beating is designated 'rhythmic mode 2a' only when the singer contrasts it with suspended slow beating (rhythmic mode 2b) within the same item. Otherwise it is simply designated 'rhythmic mode 2'. The form of uneven beating patterns is indicated using the convention x = clapstick beat; o = rest.

Table 2.1 Summary of rhythmic mode terminology, showing associated features of tempo and clapstick beating patterns.

Table 2.2 presents a different view of this data for the measured rhythmic modes (2–5), showing that some combinations (for example, uneven slow) do not occur in the *wangga* repertories under discussion. Such combinations may occur in other repertories of didjeridu-accompanied public dance-song, however (for example, slow uneven triple beating occurs in the *muyil lirrga* repertory) (Barwick, 2006). Differentiation of repertories and genres by characteristic clapstick patterns (and other musical features) assists in establishing and maintaining a clear aural identity, which Barwick has argued helps in ceremonial functions, especially in complex events like circumcision ceremonies, where there are likely to be multiple genres and repertories being performed (Barwick, 2011).

Tempo/beating style	slow	slow moderate	moderate	fast
even	2a	3a	4a	5a
even (suspended)	2b		4a (var)	5a (var)
uneven (triple)		3b	4c	5d
uneven (quadruple)			4b	5c
uneven (quadruple suspended)			4b (var)	
uneven (quintuple)			4d	
uneven (sextuple)				5e
doubled			4e	5b

Table 2.2 Measured rhythmic modes by tempo band and clapstick beating style.

Other factors help to further define rhythmic mode, including the metrical relationship between the voice and the clapsticks (Barwick, 2003; Marett, 2005). The didjeridu too has a role in defining rhythmic mode through the use of specific patterns associated with each mode. In measured rhythmic modes, the didjeridu plays almost as great a role in supporting the vocal line and defining metre as the clapsticks, while in the unmeasured rhythmic mode 1 (without clapsticks) it may maintain a degree of independence from the vocal rhythm. Rhythmic modes are also associated with affect. For example, in the Daly region, as in other areas across Arnhem Land (Anderson, 1992), unmeasured rhythmic modes are often associated with particularly serious songs. An association of fast tempo with heightened mood is reflected in the term *lerri* (Batjamalh for 'happy'), which at Belyuen is applied to several songs in fast rhythmic modes (by Barrtjap, Mandji and Muluk).

It is the association with dance (which can occur in both vocal and instrumental sections) that most strongly underpins the system of rhythmic modes. Through synchronising their movements with the clapstick beating, dancers tread in the footsteps of the ancestral ghosts summoned by the power of song. Both men and women dance, though the men's dancing is usually much more prominent—taking place in the centre of the dance ground and more likely to use mimetic movements referring to the content of the song texts. Men's dancing is based around a stamping movement, usually using alternate legs, described in Batjamalh using the verb –*mara* 'kick' (see chapter 3) (see figure 2.3). By contrast, women's dancing, which usually takes place around the edge of the dance ground, employs totally different movements (described in Batjamalh using the verb –*muya* 'sway') with alternate arms marking the beat and little if any movement of the feet (see figure 2.4).

For unmeasured and slow rhythmic modes male dancers often perform unstructured and mimetic movements, the everyday actions of ancestors—walking about, hunting, tracking, standing on one leg. By contrast, for songs in the moderate and fast rhythmic modes, accompanying male dance movements comprise a highly structured sequence of runs, stamps and flourishes (Marett, 2005, pp 101–05). The precedents for these dances lie in the ceremonies of the ancestors: that is, humans dance as the ancestors dance, and in so doing become one with them. In several songs (for example, Jimmy Muluk's 'Puliki' and 'Lame Fella') setting the same text to a different rhythmic mode is associated with changes in the described activity of the ancestral ghost. For example, in Billy Mandji's lengthy performance of 'Puliki' (chapter 5, track 2), vocal sections with slow beating refer to the slow rhythmic movements of the ancestral Buffalo swimming across the bay to Mica Beach, while fast beating is associated with the Buffalo dancing at Mica Beach.

Later in this chapter, we will discuss rhythmic mode and dance in more detail, including the distribution of rhythmic modes within each repertory. See Appendix 1 for more detailed information on the characteristics of each mode, including its relationship to dance.

Musical example: 'Tjerri', a *wangga* by Maurice Ngulkur

In this section we provide further clarification of our musical terminology and definitions of song structure through close attention to one song, Maurice Ngulkur's 'Tjerri'[6] one of the most interesting of the Ma-yawa *wangga* songs. 'Tjerri' speaks directly to the nature of Dreamings (*ngirrwat*). The composer and singer Maurice Ngulkur addresses the Sea Breeze Dreaming 'Tjerri' as 'elder brother' (*mana*) and sings of how the Sea Breeze manifests itself right here and now, as it has always done, causing waves to break at the mouth of the creek at the Tjerri Dreaming site (*kigatiya*) (see further in the notes to chapter 9, track 13).

---

6   Analyses of two other songs, 'Bangany-nyung Ngaya' and 'Yendili No. 1', which introduce the same analytical terminology, are also available in chapter 4 'Conventions of song and dance' of *Songs, dreamings and ghosts* (Marett, 2005).

Figure 2.3 Men and boys at Belyuen dancing at the launch of Allan Marett's book *Songs, dreamings and ghosts*, Belyuen, 2006. Photograph by Gretchen Miller, ABC Radio National, reproduced with the permission of Belyuen community.

Figure 2.4 A line of women dancing *wangga* at a circumcision ceremony in Wadeye, 1988. Photograph by Mark Crocombe, reproduced with the permission of Wadeye community.

Figure 2.5 Frank Dumoo executes a spectacular final flourish, dancing *wangga* at a Wadeye circumcision ceremony. Photograph by Mark Crocombe, reproduced with the permission of the Wadeye community.

Figure 2.6 Ambrose Piarlum dancing *wangga* at a Wadeye circumcision ceremony, 1992. Photograph by Mark Crocombe, reproduced with the permission of the Wadeye community.

Figure 2.7 Musical transcription of 'Tjerri' as performed by Maurice Ngulkur (rec. Marett Mar98-14-s08). Transcription by Allan Marett.

As already suggested, the musical form of 'Tjerri' is quite conventional (see figure 2.7). It begins with an instrumental introduction.[7] In this song, because the vocal sections are in rhythmic mode 1 (without

---

7   The introductory instrumental section establishes both the pitch and the tempo of the song. Where necessary (for example, when taking up a fresh song), a songman will indicate the required didjeridu pattern to the didjeridu player by singing it prior to the song beginning. Following the terminology used by Alice Moyle (AM Moyle, 1967b), we refer to these utterances as 'didjeridu mouth sounds'. If, as in 'Tjerri', the vocal sections of a song are to be performed in rhythmic mode 1 (without clapstick beating), the didjeridu will play a solo instrumental introduction. If on the other hand one of the measured rhythmic modes is used for the following vocal section, a songman will usually begin beating his clapsticks during the instrumental introduction, although it is not uncommon for him to wait until the beginning

clapsticks), the instrumental introduction is performed by the didjeridu alone. After a few seconds the singer begins vocal section 1, which comprises five text phrases sung within a single melodic section. The definition of a text phrase is somewhat loose: in the case of texts in human language, text phrases tend to comprise single units of meaning. In the text of 'Tjerri' (see table 2.3) we have defined *karra mana tjerri* and *kinyi-ni kavulh (kagan-dja)* as two text phrases, labelled text phrase 1 and text phrase 2 in the song structure summary of chapter 9, track 13, though they could have been classified as a single text phrase. In this case, the division into two was prompted by the need to treat the unit of text in text phrase 2 as a separate entity in the analysis.

VS	TP	A	B	C
1	1-2	karra mana tjerri	**kagan-dja kinyi-ni kavulh**	
	3-5	karra mana tjerri	**kinyi-ni kavulh kagan-dja**	purangang kin-pa-diyerr kagan-dja kisji
2	1-2	karra mana tjerri	**kinyi-ni kavulh**	
	3-5	karra mana tjerri	**kinyi-ni kavulh**	purangang kin-pa-diyerr kagan-dja kisji

Table 2.3 Text of 'Tjerri' as performed by Ngulkur in chapter 9, track 13, highlighting variability in text phrases. VS stands for 'vocal section', TP for 'text phrase' and the repetition pattern proposed for the units of text is indicated by the letters A, B, C. The variable text phrase B is highlighted in bold.

As usual in Ngulkur's performances, the precise form of the text within the text phrase varies from vocal section to vocal section and even from text phrase to text phrase. This variability can be observed in the placement of the word *kagan-dja* 'right here and now' in the performance (see table 2.3). In text phrase 2 of vocal section 1, he sings *kagan-dja kinyi-ni kavulh* 'right here and now he is always manifesting himself', while in text phrase 4 of the same vocal section he moves the word *kagandja* to the end of the text phrase so that it yields *kinyi-ni kavulh kagan-dja* 'he is always manifesting himself right here and now'. In text phrases 2 and 4 of vocal section 2, *kagan-dja* is omitted altogether, so the phrase becomes simply *kinyi-ni kavulh* 'he is always manifesting himself'. If we accept the basic equivalence of these variant forms of the text phrase, the textual form of each vocal section in this song is thus ABABC (as given in figure 2.1 and table 2.3). Freedom to change the position of words or to truncate a phrase stems from the fact that the song was rarely, if ever, sung in ceremony in recent times and therefore did not require exact reproduction from performance to performance (Marett, 2005, p 200). It is probably for this reason that Ngulkur's backup singer in this performance, Ambrose Piarlum, does not articulate the text very clearly, especially in vocal section 1, where he joins in mainly on the long notes.

In 'Tjerri', each vocal section comprises one melodic section, which in this case (but not in all *wangga* songs) is therefore co-terminous with the vocal section (as shown in figure 2.1 above). Melodic sections usually comprise a descent from the highest note to the lowest note. In most *wangga* the lowest note falls on the same pitch as the didjeridu. To facilitate comparison between songs, the pitch of the didjeridu is notated as C in all our transcriptions (with the original pitch of 'Tjerri', E flat, annotated above the stave in figure 2.7). Melodic sections may in some cases be further subdivided into subsections. The cadence points on F at the end of text phrases 2 and 4 in 'Tjerri' would mark such a division (and are indicated with dashed lines in figure 2.1). The melodic contour of 'Tjerri' is used in the majority of songs in the Ma-yawa *wangga* repertory, particularly those that are about Dreamings.[8]

Although not written out in full in the musical example in figure 2.7, the didjeridu always continues throughout the vocal section. In the case of a metrically free vocal section like that of 'Tjerri', where the

---

of the vocal section to begin beating the clapsticks (see for example Barrtjap's performance of 'Bangany-nyung Ngaya', chapter 4, track 5).

8 We discuss the melodies used in the Ma-yawa *wangga* in more detail below.

Figure 2.8 Maurice Ngulkur performing Ma-yawa *wangga* at Peppimenarti, 7 October 1998, during the period before the ceremony when dancers were still painting up. The didjeridu player is out of the frame to the right. Photograph by Allan Marett, reproduced with the permission of Wadeye community.

metre is underlyingly determined by speech rhythm (hence the marking of *parlando*), the didjeridu tends to mark word and morpheme boundaries with pulsations that enhance the comprehensibility of the text. The astute reader and listener may also have noticed that word boundaries are frequently marked by rhythmic prolongation of the final syllables of words (sometimes performed over several pitches as a melisma). This enhances comprehensibility.

Each vocal section is followed by an instrumental section performed by the clapsticks and didjeridu, with some vocalisation by the singer. In instrumental section 1 of 'Tjerri', this vocalisation is a held note on the vowel 'ii'; in instrumental section 2, it is a series of grunts (the latter not notated in figure 2.7).[9] Vocalisation within instrumental sections is another common but optional performance convention used by all singers from time to time, but most singers never deliver melodic text during an instrumental section.[10]

It is in the instrumental sections that the emphasis turns to dance, as the dancers enter to perform their rhythmically dynamic actions. For this reason, in instrumental section 1 of 'Tjerri' we can hear the mildly irregular metre of vocal section 1 replaced by regular even stick beating in a moderate tempo quaternary metre (rhythmic mode 4a). Even stickbeating patterns in moderate or fast tempo are used for non-final instrumental sections in all Ma-yawa *wangga* and Walakandha *wangga*[11] whose

---

9   Such vocalisations are noted but not transcribed in the song structure summaries in chapters 4–9.

10 An exception is Lambudju's performance of vocables in the lower octave of various songs (for example, 'Rak Badjalarr', chapter 7, track 2). In these cases, the vocal register clearly sets the vocable text apart from the melodic text in the vocal section proper.

11 In the Walakandha *wangga*, only fast tempo is used in this position (see chapter 8).

vocal sections are in rhythmic mode 1. The singer usually signals the end of an instrumental section with a clapstick pattern in the approximate rhythm ♫ ♩ ♫ ♩ ♩ 𝄽. Because of its pervasiveness in the Walakandha *wangga* repertory, Marett has previously termed this the 'Walakandha *wangga* cueing pattern' but in fact it occurs in other repertories including Muluk's (chapter 5) and the present Ma-yawa *wangga* (chapter 9) (Marett, 2007, p 71).[12]

In 'Tjerri', instrumental section 2 is the final instrumental section. To signal to the audience, didjeridu player and any dancers that this will be the end of the item, the lead singer Ngulkur commences a fast doubled beating pattern (rhythmic mode 5b), with interlocking beats provided by the backup singer Piarlum (in figure 2.2 we have notated this as an interlocking crotchet beat, performed by Piarlum, inserted into the quaver pattern performed by Ngulkur, the lead singer). In 'Tjerri', the crotchet tempo of the final instrumental section is approximately 130 beats per minute (bpm) (as compared to 136–40 for other fast tempo rhythmic modes in the Ma-yawa *wangga* repertory). Often final instrumental sections with interlocking beating in the fast doubled rhythmic mode (rhythmic mode 5b) are performed at a slightly slower tempo than is usual for the fast even rhythmic mode (rhythmic mode 5a), perhaps to make it easier for the backup singer to place the interlocking crotchet beats correctly, or perhaps because of the greater difficulty of performing regular fast quavers.

Cross-repertory variation

Song texts and vocal sections

Vocal sections vary a great deal in form from repertory to repertory and from song to song. Song texts may be entirely in spirit language or entirely in human language, or in a mixture of both. The number and complexity of text phrases and melodic sections too may vary. In some cases, vocal sections may contain contrasting types of text; see for example Muluk's famous 'Puliki' song (chapter 5, track 1), where a portion of text in spirit language (text phrases 1–3) is sung to the first melodic section (that is, one full melodic descent), and text that is largely in human language (text phrases 4–5) is sung to the second melodic section.

As already mentioned, some singers (for example Barrtjap and Lambudju) have quite stable texts, which are sung more or less exactly the same way from vocal section to vocal section and from performance to performance. We have already noted in the above discussion of 'Tjerri' that other singers may display considerable instability, not only from performance to performance, but also from vocal section to vocal section of the same item. Textual stability assists the singers to maintain the strong vocal unison desirable in ceremonial performance and also makes it easier to coordinate the actions of the dancers. Once a repertory is not regularly sung in ceremony, singers seem to delight in ringing the changes on their texts (see for example Ngulkur's three performances of 'Walakandha Ngindji' in chapter 9, tracks 1–3). This sort of instability is not to be confused with the highly structured variation of both text and music that an experienced singer like Muluk can use to great effect without diminishing the ability of the song to function ceremonially (as can be seen in his performance of five consecutive items of 'Piyamen.ga' in chapter 5, tracks 10–12).

Across the *wangga* corpus, the majority of songs have one or two melodic sections per vocal section (the example of 'Tjerri' discussed above had only one), although more melodically complex vocal sections are not uncommon. For example, vocal section 1 of Ngulkur's song 'Malhimanyirr' (chapter 9, track 17) has four melodic sections (in this case, formed by two repetitions of a two-melodic section text).

---

12 See further discussion of this point in the music analysis section of chapter 5.

Vocal timbre

Vocal timbre (or voice quality) is an integral quality distinguishing the different repertoires, especially at Belyuen, where singers consciously imitate the voice of their ancestral singers (whether alive or dead). Thus, when we played back Elkin's 1952 recordings, our collaborators at Belyuen were unable to distinguish the recorded voices of Tommy Barrtjap and his teacher Jimmy Bandak (Marett, 2000; 2005, p 68). We have also observed similarities in vocal quality between apprentice and master in Roger Yarrowin's performance of Lambudju's song 'Mubagandi' (chapter 7, track 25), and Colin Worumbu Ferguson's performance of songs sung by Billy Mandji (see notes to Worumbu's performance of 'Puliki', chapter 5, track 4). While each lineage at Belyuen might be said to have a characteristic vocal quality (piercing, with highly controlled vocal ornamentation for Barrtjap's lineage 1; a lighter, sweeter tone for Lambudju's lineage 2; a strong and darker toned husky quality for Muluk's lineage 3, and a forceful rounded quality for Mandji's lineage 4)[13] some songs, especially those of Billy Mandji (for example, 'Happy (*lerri*) song no. 2' in chapter 6, track 5), are notable for their systematic alteration of vocal quality within the vocal section, with prominent timbral changes giving the impression of a conversation. Marett argues that reproduction of the voice quality of deceased songmen and ancestral song-giving ghosts adds to the songs' power to create a liminal space between the worlds of the living and the dead (Marett, 2005, p 68).

At Wadeye, by contrast, there is no conscious effort to imitate the voice of the originator of the song (Marett, 2005, p 68). Rather, at least in the Walakandha *wangga* tradition, in ceremonial performances there is a preference for strong vocal unison from a rather larger number of singers (up to four or five). Perhaps this is due to singing groups of similar size in the two Wadeye sister traditions *lirrga* and *djanba*. Certainly in very large ceremonies a larger group of singers is more likely to be heard, and the content of their songs to be understood.

The power of the voice is evident in other traditional practices in the Daly region and indeed in much of Aboriginal Australia. Traditional owners often call out in their ancestral language to introduce strangers to ancestors residing in the 'sentient landscape' (Povinelli, 1993) of their homelands. Voice, like sweat,[14] has the power to penetrate bodies and landscapes, to integrate the unfamiliar and to summon the company of the ancestral ghosts to ceremony (Marett, 2003).

Melodic considerations

In this section we give more detail on the use of melody and melodic mode in defining *wangga* repertoires. We define melody as a fixed sequence of pitches that recurs regularly in each vocal section.

Sharing melody across repertoires

It is quite uncommon for a melody to be shared across repertoires. Rather, each repertory has one or more characteristic melodies that form part of its aural identity. When Maurice Ngulkur took the Walakandha *wangga* song 'Walakandha No. 2' (chapter 8, track 23) as the model for his song 'Walakandha Ngindji' (chapter 9, tracks 1-3), one of the most significant changes he made was to change the melody from one typical of the Marri Tjavin Walakandha *wangga* to one emblematic of Marri Ammu people, their country and their Dreamings (Marett, 2005, pp 137-150). Such performative gestures rest upon a convention that is widespread throughout the parts of Aboriginal Australia where song traditions are still strong, namely that melody encodes relationships between songs, totemic

---

13 These are our own characterisations of timbral characteristics—we have been unable to elicit any indigenous terminology.

14 Rubbing the sweat of traditional owners on strangers is another strategy used to introduce them to country and potentially dangerous Dreamings.

ancestors, country and kinship (Keen, 1994; RM Moyle, 1979, p 71; Toner, 2001). Given the power of melody to articulate such relationships, there was no more potent way for Ngulkur to bring the song into the Marri Ammu cultural sphere.

The melody/repertory relationship

In *wangga* generally, repertories commonly use more than one melody, but some repertories have a more restricted number of melodies than others. As already mentioned, in the Ma-yawa *wangga* (chapter 9) most songs that refer to Dreamings (*ngirrwat*) or Dreaming places (*kigatiya*) in Marri Ammu country share a melody, and most of the early Walakandha *wangga* songs use very closely related if not identical melodies. The Walakandha *wangga* repertory has a high proportion of shared melodies: 25 of its 34 songs share a melody with at least one other. By contrast, the Belyuen repertories use many different melodies, though there are still one or two examples of songs that share a melody, such as 'Tjinbarambara' and 'Wak' in Muluk's repertory.

The only repertory containing songs that may be sung to more than one melody is the Walakandha *wangga* repertory, for example 'Truwu' and 'Mirrwana'. Perhaps it was this precedent that inspired Ngulkur to set the text of the Walakandha *wangga* song 'Walakandha No. 2' to his own Marri Ammu melody in 'Walakandha Ngindji'.

The melodic mode/repertory relationship

It is common for songs within a repertory to share a melodic mode. All repertories include at least two different melodic modes (see table 2.4). In *Songs, dreamings and ghosts*, Marett demonstrated that there is a relationship between melodic mode and lineage (Marett, 2005). Marett has also shown how in performance singers can manipulate melodies in order to articulate the intersection or divergence of clan or language group interests (Marett, 2005, pp 117–21, 137–50).

Barrtjap's songs, for example, were for decades performed by a single patriline, passing from Barrtjap's classificatory father Jimmy Bandak to Barrtjap himself, and then to Barrtjap's sons, Kenny and Timothy. This straightforward transmission of the repertory has led to significant musical homogeneity. All but one of Barrtjap's songs have melodies that use a descending dorian series (B flat A G F E flat D C). This remains true today, even though, as we saw in chapter 1, these songs are now sung by singers from outside the Barrtjap lineage, such as Roger (Rossie) Yarrowin and Colin Worumbu Ferguson. The reason why this melodic homogeneity continues is probably that no new songs have been added to this set for at least a decade.

On the other hand, a complex history such as we find for Lambudju's repertory may result in a diversity of melodic modes. Marett has suggested that older songs inherited from Lambudju's father's brothers use all or part of a descending lydian series (C B A G F sharp E D C), while songs of Lambudju's own composition tend to use a dorian series (or part thereof, in the case of pentatonic or hexatonic melodies) (Marett, 2005, pp 194–95). A similarly complex musical history may underlie Jimmy Muluk's use of a mixolydian modal series for two of the older songs in his repertory, while most are in a major mode, with one sharing chromatic tendencies with two of Lambudju's songs. The distribution of melodic mode in Mandji's repertory is similar to Muluk's, perhaps reflecting their common musical history. Within the Walakandha *wangga* repertory (chapter 8) most songs composed by Stan Mullumbuk, together with those by members of the Kungiung, Dumoo and Kundjil families, have melodies in the dorian mode, while all songs composed by Mullumbuk's younger brother Philip Mullumbuk are in a major series.

	dorian	major	lydian	mixolydian	chromatic
Barrtjap	most	one			
Muluk		most		old	one
Mandji		most		one	
Lambudju	newer		older		two (new)
Walakandha	older	newer			
Ma-yawa	most	some			

Table 2.4 Distribution of melodic mode across the six repertories.

Rhythmic considerations

In this section we will examine the use of tempo, clapstick beating style and rhythmic mode across repertories, and show that certain rhythmic modes or combinations of rhythmic modes occur more frequently in certain repertories, suggesting that rhythmic mode is an important component of the aural identity of the repertory. The following consolidated data draws on the detailed information set out in the musical analysis summary for each repertory (see the relevant chapters for more detail). Additional information on the characteristics of each rhythmic mode is given in Appendix 1.

Because of significant discrepancies between the early and late repertories of the Walakandha *wangga* (see further discussion in chapter 8) we deal with them separately in this section.

Cross-repertory use of rhythmic mode and its components

For the purposes of clarifying cross-repertory variation in the use of rhythmic mode, we have found it useful to separate the rhythmic mode into its two components, tempo and clapstick beating style, to account for the fact that certain singers perform certain clapstick beating styles more commonly in one tempo than was usual in another repertory. For example, in final instrumental sections Muluk liked to employ moderate doubled beating (rhythmic mode 4e), while other repertories (such as Barrtjap and the Walakandha *wangga*) preferred fast tempo for their doubled beating (rhythmic mode 5b).

Tempo

Collating data from the various performances in chapter 4–9, we can observe that different repertories consistently use slightly different absolute tempi for the various tempo bands (see table 2.5). For example, we can observe that Mandji's slow tempo songs (with a tempo range of 46–48bpm) are considerably slower than those of Lambudju (64–69bpm). Some repertories, such as Barrtjap's, use a relatively wide range of tempi within a tempo band, while others are more restricted. Lambudju's unique use of four rather than three tempo bands means that each tempo band is relatively smaller in range.

Repertory/tempo band	Slow	Slow Moderate	Moderate	Fast
Barrtjap	58-65		117-120	126-144
Muluk	50-55		110-113	126-140
Mandji	46-48		110-116	130-140
Lambudju	64-69	99-107	110-116	120-125
Walakandha (early)	60-72		112	120-136
Walakandha (post 1986)	55-65			133-142
Ma-yawa		117-125	134-146	

Table 2.5 Tempo bands by repertory, showing range of absolute tempi used across each repertory (expressed in beats per minute).

If we examine the relative frequency of use of each tempo band by repertory, calculated by collating information on the usual tempo band for each song in the repertory (see data in the relevant chapters),[15] significant interrepertory differences again emerge (see table 2.6). For convenience of discussion we count the lack of clapstick beating as its own tempo band category.

Tempo band clapsticks	Barrtjap	Muluk	Mandji	Lambudju	Walakandha (early)	Walakandha (late)	Ma-yawa
none	3	5	8	6	18	32	13
slow	8	19	8	8	5	7	
slow mod				17			
mod	13	**40**	25	33	23		11
fast	**76**	35	**60**	**36**	**55**	**68**	**76**
TOTAL	100	100	100	100	100	100	100

Table 2.6 Proportional use of the various tempo bands across repertories (preferred tempo for each repertory highlighted in bold font). The numbers represent percentage values based on the number of times a particular tempo band occurs per song section in each repertory.

Key observations include the lack of slow tempo songs in the Ma-yawa repertory (see chapter 9) and the lack of moderate tempo songs in the late Walakandha *wangga* repertory. Each of these recent Wadeye repertories uses only three tempo bands, whereas the early Walakandha *wangga* conforms to the pattern of most Belyuen repertories in using four clapstick tempi (none, slow, moderate and fast tempo bands). Lambudju's repertory is the only one to use all five tempo bands, and the only one to include a tempo bond between slow and moderate, namely slow moderate. Muluk's repertory is the only one to use the moderate tempo band more frequently than the fast.

---

15 Source data on each song by repertory is found in tables 4.2 (Barrtjap), 5.2 (Muluk), 6.2 (Mandji), 7.2 (Lambudju), 8.3 (early Walakandha *wangga*), 8.4 (later Walakandha *wangga*), and 9.2 (Ma-yawa *wangga*). In cases where more than one rhythmic mode is performed in an item, vocal section or instrumental section, each is counted to arrive at the numbers that appear in this chapter.

Significant differences between repertories emerge when we consider the relative use of the various tempo bands by song section.

- Vocal sections: Overall, fast rhythmic modes are slightly preferred in vocal sections, with the next most common being rhythmic mode 1. Both repertories of Walakandha *wangga* display a clear preference for rhythmic mode 1 (no clapsticks). Muluk prefers slow tempo for his vocal sections, while Lambudju shows an equal preference for moderate and fast. Barrtjap displays an overwhelming preference for fast tempo in vocal sections. Mandji and Ma-yawa also prefer fast, though like Muluk and Lambudju they have a more even distribution of songs across the various tempo bands.
- Internal instrumental sections: All repertories prefer fast rhythmic modes, except for Muluk, who prefers moderate, and Lambudju, who again shows equal preference for moderate and fast tempi.
- Final instrumental sections (Barrtjap coda): All repertories prefer fast tempo, which in danced performances usually constitutes the climax and allows the most virtuosic dancers to show their ability to maximum effect.

Clapstick beating style

The other component of rhythmic mode, clapstick beating style, also shows some interesting variability across repertories (table 2.7). For convenience of discussion we count the lack of clapstick beating as its own clapstick beating style category.

clapstick beating style	Barrtjap	Muluk	Mandji	Lambudju	Walakandha (early)	Walakandha (late)	Ma-yawa
none	3	5	8	6	19	30	14
even	25	**44**	**60**	42	33	**40**	18
even (suspended)		9				1	
uneven (triple)	7		3	31			
uneven (quadruple)	**38**	9	23	22	14	0	**57**
uneven (quadruple suspended)			3				
uneven (quintuple)	10						
doubled	17	33	5		33	30	11
TOTAL	100	100	100	100	100	100	100

Table 2.7 Proportional use of the various clapstick patterns across repertories (preferred tempo for each repertory highlighted in bold font). The numbers represent percentage values based on the number of times a particular clapstick pattern occurs per song section in each repertory.

Two clapstick beating styles occur in all repertories: none, and even beating. Even patterns are preferred in all repertories except Barrtjap's and the Ma-yawa *wangga*, which prefer uneven (quadruple) beating patterns (♩ ♩ ♩ 𝄽). Barrtjap and Mandji employ the most number of different patterns (six) and Barrtjap's is the only repertory to include the uneven quintuple beating pattern (♩ ♩ 𝄽 ♩ 𝄽). Muluk uses five different beating patterns and the remaining four repertories (Lambudju, the early and late Walakandha *wangga*, and the Ma-yawa *wangga*) employ four each, though in each case a different combination.

More differentiations appear when we consider separately the distribution of clapstick beating styles across each structural division of the song.

- Vocal sections: Muluk, Mandji and Lambudju show a preference for even beating, while Barrtjap and Ma-yawa prefer the uneven (quadruple) pattern, and as already noted above, both eras of the Walakandha *wangga* prefer rhythmic mode 1. Note that it is only in vocal sections that suspended patterns occur (in Barrtjap, Muluk, Mandji and in both eras of the Walakandha *wangga* even suspended patterns occur, and in Mandji we find the sole example of uneven quadruple suspended).
- Internal instrumental sections: we again see Barrtjap and Ma-yawa grouping together in their preference for the uneven quadruple pattern, while all the remaining repertories show a strong preference for even beating.
- Final instrumental sections (Barrtjap coda): Again Barrtjap and Ma-yawa prefer the uneven quadruple pattern, while Lambudju and Mandji prefer even beating. Only Muluk and the two sub-repertories of the Walakandha *wangga* have a different preference for final instrumental sections (or coda) from internal instrumental sections. In both cases the preference clapstick beating style changes from even beating to doubled beating. Although this similarity was not singled out by Marett in his 2007 paper on the relationship between the Walakandha *wangga* and Muluk's repertory (Marett, 2007), it lends additional weight to his argument that Muluk's *wangga* was a compositional model for the Walakandha *wangga* repertory.

Combinations of rhythmic mode

We will finish our exploration of rhythmic mode across the *wangga* corpus by considering the proportion of songs in each repertory that occur in mixes of rhythmic modes.

Firstly, analysis reveals that the majority of songs (59%) in the corpus of 103 songs display some mixing of rhythmic modes, whether within sections of an item or between different performances of the same song. This is not evenly distributed between repertories, however. The repertories of Mandji, Lambudju and Ma-yawa have a preponderance of songs in the same rhythmic mode throughout (55%, 85% and 69% respectively), while the repertories of Barrtjap, Muluk and the Walakandha *wangga* have a majority of songs mixing rhythmic modes (constituting a massive 96% of songs in the late Walakandha *wangga*, due to the preponderance of vocal sections using rhythmic mode 1).

There are various ways in which different rhythmic modes can be applied to the same song. These are not mutually exclusive; indeed, Muluk's repertory in particular exhibits many different ways of combining rhythmic modes.

Presenting the same text in different rhythmic modes in successive items occurs only in the repertories of Muluk, the early Walakandha *wangga*, and the Ma-yawa *wangga*. In Muluk's repertory the songs concerned are 'Rtadi-thawara', which occurs with the vocal section set in three different rhythmic modes (2, 5c and 5b), 'Lame Fella', which occurs in two different rhythmic modes (2 and 5a), and 'Lerri', which occurs in three different rhythmic modes (2, 4a and 5b) (see table 5.1, chapter 5, for more detail). In the early Walakandha *wangga*, the songs 'Walakandha no 8' (rhythmic modes 4c and 5a) and 'Walakandha no. 9' (rhythmic modes 4a and 1) each occur in two different rhythmic modes, while in the Ma-yawa *wangga* it is 'Wulumen Tulh' (rhythmic modes 5c and 1).

Across all repertories, songs with vocal sections in rhythmic mode 1 and the slow rhythmic modes have fast or moderate tempi in the instrumental sections, required to allow the dancing characteristic of the style. There is also frequently a difference in rhythmic mode between internal and final instrumental sections (or coda), irrespective of the rhythmic mode used in the vocal sections (this feature occurs in almost half of the songs in the corpus—49 songs out of 103 songs—and is especially common in songs using rhythmic mode 1 for the vocal section).

Presentation of the same text in different rhythmic modes in different vocal sections within an item is unevenly distributed across the various repertories, with this feature being used in various ways in the Barrtjap, Muluk, Mandji, Lambudju and Ma-yawa repertories, but being absent from both eras of the Walakandha *wangga* repertory. In Barrtjap's case, six songs start out with the vocal sections set to the fast doubled rhythmic mode (5b), followed by one or more vocal sections in one of the other fast modes, most commonly by 5c (fast uneven quadruple) but in one instance by 5a (fast even) (see table 4.2 in chapter 4 for details). In the Ma-yawa, both performances of the song 'Walakandha Ngindji' (chapter 9, tracks 1–2) have the first vocal section in rhythmic mode 5c, and the second vocal section unaccompanied (rhythmic mode 1).

Mixing of rhythmic modes within a vocal section occurs most frequently in Muluk's repertory, where rather than using modes that contrast entire vocal sections, he instead uses suspension of the beating accompaniment (rhythmic modes 4a [var] and 2b) in a systematic way to differentiate the initial vocal section from subsequent vocal sections. For example, in the slow versions of both 'Lame Fella' and 'Rtadi-thawara' (chapter 5, tracks 13 and 15), he suspends beating throughout the entire first vocal section (rhythmic mode 2b throughout), whereas the second and subsequent vocal sections begin with the usual (non-suspended) slow beating (rhythmic mode 2a). In the five items of Piyamen. ga (chapter 5, tracks 10–12), we can observe a similar systematic use of the suspended form of the moderate tempo rhythmic mode (4a [var]). In these cases, the first vocal section in each item begins with the non-suspended form (rhythmic mode 4a), whereas the second and subsequent vocal sections begin with the suspended form, rhythmic mode 4a (var) (see chapter 5 for further details).

In Muluk, Mandji and the early Walakandha *wangga* repertories we find a number of songs that use contrasting rhythmic modes in different melodic sections or text phrases within the vocal section. For example, Muluk's song 'Puliki' (chapter 5, track 1) uses slow even beating (rhythmic mode 2a) in the first melodic section, and suspended slow beating in the second melodic section. We have already discussed above a number of instances in the Barrtjap, Muluk, Mandji and Walakandha *wangga* repertories in which suspended beating for part or all of a text phrase in the slow or moderate tempo bands (rhythmic modes 2b and 4a [var]) occurs in combination with the non-suspended forms (rhythmic modes 2a and 4a).

It is important to note that combinations of rhythmic modes within a vocal section only occur between the unaccompanied and slow rhythmic modes, or between the suspended and non-suspended forms of the slow and moderate rhythmic modes. The great variability in rhythmic mode we can observe in Muluk's repertory is perhaps in part attributable to his preference for moderate and slow rhythmic modes, that is, the modes with the most combinatorial possibilities. There are no instances in the corpus of vocal sections that combine moderate and fast rhythmic modes, or indeed slow and fast rhythmic modes. Indeed, one can imagine that this sort of rhythmic modal variability would be rather difficult to manage, both for musicans and dancers.

A few songs in the Muluk and early Walakandha *wangga* repertories, along with two songs in the Ma-yawa *wangga* repertory, have the feature of mixing rhythmic modes within a single instrumental section. This occurs in rhythmic modes 4* and 5*, in which internal instrumental section begins in doubled beating (rhythmic mode 4e or 5b), to be followed by a return to the even form of the same tempo band (4a or 5a). This distribution pattern confirms the influence of Muluk's repertory on the Walakandha *wangga*, and perhaps a subsequent influence of the Walakandha *wangga* on Ngulkur's performances of his Ma-yawa *wangga* repertory.[16]

---

16 Ngulkur frequently danced and sang Walakandha *wangga* songs alongside the Marri Tjavin singers.

Conclusion

We have gone into some detail on the differential use of rhythmic modes and their combinations across repertories, observing that different songmen have developed significantly different rhythmic modal profiles. We argue that, in combination with other factors (such as vocal timbre, use of a particular ancestral language, use of various melodic characteristics), these rhythmic modal characteristics contribute towards the aural identity or gestalt of the repertory, which allows it to be identified quickly in a complex ceremonial soundscape, and facilitates its function as a powerful vehicle for effecting social change through communication and danced interaction with the worlds of the living and of the dead.

Chapter 3
THE LANGUAGE OF *WANGGA*

Introduction

This chapter analyses the language of *wangga* song texts and shows a much more complex picture with regard to the differences between song language and everyday spoken language than is generally accepted. The following statement by Dixon is typical of generalisations about such differences:

> Songs that involve just everyday vocabulary tend to have quite simple grammar. There is minimal use of affixes—often in marked contrast to the everyday speech style—with, for instance, case-endings sometimes being omitted from nouns. In many languages songs just involve simple sentences, eschewing complexities. (Dixon, 1980, p 56)

We have already shown, through a linguistic analysis of Marri Ngarr *lirrga* song texts, that *lirrga* songs reveal a significantly greater degree of morphological and syntactic complexity than survives in spoken texts (Ford, 2006). In this chapter, we will show that, like *lirrga*, *wangga* song texts in the five language varieties in which *wangga* is sung contain significant complexity in their grammar and lexicon, and that they preserve features no longer present in everyday language. Some features absent in *wangga* that are present in everyday spoken language might be explained by the constraints of metre and poetry.

Most *wangga* texts come from a period when the languages in which they are sung were viable, when the songmen and their audiences had command of more than one of the Australian Indigenous languages of the Darwin-Daly River region. Most songmen sang in only one of the Daly languages, but some songmen used more than one language in a single song: Lambudju alternated languages at the level of text phrases (chapter 7, track 11) and Mandji alternated them at the level of vocal section (chapter 6, track 8). Today, the speech communities that produced *wangga* are no longer viable. Thus *wangga* texts are an important source of information about the grammar and lexicon of morphologically complex and severely endangered Australian Indigenous languages.

Wangga is sung in five language varieties from three distinct languages. These languages are:

- **Batjamalh** (the language of the Wadjiginy), still spoken at Belyuen (see figure 1.1) but with fewer than half a dozen fluent speakers
- **Emmi** (the language of the Emmiyangal people) and its closely related dialect **Mendhe** (the language of the Mendheyangal people) with only a handful of fluent speakers at Belyuen, One Mile Dam and Knuckey's Lagoon (both in Darwin) and at Balgal outstation opposite the Peron Islands
- **Marri Tjavin** (the language of the Marri Tjavin people) and its closely related dialect **Marri Ammu** (the language of the Marri Ammu people) with perhaps a dozen fluent speakers at Wadeye, Perrederr and at Knuckey's Lagoon in Darwin.

The traditional territories of these five language varieties abut each other, with Batjamalh the most northerly language, followed, along the coastal strip to the south of the Daly River mouth, by Emmi, Mendhe, Marri Ammu and finally Marri Tjavin. Emmi-Mendhe and Marri Tjavin-Marri Ammu belong to the Western Daly group of languages, a low-level linguistic subgroup (Dixon, 2002, p 675). The linguistic relationship of Batjamalh is less certain. Loans from Emmi-Mendhe into Batjamalh suggest that Batjamalh is a relative newcomer to the area, but even so it is likely that the Wadjiginy and their language have been in the Daly River region for several hundred years.

Figure 3.1 Lysbeth Ford and Kenny Burrenjuck working on Jimmy Muluk song texts, Mandorah, 1997. Photograph by Linda Barwick, reproduced with the permission of Belyuen community.

We may conclude therefore, that all five language varieties used in *wangga* are by now severely endangered. None has more than a dozen fluent speakers, and most current songmen have only imperfect command of Batjamalh. This is because of relatively recent but thoroughgoing language shifts.

As pointed out in chapter 1, the past one hundred and forty years have seen the migration of most speakers of Batjamalh and Emmi-Mendhe from their traditional territory around the mouth of the Daly River to Darwin, founded in 1867. The first recorded evidence of the presence of the Wadjiginy at Point Charles, on the west coast of Darwin Harbour, is dated 1885 (Ford, 1990). In 1937, the Wadjiginy and their Emmiyangal and Mendheyangal affines were resettled across the harbour from Darwin at Delissaville, now known as Belyuen. Today, everyone aged fifty and under at Belyuen speaks light Kriol (Sandefur, 1991) as their first language.

More recently, speakers of Marri Ammu and Marri Tjavin were brought into the Catholic mission founded in 1935 at Port Keats (known since 1979 as Wadeye). Marri Ammu and Marri Tjavin are related to the neighbouring inland language Marri Ngarr and its coastal dialect, Magati Ke. All four language varieties are generally known as Marri languages, and their speakers are known as members of the Marri language group. Marri elders tell how, as a result of intimidation by the more numerous Murriny Patha people, who own the land on which the mission stood, they started to speak Murriny Patha as their main language (Ford & Klesch, 2003). Today, there remain few fluent speakers of the Marri languages, and an unpublished sociological survey carried out in 2000 by Ford, Kungul and Jongmin showed that everyone at Wadeye aged fifty and under speaks Murriny Patha as their first language (Ford, Kungul, & Jongmin, 2000). Those whose mother tongue belonged to the Marri subgroup found this language shift expedient and relatively easy because, despite thoroughgoing lexical differences, the sound system and grammatical organisation of Murriny Patha are roughly similar to those of the Marri languages.

Overview of languages in which *wangga* is sung

Sound Systems

The languages in which *wangga* is sung have similar, but not identical, phoneme inventories. These are relatively simple. They all have a voicing contrast in stops and five series of stops and nasals. They all have two apical series of stops /**t**/, /**d**/, /**rt**/, /**rd**/, and all have two laminal series of stops (lamino-palatal /**tj**/, /**dj**/ and lamino-dental /**th**/, /**dh**/) except for Batjalmalh, which has only a lamino-palatal series. All three languages have an apical retroflex fricative /**rz**/. In addition Emmi-Mendhe and Marri Tjavin-Marri Ammu have a bilabial fricative /**v**/ and Marri Tjavin-Marri Ammu has an additional fricative, the lamino-palatal /**sj**/. All have two peripheral series of stops: labial /**p**/, /**b**/ and dorso-velar /**k**/, /**g**/. They all distinguish six nasals /**n**/, /**rn**/, /**ny**/, /**nh**/, /**m**/, /**ng**/, except for Batjamalh, which lacks /**nh**/. They all have two rhotics (apical /**rr**/ and retroflex /**r**/); three laterals (apical /**l**/, /**rl**/ and laminal /**lh**/), and two glides (lamino-palatal /**y**/ and a labial-velar /**w**/). They all have the four phonemic vowels /**i**/, /**e**/, /**a**/, /**u**/, but in addition Batjamalh has a fifth high front rounded vowel /**ü**/ and Emmi-Mendhe has a fifth mid unrounded vowel /**ö**/. These inventories are given in full below in the discussion of the sound systems of the relevant languages.

Lexicon

Each of these languages contains a lexicon of several thousand words (Ford, 1997 and in preparation). Each language uses sets of nominal and verbal classifiers to order the world around it, and contains an elaborate set of kin-terms by which it orders relationships between individuals. The number of classifying verbs ranges from ten in Batjamalh to thirty in each of Emmi-Mendhe and Marri Tjavin-Marri Ammu. Each classifying verb may co-occur with one or more of hundreds of co-verbs.

Morphology

These are morphologically complex, polysynthetic languages. This means that they contain long words consisting of ordered morphemes. Some of these morphemes are so old that they have fused, and thus convey more than one piece of meaning. Verbal affixes indicate, often redundantly, the person, number and gender of Subject and Object, and verbs inflect to show tense, aspect, mood and modality. Nominals are case-marked. A rich system of enclitics indicates direction, aspect, purpose and illocutionary force.

Word classes

Analysis of each of these languages contains the discrete word classes of nominals (nouns, pronouns, adjectives, deictics), verbals, modifiers (adverbs) and particles. Except for enclitic particles, which may attach to words of any class and are often attracted to a clause-initial host, each of these word classes behaves differently from the others and takes different affixes.

Syntax

Syntactically, each of these languages is head-marking, in that its verbs inflect for person, number, and gender. Each language is also dependent-marking, in that its nominals are, as in many Australian languages (Dixon, 1980, p 294), case-marked for core, peripheral and local relations. All sentient beings—including humans, living creatures and the land itself—qualify as Subjects.

Verbs are formally marked as transitive or intransitive by means of pronominal prefixes, which specify the person and number of the Subject and, in the case of transitive verbs, the Object of the verb. In Batjamalh, Subject and Object are fused in a portmanteau prefix. In the other languages, Subject and Object are marked by discrete prefixes. In Batjamalh, third personal minimal prefixes are also gender marked.

In each of these languages, the number system marked on verbs and free pronouns is most accurately described as Minimal versus Augmented, rather than Singular versus Plural. In each, there is a Minimal stem (glossed MIN) for: I, you (one person), you (one person + I—speaker and addressee) and he/she; and an Augmented stem (glossed AUG) for: we/us, you (more than one person) and they/them. Each language has an affix meaning 'plus one', which suffixes to a Minimal stem to augment the stem by one.[1] Each language has another affix meaning 'plus more than one', which suffixes to an Augmented stem to specify numbers greater than three.

Each of these languages has a rich system of bound pronouns describing how the action/event denoted by the verb affects a human Object, and the degree to which the person affected has control over what is happening to them. Free and bound pronouns make a distinction between including or excluding the addressee (inclusive/exclusive).

Each language employs verbless equational clauses and verbal clauses to state propositions. Verbs inflect for Realis mood to express statements whose reality can be vouched for by the speaker, and for Irrealis mood to refer to events, states or actions that he or she has not witnessed. These include things yet to happen, hearsay and hypotheticals; indeed anything whose reality the speaker cannot vouch for.

Each language has simple and complex clauses including embedded clauses. These may take the form of headless relative clauses, which omit the antecedent to the relative clause. Each language also contains serial constructions, which are conjoined clauses containing a main verb, followed by a simple intransitive verb signifying the physical orientation of the co-referential Subject, and/or adding aspectual information to the notion expressed by the verb. This aspectual information tells us whether the action/event/state expressed by the verb is habitual, repeated, deliberate, temporary or permanent. Both verbs share specification for tense (past/non-past), mood (declarative/imperative) and modality (Realis/Irrealis).

Semantics

Semantically, each of these languages incorporates body-part nominals into a verb phrase or noun phrase to signify any entity of the same shape. So, 'eye' (Batjamalh **mive**, Emmi-Mendhe and Marri Tjavin-Marri Ammu **miri**) stands for a face, a person, a window or door, a seed, a hearth or a fire. 'Belly' (Batjamalh **dawarra**, Emmi-Mendhe **mari**, and Marri Tjavin-Marri Ammu **marzi**) stands for the interior of a boat or car, or the curve of a beach. In everyday spoken language, body parts are metaphors for emotion; the belly represents anxiety, the back represents laughter and the head represents embarrassment.

In Emmi-Mendhe and Marri Tjavin-Marri Ammu, classifying verbs for the most part co-occur with semantically appropriate co-verbs. While some pairings appear anomalous, this is inevitable in a system where co-verbs require classifying verbs to specify the person, number and gender of the Subject and Object, as well as the tense, aspect, mood and modality of the action/state/event denoted by that co-verb. In Batjamalh, this system applies to some verbs, but by no means all, because many verb stems inflect for person, number, gender, tense, aspect, mood and modality without requiring a classifying verb to do this.

Song words

Each of the song repertoires discussed in this book contains, to a greater or lesser extent, words that are not part of normal spoken language. In transcription we gloss these as 'song words' (SW) and in identifying such words, we are reliant on songmen and other informants, who usually say that they are 'just for song.' In many cases vocables of this sort are identified as 'spirit language.' For example, Tommy Barrtjap told us that when he received songs from *wunymalang* ghosts in dream, they were

---

1   An anomaly of this system is that when this suffix, added to Minimal stems to mean 'plus one', is added instead to an Augmented stem, it means 'plus two.'

initially entirely in the language of the *wunymalang*, and that it was his responsibility, as songman, to 'turn over' the songs into human language. In many of his songs, only a portion of the text is rendered in human language (in this case, Batjamalh), while the remainder of the song is left in *wunymalang* language, which we, like native speakers, hear only as a string of unintelligible vocables.

Contrary to the experiences of Dixon and Koch (1996, pp 26–34), our consultants have, over several decades, steadfastly resisted our attempts to segment or assign meaning to individual song words. Moreover, there was complete clarity about what were song words and what were not, even in cases where the form of the song words bears a resemblance to words in mundane register. For example, the phrase **mele nele**—which could mean 'older brother, for him'—occurs in one of Mandji's songs within a section of the song that otherwise contains only song words (chapter 6, track 1, text phrases 1 and 2). Consultants were adamant that in this context **mele nele** are song words and not words in Mendhe. In one of Barrtjap's songs, 'Kanga Rinyala Nga-ve Bangany-nyung,' (chapter 4, track 5) the phrase **kanga rinyala** tantalisingly seems to contain the Batjamalh word for melody, **rinya**, yet attempts on our part to gloss it as Batjamalh rather than song language were strongly resisted by the songman himself.

Spirit language resists linguistic analysis, because fluent speakers of the languages under focus insist that song words are not generally understood by living humans. Moreover, song words are generally CVCV sequences that do not correspond to words in everyday register. For this reason, song words will not be dealt with in any detail in this chapter, although in the following discussion of Batjamalh, some of the difficulties of transcribing such words will be discussed.

Nevertheless, it is clear that the proportion of song words to words in everyday language differs from singer to singer. Of the two Batjamalh-speaking songmen, for example, Barrtjap uses a much higher proportion of song words than Lambudju does, and so do the other two Belyuen songmen, the Mendheyangal songman Jimmy Muluk and the Marri Tjavin speaker Billy Mandji. The Marri Tjavin and Marri Ammu *wangga* from Wadeye, on the other hand, use almost no song words at all. Although there is some overlap, the song words in the Emmi-Mendhe and Marri Tjavin-Marri Ammu *wangga* of Muluk and Mandji generally differ from those in the Batjamalh *wangga* of Tommy Barrtjap.

BATJAMALH

Detailed analysis of *wangga* song language will begin with Batjamalh, not only because the earliest *wangga* in our corpus were composed in Batjamalh, but also because its lexicon and its verbal and nominal morphology differ significantly from those of the other languages in which *wangga* is sung. That Batjamalh is the newcomer to the area is shown by its fossilised and limited use of nominals, verbal classifiers, body part noun incorporation, and, as Evans (1989) shows, Irrealis morphemes. All these grammatical categories would appear to have been borrowed from the neighbouring Marri languages. The two Batjamalh *wangga* repertories were composed and performed by Wadjiginy songmen Barrtjap (chapter 4) and Lambudju (chapter 7).

Sound system

The sound system of Batjamalh contains fewer consonant phonemes than those of the other languages in which *wangga* is sung. As table 3.1 shows, its twenty-three consonants include five full series of voiced and voiceless stops: two apical, one laminal, and two peripheral, with nasals to match. Batjamalh lacks the full lamino-dental series of stops and nasals found in Marri Tjavin-Marri Ammu, and has only one, rarely occurring, phonemic fricative, compared to the two in Emmi-Mendhe and the three in Marri Tjavin-Marri Ammu. Like the other Daly languages in which *wangga* is sung, Batjamalh has three laterals (two apical and one laminal), two apical rhotics and two semivowel continuants.

As pointed out in the previous section and set out in table 3.2, Batjamalh has five phonemic vowels, including the rounded front vowel ü.

	APICO-		LAMINO-		PERIPHERAL	
	Alveolar	Retroflex	Interdental	Palatal	Dorso-velar	Bilabial
Stops: voiceless	t	rt		tj	k	p
Stops: voiced	d	rd		dj	g	b
Fricative		rz				
Nasal	n	rn		ny	ng	m
Liquid: lateral	l	rl	lh			
Liquid: rhotic	rr	r				
Continuant/glide				y		w

Table 3.1 Batjamalh consonant phonemes.

	unrounded		rounded	
high	i		ü	u
mid	e			
low	a			
	front	back	front	back

Table 3.2 Batjamalh vowel phonemes.

Tables 3.1 and 3.2, listing Batjamalh consonant and vowel phonemes, may be compared with the inventory of Emmi-Mendhe consonant and vowel phonemes shown in tables 3.3 and 3.4, and the inventory of Marri Tjavin-Marri Ammu consonant and vowel phonemes shown in tables 3.6 and 3.7.

All Batjamalh phonemes are represented in the *wangga* song texts, except the apico-postalveolar (retroflex) fricative and lateral. The absence of these phonemes in *wangga* is not surprising, as both carry a low functional load in everyday speech. In our extensive Batjamalh corpus, /**rz**/ occurs only in the lexemes **marzanmarzan** 'barnacle' and **mürza** 'star' and its compounds **mürzarak** 'sky' and **mürzamedjem** 'egg', while /**rl**/ occurs only in the lexemes **durl** 'cranky', **durlk** 'whale; Dreaming,' **kurluk** 'blind' and **barndarla** 'stringybark.'

So as to represent as faithfully as possible the actual sounds sung, and to render the text as accessible as possible to the general reader, our transcriptions of *wangga* texts are written in a sub-phonemic orthography that shows the allophonic variants of phonemes.[2] For instance, the voiced bilabial stop phoneme /**b**/ is often realised as the allophone [**v**]. We have therefore made a decision to represent /**b**/ as [**v**] when it occurs between vowels. This can be seen in text phrases such **naya rradja bangany nye-ve** 'Naya rradja. You go for a song' (chapter 4, track 16, text phrases 1–3) and **yagarra yine nga-ve-me-nüng** 'Yagarra! What have I come to do?' (chapter 4, track 7, vocal sections 2 and 3, text phrase 2; track 22, text phrase 3).

A second example of our use of subphonemic orthography occurs where consonants show allophonic assimilation to a preceding or following consonant. A frequently occurring example of the former is where the initial consonant of the dative suffix -**nung** assimilates to the final consonant of the preceding morpheme **bangany** (song) to produce **bangany-nyung** (chapter 4, track 1; chapter 7, track 1). An

---

2   Allophonic variants do not make a difference in meaning but represent the phonetic variant of that phoneme in a particular environment.

instance of allophonic assimilation to a following consonant is found where the final apico-alveolar nasal of the pronominal prefix **ngan-** is realised as retroflex before a following stem-initial retroflex stop, see for example **ngan-rdut-mene-ng** represented as **ngarn-rdut-mene-ng** (chapter 7, track 10, text phrase 1b).

A third example of our use of subphonemic orthography concerns vowel harmony, which occurs when a vowel assimilates to a preceding or following vowel. An example of the former occurs where the initial vowel of a suffix assimilates to the vowel quality of the final vowel of the preceding morpheme, as when the suffix **-nung** becomes **-nüng** after **me**, as in **yagarra yine nga-ve-me-nüng** (chapter 4, track 7, vocal sections 2 and 3, text phrase 2; track 22, text phrase 3) or after **djü**, as in **nga-p-pindja-ng nga-p-puring-djü-nüng** (chapter 4, track 7, vocal sections 2 and 3, text phrase 3). An example of assimilation to a following vowel occurs in **bangany nye-bindja-ng nya-mu** 'Sit and sing a song!' (chapter 7, track 17, text phrase 1) where there is vowel harmony affecting the final vowel of each pronominal prefix **nyV**. The underlying vowel of this prefix is realised as [e] before **-bindja** because the first vowel of **-bindja** is a front vowel, but is realised as [a] before **-mu** because **-mu** contains a back vowel. Thus we write **nye-bindja** in the first case, but **nya-mu** in the second.

Transcribing the vocables in *wangga* song texts presents particular difficulties, because there are no equivalents in everyday language against which to check them. We write them in the same sub-phonemic orthography as the rest of the *wangga* texts. They are, however, inherently unstable as a result of the distortion brought about by the airflow of singing, which is typically very strong at the start of a breath phrase and weak towards the end. This distortion blurs the distinction made between sounds produced in the same part of the mouth (Marett & Barwick, 1993, p 21). For example, if the apico-alveolar rhotic /rr/ is, for this reason, not accurately articulated, or pushed back in the mouth, **rradja** can sound like **adja**, **dadja**, **rzadja** or even **gadja**.³ Similarly, if the lamino-palatal stop /dj/ in the same song word **rradja** is not accurately articulated, it can be lenited to **rraya** or fricativised to **rrarza**. For the same reason, nasals are more clearly articulated with the relaxation of breath towards the end of a breath-phrase, and conversely lightly articulated at the beginning of a breath-phrase. So, the first **naya** in text phrase 1 of each verse of 'Naya Rradja Bangany Nye-ve' (chapter 4, track 16) can sound like **aya**, and the quality of the nasal in **mayave** is hard to distinguish. Vowels tend to close and come forward and higher as the breath flow weakens, so that [a] becomes [e]. For this reason **bangany-nyaya** is sometimes realised as **bangany-nyaye** and **yagarra** becomes **yakerre**.

Word classes

The *wangga* texts contain examples of all Batjamalh word classes.

Nominals

A well-formed Batjamalh sentence need contain no overt nominals. Batjamalh *wangga* song texts, however, contain a higher proportion of overt nouns than is common in everyday speech. Barrtjap's 88 clauses contain 49 nominals and Lambudju's 46 clauses contain 56 nominals. Some of these nominals represent new information, some are repetitions, some are body-part nominals incorporated into the verb phrase, and others form verbless equational clauses stating the topic of the song-text, as in **anadadada bangany-nyaya nga-bindja-ya** ' "Anadadada" is the song I'm singing' (chapter 4, track 26, text phrases 1–2).

---

3   It is for these reasons that earlier published transcriptions of the vocable text varied from those presented in this work. What we previously wrote as **dadja gadja** is now **naya rradja** and what was **mayave gadja** is now **mayave rradja** (Marett, 2005, pp 175–179).

A wide range of nominals appears in the *wangga* texts. These include: proper nouns, either personal names such as **Tjerrendet** (chapter 7, track 15, text phrase 1) and **Mangalimba** (chapter 4, track 25, text phrase 1), or place names such as **Badjalarr** 'North Peron Island' (chapter 7, track 1); common nouns such as **winmedje** 'oyster' (chapter 7, track 1, text phrase 6; track 14, text phrase 1) or **kurratjkurratj** 'channel-billed cuckoo' (chapter 7, track 13, text phrases 1-4); and kin-terms such as **balhak** 'older brother' (chapter 7, track 10, text phrase 1b), **ngaradja** 'daughter' (chapter 4, track 1, text phrases 7–9) and **nedja** 'son' (chapter 4, track 20, text phrases 1-4).

An example of an adjective in Badjamalh *wangga* texts is **munguyil-malang** 'fast-paddling' (chapter 7, track 10, text phrase 3), which is derived from the noun **munguyil** 'paddle,' by adding the suffix **malang** '-FUL.' Everyday spoken Batjamalh contains several adjectives produced by adding **malang**, such as **bwikmalang** 'bony', from **bwik**, 'bone' + **-malang** '-FUL.'

Although gender and number-marked deictics occur in everyday Batjamalh to position referents in relation to the speaker, the only deictic to occur in Batjamalh *wangga* is **tjidja** 'this man near me' (chapter 4, track 23, text phrase 5 and chapter 7, track 15, text phrases 1–4). Other *wangga* repertories use deictics more freely.

Each nominal is case-marked to show its relation to other nominals in the sentence. As in everyday Batjamalh, nominals in *wangga* texts carry case-affixes encoding core syntactic, peripheral syntactic or local relations. As a core grammatical relation, a nominal in Absolutive case, which carries zero case-marking, may function as the Subject of an intransitive verb, as in **Tjerrendet-maka**[4] **ka-ngadja** 'Tjerrendet has gone back' (chapter 7, track 15, text phrase 1). A nominal in Absolutive case may also function as the Object of a transitive verb, as in **winmedje ngan-dji-nyene ngami** 'I am sitting eating oysters' (chapter 7, track 14, text phrase 1).

When first introduced into the discourse, a noun or pronoun case-marked for the core syntactic role of Agent of a transitive verb carries the affix **-garrang**, which is realised as **-karrang** after a host-final voiceless stop, as in **malvak-karrang-maka ngarn-rdut-mene-ng ka-bara** 'Malbak has gone and left me behind' (chapter 7, track 10, text phrase 1).

Batjamalh *wangga* texts also contain nominals case-marked to show dative, causative and instrumental relations. For example, a nominal is marked as a target or goal with the dative case-affix **-nyung** (chapter 4, track 1; chapter 7, track 1). The causative case-affix **-maka** denotes the reason for an action, event or state. So, for instance, **rak badjalarr-maka** means 'for the sake of [a song for] my ancestral country, North Peron Island' (chapter 7, track 1, text phrases 1-5). The instrumental case-affix **-djene** marks the floating log as a tool in **ngawardina-djene** (chapter 7, track 10, text phrase 4).

Batjamalh has two ways to show the possessive relation. The most common in everyday speech is to affix the possessive affix **-bütung** to the possessed noun. The alternative is to juxtapose possessed and possessor nouns, as always happens in Marri Tjavin and Marri Ammu. **-bütung** does not occur in Batjamalh *wangga*. When Barrtjap sings **rak-pe ngadja** 'my eternal country,' however, possessed (**rak-pe**) and possessor (**ngadja**) nominals are juxtaposed (chapter 4, track 12, text phrases 1–4).

In everyday Batjamalh, verbs may incorporate body-part nominals that represent a part of the Object (metonym). In **tjendabalhatj mive-maka nyen-ne-ne kanye-djanga** 'Tjendabalhatj, they saw you standing there' (chapter 7, track 16, text phrases 1–4), **mive** 'eye,' stands for the whole person called Tjendabalhatj. Similarly, **müng ya-mara** 'catch him up' literally means 'kick his arse (**müng**)' (chapter 7, track 10, text phrase 3).

As mentioned above, body-part nominals may also be metaphors for any entity with the same shape as the body part. In Lambudju's *wangga*, **nguk** in **nguk ka-maridje-ng ka-yeve** 'he is lying with one knee bent over the other' (chapter 7, track 10, text phrase 2), is the reduced form of the everyday word

---

4 Here **-maka** is the Perfective enclitic, not to be confused with the homophonous case-marker **maka** 'on behalf of'.

mirranguk 'knee.' While in this case the reference is to the actual body part, the knee, in everyday Batjamalh **nguk** may also signify 'pandanus fruit,' which happens to be shaped like a kneecap. Similarly, **dawarra** 'belly,' is used to refer to any concave entity. Features of the landscape are commonly referred to as the body-part whose shape they share. So, in Barrtjap's *wangga*, **dawarra wagatj** 'belly of the beach' means the hollow curve of a beach, as in **yagarra dawarra wagatj nga-bindja-ng ngami ni** 'I was sitting in the curve of the beach singing "ni"' (chapter 4, track 7, vocal section 1, text phrase 3).

Verbals

Batjamalh *wangga* texts reveal copious evidence of verbal and non-verbal clauses. Of the 103 clauses that make up Barrtjap's *wangga* corpus, 53 (51.45%) contain verbs. Of the remaining 50 non-verbal clauses, 38 (76%) consist of the free particle **yagarra** (which we never translate, although it literally means 'oh, no!'), and the rest are equational clauses, such as **nedja tjine rak-pe** 'Son, where is my camp/eternal country?' (chapter 4, track 20, text phrases 1–3).

Lambudju's *wangga* contain a slightly higher proportion of verbal clauses. Of the 62 clauses, 47 (75.8%) contain verbs. In the remaining 15 clauses, there are 6 elliptical constructions. In track 1 of chapter 7, for example, the causal noun phrase + dative noun phrase, **rak badjalarr-maka + bangany-nyung** 'for my ancestral country, North Peron Island + for the sake of a song' is repeated five times with no main verb, thus giving, 'for the sake of a song for my ancestral country, North Peron Island.' In his spoken gloss, however, Lambudju supplies the missing verb **nga-bindja-ng** 'I am singing.'

There are two types of Batjamalh verb phrase (Ford, 1990, pp 120–62). Type one consists of a single verb stem with pronominal prefixes and affixes indicating tense, aspect and modality, as in **ka-djen-mene** 'it [the tide] is coming in' (chapter 7, track 7, text phrases 1–2). Type two consists of two verb stems, one of which inflects for person, number and gender by means of pronominal prefixes. For example, in **ngala-viyitj nya-mu-nganggung** 'sit and clap hands for us both' (chapter 7, track 8, vocal section 2, text phrase 2), **nya-mu** acts as a classifier to the preceding uninflected co-verb (**-viyitj**). Both types of verb phrase may begin with an incorporated body-part nominal (in the preceding example, this is **ngala**). The great majority of Batjamalh verb phrases are of type one; only ten classifying verbs have been identified for Batjamalh (Ford, 1990).

Batjamalh has two sets of pronominal prefixes. The first shows that it is transitive, requiring a Subject and Object. The second set shows that it is intransitive, requiring only one argument, the Subject. All other *wangga* languages have only one set of Subject prefixes that serve for both transitive and intransitive verbs and show the Object simply by suffixing one of a set of Object bound pronouns to the classifier verb stem.

Examples of Batjamalh intransitive prefixes are **nga-** 'I,' as in **nga-mi** 'I sit' (many examples throughout chapter 4 and chapter 7); and **ka-** 'he,' (inflected for Realis mood), as in **bandawarra-ngalgin ka-djen-mene** 'it [the tide] is coming in at Bandawarra-ngalgin' (chapter 7, track 7, text phrases 1-2). The pronominal prefix for 'you (one person)' inflected for Irrealis mood is **nyV-**, as in **nye-bindja-ng** 'you sing' (chapter 4, track 7, vocal section 1, text phrase 2); **nya-muy-ang** 'dance' (chapter 7, track 8, text phrase 2); **nya-ngadja-barra-ngarrka** 'you (one person), come back here to me!' (chapter 4, track 24, text phrase 2).

Batjamalh has another set of portmanteau Subject or Agent plus Object (S/A + O) pronominal prefixes for transitive verbs that show who is doing what to whom. The term portmanteau means that the forms are so fused and so old that it is impossible to unpack them to distinguish Subject from Object. For example, the pronominal prefix **ngan-** on transitive verbs can mean either 'he/she does it to me' or 'I do it to them.' Although it is impossible to unpack this portmanteau morpheme further, context will often disambiguate the meaning. For example **ngan-dji-nyene** (chapter 7, track 1, text phrase 6) could mean either 'I eat them' or 'he/she eats me.' In his spoken gloss, Lambudju is careful to disambiguate this by adding the serial verb **nga-mi** (I sit) to the phrase, thus **ngan-dji-nyene nga-mi,** in order to unambiguously produce the meaning 'I [sit and] eat them.' Nevertheless, from the point of view of poetics it is interesting to reflect on why Lambudju choses to leave out the disambiguating element **nga-mi** in the sung form, particularly since in another related song 'Winmedje' (chapter 7, track 14) he retains **nga-mi** in the sung version of this phrase. Another instance from Lambudju's repertory where serial construction disambiguates a potential ambiguity with regard to **ngan-** may be seen in **ngarn-rdut-mene ka-bara** 'he has gone and left me behind' (chapter 7, track 10, text phrase 1b).

Similarly ambiguous is the pronominal prefix **yV-**, which could mean either 'you (one person) do it to him' or 'he/she does it to him.' Thus the phrase **müng ya-mara** (chapter 7, track 10, text phrase 3) could mean either 'you must catch him up!' or 'he/she must catch him up.' The presence of the serial verb **nya-buring** ('you do it deliberately'), thus **müng ya-mara nya-buring**, not only adds aspectual information—that the action is deliberate—but it also disambiguates the meaning. Because the subjects of the two verbs have to be coreferential, the meaning must be 'you must [deliberately] catch him up.' Because this is rather a mouthful, in chapter 7 we translate this with the more idiomatic 'Catch him up!'

In the other *wangga* languages, direct or indirect object bound pronominals are suffixed to the classifier verb stem. In Batjamalh, only indirect object bound pronominals are suffixed to the verb stem. Examples of these are **-ngarrka** 'for me,' (chapter 4, track 14, text phrase 4; chapter 7, track 17, text phrases 1–2); **-nganggung** 'for you and me,' (chapter 4, track 15, text phrase 5; chapter 7, track 17, text phrases 3–4) and **nüng** 'for him' (chapter 7, track 13, text phrases 1–4).

Modality expresses the attitude of the speaker towards what she or he says. Batjamalh speakers vouch for the reality of their utterances by grammaticalising modality. Pronominal prefixes to the verb are marked Realis, if the speaker can vouch for the truth of what she or he says, or Irrealis, if s/he cannot.

To complicate matters, some pronominal prefixes and many verb stems do not alter to show modality. In one conjugation, however, verb stems are suffixed with **mene/nene/nyene** to mark Realis (Ford, 1990, p 178). This is the function of **mene** in **ka-djen-mene** 'it [the tide] is coming in [and I can vouch for this]' (chapter 7, track 7 text phrases 1–2). It is also the function of **mene** in **ngarn-rdut-mene** 'he leaves me behind [and I can vouch for this]' (chapter 7, track 10, text phrase 1b), of **nyene** in **ngan-dji-nyene** 'I eat them [and I can vouch for this]' (chapter 7, track 1, text phrase 6) and of **nene** in **nyen-ne-ne**, 'they see you [and I can vouch for it]' (chapter 7, track 16).

If the speaker *cannot* vouch for the truth of what she or he says, the utterance is marked Irrealis. Thus, utterances about the future or commands (which are intrinsically not yet realised and therefore cannot be vouched for) are all marked as Irrealis.

Irrealis modality is signified by three mechanisms: by attaching Irrealis forms of the pronominal prefixes to verbs (if these forms exist), by inserting an Irrealis morpheme between the prefix and the verb stem or by changing the verb stems from a Realis to an Irrealis form (if these forms exist), sometimes by adding the verb phrase-final purpositive enclitic **-nung**.

Commands combine an Irrealis prefix and a verb stem, which if such a form exists, will be inflected for Irrealis. For example, the utterance **nye-bindja-ng nya-mu** 'you [sit and] sing!' (chapter 4, track 7, vocal section 1, text phrase 2) is a command that combines two verb stems (sit and sing), both inflected for Irrealis modality. The pronominal prefix **nye-/nya-** (you) is in Irrealis form in both verbs. The verb stem **-bindja** (sing) does not change to show Irrealis modality but the serial verb does: **mu** (sit) is an Irrealis form, whose Realis form is **-mi** (sit).

Statements of future intent combine all three mechanisms: a pronominal prefix inflected for Irrealis (if such a form exists), the Irrealis morpheme **p-** and a verb stem inflected for Irrealis (if such a form exists). For instance, **nga-p-pindja-ng nga-p-pur-ing-djü** 'I'm going to climb up and go now' (chapter 4, track 22, text phrase 4), is a serial construction containing two verbs, the stems of which are **-pindja** and **-pur**. In both verbs the pronominal prefix **nga-** is one that remains the same irrespective of modality.

Nga- is followed, in both verbs, by the Irrealis morpheme **p-**. The verb stem **-bindja** (here pronounced **-pindja** to assimilate to the previous morpheme) is one that does not change to reflect modality. The second verb **-bur** (here pronounced **-pur** to assimilate to the previous morpheme) is, however, one that does change to reflect modality, in this case by adding the suffix **-ing** as well; its Realis form is **-bara**.

Further to the use of Realis and Irrealis modalities in Batjamalh, we should note that there is an apparently anomalous construction that is unique to Batjamalh among the Daly languages, and which appears to contradict the normal semantic domains associated with Realis and Irrealis. This concerns prohibitions, which are negative commands. While Batjamalh, like all the Daly languages used in *wangga*, can express a prohibition by means of a clause-initial negator (in Batjalmalh this is **nagulhü**) and a verb inflected for Irrealis mood, Batjamalh has another productive mechanism for expressing prohibition. We see this in Barrtjap's song, 'Yagarra Delhi Nya-ngadja-barra-ngarrka' (chapter 4, track 24, text phrase 3): **nanggang-gulhü kanya-bara-m**, which consultants routinely translate as 'Don't be frightened!' Here the clause negator is realised as an enclitic particle **gulhü** and the verb is inflected for Realis (rather than the expected Irrealis) modality.

The *wangga* texts show that some Batjamalh verb stems are inherently ambiguous. Despite its intransitive prefixes, the verb **-bindja** 'sing' functions as a transitive verb when Barrtjap and Lambudju add **bangany** 'song' to the verb phrase (chapter 4, track 1, track 4, track 10; chapter 7, track 2, text phrases 1-5; track 15, text phrases 1-4). **Ka-bindja** can, however, also mean 'he climbs up' or 'he hangs something up.' Only context, such as the evidence of the songman who composed the song, or the consensus of fluent speakers, decides that in Barrtjap's song, 'Ya[garra] Nga-bindja-ng Nga-mi' (chapter 4, track 7, vocal sections 2 and 3, text phrase 4) the serial construction **nga-p-pindja-ng nga-p-puring-djü-nüng** has the meaning 'I'm going to sing and then go back,' rather than that which it has in another of Barrtjap's songs ('Yagarra Tjüt Balk-nga-me Nga-mi'); namely, 'I'm going to climb up and go now' (**nga-p-pindja-ng nga-p-puring-djü**) (chapter 4, track 22, text phrase 4). In *Song, dreamings and ghosts*, Marett discusses in considerable detail instances where the songman exploits ambiguity, often to disguise deeper meanings (see for example Marett, 2005, pp 170–71, 193–94).

Some verbs are restricted to gender-specific activities. For example, the verb stem **-muya** 'sway' is only used of women's dancing, so we can tell that the subject of the verb **nya-muy-ang** 'Dance!' must be female (chapter 7, track 8, vocal section 1, text phrase 2, track 17, text phrases 3 and 4). Similarly, the verb stem **-mara** 'kick' is only used of men's dancing, so the Subject of **ya-mara** 'Dance, man!' must be male (chapter 7, track 17, text phrases 3 and 4).

While serial constructions also occur in mundane texts and in conversation, they are especially common in Batjamalh *wangga*, amounting to 37.5% of all verbal clauses in Barrtjap's songs, and 29% of all verbal clauses in Lambudju's songs.

Serial constructions are conjoined clauses where a main verb is paired with an intransitive verb, which specifies whether the action denoted by the main verb is habitual, repeated, intentional, permanent or temporary, and may add information about the physical orientation of the co-referential Subject. Both verbs are matched for tense, aspect and modality. For example, **winmedje ngan-dji-nyene nga-mi** means both 'I'm sitting eating oysters,' and 'I'm engaged in the temporary state of eating oysters' (chapter 7, track 14, text phrase 1). In this instance, the main verb is transitive, the serial is intransitive, but both are inflected for Realis modality. In **nye-bindja-ng nya-mu** 'You [sit and] sing!' (chapter 4, track 7, text phrases 2 and 4), both verbs are intransitive, and both are inflected for Irrealis modality.

In many Batjamalh serial constructions, the main verb is suffixed by the simultaneous marker **-ng**, glossed SIM, to show that the actions or states denoted by both main and serial verb occur at the same time. This marker does not occur in serial constructions in any other Daly language *wangga*.

Modifiers

The Batjamalh mundane register contains at least 40 adverbial modifiers (Ford, 1990, pp 163–66). Batjamalh *wangga* texts contain just two, the modal adverb **werret** 'quickly' (chapter 4, track 24, text phrase 4; chapter 7, track 10, text phrase 3) and the temporal adverb **yangarang** 'today' (chapter 4, track 26, text phrase 4).

Particles

Of the fifteen free particles that occur in the Batjamalh mundane register (Ford, 1990, pp 166-69), ten are exclamations, two are negators, two interrogatives, and two are continuant particles.

Batjamalh *wangga* texts contain only three free particles: **delhi** 'Wait!' (chapter 4, track 24, text phrase 2); **yagarra**, literally 'oh no!' but untranslated in our song texts (chapter 4, tracks 1, 2, 3), with its allomorph **yakerre** (chapter 4, track 4, text phrase 3; chapter 7, track 28, text phrase 5); and **karra** (chapter 4, track 13, track 23; chapter 7, tracks 10, 11, 17, 23, 25) that always occurs at the start of a line and alerts the audience to the fact that what follows is sung by the dead (Marett, 2005, p 43). While **karra** is ubiquitous in the Marri Tjavin-Marri Ammu *wangga*, it occurs in only two of Barrtjap's songs and only five of Lambudju's songs. Because it occurs so frequently in the Marri Tjavin-Marri Ammu *wangga*, we do not in general include **karra** in our translations,

Fluent speakers of Batjamalh assured us that in the songs of Barrtjap the song word **ya** (chapter 4, tracks 1, 2, 3) is not the particle **ya** 'I don't know' which occurs in the mundane register. It is a vocable to fill out the rhythm, to provide a vehicle for extended vocalisations and to provide rhyme, as does the vocable **ngaya** in **bangany-nyung ngaya** (chapter 4, track 4, text phrase 1).

Fourteen enclitic particles occur in the Batjamalh mundane register. The six most common of these enclitic particles also appear in *wangga* texts. They are:

- the directional enclitic -**barra** 'towards speaker' (chapter 4, track 24, text phrase 2)
- the continuant particle -**djü** (chapter 4, track 7, vocal sections 2 and 3, text phrase 3)
- the present enclitic -**m** (chapter 4, track 24, text phrase 3)
- the perfective enclitic -**maka** (chapter 4, track 14, text phrase 2; chapter 7, tracks 10, text phrase 1b, 13, text phrases 1–4)
- the purposive enclitic -**nung** (chapter 7, track 10), which Barrtjap habitually pronounces -**nüng** (chapter 4, tracks 7, 10, 15)
- the temporal enclitic -**bende**[5] (chapter 7, tracks 10, 11, 12, 25) and its allomorph -**nde** 'now' (chapter 7, track 15)
- the nostalgic enclitic -**ve** 'my eternal' (chapter 4, tracks 20[6], 22; chapter 7, track 11, 23).

Batjamalh *wangga*

Although Barrtjap and Lambudju were both Wadjiginy songmen living and performing at Belyuen in the same time period, their *wangga* are very different. Marett (2005, p 92) points to Barrtjap's economy of lexicon, and contrasts it with Lambudju's texts which he characterises as 'highly varied in terms of both lexicon and structure' (Marett, 2005, p 182). Another way in which Lambudju differs strikingly from Barrtjap is in his use of two languages in a single text. He does this in track 11 of chapter 7, where he alternates text phrase in Emmi and Batjamalh. He is able to do this because the words make perfect sense to his multilingual audience. He begins with an expression that is the same in both languages,

---

5 The unrelated vocable **bende** is used as a song word in chapter 7, track 28.

6 In these cases the form is **pe** because the initial consonant assimilates to the consonant of the previous morpheme **rak**.

karra-ve 'SW + forever', and continues with a serial construction in Emmi, **kanya-verver-rtedi kaya-ndhi** 'it [a breeze] is alway cooling my back'. The next text phrase begins with the same formulaic expression, **karra-ve**, and continues with the Batjamalh phrase **kak-ung-bende badjalarr** 'away now to Badjalarr'. He continues with a text phrase comprising the song words **ribene ribene**.[7] He concludes the song by reprising the opening line. For a possible explanation as to why he uses two languages in this song, see chapter 7, tracks 11 and 12.

We may conclude that Batjamalh *wangga* texts contain valuable evidence of the complex structures of this endangered language. The most recently composed songs also contain evidence that the language is moribund. For example, the text of 'Mubagandi' (chapter 7, tracks 25, 26), which according to the singer, Roger Yarrowin, was given to him some time before the death of his brother-in-law Lambudju, contains a verb phrase **yeme-ngadja** 'tell him to come back,' which fluent speakers of Batjamalh condemned as unacceptable in Batjamalh. Each of the component morphemes are perfectly good Batjamalh, but they are combined in an impossible way, in that the classifying verb precedes the intransitive co-verb. While this is common in Emmi, classifying verbs always *follow* their co-verb in Batjamalh. It looks as if Roger Yarrowin has misremembered a Batjamalh verb in a way that would be grammatical in Emmi, his mother tongue. This is very different from the way Lambudju mixes languages. When Lambudju alternates text phrases in Emmi and Batjamalh they show no sign of mother tongue interference. Rather the macaronic nature of the text reflects a period when there was a viable speech community bilingual in Batjamalh and Emmi, as evidenced by Lambudju's own history as a Batjamalh man who was brought up in an Emmiyangal family.

EMMI-MENDHE

Emmi is the language of the Emmiyangal, whose traditional territory adjoined that of the Wadjiginy, and stretched south-west from the mouth of the Daly River to Mabulhuk (Cape Ford). Emmi has a closely-related dialect, Mendhe, the language of the Mendheyangal, whose territory adjoins Emmiyangal country, along the coast from Cape Ford to Cape Scott in the west and Nandhiwudi in the south. Inland of Mendhe country lie the Dashwood plains, which is Marrithiyel country. South of Nandhiwudi is Marri Ammu country.

Muluk (chapter 5) sang only in Mendhe, while Mandji (chapter 6) sang in Emmi, Mendhe and in Marri Tjavin (for example, chapter 6, track 8 is in a mixture of Mendhe and Marri Tjavin).

As noted earlier, over at least the past hundred and forty years, the Emmiyangal and Mendheyangal have, with their Wadjiginy affines, migrated from their traditional country to live in the Darwin region; specifically, on the coast of the Cox Peninsula, and since 1937, at the community of Delissaville, now known as Belyuen. There are Mendheyangal and Emmiyangal families at Belyuen, but very few fluent speakers of either Emmi or Mendhe. Due to the proximity of Darwin, only twenty minutes away by hydrofoil, at Belyuen there has been a gradual language shift to light Kriol, which is the first language of everyone aged fifty or below, and the language of daily social intercourse between Belyuen residents.

As also noted earlier, Emmi and Mendhe belong to the Western Daly linguistic subgroup, whose other members are Marranunggu, Marri Ammu and its closely related dialect Marri Tjavin, and Marri Ngarr and its dialect Magati Ke. This subgroup appears to go back several hundred years to a common mother language. Emmi and Mendhe have, however, diverged from these related languages because they have been influenced by, and have borrowed from, Batjamalh, the language of the Wadjiginy affines of Emmiyangal and Mendheyangal people. Geographical separation from Marranunggu, the closest linguistic relative to Emmi and Mendhe, has resulted in the loss of a phoneme and the initial segment of a pronominal. While Emmi and Mendhe share identical sound systems and grammar, they differ

---

7 This song word also appears in his song 'Bende Ribene' (chapter 7, track 28), which is entirely in Batjamalh.

slightly in lexicon and morphology. Because the two language varieties are so close they are henceforth referred to as Emmi-Mendhe, except where relevant.

In regards to phonemes, Emmi-Mendhe has lost Marranunggu's prestopped lateral, so Marranunggu **pedle**, 'white,' is **pele** in Emmi-Mendhe, and the Marranunggu bound pronominal -**nedla**, 'for his benefit,' is **nela** in Emmi-Mendhe. As regards morphology, in current everyday Emmi-Mendhe, **nginen** means 'I sit', but Emmiyangal and Mendheyangal elders told me that **anginen** is the old-fashioned form. **Anginen** is transparently derived from **ganginen**, the Marranunggu form for 'I sit,' from which the Marri Tjavin-Marri Ammu and Marri Ngarr-Magati Ke form **gangi** is also derived.

Sound system

Emmi and Mendhe share identical sound systems, shown in tables 3.3 and 3.4. These consonant systems differ from Batjamalh only in having a laminal dental series (stops and nasals), which are missing in Batjamalh. There is also a minor difference in vowel quality: where Batjamalh has a front rounded vowel /**ü**/, Emmi and Mendhe have a central unrounded vowel /**ö**/.

Emmi and Mendhe each have twenty-two consonant phonemes, including six full series of stops and nasals, which contrast for voicing. There are two apical series of stops and nasal (apico-alveolar and apico postalveolar or retroflex), two laminal series (lamino-dental and lamino-palatal), and two peripheral series (dorso-velar and bilabial). There are two phonemic fricatives: an apical /**rz**/ and a bilabial /**v**/. There are two laterals: one apico-alveolar, one retroflex and one lamino-dental. There are two rhotics: one apico-alveolar trill, and one retroflex continuant. There are two semi-vowels: one labial, one lamino-palatal. There are five phonemic vowels: high front /**i**/, low /**a**/, high back rounded /**u**/, open mid vowel /**e**/ and, unusually, central unrounded /**ö**/.

	APICO-		LAMINO-		PERIPHERAL	
	Alveolar	Retroflex	Dental	Palatal	Dorso-velar	Bilabial
Stops: voiceless	t	rt	th	tj	k	p
Stops: voiced	d	rd	dh	dj	g	b
Fricative		rz				v
Nasal	n	rn	nh	ny	ng	m
Liquid: lateral	l	rl	lh			
Liquid: rhotic	rr	r				
Continuant/glide				y		w

Table 3.3 Emmi-Mendhe consonant phonemes

	unrounded		rounded
high	i		u
mid	e	ö	
low	a		
	front	central	back

Table 3.4 Emmi-Mendhe vowel phonemes.

All these phonemes occur in Emmi-Mendhe *wangga*.

Differences between Emmi and Mendhe

Lexicon

While Emmi-Mendhe and Batjamalh have little vocabulary in common, sharing only 12% cognates in Dixon's 90-item Comparative Australian word list and 11% in the 400-item Comparative Australian word list, Emmi and Mendhe share 93% cognates from the 90-item word list and 96% cognates from the 400-item word list. Table 3.5 lists the lexical variants that exist in everyday Emmi and Mendhe. The bolded variants show up in *wangga* texts.

Emmi	Mendhe	English gloss
derivirin	derivun	'skin'
kaderrem	pin.gurrutuk	'freshwater catfish'
kudjala	yangu	'today'
man.garra	**kuluguluk**	'catarrh'
mele	**mana**	'older brother'
meyidja	meyida	'two'
mirinnga	amanga	'raw'
munymutj	luk	'edible grub'
ngala	ngula	'I use fingers'
ngarrinye-gurriny	tjanggurriny	'Belong to us, but not you (the addressee)'
ngula	ngala	'I chop it'
nirr	ninirr	'vein'
rimi	rimu	'forehead'
rungurungurr	**wörörö**	'mudcrab'
tjinytji	wilhyirri	'tree sp.'
tjirrkinin	kunarra	'witchetty grub tree'
werrerdje	perridje	'heavy'
wunggula	naka	'older sister'
wurrum	wudut	'wet season; year'
wutharr	pörrme	'sea'
yerrangöya	emörru	'yesterday'

Table 3.5 Lexical variants between Emmi and Mendhe.

Morphology

Like Batjamalh, Emmi and Mendhe distinguish Realis from Irrealis modality. While they use the same basic mechanisms—changing pronominal prefixes, changing the main verb stem, inserting an Irrealis morpheme and adding a verb phrase-final purpositive enclitic—the forms have little in common.[8]

Emmi and Mendhe, on the other hand, use virtually identical forms to mark Irrealis except that Mendhe omits the Irrealis morpheme. So the Emmi verb **nga-wa-ni** 'I will walk' is rendered in Mendhe as **nga-ni**. We see this in Muluk's famous Puliki song (chapter 5, track 1, text phrase 4): **nga-ni-purr-mbele ngayi-nö alawa mari-pinindjela** 'I will always dance for you at Mari-pinindjela (Mica Beach)'.

---

8 Batjamalh appears to have borrowed its Irrealis morpheme from Emmi-Mendhe (Evans, 1989).

Word classes

Like Batjamalh, Emmi and Mendhe distinguish nominals (noun, adjective, pronoun, deictic), verbals, modifiers and particles. All these word classes are represented in the *wangga* song texts.

Nominals

Although, as in Batjamalh, a well-formed Emmi or Mendhe sentence need not contain an overt nominal, most Emmi-Mendhe *wangga* texts, like those in Batjamalh, present a significant proportion of overt nominals. Mandji's seventeen clauses contain twenty-two nominals, eight of which are incorporated into the verb. Muluk's seventy-two clauses contain one hundred and eighteen nominals, twenty-one of which are incorporated into the verb.

There is a wide range of nominals in these *wangga* texts, from the place names that locate the songs—**duwun** 'Duwun (Indian Island)' (chapter 6, track 1, text phrase 4); **mari-pinindjela** 'Mica Beach' (chapter 5, track 1, text phrase 4); and **pumandjin** 'Pumandjin Hill' (chapter 5, track 9, vocal section 1, text phrase 2)—to the common nouns **alawa** 'beach' (chapter 5, track 1, text phrase 4); **piyamen.ga** 'shady tree'(chapter 5, track 11, vocal section 3, text phrase 5); **thawara** 'mangrove sprout' (chapter 5, track 15, vocal section 1, text phrase 5); and **dörr** 'ground' (chapter 5, track 11). Some nouns, for example **tjinbarambara** 'seagull' (chapter 5, track 5, text phrase 1), and **wak** 'crow' (chapter 5, track 7, vocal section 1, text phrase 2) refer to Dreamings. Taken together these nominals reveal detailed knowledge of the totemic landscape known to songmen and their audience.

As in Batjamalh *wangga*, Emmi and Mendhe *wangga* use personal pronouns to draws the audience in and link them with the subject of the songs. The most common of these are: **ngany** 'I' (chapter 6, track 8, vocal section 1, text phrase 2), and the first person dual inclusive form **nganggu-ga** 'yours and mine' (chapter 5, track 7). The use of the anaphoric deictic **yawa** 'that place we know about' (chapter 5, track 7) heightens this intimacy.

Unlike the Batjamalh *wangga*, Emmi-Mendhe song texts contain no names of individuals, but like Batjamalh *wangga*, they do contain kin-terms, for example, **mele** 'elder brother' (chapter 6, track 8, vocal section 1, text phrase 2), which for an informed audience would normally be enough to identify a particular individual.

Complex noun-phrases

As in Batjamalh, Emmi-Mendhe nominals are marked for case and tense by ordered enclitics, for example:

- the dative case marker **-nö** 'for' and the temporal enclitic **-endheni** 'now' both of which appear in the following phrase from Mandji's *wangga*: **mele ngany-endheni-nö** 'for my older brother now' (chapter 6, track 8, vocal section 1, text phrase 2)
- the ablative/causal marker **-ngana** 'from' and the perfective enclitic **yi**, both of which appear in the following phrase from Muluk's *wangga*: **wak-ngana-yi** 'it came from crow' (chapter 5, track 7, vocal section 2, text phrase 1)
- the illocutionary enclitic **-ndha** 'really,' as in the expression **yawa-ndha** 'that place we really know about,' which occurs particularly frequently in Mendhe *wangga* texts.

Like Batjamalh, Emmi and Mendhe have a possessive pronoun, but the Emmi-Mendhe pronoun (unlike the Batjamalh pronoun) is marked for number and gender. Its base form is **gurriny** 'belonging to.' This occurs in the following phrase from Mandji's *wangga*: **ngandhi mandha na-gurriny** 'that song of his' (chapter 6, track 3, text phrase 3), where the possessive pronoun is marked by the pronominal **na-** to specify third singular male possessor. Another example is where Muluk signals his Mendhe identity by using the possessive pronoun to express his relationship to the shady tree that is the focus of his song: **piyamen.ga ngani-gurriny** 'my shady tree' (chapter 5, track 11, vocal section 3, text phrase 5).

All languages used in *wangga* that are discussed in this book have another mechanism to express the possessive relation, whereby the possessed noun is juxtaposed with a free pronoun denoting the possessor, as in **mele ngany** 'my older brother' (chapter 6, track 8, vocal section 1, text phrase 2) and **viye pumandjin** 'the top of Pumandjin Hill' (chapter 5, track 9, vocal section 1, text phrase 2).

Incorporated body-part nouns

As is common in the everyday usage of all the languages used in *wangga*, Emmi-Mendhe *wangga* songs may incorporate body-part nominals into the verb phrase. Generally these are reduced forms of nouns denoting body parts. These incorporated body parts are sometimes used literally, as for example in **ngammanya-mu-viye** 'let's both always keep dancing (with our hands above our heads)' (literally, let's both do it, do it to the head) (chapter 6, track 3, text phrase 3) and **kana-nga-mu-viye karru** 'she [Numbali] is dancing, making a deliberate movement of her hands above her head' (literally, 'she's walking, doing it to her head as she goes') (chapter 5, track 9, vocal section 1, text phrase 2). Body-part nominals may also be used metaphorically, as when the idiom **mörö-gumbu** (literally, 'buttock-foot') is used to mean 'from top to toe' or 'right through' in the serial construction **nganya-bet-mörö-gumbu ngayi** 'let me always sing it for him "right through the night" [ie all night long]' (chapter 6, track 8, vocal section 1, text phrase 2). Mandji also incorporates the non-body-part nominal **mandha** 'song' in **gidji-djedjet-mandha-ya** 'he sings out that song' (chapter 6, track 1, text phrase 4).

Verbals and Verb phrase structure

Ford (2007) compared three Mendhe *wangga* texts with the prose versions of their subject matter, which had been provided as explanation to Alice Moyle and recorded by her immediately after the *wangga* songs had been performed. That paper, showed that the spoken text reveals significantly less complexity with regard to verbal clauses than the *wangga* texts. These texts are reproduced in chapter 5 in the notes to tracks 1, 7 and 8.

In Batjamalh, Subject or Agent (S/A) and Object (O) are combined in a single portmanteau pronominal prefix to the verb. Emmi-Mendhe verbs are quite different in that the Subject is marked separately from the Object. Emmi-Mendhe verbs begin with a pronominal prefix that specifies the person, number and modality of the Subject or Agent (S/A) of the verb. This is followed by a verb stem, which in turn is followed by a bound pronominal specifying the person, number and gender of the Direct Object (O) or Indirect Object (IO). There is no simple example of this construction in the Emmi-Mendhe *wangga*. An example from everyday speech might be, however: **ka-ya-na-wut** 'he always gives it to him,' where the classifying verb stem is **-ya** 'lie down/always do' and the co-verb is **-wut** 'give.' The third person subject is marked by **ka** 'he,' the third person and the indirect object is marked by **-na** 'to him.'

As in Batjamalh, the verb paradigms are irregular and cannot be fully predicted, and ordered verb-final enclitics signal aspect, tense, mood, modality, direction and degrees of illocutionary force. Unlike Batjamalh, however, the majority of Emmi-Mendhe verbs are inflected classifying verbs, which co-occur with an uninflected co-verb. The classifying verb describes the type of action/event or state specified by the co-verb. The complex verb phrases **ka-na-kalkal-rtadi** (chapter 5, track 7, vocal section 1, text phrase 1) and **ka-na-putput-rtadi** (chapter 5, track 7, vocal section 4, text phrase 1) both have **-na** 'go/walk' as the classifying verb, which here co-occurs with the co-verbs **-kalkal** 'climb' or **-putput** 'walk'. When used as a classifying verb, **-na** 'go/walk' also conveys aspectual information, specifying the action denoted by the co-verb as ongoing. Some classifying verbs, like **-me** 'say/do/feel' and **-nya** 'make/cook it' may co-occur with any of dozens of co-verbs; other classifying verbs are attested as co-occurring only with a single co-verb. Twenty-seven of the thirty classifying verbs may also occur on their own, without a co-verb, as fully-inflected simple verbs.

Some simple verbs are more common than others. For example, the five intransitive verbs **-nen** 'sit'; **-ma** 'stand'; **-ya** 'lie down', **-na** 'walk' and **-rru** 'travel' may also function as the second verb in serial verb constructions. Only two of these occur in Emmi-Mendhe *wangga* as the second verb in a serial construction. They are **-ya** 'lie down/always do' and **-rru** 'travel/do deliberately.' Ya occurs in thirty-five serial constructions, that is, in every Emmi or Mendhe *wangga* text except one, while **-rru** occurs three times, on each occasion with reference to a dance movement. **Ya** is the verb of choice because it underscores the never-ending nature of the events celebrated in *wangga*.

Headless relative clauses

In spoken Emmi-Mendhe, as in spoken Batjamalh, headless relative clauses most often occur with a locative sense. This is true of some but not all relative clauses in the Emmi-Mendhe *wangga* texts. Consider, for example, Muluk's phrase **nganggu-ga kaya yawa-ndha** 'our X that is always in that place we know about.' Just what that X is, is clarified by the context. In one of Muluk's songs it is 'our seagull', but in another it is 'our stuff' (chapter 5, tracks 5 and 7). Other relative clauses provide information about the Subject of the verb, for example **ka-me-ngana-yi ka-ya** 'this [song] came from the one who always sings this' (chapter 6, track 7, text phrase 2).

Modifiers

Like Batjamalh, Emmi-Mendhe has a small closed class of words that modify the verb as temporal, locational or manner adverbs. None of these appear in the *wangga* texts of either Muluk or Mandji.

Particles

Like Batjamalh, Emmi-Mendhe has a small closed class of particles, which are of two types; 'free particles,' which occur as independent words, and 'enclitic particles,' which must attach to a host word, which can be from any word class.

While in general free particles are exclamations, like **Puvuy!** 'Keep going!' or tags such as **ening** 'is it?' or **wakkay** 'it's finished,' they may also include polarity markers such as **Yu** 'yes!', or clause negators such as **way**. However, **yakarre** (literally, 'oh, no!', but untranslated in our texts) (chapter 5, track 9, vocal section 1, text phrase 2; chapter 6, track 3, text phrase 3) is the only free particle to appear in Emmi-Mendhe *wangga*.

Twenty-three ordered enclitic particles have been identified for the Emmi-Mendhe mundane register. Nine of these are adnominal enclitics, which attach to the end of a nominal phrase, where they generally mark case (see above under Nominals). The remaining fourteen are propositional enclitics, which attach to the end of a verb phrase, and modify the whole clause, providing information about direction, aspect, tense, modality, mood and illocutionary force. Adnominal enclitics precede propositional enclitics.

In Emmi-Mendhe *wangga* the only adnominal enclitic to occur is **ngana** 'from' as in **ngany-ngana-yi** 'it is from me' (chapter 5, track 11, vocal section 3, text phrase 4). Here, as in mundane usage, the adnominal enclitic -**ngana** precedes the propositional perfective enclitic -**yi.**

Six of the fourteen possible propositional enclitics occur in the *wangga* corpus. These are:

- the tense marker -**endheni** 'now' (chapter 6, track 8, vocal section 1, text phrase 2)
- the perfective marker -**(e)yi** (chapter 5, track 7, vocal section 2, text phrase 1; chapter 6, track 1, text phrase 4)
- the purposive marker -**(e)nö** (chapter 5, track 1, vocal section 1, text phrase 2; chapter 6, track 8, vocal section 1, text phrase 2)
- the topic marker -**ga** (chapter 5, track 5, text phrase 2)

- the illocutionary marker **-ndha** (chapter 5, track 2, vocal section 1, text phrase 2)
- the directional marker **-ya** 'thither' (chapter 6, track 1, text phrase 4).

MARRI AMMU AND MARRI TJAVIN

The Marri Ammu people have as their ancestral country the coastal strip south from Ngandhiwudi to Anggileni (Cape Dombey). Their territory abuts that of the Mendheyangal to the north, the Marrithiyel people to the east, and the Marri Tjavin people to the south. Marri Tjavin territory stretches from Nadirri at the mouth of the Moyle River, inland to Perrederr, Yendili and Yenmilhi. It is bounded on the east by Marri Ngarr country and on the south by Magati Ke country. Today, almost all Marri Ammu and Marri Tjavin families live at Wadeye, but they visit their country regularly when, as in the dry season, the weather and finances permit.

The Walakandha *wangga* (chapter 8) has been composed by a number of Marri Tjavin songmen over the past four decades or so. It is the main song series for many of the Marri language groups resident at Wadeye, including the Marri Ammu who participate in ceremonies primarily as dancers. The Marri Ammu have their own series, the Ma-yawa *wangga* (chapter 9), but this is no longer performed today, and has probably not been used in ceremony for several decades (Marett, 2005, p 135).

Marri Ammu and Marri Tjavin are very closely related dialects, differentiated by only a few lexical items. Their closest linguistic relative is Marrithiyel, which has independently undergone some minor sound changes and diverged in its lexicon. Less closely related is Marri Ngarr and its dialect Magati Ke, and related more distantly still are Marranunggu and Emmi-Mendhe. All these language varieties have been identified by Ian Green as belonging to the Western Daly linguistic subgroup (Green, 1994).

Members of the Marri Ammu and Marri Tjavin language groups differentiate themselves from these other groups by calling themselves **Ma Thanggural**. Marri Ammu *wangga* are known as **wangga ma-yawa** '*wangga* belonging to the *ma-yawa*'. Marri Tjavin *wangga* are known as **wangga ma walakandha** '*wangga* belonging to the *ma walakandha*.' *Ma-yawa* and *ma walakandha* are the spirits who gave the songs to the songmen (Marett, 2005).

Marri Tjavin and Marri Ammu are so similar in phonology, morphology and syntax that they can be discussed as one system. We will, however, point out the small differences that do exist where relevant. We will show what we can learn of this system first from Walakandha *wangga* texts, and then from Ma-yawa *wangga* texts.

Sound system

Marri Ammu and Marri Tjavin share identical sound systems, as shown in tables 3.6 and 3.7. This differs from the Emmi-Mendhe sound system only in having an extra fricative, the lamino-palatal /sj/ and in lacking Emmi-Mendhe's fifth vowel, the unrounded /ö/. They each have twenty-eight consonant phonemes, including six full series of stops and nasals, which contrast for voicing. There are two apical series of stops and nasal (apico-alveolar and apico postalveolar or retroflex), two laminal series (lamino-dental and lamino-palatal, and two peripheral series (dorso-velar and bilabial). There are three phonemic fricatives: an apical /rz/, a laminal /sj/ and a bilabial /v/. There are three laterals: one apico-alveolar, one apico-postalveolar and one lamino-dental. There are two rhotics: one apico-alveolar trill, and one retroflex continuant. There are two semi-vowels: one labial, one lamino-palatal. There are four phonemic vowels: high front /i/, low /a/, high back rounded /u/ and the open mid vowel /e/. Before a following high front vowel /i/, the velar nasal /ng/ becomes palatalised, and sounds like **ngyi**, as happens in the neighbouring language, Murriny Patha.

All these phonemes occur in Marri Tjavin and Marri Ammu *wangga*.

	APICO-		LAMINO-		PERIPHERAL	
	Alveolar	Retroflex	Dental	Palatal	Dorso-velar	Bilabial
Stops: voiceless	t	rt	th	tj	k	p
Stops: voiced	d	rd	dh	dj	g	b
Fricative		rz		sj		v
Nasal	n	rn	nh	ny	ng	m
Liquid: lateral	l	rl	lh			
Liquid: rhotic	rr	r				
Continuant/glide				y		w

Table 3.6 Marri Tjavin-Marri Ammu consonant phonemes.

	unrounded	rounded
high	i	u
mid	e	
low	a	
	front	back

Table 3.7 Marri Tjavin-Marri Ammu vowel phonemes.

Lexicon

Marri Tjavin and Marri Ammu share 98% cognates from Dixon's 90-item Comparative Australian word list and 98% cognates from Dixon's 400-item comparative Australian word list. Table 3.8 lists the lexical variants between mundane Marri Ammu and Marri Tjavin. The bolded variants show up in *wangga* texts.

According to Tryon (1974, p xiv), Marri Tjavin-Marri Ammu share approximately 43% cognates with Emmi-Mendhe and approximately 18% cognates with Batjamalh. However, Tryon's early work was based on a limited sample. No later comparative data exists.

Marri Tjavin	Marri Ammu	English gloss
thidha	dirral	'father'
kila	kindal	'mother'
mangga	manggerral	'mother's mother'
ngaya	ngayerral	'father's sister'
kaga	karral	'mother's brother'
yeri	**ngatja**	'child'
-nginanga	-nginyanga	'against my will'

Table 3.8 Lexical variants between Marri Ammu and Marri Tjavin (bolded forms occur in *wangga*).

Where forms peculiar to Marri Ammu occur in *wangga*, as they do in 'Yendili No. 5' (chapter 8, track 29), they serve to emphasise the Marri Ammu identity of the speaker, in this instance, Honorata Ngenawurda, Frank Dumoo's mother.

Word classes

Marri Tjavin and Marri Ammu distinguish the same word classes as Batjamalh and Emmi-Mendhe. These are all represented in Walakandha *wangga* and Ma-yawa *wangga*.

Nominals

As in Batjamalh and Emmi-Mendhe *wangga*, there are more overt nominals in Walakandha *wangga* than one would normally expect in a mundane text (see 4.5 below). For instance, the earliest Walakandha *wangga* songs (composed by Stan Mullumbuk), comprise five clauses containing fourteen nominals. Seven of these (50%) are nouns that introduce the Subject of the clause, two are body-part nouns incorporated into the verb phrase, four are locative noun phrases incorporating a body-part noun, and one is a deictic marked with **-gu** as a different topic.

The range of nominals is similar to that seen in *wangga* already analysed. As in other *wangga* repertories, proper nouns frequently occur in Walakandha *wangga*, whether they be names of people—for example, **Wutjelli** (chapter 8, tracks 3, 22); **Berrida**, **Munggumurri** (chapter 8, track 35); **Tjagawala** (chapter 8, track 27)—or of places—for example, **Yendili** (chapter 8, tracks 10, 13, 14, 29, 30, 32, 35); **Yenmilhi** (chapter 8, tracks 11, 20); **Truwu** (chapter 8, tracks 16–18, 22); **Kubuwemi** (chapter 8, tracks 12, 33); **Nadirri** (chapter 8, track 19); **Yenmungirini** (chapter 8, track 34); **Pelhi** (chapter 8, track 20); **Pumurriyi** (chapter 8, track 24); **Lhambumen** (chapter 8, track 31); **Ngumali** (chapter 8, track 36); **Kinyirr** (chapter 8, track 37); **Namadjawalh, Yimurdigi, Kanbirrin, Lhambudinbu** (chapter 8, track 38); **Rtadi-wunbirri** (chapter 8, track 39). A frequently used non-specific reference to place is the important phrase **nidin-ngina**, which has been various translated as 'poor fellow my country,' 'poor bugger my country,' and 'my dear country.' It is a powerfully emotive articulation of people's attachment to country.

Some common nouns provide situational context, for example **mirrwana** 'cycad palm' (chapter 8, track 21), which is traditionally associated with Walakandha, and **ngatha devin bugim rtadi** 'a solitary house with a white roof' (chapter 8, track 23), which refers to a particular house at the Nadirri outstation.

Kin-terms also occur in Walakandha *wangga*, including **mana** 'older brother' (chapter 8, track 20, text phrase 1); **angga** 'grandfather/grandson' (chapter 8, track 27, text phrase 3), **thidha** 'father' (chapter 8, track 25, text phrase 1), **ngatja** 'child' (in Marri Ammu) (chapter 8, track 29, text phrase 3). The composers of Walakandha *wangga* use these to draw the audience in, just as Barrtjap and Lambudju did in Batjamalh *wangga*. Like Barrtjap, Muluk and Mandji (discussed above), they also create intimacy by using cardinal pronouns, for example **nany** your (chapter 8, track 25, text phrase 1), **yigin** 'I' (chapter 8, track 25, text phrase 2), **ngangga-nim** 'for all of us' (chapter 8, track 20, text phrase 4).

The densest use of nominals occurs in the songs of the late Marlip Philip Mullumbuk. His fifty-six clauses contain sixty-nine nominals, an average of 1.25 nominals per clause. Most of these are place names, and thirty-nine occurrences of the place name **Namadjawalh** come from a single *wangga* text 'Wedjiwurang' (chapter 8, track 38), about **wedjiwurang** 'wallaroo', the totem whose dreaming-site is Namadjawalh. Mullumbuk's use of the anaphoric locative **yivi-ndja** (chapter 8, track 38, vocal section 1, text phrase 2) is cognate with Muluk's formulaic noun phrase **yawa-ndha** 'that place we know about.'[9]

---

9   The anaphoric locative **yivi** (Emmi-Mendhe **yawa**) 'that place we know about', the anaphoric deictic **kan**, 'that one we know about' and the locative deictic **kagan** 'right here' can be used to refer obliquely to things that are known to the audience but not to outsiders. These may include Dreamings and Dreaming places, as well as people and ritual

Noun classifiers

Like Batjamalh and Emmi-Mendhe, Marri Tjavin-Marri Ammu has a system of noun classifiers, but its system is much more comprehensive and exact. Its twelve noun classifiers differentiate male from female, edible vegetables from meat, edible vegetables from grasses, fire, danger, liquids, language, spears, inanimate objects, and location in time or space. Each of these categories of nominal has its own classifier. When first introduced into mundane discourse, a species item is always preceded by an appropriate noun classifier. Thereafter, the referent may occur without the classifier, or be referred to by the noun classifier without the species name. For instance, **walakandha** 'ancestral dead' would in mundane register be first introduced into the text with the male human classifier **ma**, as **ma walakandha**. In Walakandha *wangga* texts, however, it never occurs with a noun classifier. Indeed, except for Marlip Philip Mullumbuk's anomalous[10] song 'Wedjiwurang' (chapter 8, track 38), there are no noun classifiers in the Walakandha *wangga* texts. In this song Marlip introduces the topic with the generic animal classifier **awu** without the species name; only in the next text phrase does he name the species as the topic **wedjiwurang-ga**, marking it with the topic marker **-ga** (chapter 8, track 38, vocal section 1, text phrases 1 and 2).

Complex noun phrases

Unlike Emmi-Mendhe, Marri Tjavin-Marri Ammu has only one way to express the possessive relation. This is by juxtaposing possessed and possessor nominals, as in **thidha ngany** 'your father' (literally 'you father') (chapter 8, track 25, text phrase 1) and **yeri meri yigin** 'my children' (literally 'children males I' (chapter 8, track 34, text phrase 2). **Marzi mungirini** 'deep inside the jungle' (chapter 8, track 2, text phrase 2) is a possessive noun phrase where the possessed entity is a body part used metaphorically to represent a geographical feature shaped like the body part.

Verbals

Verb phrase structure

Like Batjamalh and Emmi-Mendhe, Marri Tjavin-Marri Ammu verb phrases consist of a series of ordered morphemes. Marri Tjavin-Marri Ammu and Emmi-Mendhe verb phrases have identical structures, in that they begin with a pronominal prefix that specifies the person, number and modality of the Subject/Agent of the verb.

Then comes the main verb stem, which is followed by a slot for the Object of the verb. If there is a co-verb, this will come next. Then comes a slot for an incorporated noun, followed by a slot for a benefactive bound pronominal, followed by a slot for an adversative bound pronominal. This is followed by a series of ordered slots for enclitic particles, which specify number and gender of Subject and/or Object, tense and aspect.

In Walakandha *wangga*, a noun incorporated into the verb phrase conveys more than just the literal meaning. For example, when **venggi** 'knee' is incorporated into the verb-phrase **ki-nyi-ni-venggi-tit** 'he bent his leg', it means one knee bent over the other, in the position known in Aboriginal English as 'number four leg'. Similarly, the noun **mi** 'eye' incorporated into the verb phrase in 'Yendili No. 5'

---

events. Such expressions, which convey a world of meaning in a word, are termed 'cultural schemas.' Similar cultural schemas have been identified in the non-standard English dialect of Aboriginal children in Geraldton, WA (Sharifian, 2005, 2006). For these Aboriginal children, who have never heard of *wangga* let alone Mendhe or Marri Tjavin, 'dis ting' and 'dat ol' man' may be used to refer to Dreaming sites and Dreamings. The survival of these cultural schemas testifies to the dynamism of Aboriginal cultural transmission.

10 For discussion of this song and some of its unusual features, see the relevant section of chapter 8 (track 38), and Ford (2007, pp 76-89).

(**wudi yendili ngil-dim-mi-nginyanga**[11]**-ndjen** 'I'm closing down the spring at Yendili against my will'; (chapter 8, track 29, text phrase 4) it refers to the round, eye-shaped heart of the water-hole.

Unlike Emmi-Mendhe *wangga*, Walakandha *wangga* contain no benefactive bound pronominals; on the other hand, unlike all other *wangga*, a significant proportion of Walakandha *wangga* contain adversative bound pronominals. The most commonly occurring form is **nginyanga** 'I couldn't stop it' (chapter 8, track 29, text phrase 4).

Inflected verbs

Like Emmi-Mendhe, Marri Tjavin-Marri Ammu has thirty inflected verbs, but their forms are only distantly related. In both languages the verb paradigms are irregular and cannot be fully predicted. Many of the Marri Tjavin-Marri Ammu forms have neutralised. Twenty-seven of these inflected verbs may co-occur with a following uninflected co-verb.

Classifying verbs

As in Emmi-Mendhe, the classifying verb describes the type of action/event or state specified by the co-verb. For instance, the intransitive verb **-wa** 'stand' classifies co-verbs that involve vertical action. Many collocations are transparent. For example, **purangang kuwa-vapa** 'the waves are crashing' (literally, 'the salt water stands up and crashes') (chapter 8, track 16, text phrase 1).

In addition to their primary meaning, classifying verbs may also provide aspectual information. So, for example, the primary meaning of the intransitive verb **ka-ni**[12] is 'go/walk'. The first person Irrealis form of this is **ngumbu** and this is what it means in **ngumbu-vup-nim** 'let's all get going now' (chapter 8, track 26, text phrases 1-2). But **ka-ni** 'go/walk' also renders an action ongoing, so **ka-ni-wurr-a** means 'he was dying' (chapter 8, track 38, vocal section 4, text phrase 5). Likewise, the transitive classifying verb **ka-rri** 'use hands' co-occurs with co-verbs denoting actions done with the hands. **Ka-rri-wuwu** 'it flies' (chapter 8, track 39, text phrase 2) is a transparent collocation meaning that the bird is using its wings (hands) to fly. But **ka-rri** is also used of an external agency forcing an intransitive action, so **ka-rri-tik** 'the tide goes out' (chapter 8, track 19, text phrase 1), which is a metaphor for dying, means an external force makes the tide go out or the person die. Likewise again, the primary sense of the transitive classifying verb **ki-nyi** is to 'make something', but this verb is also a causative verb, meaning 'make something happen'. So **ki-nyi-ng-kurr-a** means literally 'it [a breaker] made me get hit' (chapter 8, track 27, text phrases 1-2). **Ki-nyi** also transitivises intransitive verbs. So, for example, **ki-nyi-ni venggi-tit** means 'he makes himself bend his knee' (chapter 8, track 2, text phrase 2).

Some classifying verbs, like **ki-nyi** 'make something', **ka-rri** 'use hands', **kin** 'paint, draw' and the zero stem inflected verb **ki-Ø**, may co-occur with any of several co-verbs, but there are many more co-occurrence restrictions in Marri Tjavin-Marri Ammu than in Emmi-Mendhe, and some classifying verbs are attested as co-occurring only with a single co-verb.

The Walakandha *wangga* texts contain a small subset of inflected verbs, twelve out of a possible thirty. They are: **ku-rzi** 'sit'; **ku-wa** 'stand'; **ka-vulh** 'lie down'; **ka-ni** 'go/walk'; **ka-yirr** 'go/travel'; **ki-l** 'chop'; **ki-n** 'paint, draw'; **ki-nyi** 'make something'; **ka-rri** 'use hands'; **ki-din** 'see'; **ku-munit** 'pick up'; and **ku-muyi** 'emerge'. Ten of these inflected verbs function as classifying verbs to one or more co-verbs in the *wangga* texts. **Ka-vulh** 'lie down'; **ku-munit** 'pick up'; and **ku-muyi** 'emerge' occur only as simple verbs.

---

11 -**nginyanga** is the Marri Ammu equivalent of Marri Tjavin -**nginanga** 'against my will'. Its use emphasises the Marri Ammu identity of the speaker, as does the Marri Ammu word **ngatja** 'child' in the previous text phrase.

12 Because the forms of these inflected verbs are so irregular, and the differences between forms have been neutralised in so many of the thirty paradigms, in these examples we have used the third person minimal to characterise each verb because this is the form most likely to tell you which verb you are dealing with.

Simple verbs as serial verbs

In mundane usage, the five intransitive verbs—**ku-rzi** 'sit', **ku-wa** 'stand', **ka-vulh** 'lie down', **ka-ni** 'go/walk' and **ka-yirr** 'go/travel'—also function as the second verb in serial verb constructions. Only three of these occur as the second verb in *wangga* serial constructions. These verbs are; **ka-vulh** 'lie down/always happen', which occurs in twenty-one serial constructions; **ka-ni** 'go/walk; keep on doing', which occurs in eight serial constructions; and **ku-wa** 'stand', which occurs in four serial constructions.

The second verb in a serial construction provides aspectual information about the action denoted in the co-verb, and also specifies the physical orientation of the co-referential Subject of the two conjoined clauses. For example, where **ka-ni** is the second verb, the repetitive nature of the action expressed in the co-verb is emphasised; where **ka-vulh** 'lie down/do always' is used, the permanence of the action is stressed. When **ku-wa** is used, only vertical orientation is stressed.

Sometimes this physical orientation is incompatible with the meaning of the co-verb, in which case the aspectual information overrides the literal meaning. Sometimes it is merely ambiguous whether the literal or aspectual meaning should prevail—and this ambiguity is frequently exploited in *wangga* texts.

Walakandha songmen, like the Ma-yawa *wangga* songmen to be discussed below, frequently emphasise the everlasting quality of the actions they describe by using **ka-vulh** 'lie down/do always' as the second verb in most of these serial constructions.

Headless relative clauses

The only Walakandha *wangga* composer to use headless relative clauses is Marlip Philip Mullumbuk. This is a locative relative clause that provides information about Yenmungirini: **kangi-nginanga yenmungirini na pumut-pumut kurzi**, 'I've got to stay here at Yenmungirini where the Headache Dreaming is' (chapter 8, track 34, text phrase 2).

Modifiers

Like Emmi-Mendhe, Marri Tjavin-Marri Ammu has a small closed class of words that modify the verb as temporal, locational or manner adverbs. The only ones to occur in the Walakandha *wangga* are **wandhi** 'behind' (chapter 8, track 20, text phrase 3; track 34, text phrase 1) and **warambu** 'high up' (chapter 8, track 36, text phrase 1). In track 20, **wandhi** occurs outside the verb phrase. In track 34, **wandhi** is incorporated into the verb phrase, as is **warambu** in track 36. The absence of other independent modifiers is accounted for by the incorporation within noun phrases and verb phrases of spatial nouns such as **rtadi** 'back/top surface' and **marzi** 'belly/inside'.

Particles

Like Emmi-Mendhe, Marri Tjavin-Marri Ammu has a small closed class of particles, which are of two types: 'free particles,' which occur as independent words; and 'enclitic particles,' which must attach to a host word that can be from any word class. Few free particles occur in Walakandha *wangga*. They are; the negator **ambi** 'not' (chapter 8, track 25, text phrase 1); the exclamations **wakkay** 'it's finished!' (chapter 8, track 27, text phrase 3) and **yakerre** (chapter 8, track 36, text phrase 3); and the song word **karra**, which begins many grammatical text phrases in Walakandha *wangga* and is absent in only three songs.

Ordered enclitic particles occur in all Walakandha *wangga*. They are all propositional enclitics, which attach to the end of a verb phrase, and modify the whole clause, providing information about direction, aspect, tense, modality, mood and illocutionary force. One propositional enclitic, the directional **-wurri** 'to me', occurs in half (nineteen) of the thirty-eight *wangga* songs in chapter 8. The other enclitics that occur in Walakandha *wangga* are:

- the perfective marker **-(ey)a** 'it is over' (chapter 8, track 1, text phrase 1)
- the tense marker **-ndjen** 'now/then' (chapter 8, track 26, text phrase 1)

- the purposive enclitic -(**e**)**ni** (chapter 8, track 32, text phrase 1-2)
- the illocutionary marker –(**a**)**ndja** (chapter 8, track 33, text phrase 1)
- the ablative/causal enclitic -**nganan**, which occurs in Marlip Philip Mullumbuk's 'Walakandha No. 5': **kurriny-rtadi-warambu-nganan-wurri-ya** 'they came towards me from high in the inland country' (chapter 8, track 36, text phrase 1)
- the allative enclitic -**rzan** (chapter 8, track 25, text phrase 2)
- the reiterative enclitic 'again' -**da** (chapter 8, track 38, vocal section 1, text phrase 3).

The topic marker -**ga** occurs only in the *wangga* of Marlip Philip Mullumbuk, where it modifies a noun (chapter 8, track 33, text phrase 1). Different topic -**gu** also modifies a nominal (chapter 8, track 33, text phrase 1), but is used propositionally elsewhere (chapter 8, track 7, text phrase 1). Marlip Philip Mullumbuk is the only composer to contrast -**ga** and -**gu** (chapter 8, track 33, text phrase 1).

Song words

A conspicuous feature of the Walakandha *wangga* texts is that they do not contain the song words that play such an integral role in Batjamalh and Emmi-Mendhe *wangga*. The only song word used in the Walakandha *wangga* is **karra**, which is used to signal that the following statement has emanated from the ancestral realm. In one instance (chapter 8, track 28), the text contains no words other than **karra**.

Anomalous texts

We will conclude our discussion of Walakandha *wangga* by noting three unusual texts. The first text, 'Yendili No. 2' (chapter 8, track 14), breaks with convention, in that it was composed in Marri Ngarr[13] by a Marri Ngarr woman, Maudie Attaying Dumoo, about a Walakandha Dreaming site in Marri Tjavin country for which her Marri Tjavin husband had responsibility. The song is addressed to the couple's children, who are bilingual in Marri Ngarr and Marri Tjavin and inheritors of responsibility for the site. It addresses the children directly, and orders them to keep hold of the place named in the song. For more esoteric meanings, see the notes to track 14 in chapter 8.

The first two text phrases are identical and consist of a pair of complex verb phrases inflected for Irrealis modality; the final clause is a verbless vocative phrase: **aa ye-ngin-a** 'Ah, my dear children.' The first two text phrases begin with **karra** followed by the reduplicated place name 'Yendili.' Even though the text is in Marri Ngarr rather than Marri Tjavin, its structure follows that of other Walakandha *wangga* (Marett, 2005, pp 125–26).

The second unusual *wangga* text, Mandji's 'Karra Mele Ngany-endheni-nö' combines features of Mendhe *wangga* and Marri Tjavin *wangga* (chapter 6, track 8). Here Mandji alternates vocal sections in Mendhe and Marri Tjavin. The Marri Tjavin vocal section includes an adversative bound pronominal -**ngangga**, the directional enclitic -**wurri**, a serial construction and a headless relative clause, all of which also occur in the Walakandha *wangga*.

A third anomalous text, Philip Mullumbuk's 'Wedjiwurang' has been discussed in detail elsewhere (see Ford 2007 and notes to track 38 in chapter 8).

Differences between the Ma-yawa *wangga* and the Walakandha *wangga*

The twenty-nine Ma-yawa *wangga* tracks comprise twelve songs. We exclude from our analysis 'Walakandha Ngindji' (chapter 9, tracks 1 to 3), because it is borrowed wholesale from a Walakandha *wangga* text (chapter 8, track 23). Nor do we take into account the performance of 'Thalhi-ngatjpirr'

---

13 Marri Ngarr has its own song genre, *lirrga*, which is very different from *wangga*. The two genres are contemporary with each other, but mutually exclusive.

sung by Frank Dumoo and Colin Worumbu Ferguson (chapter 9, track 24), in which a Marri Tjavin songman borrows wholesale a Ma-yawa *wangga* text.

The remaining texts reveal the following differences from the Walakandha *wangga* texts.

Nominals

The texts contain 224 nominals in 146 clauses, approximately 1.5 overt nominals per clause, much higher than in mundane usage, but roughly comparable in frequency to the nominals in Walakandha *wangga* texts.

These texts contain fewer place names than the Walakandha *wangga*, but the occurrence in them of geographical terms such as **mungirini** 'jungle' (chapter 9, track 16, text phrase 2), **diyerr** 'cliff' (chapter 9, track 20, vocal section 1, text phrase 1), **wudi-pumininy** 'freshwater spring' (chapter 9, track 21, vocal section 1, text phrase 1) and **purangang** 'salt water' (chapter 9, track 20, vocal section 3, text phrase 1) fixes the location of the songs, as does the anaphoric locative **kagan-dja** 'that place we know about' (chapter 9, track 13, vocal section 1, text phrase 2).

As in other *wangga* repertories, intimacy is conveyed by the use of kin-terms, but these texts contain only the kin-term **mana** 'elder brother', which occurs 21 times, almost always introduced by the song word **karra**. In all these cases **mana** refers to Dreaming beings, which are commonly referred to as 'elder brother' throughout the Daly. As Marett has noted (2005, p 135), the Ma-yawa *wangga* focuses on Dreamings (*ngirrwat*) and Dreaming places (*kigatiya*) to a much greater extent than other *wangga* repertories. Of the seven place names that occur in the texts, one, **menggani** 'butterfly Dreaming', is also the name of a Dreaming place; in all, six Dreamings—**Menggani, Malhimanyirr, Tjerri, Tjiwilirr, Tulh, Ma-yawa**—are named. In one text, 'Malhimanyirr,' the Dreaming is explicitly described as **kanyi-ngin** 'my totem' (chapter 9, track 17, vocal section 1, text phrase 1).

Noun classifiers

Unlike the Walakandha *wangga*, these texts contain a range of generic nouns that function as classifiers. These are: **ma** 'male human' (chapter 9, track 20, vocal section 1, text phrase 2), **wulumen** 'old man' (chapter 9, track 4, vocal section 1, text phrase 1, track 28), **miyi** 'edible vegetable' (chapter 9, track 28, vocal section 1, text phrase 3), **nidin** 'place' (chapter 9, track 25, vocal section 1, text phrase 1), **thawurr** 'inanimate' (chapter 9, track 27, vocal section 1, text phrase 1).

Complex noun phrases

Like the Walakandha *wangga*, these texts contain adjectival noun phrases: **meri ngalvu** 'many people' (chapter 9, track 22, vocal section 1, text phrase 1), **mungirini kapil** 'big jungle' (chapter 9, track 16, vocal section 1, text phrase 2), **mungarri kapil** 'deep sleep' (chapter 9, track 18, vocal section 1, text phrase 4); and possessive noun phrases: **mana nganggi** 'our brother' (chapter 9, track 20, vocal section 3, text phrase 2).

Verbals

Out of a total of 146 clauses, only 12 are verbless. Seventy-seven are simple clauses containing only one verb, and 59 are complex clauses that combine two verbs in a serial construction. The verb **ka-vulh**, 'he lies/does it forever' occurs as the serial verb in 45 of these constructions; **ka-yirr** 'he travels/does deliberately,' occurs in four; **ka-ni** 'he goes/keeps on doing' in four and **ku-wa** 'he stands up,' and its Irrealis form **ngunda** in six. There are only four embedded, locative, headless relative clauses and these all express locative information. For example:

- **kani-djet diyerr kuwa** ' he sits where the cliff stands up [i.e., at the foot of the cliff]' (chapter 9, track 20, vocal section 1, text phrase 1)

- **kani-djet kuwa kagan-dja** 'he is sitting right here where it [the cliff] stands up' (chapter 9, track 20, vocal section 2, text phrase 1)
- **nidin na kaddi devin kurzi** 'country that is just for us' (chapter 9, track 22, vocal section 1, text phrase 1).

Modifiers

The texts contain a limited range of adverbs: **nal** 'just' (chapter 9, track 28, vocal section 2, text phrase 3); **kisji** 'just like this' (chapter 9, track 28, vocal section 1, text phrase 4) and **wandhi** 'behind' (chapter 9, track 15, vocal section 1, text phrase 2).

Particles

Ma-yawa *wangga* texts use only two enclitic particles: **-dja** 'really' (chapter 9, track 12, vocal section 1, text phrase 3); and **-gu** 'different topic' (chapter 9, track 22, text phrase 2). But **-gu** is not used in Ma-yawa *wangga* as it would be in mundane usage, where **-gu** only occurs to mark a switch of topic, to contrast with an earlier topic, marked with **-ga**. In Ma-yawa w*angga*, the distinction between Topic marker **-ga** and Different Topic marker **-gu** is neutralised; **-gu** marks any topic, occurring frequently—in 46 clauses—but never in contrast with a preceding **-ga**.

This is also true of early Walakandha *wangga* texts—for example, in Stan Mullumbuk's songs 'Nginimb-andja' (chapter 8, track 4, text phrase 1) and 'Walakandha No. 8b' (track 7, text phrase 1)—but not of the most recently composed Walakandha *wangga*, where Philip Mullumbuk always conforms to mundane usage. For example, in 'Karra Yeri-ngina' (chapter 8, track 34, verse 1, text phrase 1) the sole topic of the text phrase is marked by **-ga**, but in 'Walakanda No. 3' (track 33, text phrase 1) and 'Wedjiwurang' (track 38 vocal section 3, text phrase 3, and vocal section 4, text phrases 4-5) the first topic is marked by **-ga**, and the second by **-gu**.

In Ma-yawa *wangga* and Stan Mullumbuk's Walakandha *wangga*, **-gu** always occurs at the end of a text phrase, so, in early Walakandha *wangga*, **-gu** appears to function primarily as a metric filler. Only in later Walakandha *wangga* does its use conform with mundane usage. Maybe Philip Mullumbuk alludes to this by ending the final text phrase of the final vocal phrase of 'Wedjiwurang' (track 38) with **-gu.**

In Ma-yawa *wangga,* **-gu** appears to be used both as neutralised topic marker and as metric filler. It occurs 46 times, in most instances (31, or 66%), at the end of a text phrase. But in 14 instances (30% of the total), it marks the noun phrase that begins the text phrase, and in one instance it marks the verb phrase at the beginning of the text phrase, in other words, the topic. Modern mundane usage would omit it, but Ngulkur plays with poetic and mundane usages, like a signature.

Reduplication

The Ma-yawa *wangga* contain a significant number of simple and reduplicated forms, ranging from the adverbial **wandhi-wandhi** 'behind' (chapter 9, track 14, vocal section 1, text phrase 2) and **kisji-gisji** 'like this' (chapter 9, track 6, vocal section 1, text phrase 4), to the verbal **kimi-gimi** 'he does/says/sings' (chapter 9, track 10, vocal section 1, text phrase 1) and the partial reduplication **ga-kap** 'call out' (chapter 9, track 16, vocal section 1, text phrase 1). This use of reduplication extends to place-names, for example **wudi-pumininy-pumininy** (chapter 9, track 20, vocal section 2, text phrase 2) and **rtadi-wunbirri-wunbirri** (chapter 9, track 6, vocal section 1, text phrase 3)**.**

Conclusion

To summarise, the evidence presented in this chapter shows that *wangga* song texts in the five language varieties in which *wangga* is sung, contain significant complexity in their grammar and lexicon, and preserve features no longer present in everyday language.

Figure 4.1 Portrait of Tommy Barrtjap (Burrenjuck), photograph by Alice Moyle, Delissaville (Belyuen), 1976. Photograph by Alice Moyle, courtesy of Alice Moyle family and AIATSIS (Moyle. A3.Cs - 6412), reproduced with the permission of Belyuen community.

Chapter 4
BARRTJAP'S REPERTORY

Tommy Barrtjap (Burrenjuck, also spelled Barandjak, Barradjap) (c. 1925–1992), a Wadjiginy songman resident at Belyuen on the Cox Peninsula, Northern Territory, was well known throughout the Daly region and Australia's Top End as a ritual leader, *wangga* composer, and, in his youth, a talented football player. He frequently visited Darwin and performed for public concerts as well as ceremonial occasions. With other performers from Belyuen (Delissaville) he performed 'tourist corroborees' at Mica Beach (Talc Head) and later at Mandorah. As a young man, he was taught to sing by his father's brother, Jimmy Bandak, and after the latter's death inherited his repertory and continued to receive songs from him in dream. Bandak's and Barrtjap's musical activities at Belyuen in this early period are described in Ewers (1954), Simpson (1951) and Elkin and Jones (1958); see also Barwick and Marett (2011) for comparison of musical practice at Belyuen in 1948 to that of recent times.

Marett first met Tommy Barrtjap in 1986 on a visit to Belyuen. He was a tall rather severe man, in his mid-sixties, the men's ritual leader at Belyuen. At that time he was the senior *wangga* singer in the Daly region, and even today, some eighteen years after his death, his memory is held in the highest regard and his songs remain popular. Barrtjap's repertory was passed on to his sons Kenny (1949–2008) and Timothy (b.1953), and some Barrtjap songs are featured in the repertory of the Kenbi Dancers, a group of Belyuen performers who continue to perform tourist corroborees around Darwin.

When listening to songs recorded by A.P. Elkin at Delissaville (Belyuen) in 1949, Belyuen people today find it difficult to distinguish the voices of Jimmy Bandak and Tommy Barrtjap; they are described as having 'the same voice'. Barrtjap helped us to transcribe and translate the texts of his songs, which are in a mixture of his own language Batjamalh and the language of *wunymalang* ghosts, but he was never able to speak the words of his songs, preferring to sing them for us (very slowly, at our request, causing great hilarity amongst those present at the sessions).

Notes on the recording sample

Table 4.1 summarises the songs from the Barrtjap repertory discussed in this chapter, using the same system of numbering as in *Songs, dreamings and ghosts* (Marett, 2005). We provide at least one recorded example, together with transcribed, glossed and translated texts, for all but three of Barrtjap's songs.[1] Where more than one version of a song is provided, it is normally because, unusually for Barrtjap, there are significant differences between two versions of a song, or because there are a number of versions of the song by different singers. For example, the four tracks of 'Naya Rradja Bangany Nye-ve' (tracks 16–19) were recorded by four different singers: Jimmy Bandak, Lawrence Wurrpen, Tommy Barrtjap and Kenny Burrenjuck. Considering that these performances range over almost fifty years, the versions are remarkably similar.

---

[1] Note that three song titles (11, 13 and 17) are transcribed differently from in *Songs, dreamings and ghosts*. Three additional songs, 'Ngaya Lima Bangany-nyaya' (song 20 in Marett, 2005), 'Nyala Nga-ve Bangany' (song 21), and 'Karra Bangany-nyaya Nga-p-pindja' (song 23), which were performed only rarely by Kenny Burrenjuck or Timothy Burrenjuck, are not included here because of the poor quality of the relevant recordings.

Track	Song #	Title	Singer	Recording
Track 01	1	'Ya Bangany-nyung Nga-bindja Yagarra'	Barrtjap	Moy68-05-s02
Track 02	2	'Yagarra Nga-bindja-ng Nga-mi Ngayi'	Barrtjap	Moy68-05-s03
Track 03	3*	'Bangany-nyung Ngaya'	Barrtjap	Moy68-05-s04
Track 04		'Bangany-nyung Ngaya'	Barrtjap	Moy68-05-s05
Track 05	4*	'Kanga Rinyala Nga-ve Bangany-nyung'	Barrtjap	Moy68-05-s06
Track 06		'Kanga Rinyala Nga-ve Bangany-nyung'	Barrtjap	Moy68-05-s07
Track 07	5	'Ya[garra] Nga-bindja-ng Nga-mi'	Barrtjap	Moy68-05-s08
Track 08		'Ya[garra] Nga-bindja-ng Nga-mi'	Barrtjap	Moy68-05-s09
Track 09	6	'Yagarra Bangany Nye-ngwe'	Barrtjap	Moy68-05-s10
Track 10	7	'Be Bangany-nyaya'	Barrtjap	Moy68-05-s11
Track 11	8*	'Nyere-nyere Lima Kaldja'	Barrtjap	Mar88-04-s02
Track 12	9*	'Nyere-nye Bangany Nyaye'	Barrtjap	Mar88-04-s03
Track 13	10*	'Karra Ngadja-maka Nga-bindja-ng Ngami'	Barrtjap	Mar88-04-s07
Track 14	11*	'Yerre Ka-bindja-maka Ka-mi'	Barrtjap	Mar88-05-s11
Track 15	12	'Yagarra Ye-yenenaya'	Barrtjap	Mar88-05-s02
Track 16	13*	'Naya Rradja Bangany Nye-ve'	Bandak	Elk52-19B-s04
Track 17		'Naya Rradja Bangany Nye-ve'	Wurrpen	Mad64-02-s15
Track 18		'Naya Rradja Bangany Nye-ve'	Barrtjap	Mar88-05-s03
Track 19		'Naya Rradja Bangany Nye-ve'	Burrenjuck	Mar97-04-s16
Track 20	14	'Yagarra Nedja Tjine Rak-pe'	Barrtjap	Mar88-05-s06
Track 21	15*	'Ya Rembe Ngaya Lima Ngaya'	Barrtjap	Mar88-05-s13
Track 22	16	'Yagarra Tjüt Balk-nga-me Nga-mi'	Barrtjap	Mar86-03-s04
Track 23	17	'Yagarra Tjine Rak-pe'	Barrtjap	Mar86-03-s06
Track 24	18*	'Yagarra Delhi Nya-ngadja-barra-ngarrka'	Barrtjap	Mar86-03-s05
Track 25	19*	'Nga-ngat-pat-pa Mangalimba'	Burrenjuck	Mar97-04-s07
Track 26	22*	'Anadadada Bangany-nyaya'	Burrenjuck	Mar97-04-s04

Table 4.1 Songs from the Barrtjap repertory discussed in this chapter. Songs known to have been sung by Kenny Burrenjuck are asterisked.

Tracks 1–10 are taken from a recording session made with Barrtjap in 1968 by Alice Moyle (Moy68-05) (some of these recordings were published by AM Moyle, 1992 [1977], track 3). Because of the historical importance of this recording session, here we have included most of the songs recorded by Moyle on that occasion and present them in the order in which they were recorded. There then follows a sequence of tracks recorded by Marett in 1988 (tracks 11–15, 18, 20–21). This sequence is interrupted by a number of tracks included for comparative purposes made by Elkin in 1952 (track 16, Elk52-19B), Maddock in 1964 (track 17, Mad64-02) and Marett in 1997 (track 19, Mar97-04). The remaining tracks are all taken from recordings made by Marett in 1986 (tracks 22–24, Mar86-03) and 1997 (tracks 25–26, Mar97-04). Three Barrtjap songs (numbers 20 'Ngaya Lima Bangany-nyaya', 21 'Nyala Nga-ve Bangany' and 23 'Karra Bangany-nyaya' in table 3.2 in Marett, 2005, p 247) are omitted here because the quality of performance and/or recording was insufficient for publication.

Figure 4.2 Tommy Barrtjap (seated) singing for a group of dancers at Belyuen, 1952, including from left: John Scroggi, David Woodie, [boy obscured], George Munggulu, George Manbi, Jimmy Havelock, Nipper Rankin, Ginger Moreen, Brucie Pott, Harold Woodie, Mosek Manpurr, Prince of Wales. Courtesy of University of Sydney Archives, reproduced with the permission of Belyuen community.

Figure 4.3 Tommy Barrtjap standing and singing, with dancers Tommy Lippo and Brucie Pott, and audience including George Munggulu, Mosek Manpurr, Prince of Wales (at rear), George Manbi, Nipper Rankin and Ginger Moreen. Courtesy of University of Sydney Archives, reproduced with the permission of Belyuen community.

TRACK 1 (Moy68-05-s02)

Song 1: Ya Bangany-nyung Nga-bindja Yagarra

Sung text	Free translation
ya!	Ya!
bangany-nyung nga-bindja yagarra	I'm singing in order to give you this song, yagarra!
bangany-nyung nga-bindja ngaradj[a]	I'm singing in order to give you this song, daughter
bangany-nyung nga-bindja yagarra	I'm singing in order to give you this song, yagarra!
bangany-nyung nga-bindja-ya	I'm singing in order to give you this song, ya!
ya!	Ya!
ngaradja bangany nga-bindja	Daughter! I'm singing a song
ngaradja bangany nga-bindja	Daughter! I'm singing a song
ngaradja bangany nga-bindja	Daughter! I'm singing a song
yagarra!	Yagarra!
ya di	Ya di

All *wangga* songs originate as the utterances of song-giving *wunymalang* ghosts singing to the songman in his dream. But the words that we hear are also the words of the songman as he reproduces what the *wunymalang* has taught him for an audience of living humans. In the course of rendering the song suitable for human consumption the songman massages what he has received from the ghost in a variety of ways. For example, all or part of the original song language of the *wunymalang* may be 'turned over' into human language and references to individuals or local events may be added. In this song, almost all the words of the *wunymalang* are rendered in Batjamalh. In text phrases 1–2 he announces that he is appearing (in the songman's dream) in order to give this new song: 'I [the *wunymalang*] am singing in order to give you [the songman] this song, Yagarra!' *Yagarra*, an exclamation expressing strong emotion, is often used in Barrtjap's songs. These same words can be heard by the living audience as meaning, 'I [the songman] am singing in order to provide this song [for ceremony or for entertainment], Yagarra!' In text phrase 3, the *wunymalang* (or the songman) addresses this comment directly to his daughter and in text phrase 7 he again addresses her directly, 'Daughter! I'm singing a song.' Perhaps the *wunymalang's* daughter was also present in the songman's dream; certainly in many performances one of the Barrtjap's daughters would have been amongst those dancing.

Just as the didjeridu begins, we hear the dancers perform a *malh*, that is, a ritual invocation in which the performers call to attention the living, sentient ground upon which they dance.

SONG STRUCTURE SUMMARY

VOCAL SECTIONS 1–2

Melodic section 1

Text phrase 1

Rhythmic mode 5b (fast doubled)
ya
SW

Ya!

Text phrase 2

Rhythmic mode 5b (fast doubled)

bangany	-nyung	nga	-bindja	yagarra
song	DAT	1MIN.S	sing	EXCL

I'm singing in order to give you this song, yagarra!

Text phrase 3

Rhythmic mode 5b (fast doubled)

bangany	-nyung	nga	-bindja	ngaradj[a]
song	DAT	1MIN.S	sing	daughter

I'm singing in order to give you this song, daughter

Text phrase 4

Rhythmic mode 5b (fast doubled)

bangany	-nyung	nga	-bindja	yagarra
song	DAT	1MIN.S	sing	EXCL

I'm singing in order to give you this song, yagarra!

Text phrase 5

Rhythmic mode 5b (fast doubled)

bangany	-nyung	nga	-bindja	-ya
song	DAT	1MIN.S	sing	SW

I'm singing in order to give you this song

Melodic section 2

Text phrase 6

Rhythmic mode 5b (fast doubled)

ya
SW

Ya!

Text phrases 7–9

Rhythmic mode 5b (fast doubled)

ngaradja	bangany	nga	-bindja
daughter	song	1MIN.S	sing

Daughter! I'm singing a song

Melodic section 3

Text phrase 10

Rhythmic mode 5b (fast doubled)

yagarra
EXCL

Yagarra!

Text phrase 11

Rhythmic mode 5b (fast doubled)

ya	**di**
SW	SW

Ya di

INSTRUMENTAL SECTIONS 1–2

Rhythmic mode 5b (fast doubled). Changes to Rhythmic mode 5a (fast even) towards the end of instrumental section 2.

VOCAL SECTION 3

Melodic section 1

Text phrase 1

Rhythmic mode 5a (fast even)

ya
SW

Ya!

Text phrase 2

Rhythmic mode 5a (fast even)

bangany	**-nyung**	**nga**	**-bindja**	**yagarra**
song	DAT	1MIN.S	sing	EXCL

I'm singing in order to give you this song, yagarra!

Text phrase 3

Rhythmic mode 5a (fast even)

bangany	**-nyung**	**nga**	**-bindja**	**ngaradj[a]**
song	DAT	1MIN.S	sing	daughter

I'm singing in order to give you this song, daughter

Text phrase 4

Rhythmic mode 5a (fast even)

bangany	**-nyung**	**nga**	**-bindja**	**yagarra**
song	DAT	1MIN.S	sing	EXCL

I'm singing in order to give you this song, yagarra!

Text phrase 5

Rhythmic mode 5a (fast even)

bangany	**-nyung**	**nga**	**-bindja**	**-ya**
song	DAT	1MIN.S	sing	SW

I'm singing in order to give you this song

Melodic section 2

Text phrase 6

Rhythmic mode 5a (fast even)

ya
SW

Ya!

Text phrases 7–9

Rhythmic mode 5a (fast even)

ngaradja	**bangany**	**nga**	**-bindja**
daughter	song	1MIN.S	sing

Daughter! I'm singing a song

Melodic section 3

Text phrase 10

Rhythmic mode 5a (fast even)

yagarra
EXCL

Yagarra!

Text phrase 11

Rhythmic mode 5a (fast even)

da	**ni**
SW	SW

Da ni

INSTRUMENTAL SECTION 3

Rhythmic mode 5a (fast even)

CODA

Rhythmic mode 5a (fast even)

yit ngayi ngayi …

TRACK 2 (Moy68-05-s03)

Song 2: Yagarra Nga-bindja-ng Nga-mi Ngayi[2]

Sung text	Free translation
yagarra nga-bindja-ng nga-mi ngayi ngayi yit ngayi	Yagarra! I'm singing 'ngayi ngayi yit ngayi'
yagarra yine ngadja ya di di	Yagarra! What am I? Ya di di …

Here the text states that the utterer (the song-giving *wunymalang*, or the songman) is singing the didjeridu mouth sounds, 'ngayi ngayi yit ngayi' and then, in text phrase 2, poses the question, 'what am I?' This question points to the fact that singers deliberately obscure the distinction between themselves and their song-giving *wunymalang*. Between vocal sections 2 and 3 Barrtjap performs a high call, which represents the voice of the *wunymalang* (such calls may be performed either by the singer or by someone else). Whose voice are we hearing here: the voice of the ghost or the voice of the man? This is one of the means by which the singer creates a liminal space that, in the context of *kapuk* (mortuary) ceremonies, facilitates the passing of the deceased from the world of the living to the world of the dead (Marett, 2000).

The text is relatively stable; apart from variability in the number of iterations of the didjeridu mouth sounds and in the concluding vocables, the song is the same from vocal section to vocal section and from performance to performance. The didjeridu mouth sounds are performed cyclically to the same rhythm and set isorhythmically.

In addition to this single performance from 1968, there are three from the 1980s: Mar86-03-s01 and Mar88-04-s08 and –s09. These show that Barrtjap was still singing the song in almost exactly the same way twenty years later.

This song is one of two in moderate quintuple metre (defined by the stick beat pattern ♩♩ ♪ ♩ ♪, performed in the moderate tempo band). The other is song 16, 'Yagarra Tjüt Balk-nga-me Nga-mi' (track 22). Typically for quintuple metre, the coda uses the didjeridu mouth sounds 'yit ngayi yit ngowe yit ngowe.'

---

2 This song was given the title 'Yagarra Nga-bindja-ng Nga-mi-ngaye' in Marett, 2005.

SONG STRUCTURE SUMMARY

VOCAL SECTIONS 1–3

Melodic section 1

Text phrase 1

Rhythmic mode 4d (moderate uneven quintuple)

yagarra	nga	-bindja	-ng	nga	-mi	ngayi	ngayi	yit ngayi
EXCL	1MIN.S	sing	SIM	1MIN.S	sit	SW	SW	SW

Yagarra! I'm singing 'ngayi ngayi yit ngayi'

Melodic section 2

Text phrase 2

Rhythmic mode 4d (moderate uneven quintuple)

yagarra	yine	ngadja	ya	di	di
EXCL	what	1MIN.S.PRO	SW	SW	SW

Yagarra! What am I? Ya di di …

INSTRUMENTAL SECTIONS 1–3

Rhythmic mode 4d (moderate uneven quintuple)

CODA

Rhythmic mode 4d (moderate uneven quintuple)

yit ngayi yit ngowe yit ngowe …

TRACK 3 (Moy68-05-s04)

Song 3: Bangany-nyung Ngaya

Sung text	Free translation
bangany-nyung ngaya bangany-nyung nga-bindja-ya	For a song, ngaya, I'm singing in order to give you a song
bangany-nyung ngaya bangany-nyung nga-bindja-ya	For a song, ngaya, I'm singing in order to give you a song
yagarra nga-bindja-ng nga-mi yakerre ye di di	yagarra! I'm singing, yakerre! ye di di
ii	ii
yagarra nga-bindja-ya nye nye nye	yagarra! I sing 'nye nye nye'
yagarra nga-bindja-ya	yagarra! I sing

This is one of several songs in Barrtjap's repertory (we have already encountered one in song 1) that reproduce the words of a song-giving *wunymalang* ghost singing to the songman in his dream and telling him that he has come to give him a song. When sung in ceremony by a living songman, the same words convey the fact that he, the songman, has come to the ceremony ground in order to sing the song for the dancers and audience there.

This is the most popular of Barrtjap's songs. There are dozens of recordings of 'Bangany-nyung Ngaya,' sung by a range of different performers, including Marett. The song has been discussed in chapter 4 of Marett's book (2005) in far more detail than is possible here.

The song text is almost identical from performance to performance, although as in most oral cultures, there is scope for variation: the number of vocal sections may vary (in addition to performances such as this with two vocal sections, performances with three vocal sections are also common), the precise form of some song words may also vary, and in the case of those sections of text which are set as continuous isorhythm, the number of cycles and the precise place in the text where the singer stops is also variable. For example, in this track, Barrtjap truncates text phrase 6, stopping halfway through the text phrase. Another performance of this song where he sings the whole text phrase in this position can be heard on the next track.

In most performances, the song is performed with fast uneven quadruple beating (♩ ♩ ♩ 𝄽) for all vocal and instrumental section and for the coda, but Barrtjap's son Kenny Burrenjuck occasionally used fast doubled beating for some vocal and instrumental sections.

SONG STRUCTURE SUMMARY

VOCAL SECTIONS 1–2

Melodic section 1

Text phrases 1–2

Rhythmic mode 5c (fast uneven quadruple)

bangany	**-nyung**	**ngaya**	**bangany**	**-nyung**	**nga**	**-bindja**	**-ya**
song	DAT	SW	song	DAT	1MIN.S	sing	SW

For a song, ngaya, I'm singing in order to give you a song

Melodic section 2

Text phrase 3

Rhythmic mode 5c (fast uneven quadruple)

yagarra	**nga**	**-bindja**	**-ng**	**nga**	**-mi**	**yakerre**	**ye**	**di**	**di**
EXCL	1MIN.S	sing	SIM	1MIN.S	sit	EXCL	SW	SW	SW

Yagarra! I'm singing, yakerre! Ye di di …

Melodic section 3

Text phrase 4

Rhythmic mode 5c (fast uneven quadruple)

ii
SW

Ii

Text phrase 5

Rhythmic mode 5c (fast uneven quadruple)

yagarra	nga	-bindja	-ya	nye	nye	nye
EXCL	1MIN.S	sing	SW	SW	SW	SW

Yagarra! I sing, 'nye nye nye'

Text phrase 6

Rhythmic mode 5c (fast uneven quadruple)

yagarra	nga	-bindja	-ya
EXCL	1MIN.S	sing	SW

Yagarra! I sing

INSTRUMENTAL SECTIONS 1-2

Rhythmic mode 5c (fast uneven quadruple)

CODA

Rhythmic mode 5c

yit ngayi ngayi yit ngowe …

TRACK 4 (Moy68-05-s05)

Song 3: Bangany-nyung Ngaya

Sung text	Free translation
bangany-nyung ngaya bangany-nyung nga-bindja-ya	For a song, ngaya, I'm singing in order to give you a song
bangany-nyung ngaya bangany-nyung nga-bindja-ya	For a song, ngaya, I'm singing in order to give you a song
yagarra nga-bindja-ng nga-mi yakerre ye di di	Yagarra! I'm singing, yakerre! Ye di di
ii	Ii
yagarra nga-bindja-ya nye nye nye	Yagarra! I sing 'nye nye nye'
yagarra nga-bindja-ya (nye nye nye)	Yagarra! I sing ('nye nye nye')

Apart from some inconsistency in the length of text phrase 6, and the use of an extended coda, this version is virtually identical to the version of song 3 presented on track 3.

SONG STRUCTURE SUMMARY

VOCAL SECTIONS 1–2

Melodic section 1

Text phrases 1–2

Rhythmic mode 5c (fast uneven quadruple)

bangany	-nyung	ngaya	bangany	-nyung	nga		-bindja	-ya
song	DAT	SW	song	DAT	1MIN.S		sing	SW

For a song, ngaya, I'm singing in order to give you a song

Melodic section 2

Text phrase 3

Rhythmic mode 5c (fast uneven quadruple)

yagarra	nga	-bindja	-ng	nga	-mi	yakerre	ye	di	di
EXCL	1MIN.S	sing	SIM	1MIN.S	sit	EXCL	SW	SW	SW

Yagarra! I'm singing, yakerre! Ye di di …

Melodic section 3

Text phrase 4

Rhythmic mode 5c (fast uneven quadruple)

ii
SW

Ii

Text phrase 5

Rhythmic mode 5c (fast uneven quadruple)

yagarra	nga	-bindja	-ya	nye	nye	nye
EXCL	1MIN.S	sing	SW	SW	SW	SW

Yagarra! I sing 'nye nye nye'

Text phrase 6

Rhythmic mode 5c (fast uneven quadruple)

yagarra	nga	-bindja	-ya	nye	nye	nye
EXCL	1MIN.S	sing	SW	SW	SW	SW

Yagarra! I sing ('nye nye nye') [truncated in vocal section 2]

INSTRUMENTAL SECTIONS 1–2

Rhythmic mode 5c (fast uneven quadruple)

CODA

Rhythmic mode 5c
yit ngayi ngayi yit ngowe …

TRACK 5 (Moy68-05-s06)

Song 4: Kanga Rinyala Nga-ve Bangany-nyung

Sung text	Free translation
kanga rinyala nga-ve bangany-nyung	Kanga rinyala, I've come for a song
ngwe ngwe ngwe ngwe ngwe ngwe ni	Ngwe ngwe ngwe ngwe ngwe ngwe ni
kanga rinyala nga-ve bangany-nyung yagarra	Kanga rinyala, I've come for a song, yagarra!

'Kanga Rinyala' is another of the most frequently performed and important of Barrtjap's songs. It is the song that is sung in *kapuk* ceremonies at the point at which the spirit of the deceased is driven out of his or her belongings by burning them, and conducted, with encouragement from the singers, dancers and audience, to the world of the dead. The recorded corpus includes a large number of performances (two of which are included here—see also track 6) by a range of different performers, including Barrtjap's son Kenny Burrenjuck. Apart from some variability in the stick beating (see below) this song is very stable from performance to performance.

The vocal section once again comprises the words of the song-giving *wunymalang* ghost, stating that he has come to give the songman the song. The text also includes a significant amount of 'ghost language,' which includes 'ngwe ngwe' and 'ni,' but it is the two vocables, 'kanga rinyala,' that begin the song that are particularly interesting, first because they are unique to this song, and secondly, because one of the ghost words has a tangential relationship to human language (Batjamalh). Lysbeth Ford suggests that the 'ghost language' word 'rinyala' may be related to the Batjamalh word 'riny-malh' (sung melody). Barrtjap and others we have consulted over the years have, however, been adamant about the fact that these are song words and not words in normal spoken language.

The song is usually accompanied by slow even beating (rhythmic mode 2), a rhythmic mode reserved for deeply serious moments. In some performances the mood of deep seriousness is further intensified by suspending the stick beating entirely: it is almost as if time stands still. The performance of 'Kanga rinyala Nga-ve Bangany-nyung' on track 6 shows an example of this practice.

In the coda the stick beating changes from slow even to fast triple beating (accompanied by the didjeridu mouth sounds 'yit ngayi yit ngowe ... ').

SONG STRUCTURE SUMMARY

VOCAL SECTIONS 1–2

Melodic section 1

Text phrase 1

Rhythmic mode 2 (slow even)

kanga	rinyala	nga	-ve	bangany	-nyung
SW	SW	1MIN.S	come	song	DAT

Kanga rinyala, I've come for a song

ngwe	ngwe	ngwe	ngwe	ngwe	ngwe	ni
SW	SW	SW	SW	SW	SW	SW

ngwe ngwe ngwe ngwe ngwe ngwe ni

Melodic section 2

Text phrase 2

Rhythmic mode 2 (slow even)

kanga	rinyala	nga	-ve	bangany	-nyung	yagarra
SW	SW	1MIN.S	come	song	DAT	EXCL

Kanga rinyala, I've come for a song, yagarra!

INSTRUMENTAL SECTIONS 1–2

Rhythmic mode 2 (slow even)

CODA

Rhythmic mode 5d (fast uneven triple)

yit ngayi yit ngowe, ngayi yit ngayi yit ngowe …

TRACK 6 (Moy68-05-s07)

Song 4: Kanga Rinyala Nga-ve Bangany-nyung

Sung text	Free translation
kanga rinyala nga-ve bangany-nyung	Kanga rinyala, I've come for a song
ngwe ngwe ngwe ngwe ngwe ngwe ni	Ngwe ngwe ngwe ngwe ngwe ngwe ni
kanga rinyala nga-ve bangany-nyung yagarra	Kanga rinyala, I've come for a song, yagarra!

As indicated in the notes to track 5, this version of song 4 'Kanga Rinyala' suspends the stick beating in the first text phrase of vocal section 2, although clapping accompaniment in the same tempo can be heard in the background (for a musical transcription see (for a musical transcription, see Marett, 2005, p 165). Song structure summary below marks this stick suspension by labelling it 'rhythmic mode 2b' and contrasting it with the normal rhythmic mode 2 beating (here labelled 'rhythmic mode 2a').

SONG STRUCTURE SUMMARY

VOCAL SECTION 1

Melodic section 1

Text phrase 1

Rhythmic mode 2a (slow even)

kanga	rinyala	nga	-ve	bangany	-nyung
SW	SW	1MIN.S	come	song	DAT

Kanga rinyala, I've come for a song

ngwe	ngwe	ngwe	ngwe	ngwe	ngwe	ni
SW	SW	SW	SW	SW	SW	SW

ngwe ngwe ngwe ngwe ngwe ngwe ni

Melodic section 2

Text phrase 2

Rhythmic mode 2a (slow even)

kanga	rinyala	nga	-ve	bangany	-nyung	yagarra
SW	SW	1MIN.S	come	song	DAT	EXCL

Kanga rinyala, I've come for a song, yagarra!

INSTRUMENTAL SECTION 1

Rhythmic mode 2 (slow even)

VOCAL SECTION 2

Melodic section 1

Text phrase 1

Rhythmic mode 2b (slow even—stick beating suspended)

kanga	rinyala	nga	-ve	bangany	-nyung
SW	SW	1MIN.S	move	song	DAT

Kanga rinyala, I've come for a song

ngwe	ngwe	ngwe	ngwe	ngwe	ngwe	ni
SW	SW	SW	SW	SW	SW	SW

ngwe ngwe ngwe ngwe ngwe ngwe ni

Melodic section 2

Text phrase 2

Rhythmic mode 2a (slow even)

kanga	rinyala	nga	-ve	bangany	-nyung	yagarra
SW	SW	1MIN.S	come	song	DAT	EXCL

Kanga rinyala, I've come for a song, yagarra!

INSTRUMENTAL SECTION 2

Rhythmic mode 2 (slow even)

CODA

Rhythmic mode 5d (fast uneven triple)

yit ngayi yit ngowe, ngayi yit ngayi yit ngowe …

TRACK 7 (Moy68-05-s08)

Song 5: Ya[garra] Nga-bindja-ng Nga-mi

Sung text	Free translation
ya[garra]	Ya[garra]!
nga-bindja-ng nga-mi	I'm singing
(yagarra yine nga-ve-me-nüng	(Yagarra! What have I come to do?
nga-p-pindja-ng nga-p-pur-ing-djü-nüng)	I'm going to sing and then go back)
yagarra nye-bindja-ng nya-mu	Yagarra! You sing
yagarra	Yagarra!
dawarra wagatj-maka nga-bindja-ng nga-mi ni	I was sitting on the curve of the beach singing 'ni'
yagarra nye-bindja-ng nya-mu	Yagarra! You sing

The text of this song, which is the most complex in Barrtjap's repertory, contains the most explicitly sung depiction that we have of the interaction between a song-giving ghost and a song man. Thus, in melodic section 1 (except in the truncated vocal section 1 of track 7) the ghost sings, 'I'm singing. What have I come to do? I'm going to sing and then go back,' and then commands the singer, 'you sing.' In melodic section 2 the ghost sings 'I was sitting on the curve of the beach singing "ni"', and then once again commands the singer, 'you sing.'

This is one of only two songs in Barrtjap's repertory to use the unmeasured rhythmic mode 1 (without clapsticks). In Barrtjap's practice, rhythmic mode 1, like rhythmic mode 2, is associated with gravity and seriousness. While this song is no longer sung today, the other song with an unmeasured vocal section, song 10 'Karra Ngadja-maka Nga-bindja Nga-mi' (track 13) remains part of the repertory of Roger (Rossie) Yarrowin.

Because there are the only two examples of Barrtjap performing this extremely moving song, and because of some variation in the way that they are performed, both of the extant recordings (tracks 7 and 8) have been included here. Vocal section 1 of track 7 has a truncated form of the text; it is as if Barrtjap were working his way into the song. Moreover, the use in instrumental section 1 of a unique form of beating that moves from very fast to fast and then to slow marks vocal section 1 off from those that follow, suggesting that the truncation might be a quite deliberate strategy.

SONG STRUCTURE SUMMARY

VOCAL SECTION 1

Melodic section 1

Text phrase 1

Rhythmic mode 1 (without clapsticks)

ya

SW

Ya!

nga	-bindja	-ng	nga	-mi
1MIN.S	sing	SIM	1MIN.S	sit

I'm singing

Text phrase 2

Rhythmic mode 1 (without clapsticks)

yagarra	nye	-bindja	-ng	nya	-mu
EXCL	2MIN.IR	sing	SIM	2 MIN.IR	sit.IR

Yagarra! You sing

Melodic section 2

Text phrase 3

Rhythmic mode 1 (without clapsticks)

yagarra
EXCL

Yagarra!

dawarra	wagatj	-maka	nga	-bindja	-ng	nga	-mi	ni
belly	beach	PERF	1MIN.S	sing	SIM	1MIN.S	sit	SW

I was sitting in the curve of the beach singing 'ni'

Text phrase 4

Rhythmic mode 1 (without clapsticks)

yagarra	nye	-bindja	-ng	nya	-mu
EXCL	2MIN.IR	sing	SIM	2 MIN.IR	sit.IR

Yagarra! You sing

INSTRUMENTAL SECTION 1

Rhythmic mode 5b (fast doubled) followed by rhythmic mode 5a (fast even) followed by rhythmic mode 2 (slow even)

VOCAL SECTIONS 2–3

Melodic section 1

Text phrase 1

Rhythmic mode 1 (without clapsticks)

yagarra
EXCL

Yagarra!

nga	-bindja	-ng	nga	-mi
1MIN.S	sing	SIM	1MIN.S	sit

I'm singing

Text phrase 2

Rhythmic mode 1 (without clapsticks)

yagarra	yine	nga	-ve	-me	-nüng
EXCL	what	1MIN.S	comeIR	do	PURP

Yagarra! What have I come to do?

Text phrase 3

Rhythmic mode 1 (without clapsticks)

nga	-p	-pindja	-ng	nga	-p	-pur	-ing	-djü	-nüng
1MIN.S	IR	sing	SIM	1MIN.S	IR	go IR	IR	CONT	PURP

I'm going to sing and then go back

Text phrase 4

Rhythmic mode 1 (without clapsticks)

yagarra	nye	-bindja	-ng	nya	-mu
EXCL	2MIN.IR	sing	SIM	2 MIN.IR	sit.IR

Yagarra! You sing

Melodic section 2

Text phrase 5

Rhythmic mode 1 (without clapsticks)

yagarra
EXCL

Yagarra!

dawarra	wagatj	-maka	nga	-bindja	-ng	nga	-mi	ni
belly	beach	PERF	1MIN.S	sing	SIM	1MIN.S	sit	SW

I was sitting on the curve of the beach singing 'ni'

Text phrase 6

Rhythmic mode 1 (without clapsticks)

yagarra	nye	-bindja	-ng	nya	-mu
EXCL	2MIN.IR	sing	SIM	2 MIN.IR	sit.IR

Yagarra! You sing

INSTRUMENTAL SECTIONS 2–3

Rhythmic mode 5d (fast uneven triple)

CODA

Rhythmic mode 5d (fast uneven triple)

yit ngayi yit ngowe, ngayi yit ngayi yit ngowe …

TRACK 8 (Moy68-05-s09)

Song 5: Ya[garra] Nga-bindja-ng Ngami

Sung text	Free translation
yagarra	Yagarra!
nga-bindja-ng nga-mi	I'm singing
yagarra yine nga-ve-me-nüng	(Yagarra! What have I come to do?)
nga-p-pindja-ng nga-p-pur-ing-djü-nüng	I'm going to sing and then go back)
yagarra nye-bindja-ng nya-mu	Yagarra! You sing
yagarra	Yagarra!
dawarra wagatj-maka nga-bindja-ng nga-mi ni	I was sitting on the curve of the beach singing 'ni'
yagarra nye-bindja-ng nya-mu	Yagarra! You sing

This version lacks the introductory vocal section and associated instrumental section of the previous performance but is otherwise identical (a musical transcription of vocal section 2 of this performance is given in Marett, 2005, p 163).

SONG STRUCTURE SUMMARY

VOCAL SECTIONS 1–2

Melodic section 1

Text phrase 1

Rhythmic mode 1 (without clapsticks)

yagarra
EXCL

Yagarra!

nga	-bindja	-ng	nga	-mi
1MIN.S	sing	SIM	1MIN.S	sit

I'm singing

Text phrase 2

Rhythmic mode 1 (without clapsticks)

yagarra	**yine**	**nga**	**-ve**	**-me**	**-nüng**
EXCL	what	1MIN.S	comeIR	do	PURP

Yagarra! What have I come to do?

Text phrase 3

Rhythmic mode 1 (without clapsticks)

nga	**-p**	**-pindja**	**-ng**	**nga**	**-p**	**-pur**	**-ing**	**-djü**	**-nüng**
1MIN.S	IR	sing	SIM	1MIN.S	IR	go IR	IR	CONT	PURP

I'm going to sing and then go back

Text phrase 4

Rhythmic mode 1 (without clapsticks)

yagarra	**nye**	**-bindja**	**-ng**	**nya**	**-mu**
EXCL	2MIN.IR	sing	SIM	2 MIN.IR	sit.IR

Yagarra! You sing

Melodic section 2

Text phrase 5

Rhythmic mode 1 (without clapsticks)

yagarra
EXCL

Yagarra!

dawarra	**wagatj**	**-maka**	**nga**	**-bindja**	**-ng**	**nga**	**-mi**	**ni**
belly	beach	PERF	1MIN.S	sing	SIM	1MIN.S	sit	SW

I was sitting on the curve of the beach singing 'ni'

Text phrase 6

Rhythmic mode 1 (without clapsticks)

yagarra	**nye**	**-bindja**	**-ng**	**nya**	**-mu**
EXCL	2MIN.IR	sing	SIM	2 MIN.IR	sit.IR

Yagarra! You sing

INSTRUMENTAL SECTIONS 1-2

Rhythmic mode 5d (fast uneven triple)

CODA

Rhythmic mode 5d (fast uneven triple)

yit ngayi yit ngowe, ngayi yit ngayi yit ngowe …

TRACK 9 (Moy68-05-s10)

Song 6: Yagarra Bangany Nye-ngwe

Sung text	Free translation
yagarra	Yagarra!
bangany-nye ngwe binya ranga binya guyanaye naye	Song-nye ngwe binya ranga binya guyanaye naye
yagarra	Yagarra!
bangany-nye ngwe binya ranga binya guyanaye naye	Song-nye ngwe binya ranga binya guyanaye naye
yagarra da nn	Yagarra! Da nn

Apart from the words 'yagarra' (an exclamation) and 'bangany' (song), both of which occur liberally throughout Barrtjap's repertory, the remaining words of this song are in 'ghost language', that is, they are not comprehensible to ordinary human beings. As is often the case with text that has no semantic content, the precise form of the words has been difficult to elicit. There is only one recording of this song, which is no longer sung today.

Towards the end of the first melodic section of vocal section 2, and during the coda, the sound of the dancers stamping as they advance in the direction of the singer can be clearly heard.

SONG STRUCTURE SUMMARY

VOCAL SECTIONS 1–2

Melodic section 1

Text phrase 1

Rhythmic mode 5a (fast even)

yagarra
EXCL

Yagarra!

bangany	**-nye**	**ngwe**	**binya**	**ranga**	**binya**	**guyanaye**	**naye**
song	SW	SW	SW	SW	SW	SW	SW

Song-nye ngwe binya ranga binya guyanaye naye

Text phrase 2

Rhythmic mode 5a (fast even)

yagarra
EXCL

Yagarra!

bangany	**-nye**	**ngwe**	**binya**	**ranga**	**binya**	**guyanaye**	**naye**
song	SW	SW	SW	SW	SW	SW	SW

Song-nye ngwe binya ranga binya guyanaye naye

Text phrase 3

Rhythmic mode 5a (fast even)

yagarra	da	nn
EXCL	SW	SW

Yagarra! Da nn

INSTRUMENTAL SECTIONS 1–2

Rhythmic mode 5a (fast even)

CODA

Rhythmic mode 5a (fast even)

yit ngayi ngayi …

TRACK 10 (Moy68-05-s11)

Song 7: Be Bangany-nyaya

Sung text	Free translation
be bangany-nyaya	Be! Song-nyaya
nga-bindja-aya	I sing-aya
bangany bangany-nyaya	Song, song-nyaya
nga-bindja-ya-nyaya	I sing-ya-nyaya
bangany-nya	Song-nya
yine nga-ve me-nüng	What am I going to do?
be bangany-nye-nye	Be! Song-nye-nye
bangany-nye	Song-nye
nga-bindja-nye	I sing-nye
bangany-nyaya	Song-nyaya
ii be bangany-nyaya	Ii! Be! Song-nyaya
nga-bindja-ya-nyaya	I sing-ya-nyaya
bangany-nya	Song-nya
yine nga-ve me-nüng	What am I going to do?
be bangany-nye-nye	Be! Song-nye-nye
bangany-nye	Song-nye
nga-bindja-nye	I sing-nye
bangany-nyaya	Song-nyaya

In the first part of this song (text phrases 1-5), Barrtjap plays creatively with the phrase 'bangany nga-bindja' (I'm singing a song), splitting it into separate elements and re-combining them with the text phrase-final vocables *-nyaya* and *-aya* to create a series of short rhyming text phrases. Text phrase 6 comprises the same ghostly question that was found in 'Yagarra Nga-bindja-ng Nga-mi' (tracks 7 and 8)—namely, 'yine nga-ve-me-nüng' (what have I come to do?). This is answered (text phrases 7–10) with further use of elements from 'bangany nga-bindja' (I'm singing a song),' now combined with rhyming text phrase-vocables ending in –nye. All ten text phrases are sung to the same melodic section, that is, within one descent. The structure of text and rhythm set to melodic section 2 is a truncated version of melodic section 1 (it omits text phrases 3 and 4 of melodic section 1). Significantly, Barrtjap renders this complex text identically in both vocal sections.

We have only one recording of Barrtjap singing this song. More recently we have heard Roger Yarrowin sing it, but have not yet analysed the extent to which he conforms to Barrtjap's model.

SONG STRUCTURE SUMMARY

VOCAL SECTIONS 1–2

Melodic section 1

Text phrase 1

Rhythmic mode 5a (fast even)

be	**bangany**	**-nyaya**
SW	song	SW

Be! Song-nyaya

Text phrase 2

Rhythmic mode 5a (fast even)

nga	**-bindja**	**-aya**
1MIN.S	sing	SW

I sing-aya

Text phrase 3

Rhythmic mode 5a (fast even)

bangany	**bangany**	**-nyaya**
song	song	SW

Song, song-nyaya

Text phrase 4

Rhythmic mode 5a (fast even)

nga	**-bindja**	**-ya**	**-nyaya**
1MIN.S	sing	SW	SW

I sing-ya-nyaya

Text phrase 5

Rhythmic mode 5a (fast even)

bangany	**-nya**
song	SW

Song-nya

Text phrase 6

Rhythmic mode 5a (fast even)

yine	nga	-ve	me	-nüng
what	1MIN.S	comeIR	do	PURP

What am I going to do?

Text phrase 7

Rhythmic mode 5a (fast even)

be	bangany	-nye	-nye
SW	song	SW	SW

Be! Song-nye-nye

Text phrase 8

Rhythmic mode 5a (fast even)

bangany	-nye
song	SW

Song-nye

Text phrase 9

Rhythmic mode 5a (fast even)

nga	-bindja	-nye
1MIN.S	sing	SW

I sing-nye

Text phrase 10

Rhythmic mode 5a (fast even)

bangany	-nyaya
song	SW

Song-nyaya

Melodic section 2

Text phrase 11

Rhythmic mode 5a (fast even)

ii	be	bangany	-nyaya
SW	SW	song	SW

Ii! Be! Song-nyaya

Text phrase 12

Rhythmic mode 5a (fast even)

nga	-bindja	-ya	-nyaya
1MIN.S	sing	SW	SW

I sing-ya-nyaya

Text phrase 13

Rhythmic mode 5a (fast even)

bangany	**-nya**
song	SW

Song-nya

Text phrase 14

Rhythmic mode 5a (fast even)

yine	**nga**	**-ve**	**me**	**-nüng**
what	1MIN.S	comeIR	do	PURP

What am I going to do?

Text phrase 15

Rhythmic mode 5a (fast even)

be	**bangany**	**-nye**	**-nye**
SW	song	SW	SW

Be! Song-nye-nye

Text phrase 16

Rhythmic mode 5a (fast even)

bangany	**-nye**
song	SW

Song-nye

Text phrase 17

Rhythmic mode 5a (fast even)

nga	**-bindja**	**-nye**
1MIN.S	sing	SW

I sing-nye

Text phrase 18

Rhythmic mode 5a (fast even)

bangany	**-nyaya**
song	SW

Song-nyaya

INSTRUMENTAL SECTIONS 1–2

Rhythmic mode 5a (fast even)

CODA

Rhythmic mode 5a (fast even)

yit ngayi yit ngayi ngayi yit ngayi ngayi …

TRACK 11 (Mar88-04-s02)

Song 8: Nyere-nyere Lima Kaldja

Sung text	Free translation
nyere nyere lima kaldja lima bangany-ya lima kaldja (repeated)	Nyere nyere lima kaldja Lima song-ya lima kaldja

Barrtjap said that this song refers to Banakula, the red cliffs in his country just south of the Daly River mouth. Barrtjap never included the names of specific sites in his songs, preferring to spell out the associations through verbal exegesis. The song is almost entirely in 'ghost language', with the exception of the Batjamalh word 'bangany' (song).

This song belong to a category of songs termed in Batjamalh *lerri* 'happy' (see additional discussion in the music analysis section of this chapter for further details).

SONG STRUCTURE SUMMARY

VOCAL SECTIONS 1–2

Melodic section 1

Text phrases 1–4 *

Rhythmic mode 5b (fast doubled)

nyere	**nyere**	**lima**	**kaldja**
SW	SW	SW	SW

Nyere nyere lima kaldja

lima	**bangany**	**-ya**	**lima**	**kaldja**
SW	song	SW	SW	SW

lima song-ya lima kaldja

*text phrase 4 is truncated

Melodic section 2

Text phrases 5–7*

Rhythmic mode 5b (fast doubled)

nyere	**nyere**	**lima**	**kaldja**
SW	SW	SW	SW

nyere nyere lima kaldja

lima	**bangany**	**-ya**	**lima**	**kaldja**
SW	song	SW	SW	SW

lima song-ya lima kaldja

*text phrase 7 is truncated in vocal section 2

INSTRUMENTAL SECTIONS 1–2

Rhythmic mode 5b (fast doubled)

VOCAL SECTION 3

Melodic section 1

Text phrases 1–4*

Rhythmic mode 5c (fast uneven quadruple)

nyere	**nyere**	**lima**	**kaldja**
SW	SW	SW	SW

Nyere nyere lima kaldja

lima	**bangany**	**-ya**	**lima**	**kaldja**
SW	song	SW	SW	SW

lima song-ya lima kaldja

*text phrase 4 is truncated

Melodic section 2

Text phrases 5-7

Rhythmic mode 5c (fast uneven quadruple)

nyere	**nyere**	**lima**	**kaldja**
SW	SW	SW	SW

Nyere nyere lima kaldja

lima	**bangany**	**-ya**	**lima**	**kaldja**
SW	song	SW	SW	SW

lima song-ya lima kaldja

INSTRUMENTAL SECTION 3

Rhythmic mode 5c (fast uneven quadruple)

CODA

Rhythmic mode 5c (fast uneven quadruple)

yit ngayi yit ngayi yit ngowe, ngayi yit ngayi yit ngayi yit ngowe …

TRACK 12 (Mar88-04-s03)

Song 9: Nyere-nye Bangany Nyaye

Sung text	Fre translation
nyere nye bangany nyaye	Nyere nye song nyaye
lima rak-pe ngadja ngaye	Lima my eternal country ngaye
(repeated)	
ii	Ii

This is another *lerri* 'happy' song. In this song Barrtjap refers once again to his country, 'my eternal country,' but without naming it.

SONG STRUCTURE SUMMARY

VOCAL SECTIONS 1–2

Melodic section 1

Text phrases 1–4

Rhythmic mode 5b (fast doubled)

nyere	**nye**	**bangany**	**nyaye**
SW	SW	song	SW

Nyere nye song nyaye

lima	**rak**	**-pe**	**ngadja**	**ngaye**
SW	country	forever	1MIN.S.PRO	SW

lima my eternal country ngaye

Melodic section 2

Text phrase 5

Rhythmic mode 5b (fast doubled)

ii
SW

Ii

INSTRUMENTAL SECTIONS 1–2

Rhythmic mode 5b (fast doubled) [moves into rhythmic mode 5c at the very end of instrumental section 2]

VOCAL SECTIONS 3–4

Melodic section 1

Text phrases 1-4

Rhythmic mode 5c (fast uneven quadruple)

nyere	nye	bangany	nyaye
SW	SW	song	SW

Nyere nye song nyaye

lima	rak	-pe	ngadja	ngaye
SW	country	forever	1MIN.S.PRO	SW

Lima my eternal country ngaye

Melodic section 2

Text phrase 5

Rhythmic mode 5c (fast uneven quadruple)

ii
SW

Ii

INSTRUMENTAL SECTIONS 3–4

Rhythmic mode 5c (fast uneven quadruple)

CODA

Rhythmic mode 5c (fast uneven quadruple)

yit ngayi yit ngayi yit ngowe, ngayi yit ngayi yit ngayi yit ngowe …

TRACK 13 (Mar88-04-s07)

Song 10: Karra Ngadja-maka Nga-bindja-ng Ngami

Sung text	Free translation
yagarra nga mm	Yagarra! Nga mm
karra ngadja-maka nga-bindja-ng nga-mi	I'm singing for myself
nye-bindja-ng nya-mu	You sing

In this song, once again, we hear the words of a song-giving ghost, first explaining that he is singing for his own sake, then commanding the songman to take up the song.

SONG STRUCTURE SUMMARY

VOCAL SECTIONS 1–3

Melodic section 1

Text phrase 1

Rhythmic mode 1 (without clapsticks)

yagarra	**nga**	**mm**
EXCL	SW	SW

Yagarra! Nga mm

Melodic section 2

Text phrase 2

Rhythmic mode 1 (without clapsticks)

karra	**ngadja**	**-maka**	**nga**	**-bindja**	**-ng**	**nga**	**-mi**
SW	1MIN.S.PRO	for	1MIN.S	sing	SIM	1MIN.S	sit

I'm singing for myself

Text phrase 3

Rhythmic mode 1 (without clapsticks)

nye	**-bindja**	**-ng**	**nya**	**-mu**
2MIN.IR	sing	SIM	2MIN.IR	sit IR

You sing

INSTRUMENTAL SECTIONS 1–2

Rhythmic mode 5a (fast even) followed by rhythmic mode 2 (slow even) followed by rhythmic mode 5d (fast uneven triple)

yit ngayi ngayi … ii … nn

CODA

Rhythmic mode 5d (fast uneven triple)

yit ngayi yit ngowe, ngayi yit ngayi yit ngowe …

TRACK 14 (Mar88-05-s11)

Song 11: Yerre Ka-bindja-maka Ka-mi

Sung text	Free translation
(Vocal section 1)	
yerre	Yerre
ka-bindja-maka ka-mi	He was singing
ii	Ii
nye-bindja nya-mu-ngarrka nn	You sing it for me, nn
(Vocal section 2-3)	
yerre	Yerre
nye-bindja nya-mu-ngarrka nn	You sing it for me, nn
ii	Ii
ka-bindja-maka ka-mi	He was singing

This song is unusual in two respects. First of all, the song-giving ghost seems to be referring to a third person, perhaps another singer present in the dream. Some doubt remains, because the high degree of nasalisation in the vocal production when singing makes it difficult to distinguish between the first and third person forms of the verb –*mi* 'to sit' (*nga-mi* versus *ka-mi*). Nevertheless, we have regularly been given the translation 'he sings' rather than 'I sing' for vocal section 1. Secondly, in vocal sections 2 and 3 the singers reverse the order of the two text phrases from that occurring in vocal section 1. The significance (if any) of this shift from 'he was singing it, you sing it for me' to 'you sing it for me, he was singing it' is unclear. At the beginning of the third vocal section Barrtjap gives a high call (representing the voice of the *wunymalang* ghost) while the backup singer, Lambudju, continues to sing the text.

SONG STRUCTURE SUMMARY

VOCAL SECTION 1

Melodic section 1

Text phrase 1

Rhythmic mode 5c (fast uneven quadruple)

yerre
SW

Yerre

Text phrase 2

Rhythmic mode 5c (fast uneven quadruple)

ka	-bindja	-maka	ka	-mi	nn
3MIN.S	sing	PERF	3MIN.S	sit	SW

He was singing

Melodic section 2

Text phrase 3

Rhythmic mode 5c (fast uneven quadruple)

ii
SW

Ii

Text phrase 4

Rhythmic mode 5c (fast uneven quadruple)

nye	**-bindja**	**nya**	**-mu**	**-ngarrka**	**nn**
2MIN.IR	sing	2MIN.IR	sit IR	1MIN.IO	SW

You sing it for me, nn

INSTRUMENTAL SECTION 1

Rhythmic mode 5c (fast uneven quadruple)

VOCAL SECTIONS 2–3

Melodic section 1

Text phrase 1

Rhythmic mode 5c (fast uneven quadruple)

yerre
SW

Yerre

Text phrase 2

Rhythmic mode 5c (fast uneven quadruple)

nye	**-bindja**	**nya**	**-mu**	**-ngarrka**	**nn**
2MIN.IR	sing	2MIN.IR	sit IR	1MIN.IO	SW

You sing it for me, nn

Melodic section 2

Text phrase 3

Rhythmic mode 5c (fast uneven quadruple)

ii
SW

Ii

Text phrase 4

Rhythmic mode 5c (fast uneven quadruple)

ka	-bindja	-maka	ka	-mi
3MIN.S	sing	PERF	3MIN.S	sit

He was singing

INSTRUMENTAL SECTIONS 2–3

Rhythmic mode 5c (fast uneven quadruple)

CODA

Rhythmic mode 5c (fast uneven quadruple)

yit ngayi ngayi yit ngowe …

TRACK 15 (Mar88-05-s02)

Song 12: Yagarra Ye-yenenaya

Sung text	Free translation
yagarra ye-yenenaya	Yagarra! Ye-yenenaya
ye-yeneyene kavemaye	Ye-yeneyene kavemaye
yeneyene yenenaya	Yeneyene yenenaya
yeneyene kavemaye	Yeneyene kavemaye
yeneyene yenenaya	Yeneyene yenenaya
yagarra nye -me -nüng	Yagarra! You have to do it
nye-bindja-ng nya-mu-nganggung-djü	Sing for us both (you and me) right now
ye-yeneyene yenenaya	Ye-yeneyene yenenaya
yeneyene kavemaye	Yeneyene kavemaye
yeneyene	Yeneyene
ii	Ii

This is another *lerri* 'happy' song, but unlike some of the others, here melodic section 2 includes some text in Batjamalh. Here the song-giving ghost is telling the songman that he has to sing the song for both of them.

SONG STRUCTURE SUMMARY

VOCAL SECTIONS 1–2

Melodic section 1

Text phrase 1

Rhythmic mode 5b (fast doubled)

yagarra	**ye**	**-yenenaya**
SW	SW	SW

Yagarra! Ye-yenenaya

ye	**-yeneyene**	**kavemaye**
SW	SW	SW

ye-yeneyene kavemaye

Text phrase 2

Rhythmic mode 5b (fast doubled)

yeneyene	**yenenaya**
SW	SW

Yeneyene yenenaya

yeneyene	**kavemaye**
SW	SW

yeneyene kavemaye

Text phrase 3

Rhythmic mode 5b (fast doubled)

yeneyene	**yenenaya**
SW	SW

yeneyene yenenaya

Melodic section 2

Text phrase 4

Rhythmic mode 5b (fast doubled)

yagarra	**nye**	**-me**	**-nüng**
EXCL	2MIN.IR	do	PURP

Yagarra! You have to do it

Text phrase 5
Rhythmic mode 5b (fast doubled)

nye	-bindja	-ng	nya	-mu	-nganggung	-djü
2MIN.IR	sing	SIM	2MIN.IR	sit IR	1/2.MIN.IO	CONT

Sing for us both (you and me) right now

Text phrase 6
Rhythmic mode 5b (fast doubled)

ye	-yeneyene	yenenaya
SW	SW	SW

Ye-yeneyene yenenaya

yeneyene	kavemaye
SW	SW

yeneyene kavemaye

Text phrase 7
Rhythmic mode 5b (fast doubled)

yeneyene
SW

Yeneyene

Melodic section 3

Text phrase 8
Rhythmic mode 5b (fast doubled)

ii
SW

ii

INSTRUMENTAL SECTIONS 1–2
Rhythmic mode 5b (fast doubled) [changes to rhythmic mode 5c at end of Instrumental section 2]

VOCAL SECTION 3
Melodic section 1

Text phrase 1
Rhythmic mode 5c (fast uneven quadruple)

yagarra	ye	-yenenaya
SW	SW	SW

Yagarra! Ye-yenenaya

ye	**-yeneyene**	**kavemaye**
SW	SW	SW

Ye-yeneyene kavemaye

Text phrase 2

Rhythmic mode 5b (fast doubled)

yeneyene	**yenenaya**
SW	SW

Yeneyene yenenaya

yeneyene	**kavemaye**
SW	SW

Yeneyene kavemaye

Text phrase 3

Rhythmic mode 5c (fast uneven quadruple)

yeneyene	**yenenaya**
SW	SW

Yeneyene yenenaya

Melodic section 2

Text phrase 4

Rhythmic mode 5c (fast uneven quadruple)

yagarra	**nye**	**-me**	**-nüng**
EXCL	2MIN.IR	do	PURP

Yagarra! You have to do it

Text phrase 5

Rhythmic mode 5c (fast uneven quadruple)

nye	**-bindja**	**-ng**	**nya**	**-mu**	**-nganggung**	**-djü**
2MIN.IR	sing	SIM	2MIN.IR	sit IR	1/2.MIN.IO	CONT

Sing for us both (you and me) right now

Text phrase 6

Rhythmic mode 5c (fast uneven quadruple)

ye	**-yeneyene**	**yenenaya**
SW	SW	SW

Ye-yeneyene yenenaya

yeneyene	**kavemaye**
SW	SW

yeneyene kavemaye

Text phrase 7

Rhythmic mode 5c (fast uneven quadruple)

yeneyene
SW

Ye-yeneyene

Melodic section 3

Text phrase 8

Rhythmic mode 5c (fast uneven quadruple)

ii
SW

Ii

INSTRUMENTAL SECTION 3

Rhythmic mode 5c (fast uneven quadruple)

CODA

Rhythmic mode 5c (fast uneven quadruple)

yit ngayi yit ngayi yit ngowe, ngayi yit ngayi yit ngayi yit ngowe …

TRACK 16 (Elk52-19B-s04)
Song 13: Naya Rradja Bangany Nye-ve

Sung text	Free translation
naya rradja bangany nye-ve	Naya rradja. You go for a song
mayave rradja bangany nye-ve	Mayave rradja. You go for a song
(three times)	
yene bangany nye-ve	Yene. You go for a song
yenene didjeremu	Yenene didjeremu
limarenye limarenye	Limarenye limarenye
limarenye limarenye	Limarenye limarenye
ii	Ii

This *lerri* song has an isorhythmic text composed largely of vocables interspersed with the Batjamalh statement 'bangany nye-ve' (you go for a song). In chapter 3 (p 71) Ford discusses the difficulties of transcribing vocable texts with special reference to this song. These difficulties should be borne in mind while listening to the following four tracks.[3]

In *Songs, dreamings and ghosts*, Marett drew attention to the high degree of stability exhibited by this song over a period of almost fifty years (see discussion and musical transcriptions in Marett, 2005, pp 174–79). The four recordings discussed in *Songs, dreamings and ghosts*—the earliest from 1952 and

---

3   In Marett, 2005, chapter 3, Marett and Ford transcribed the vocables 'naya rradja' as 'dadja kadja' and the vocables 'mayave rradja' as 'mayave kadja'.

Figure 4.4 Jimmy Bandak singing at a *burnim-rag* ceremony at Bagot, 1953. Left to right: Dolly Garinyi, Maggie Woodie, Jimmy Bandak, Maudie Woodie, George Munggulu. Courtesy of University of Sydney Archives, reproduced with the permission of Belyuen community.

the latest from 1997—are here presented in chronological order, beginning with a recording made by Elkin in 1952. The performer is Jimmy Bandak, Barrtjap's father's brother, who in the Aboriginal way Barrtjap called 'father.' Towards the end of this track the sound of the dancers advancing can be clearly heard. Bandak performs the whole item in a single rhythmic mode (5c, fast uneven quadruple).

This song continues to be sung today; indeed, in 2008 Marett sang it alongside Barrtjap's son Timothy at the *kapuk* ragburning ceremony for the late Kenny Burrenjuck, Barrtjap's eldest son and Marett's teacher (see discussion in Barwick & Marett, 2011).

SONG STRUCTURE SUMMARY

VOCAL SECTIONS 1–3

Melodic section 1

Text phrases 1–3

Rhythmic mode 5c (fast uneven quadruple)

naya	**rradja**	**bangany**	**nye**	**-ve**
SW	SW	song	2MIN.IR	go

Naya rradja. You go for a song

mayave	**rradja**	**bangany**	**nye**	**-ve**
SW	SW	song	2MIN.IR	go

Mayave rradja. You go for a song

130 • For the sake of a song

Text phrase 4

Rhythmic mode 5c (fast uneven quadruple)

yene	bangany	nye	-ve
SW	song	2MIN.IR	go

Yene. You go for a song

yenene	didjeremu
SW	SW

Yenene didjeremu

Text phrase 5

Rhythmic mode 5c (fast uneven quadruple)

limarenye	limarenye	limarenye	limarenye
SW	SW	SW	SW

Limarenye limarenye lima renye limarenye

Melodic section 2

Text phrase 6

Rhythmic mode 5c (fast uneven quadruple)

ii
SW

ii

INSTRUMENTAL SECTIONS 1-3

Rhythmic mode 5c (fast uneven quadruple)

CODA

Rhythmic mode 5c (fast uneven quadruple)

yit ngayi ngayi yit ngayi ngayi …

TRACK 17 (Mad64-02-s15)[4]

Song 13: Naya Rradja Bangany Nye-ve

Sung text	Free translation
naya rradja bangany nye-ve	Naya rradja. You go for a song
mayave rradja bangany nye-ve	Mayave rradja. You go for a song
(three times)	
yene bangany nye-ve	Yene. You go for a song
yenene bangany nye-ve	Yenene. You go for a song
bangany nye-ve limarenye	You go for a song. Limarenye
bangany nye-ve limara	You go for a song. Limara
ii	Ii

Lawrence Wurrpen was a man from Delissaville (present-day Belyuen) who moved to Beswick Creek (present-day Barunga) after he married a woman from there. He was recorded at Beswick Creek by Kenneth Maddock in 1964. Like Bandak, he uses only rhythmic mode 5c (fast uneven quadruple) but note that his tempo is a significantly slower than the other performances, with clapsticks at 126 beats per minute (as opposed to approximately 135 beats per minute). The melody in melodic section 1 is almost identical to that of Bandak, but he uses a significantly different, longer, contour for melodic section 2. Although the exact syllables pronounced are difficult to hear in this recording, text phrases 4 and 5 differ from Bandak's performance, and the didjeridu mouth sounds in the coda are also a little different. Overall, however, the two performances are very similar, despite Wurrpen living in a relatively distant community and therefore we have not included a song structure summary for this track.

TRACK 18 (Mar88-05-s03)

Song 13: Naya Rradja Bangany Nye-ve

Sung text	Free translation
naya rradja bangany nye-ve	Naya rradja. You go for a song
mayave rradja bangany nye-ve	Mayave rradja. You go for a song
(three times)	
yene bangany nye-ve	Yene. You go for a song
yenene didjeremu	Yenene didjeremu
limarenye limarenye	Limarenye limarenye
limarenye	Limarenye
ii	Ii

The main point of difference in Barrtjap's performance of song 13, recorded by Marett in 1988, is his initial use of fast doubled beating, which later changes to the same uneven quadruple (rhythmic mode 5c) as used by Bandak and Wurrpen throughout their performances. Apart from this, Barrtjap's performance is very similar to that of Bandak in both text and melody, as was pointed out in *Songs, dreamings and ghosts* (Marett, 2005, p 178, ex. 7.6).[5] Barrtjap also uses a slightly different form of didjeridu mouth sounds in the coda.

---

4 This is the track transcribed in Marett, 2005, Ex. 7.6 (pp 178-9), where it is labelled as Mad64-01-12.

5 The musical example 7.6 (Marett, 2005, p 178) wrongly transcribes Barrtjap's version with rhythmic mode 5c (fast uneven quadruple) throughout.

SONG STRUCTURE SUMMARY

VOCAL SECTIONS 1–2

Melodic section 1

Text phrases 1–3
Rhythmic mode 5b (fast doubled)

naya	**rradja**	**bangany**	**nye**	**-ve**
SW	SW	song	2MIN.IR	go

Naya rradja. You go for a song

	mayave	**rradja**	**bangany**	**nye**	**-ve**
	SW	SW	song	2MIN.IR	go

    Mayave rradja. You go for a song

Text phrase 4
Rhythmic mode 5b (fast doubled)

yene	**bangany**	**nye**	**-ve**
SW	song	2MIN.IR	go

Yene. You go for a song

	yenene	**didjeremu**
	SW	SW

    Yenene didjeremu

Text phrase 5
Rhythmic mode 5b (fast doubled)

limarenye	**limarenye**	**limarenye**
SW	SW	SW

Limarenye limarenye limarenye

Melodic section 2

Text phrase 6
Rhythmic mode 5b (fast doubled)

ii
SW

ii

INSTRUMENTAL SECTIONS 1–2

Rhythmic mode 5b (fast doubled)

VOCAL SECTION 3

Melodic section 1

Text phrases 1–2

Rhythmic mode 5c (fast uneven quadruple)

naya	**rradja**	**bangany**	**nye**	**-ve**
SW	SW	song	2MIN.IR	go

Naya rradja. You go for a song

	mayave	**rradja**	**bangany**	**nye**	**-ve**
	SW	SW	song	2MIN.IR	go

Mayave rradja. You go for a song

Text phrase 4

Rhythmic mode 5c (fast uneven quadruple)

yene	**bangany**	**nye**	**-ve**
SW	song	2MIN.IR	go

Yene. You go for a song

yenene	**didjeremu**
SW	SW

Yenene didjeremu.

Text phrase 5

Rhythmic mode 5c (fast uneven quadruple)

limarenye	**limarenye**	**limarenye**	**limarenye**
SW	SW	SW	SW

Limarenye limarenye limarenye limarenye.

Melodic section 2

Text phrase 6

Rhythmic mode 5c (fast uneven quadruple)

ii
SW

ii

INSTRUMENTAL SECTION 3

Rhythmic mode 5c (fast uneven quadruple)

CODA

Rhythmic mode 5c (fast uneven quadruple)

yit ngayi yit ngayi yit ngowe, ngayi yit ngayi yit ngayi yit ngayi …

TRACK 19 (Mar97-04-s16)

Song 13: Naya Rradja Bangany Nye-ve

Sung text	Free translation
naya rradja bangany nye-ve	Naya rradja. You go for a song
mayave rradja bangany nye-ve	Mayave rradja. You go for a song
(three times)	
yagarra bangany nye-ve	Yagarra! You go for a song
[yenene] didjeremu	[Yenene] didjeremu
limarenye limarenye	Limarenye limarenye
limarenye limarenye	Limarenye limarenye
ii	Ii

This lively performance by Barrtjap's son, Kenny Burrenjuck, follows the precedent set by Barrtjap. The performance begins with a ritual call (*malh*) followed by exhortations in both Batjamalh and English for the audience to clap along. With the exception of the exclamation 'yagarra!' in place of the vocable 'yene' to start text phrase 4, the text and melody are close to identical to Barrtjap's version, as is the sequence of clapstick beating patterns (fast doubled beating (rhythmic mode 5b) in vocal section 1, and fast uneven beating (rhythmic mode 5c) for the later vocal sections). Note that this is not the version transcribed in Marett, 2005, pp 178–79, which Marett recorded on another occasion in the same year (Mar97-07-s09).

TRACK 20 (Mar88-05-s06)

Song 14: Yagarra Nedja Tjine Rak-pe

Sung text	Free translation
yagarra nedja tjine rak-pe	Yagarra! Son, where is my camp/eternal country?
yagarra rama rama gama	Yagarra! Rama rama gama
(three times)	
yagarra nedja	Yagarra! Son!
ii	Ii!

Here the song-giving ghost addresses the songman directly as 'son.' Not long before his death in 1993, Barrtjap told Marett that this text referred to 'my place … my country long way back,' by which he seemed to mean both that the country lay at a great distance, and that it had been his since time immemorial. When he was asked the name of the country he gave four place-names: Djakaldja, Barakbana (South Peron Island), Barrabumalh and Djedjekana, all places that lie in his ancestral country near the Daly River.

In 2002, however, Barrtjap's widow Esther Burrenjuck gave another interpretation, namely, that the song had been given to Barrtjap by the ghost of his mother when she returned to the family camp at Milik on the west coast of the Cox Peninsula and found it deserted; the family had moved from there into the community of Delissaville (Belyuen).

The two interpretations rest upon an ambiguity inherent in the word *rak*, which can mean both ancestral country and camp (we are grateful to Nicholas Evans for this insight). It is not unusual for Aboriginal songs to exploit ambiguity and opacity in song texts in order to generate different exegeses according to different circumstances. The circumstances surrounding these two exegeses are discussed more fully in Marett, 2005, p 35.

Note that David Woody, the second 'singer' (in fact he is only playing part of the interlocking stick pattern), makes a mistake (filling in one of the empty beats) at the point where the rhythmic mode changes at the end of instrumental section 2.

This is another *lerri* 'happy' song deploying isorhythmic text and presenting the vocal section first in fast doubled beating (rhythmic mode 5b) and later in fast uneven quadruple beating (rhythmic mode 5c).

SONG STRUCTURE SUMMARY

VOCAL SECTIONS 1–2

Melodic section 1

Text phrases 1–3

Rhythmic mode 5b (fast doubled)

yagarra	**nedja**	**tjine**	**rak**	**-pe**
EXCL	son	where	camp/country	forever

Yagarra! Son, where is my camp/eternal country?

yagarra	**rama**	**rama**	**gama**
EXCL	SW	SW	SW

Yagarra! Rama rama gama

Text phrase 4

Rhythmic mode 5b (fast doubled)

yagarra	**nedja**
EXCL	son

Yagarra! Son!

Melodic section 2

Text phrase 5

Rhythmic mode 5b (fast doubled)

ii
SW

ii

INSTRUMENTAL SECTIONS 1–2

Rhythmic mode 5b (fast doubled) (changes to rhythmic mode 5c (fast uneven quadruple towards the end of instrumental section 2)

VOCAL SECTION 3

Melodic section 1

Text phrases 1–3

Rhythmic mode 5c (fast uneven quadruple)

yagarra	**nedja**	**tjine**	**rak**	**-pe**
EXCL	son	where	camp/country	forever

Yagarra! Son, where is my camp/eternal country?

yagarra	**rama**	**rama**	**gama**
EXCL	SW	SW	SW

Yagarra! Rama, rama, gama

Text phrase 4

Rhythmic mode 5c (fast uneven quadruple)

yagarra	**nedja**
EXCL	son

Yagarra! Son!

Melodic section 2

Text phrase 5

Rhythmic mode 5c (fast uneven quadruple)

ii
SW

Ii

INSTRUMENTAL SECTION 3

Rhythmic mode 5c (fast uneven quadruple)

CODA

Rhythmic mode 5c (fast uneven quadruple)

yit ngayi yit ngayi yit ngowe, ngayi yit ngayi yit ngayi yit ngowe …

TRACK 21 (Mar88-05-s13)

Song 15: Ya Rembe Ngaya Lima Ngaya

Sung text	Free translation
ya rembe ngaya	Ya rembe ngaya
lima ngaya rembe ngaya	Lima ngaya rembe ngaya
lima ngaya rembe ngaya	Lima ngaya rembe ngaya
lima ngaya rembe ngaya	Lima ngaya rembe ngaya
lima ngaya rembe ngaya	Lima ngaya rembe ngaya
lima ngaya rembe ng	Lima ngaya rembe ng
(twice in vocal section 1)	
yagarra yine nga-bindja-ya	Yagarra! What am I singing?
yine nga-bindja-ya	What am I singing?
yagarra rembe ngaya	Yagarra rembe ngaya
lima ngaya rembe ngaya	Lima ngaya rembe ngaya
lima ngaya rembe ngaya	Lima ngaya rembe ngaya
lima ngaya (rembe ng)	Lima ngaya (rembe ng)

This song is performed in the moderate tempo band. You can hear the slightly more relaxed feeling that it has compared with the energetic fast rhythmic modes of the previous *lerri* 'happy' songs (in Marett, 2005, it was wrongly described as being in the fast tempo band). Even though the beating is even, and the repeated vocable text elements ('rembe ngaya' and 'lima ngaya') of melodic sections 1 and 2 are each set to two beats, the addition of 'ya' at the beginning of the melodic sections creates a three-beat feel.

Another interesting feature of this song is that melodic section 1 is sung twice in vocal section 1.

SONG STRUCTURE SUMMARY

VOCAL SECTIONS 1–2

Melodic section 1 (repeated in vocal section 1)

Text phrase 1

Rhythmic mode 4a (moderate even)

ya	rembe	ngaya
SW	SW	SW

Ya rembe ngaya

Text phrases 2–5

Rhythmic mode 4a (moderate even)

lima	ngaya	rembe	ngaya
SW	SW	SW	SW

Lima ngaya rembe ngaya

Text phrase 6
Rhythmic mode 4a (moderate even)

lima	**ngaya**	**rembe**	**ng**
SW	SW	SW	SW

Lima ngaya rembe ng

Melodic section 2

Text phrase 7
Rhythmic mode 4a (moderate even)

yagarra	**yine**	**nga**	**-bindja**	**-ya**
EXCL	what	1MIN.S	sing	SW

Yagarra! What am I singing? What am I singing?

Text phrase 8
Rhythmic mode 4a (moderate even)

yine	**nga**	**-bindja**	**-ya**
what	MIN.S	sing	SW

What am I singing?

Text phrase 9
Rhythmic mode 4a (moderate even)

yagarra	**rembe**	**ngaya**
EXCL	SW	SW

Yagarra rembe ngaya

Text phrases 10–11
Rhythmic mode 4a (moderate even)

lima	**ngaya**	**rembe**	**ngaya**
SW	SW	SW	SW

Lima ngaya rembe ngaya

Text phrase 12
Rhythmic mode 4a (moderate even)

lima	**ngaya**
SW	SW

Lima ngaya

(vocal section 2 only)

(rembe	**ng)**
SW	SW

(rembe ng)

INSTRUMENTAL SECTIONS 1–2

Rhythmic mode 4a (moderate even)

CODA

Rhythmic mode 4d (moderate uneven quintuple)

yit ngayi yit ngowe yit ngowe …

TRACK 22 (Mar86-03-s04)

Song 16: Yagarra Tjüt Balk-nga-me Nga-mi

Sung text	Free translation
yagarra nn	Yagarra! Nn
yagarra tjüt balk-nga-me nga-mi yagarra nn	Yagarra! My foot has swollen up, yagarra! Nn
yagarra yine nga-ve-me-nüng	Yagarra! What am I going to do?
nga-p-pindja-ng nga-p-pur-ing-djü	I'm going to climb up and go now

As in 'Yagarra Nedja Tjine Rak-pe' (track 20), this song has two alternative interpretations. Both agree that Jimmy Bandak composed it for his 'son,' Jimmy Havelock. The first interpretation, given to Marett by Barrtjap, asserts that the song refers to an event when Havelock was working at Murgenella on the Coburg Peninsula. After getting an infected foot from a cypress pine splinter, Havelock had to 'climb up' into an aeroplane and return to Belyuen. The second explanation was that Havelock had hurt his foot in Belyuen, and had to 'climb up' onto a tractor in order to be taken to the clinic. This second explanation, which emerged at the time of the Kenbi Land Claim, emphasises links between the Wadjiginy people and Belyuen.

Observant readers might note that the question and answer in the final two text phrases *yine nga-ve-me-nüng / nga-p-pindja-ng nga-p-pur-ing-djü* has been translated elsewhere (song 5, tracks 7–8) as the utterance of a song-giving ghost meaning 'What have I come to do? I'm going to sing and then go back.' This third possible interpretation rests on the fact that the verb *-bindja* (*-pindja*) means both 'to sing' and 'to climb up'.

Like 'Yagarra Nga-bindja-ng Nga-mi Ngayi' (track 2), this song uses moderate quintuple beating (rhythmic mode 4d). Barrtjap is the only *wangga* singer to use quintuple beating.

SONG STRUCTURE SUMMARY

VOCAL SECTIONS 1–2

Melodic section 1

Text phrase 1

Rhythmic mode 4d (moderate uneven quintuple)

yagarra   nn
SW   SW

Yagarra! Nn

Text phrase 2

Rhythmic mode 4d (moderate uneven quintuple)

yagarra	tjüt	balk	-nga	-me	nga	-mi	yagarra	nn
EXCL	foot	swollen	1MIN.S	do	1MIN.S	sit	SW	SW

Yagarra! My foot has swollen up, yagarra! Nn

Melodic section 2

Text phrase 3

Rhythmic mode 4d (moderate uneven quintuple)

yagarra	yine	nga	-ve	-me	-nüng
EXCL	what	1MIN.S	IR	do	PURP

Yagarra! What am I going to do?

Text phrase 4

Rhythmic mode 4d (moderate uneven quintuple)

nga	-p	-pindja	-ng	nga	-p	-pur	-ing	-djü
1MIN.S	IR	climb up	SIM	1MIN.S	IR	go IR	IR	CONT

I'm going to climb up [into the tractor/plane] and go now [I'm going to sing and then go back]

INSTRUMENTAL SECTIONS 1–2

Rhythmic mode 4d (moderate uneven quintuple)

CODA

Rhythmic mode 4d (moderate uneven quintuple)

yit ngayi yit ngowe yit ngowe …

TRACK 23 (Mar86-03-s06)

Song 17: Yagarra Tjine Rak-pe

Sung text	Free translation
yagarra tjine rak-pe	Yagarra! Where is my eternal country?
karra tjine ka-yewe	Where does it lie?
karra tjine ka-yewe	Where does it lie?
karra tjine ka-yewe	Where does it lie?
yagarra tjidja ka-bindja-ng ka –mi	Yagarra! This [man/*wunymalang*] is singing

This song refers to Barrtjap's distant ancestral country near the Daly river mouth. It expresses the pain that people feel when, as is the case of the Wadjiginy at this time, they have lost contact with the country of their forefathers. Note that, as is often the case with songs that use rhythmic modes 1 or 2 for the vocal sections, the coda is in a fast rhythmic mode. This is to facilitate the dancing, which is most prominent and energetic in this section of the song.

SONG STRUCTURE SUMMARY

VOCAL SECTIONS 1–3

Melodic section 1

Text phrase 1

Rhythmic mode 2 (slow even)

yagarra	**tjine**	**rak**	**-pe**
EXCL	where	country	forever

Yagarra! Where is my eternal country?

Text phrases 2–4

Rhythmic mode 2 (slow even)

karra	**tjine**	**ka**	**-yewe**
SW	where	3MIN.S	lie

Where does it lie?

Melodic section 2

Text phrase 5

Rhythmic mode 2 (slow even)

yagarra	**tjidja**	**ka**	**-bindja**	**-ng**	**ka**	**-mi**
EXCL	3MIN.M.DEIC	3MIN.S/A	sing	SIM	3MIN.S/A	sit

Yagarra! This [man/*wunymalang*] is singing

INSTRUMENTAL SECTIONS 1–3

Rhythmic mode 2 (slow even)

CODA

Rhythmic mode 5d (fast uneven triple)

yit ngayi yit ngowe, ngayi yit ngayi yit ngowe …

TRACK 24 (Mar86-03-s05)

Song 18: Yagarra Delhi Nya-ngadja-barra-ngarrka

Sung text	Free translation
ya yagarra delhi nya-ngadja-barra-ngarrka nanggang-gulhü kanya-bara-m	Ya! Yagarra! Wait! Come back here to me Don't be frightened
kuu yagarra nye-bindja-ng werret bangany ngwe ngwe yagarra dü	Kuu. Yagarra! Climb up, quick now! Song! Ngwe ngwe Yagarra! Dü!

This song is connected with a powerful and dangerous Dreaming, the Cheeky Yam, Wilha, who lives in the Bynoe Harbour, close to Belyuen. Barrtjap told Marett that it was about an event that occurred when he and a group of other people went hunting on Indian Island to the west of the Cox Penisula. There was a strong tide running and because the Wilha Dreaming is known to travel on the tide, Barrtjap and his party climbed up on a small hill to wait out the danger. The husband of one of the women—a man who was not a local, but from the Tiwi Islands—went to the southern tip of the island, from where he thought he saw the Wilha Dreaming coming after him. Barrtjap calls him up to the safety of the hill. The high calls heard in the song seem to indicate not only Barrtjap's calls to the frightened man, but also (perhaps) the high call uttered by the Wilha Dreaming itself.

This song is discussed in more detail in Marett, 2005, pp 167–70, where there is also a transcription of the first part of the song.

SONG STRUCTURE SUMMARY

VOCAL SECTIONS 1–2

Melodic section 1

Text phrase 1

Rhythmic mode 2a (slow even)

ya
SW

Ya!

Text phrase 2

Rhythmic mode 2b (slow even, stick beating suspended)

yagarra	**delhi**	**nya**	**-ngadja**	**-barra**	**-ngarrka**
EXCL	wait	2 MIN.IR	come back	towards speaker	1MIN.IO

Yagarra! Wait! Come back here to me

Text phrase 3

Rhythmic mode 2b (slow even, stick beating suspended)

nanggang	**-gulhü**	**kanya**	**-bara**	**-m**
frightened	NEG	2MIN.S.R	travel	PRES

Don't be frightened

Melodic section 2

Text phrase 4

Rhythmic mode 2b (slow even, stick beating suspended)

kuu	**yagarra**	**nye**	**-bindja**	**-ng**	**werret**	**bangany**	**ngwe**	**ngwe**
SW	EXCL	2MIN.S.IR	climb	SIM	quick	song	SW	SW

Kuu. Yagarra! Climb up, quick now! Song! Ngwe ngwe

Melodic section 3

Text phrase 5

Rhythmic mode 2a (slow even)

yagarra	**dü**
EXCL	SW

Yagarra! Dü!

INSTRUMENTAL SECTIONS 1-2

Rhythmic mode 2a (slow even)

CODA

Rhythmic mode 5a (fast even)

yit ngayi ngayi …

TRACK 25 (Mar97-04-s07)

Song 19: Nga-ngat-pat-pa Mangalimba

Sung text	Free translation
nga-ngat-pat-pa mangalimba	Nga-ngat-pat-pa Mangalimba
nga-ngat-pat-pa mangalimba	Nga-ngat-pat-pa Mangalimba
yagarra nye-bindja-ya nye-bindja-ya	Yagarra! You sing, you sing
yagarra nye-bindja-ya	Yagarra! You sing
bangany nye-bindja-ya	You sing the song
yagarra nye-bindja-ya	Yagarra! You sing
(nga-ngat-pat-pa)	(Nga-ngat-pat-pa)
ii bangany-nye nye-bindja-ya nye-bindja-ya	Ii! You sing the song, you sing
bangany nye-bindja-ya	You sing the song

Although this song was composed by Tommy Barrtjap, he was never recorded singing it. This performance is by his son, Kenny Burrenjuck, for whom it was a favorite. Mangalimba is the name of a woman. The word 'nga-ngat-pat-pa' is said to be just for song, but it is unlike any other vocables that we have encountered, and like 'rinyala' (song 4, tracks 5 and 6) it sounds like, but isn't, a Batjamalh word. This lively performance was recorded at the launch of Lysbeth Ford's Batjamalh Dictionary at Belyuen.

Figure 4.5 Kenny Burrenjuck singing for the launch of Lysbeth Ford's Batjamalh dictionary, Belyuen, 1997. Photograph by Linda Barwick, reproduced with the permission of Belyuen community.

SONG STRUCTURE SUMMARY

VOCAL SECTIONS 1–2

Melodic section 1

Text phrases 1–2

Rhythmic mode 5c (fast uneven quadruple)

nga-ngat-pat-pa	**mangalimba**
SW	person's name

Nga-ngat-pat-pa Mangalimba

Text phrase 3

Rhythmic mode 5c (fast uneven quadruple)

yagarra	**nye**	**-bindja**	**-ya**	**nye**	**-bindja**	**-ya**
EXCL	2MIN.IR	sing	SW	2MIN.IR	sing	SW

Yagarra! You sing, you sing

Barrtjap's repertory • 145

Text phrase 4

Rhythmic mode 5c (fast uneven quarduple)

yagarra	**nye**	**-bindja**	**-ya**
EXCL	2MIN.IR	sing	SW

Yagarra! You sing

Text phrase 5

Rhythmic mode 5c (fast uneven quadruple)

bangany	**nye**	**-bindja**	**-ya**
song	2MIN.IR	sing	SW

You sing the song

Text phrase 6

Rhythmic mode 5c (fast uneven quadruple)

yagarra	**nye**	**-bindja**	**-ya**
EXCL	2MIN.IR	sing	SW

Yagarra! You sing

Text phrase 7 (vocal section 2 only)

Rhythmic mode 5c (fast uneven quadruple)

nga-ngat-pat-pa
SW

Nga-ngat-pat-pa

Melodic section 2

Text phrase 8

Rhythmic mode 5c (fast uneven quadruple)

ii	**bangany**	**-nye**	**nye**	**-bindja**	**-ya**
SW	song	SW	2MIN.IR	sing	SW

Ii! You sing the song, you sing

Text phrase 9

Rhythmic mode 5c (fast uneven quadruple)

yagarra	**nye**	**-bindja**	**-ya**	**nye**	**-bindja**	**-ya**
EXCL	2MIN.IR	sing	SW	2MIN.IR	sing	SW

Yagarra! You sing, you sing

Text phrase 10

Rhythmic mode 5c (fast uneven quadruple)

bangany	**nye**	**-bindja**	**-ya**
song	2MIN.IR	sing	SW

You sing the song

INSTRUMENTAL SECTIONS 1–2

Rhythmic mode 5c (fast uneven quadruple)

CODA

Rhythmic mode 5c (fast uneven quadruple)

yit ngayi yit ngayi yit ngowe, ngayi yit ngayi yit ngayi yit ngowe …

TRACK 26 (Mar97-04-s04)

Song 22: Anadadada Bangany-nyaya

Sung text	Free translation
anadadada bangany-nyaya nga-bindja–ya	'Anadadada' is the song I'm singing
anadadada bangany-nyaya nga-bindja–ya	'Anadadada' is the song I'm singing
dengalma dengalma nga-ve	I'm out of breath
yangarang nga -bindja -ya	Today I'm singing
bangany nga-bindja-ya	I'm singing the song
ngwe ngwe ngwe	Ngwe ngwe ngwe

This song was composed by Kenny Burrenjuck, who 'made up' rather than dreamed his songs. The reason for this was that he lived at the community of Milikapiti on Melville Island, away from his community of Belyuen and hence his familial ghosts. Kenny was nonetheless acknowledged as Barrtjap's main heir in the matter of songs and he frequently visited Belyuen for ceremonial and other reasons, hence his nickname, 'Come and go.'

Kenny was asthmatic and this sometimes made singing difficult, hence the song's reference to breathlessness. At his rag burning ceremony in August 2008 this song was frequently sung, making it particularly poignant when his 'puffer' (inhaler) was thrown into the fire along with his other belongings (Barwick & Marett, 2011).

SONG STRUCTURE SUMMARY

VOCAL SECTIONS 1–3

Melodic section 1

Text phrases 1–2

Rhythmic mode 5c (fast uneven quadruple)

anadadada	bangany	-nyaya	nga	-bindja	-ya
SW	song	SW	1MIN.S.R	sing	SW

'Anadadada' is the song I'm singing

Text phrase 3

Rhythmic mode 5c (fast uneven quadruple)

dengalma	**dengalma**	**nga**	**-ve**
breathless	breathless	1MIN.S.R	move

I'm out of breath

Text phrase 4

Rhythmic mode 5c (fast uneven quadruple)

yangarang	**nga**	**-bindja**	**-ya**
today	1.MIN.S.R	sing	SW

Today I'm singing

Text phrase 5

Rhythmic mode 5c (fast uneven quadruple)

bangany	**nga**	**-bindja**	**-ya**
song	1.MIN.S.R	sing	SW

I'm singing the song

Text phrase 6

Rhythmic mode 5c (fast uneven quadruple)

ngwe	**ngwe**	**ngwe**
SW	SW	SW

Ngwe ngwe ngwe

INSTRUMENTAL SECTIONS 1–3

Rhythmic mode 5c (fast uneven quadruple)

CODA

Rhythmic mode 5c (fast uneven quadruple)

yit ngayi ngayi yit ngowe …

MUSICAL ANALYSIS OF BARRTJAP'S REPERTORY

This section of the chapter provides an overview of Barrtjap's song structures, text structures and use of rhythmic and melodic mode across his repertory, as well as additional musical detail on some of the tracks.

Song structure overview

All Barrtjap's songs take the form of an introductory instrumental section, followed by a number of vocal plus instrumental section pairs, followed by a coda. The coda, a structural constituent unique to Barrtjap's repertory, is accompanied by characteristic vocables (didjeridu mouth sounds), which vary according to its rhythmic mode. Not infrequently the coda is in a different mode from the immediately preceding instrumental section, and because it ends the song item, in several respects it may be viewed as structurally equivalent to the final instrumental section in the other repertories (Marett, 2005, p 93).

All but two of the songs discussed here have either two or three paired vocal+instrumental sections. Barrtjap's songs tend to be very stable in their vocal sections, with very little textual variation. They also tend to maintain the same melody and rhythmic treatment from one vocal section to another, and from one song item to another, even over long periods of time.

Most Barrtjap songs have two or three melodic sections within the vocal section, the exception being 'Anadadada Bangany-nyaya' (track 26), which has only one melodic section. Melodic sections normally begin on a high pitch and descend to cadence on the note articulated by the didjeridu tonic. In most cases melodic sections are sung in one breath, though in unusually long melodic sections, such as that in 'Ya[garra] Nga-bindja-ng Nga-mi' (track 7), the singer may be forced to subdivide the melodic section by taking a breath.

Text structure overview

The predominant themes of his songs are acts of song-giving—where we hear the words of the song-giving ghost as he or she addresses the songman in his dream, as in 'Ya[garra] Nga-bindja-ng Nga-mi' (chapter 4, track 7)— and the act of singing itself. There are a number of generic references to country: for example, in 'Yagarra Nedja Tjine Rak-pe' (chapter 4, track 20), the ghost is asking the singer (addressed as 'son') where his ancestral country lies. Barrtjap's repertory is nevertheless conspicuous for its lack of references to specific named places. This is undoubtedly because Barrtjap and his kin were living far from their traditional country on Anson Bay.

Most of Barrtjap's texts comprise both ghost language (or other forms of unintelligible vocables such as didjeridu mouth sounds) and Batjamalh. A distinctive feature of Barrtjap's style is that that the text in human language (Batjamalh) comprises a limited number of text formulae (Marett, 2005, pp 156–58). His songs are quite diverse in text structure. Some of his songs, for example 'Ya[garra] Nga-bindja-ng Nga-mi' (track 7), have through-composed text (with no repeated text material within the vocal section), while others, for example 'Nyere-nyere Lima Kaldja' (track 11), are made up entirely of cyclical text that is sung isorhythmically (that is, several repeats of the same text string within a vocal section, using the same rhythmic setting each time). The vast majority of songs, however, use both types of text, sometimes using cyclic text for one melodic section and through-composed text in the next. An example is 'Yagarra Ye-yenenaya' (track 15).

Rhythmic mode overview

Table 4.2 shows that Barrtjap used no fewer than nine different rhythmic modes. Barrtjap was generally very consistent in his use of rhythmic mode from performance to performance of the same song, both for vocal sections and instrumental sections.

Tempo band of vocal section	#	Song title	Rhythmic mode of VS	Rhythmic mode of IIS	Rhythmic mode of coda
Unmeasured					
Without clapsticks	5	'Ya[garra] Nga-bindja-ng Nga-mi' (tracks 7-8)	1	5b+5a+2, 5d	5d
	10	'Karra Ngadja-maka Nga-bindja-ng Nga-mi' (track 13)	1	5a+2+5d	**5d**
Measured					
Slow (58–65bpm)	4	'Kanga Rinyala Nga-ve Bangany-nyung' (tracks 5-6)	2	2	**5d**
	17	'Yagarra Tjine Rak-pe' (track 23)	2	2	**5d**
	18	'Yagarra Delhi Nya-ngadja-barra-ngarrka' (track 24)	2a, 2b+2a	2	**5a**
Moderate (117–20bpm)	2	'Yagarra Nga-bindja-ng Nga-mi Ngayi' (track 2)	4d	4d	4d
	15	'Ya Rembe Ngaya Lima Ngaya' (track 21)	4a	4a	**4d**
	16	'Yagarra Tjüt Balk-nga-me Nga-mi' (track 22)	4d	4d	4d
Fast (126–44bpm)	6	'Yagarra Bangany Nye-ngwe' (track 9)	5a	5a	5a
	7	'Be Bangany-nyaya' (track 10)	5a	5a	5a
	3	'Bangany-nyung Ngaya' (tracks 3-4)	5c	5c	5c
	11	'Yerre Ka-bindja-maka Ka-mi' (track 14)	5c	5c	5c
	19	'Nga-ngat-pat-pa Mangalimba' (track 25)	5c	5c	5c
	22	'Anadadada Bangany-nyaya' (track 26)	5c	5c	5c
Fast doubled (268–88/134–44bpm)	1	'Ya Bangany-nyung Nga-bindja Yagarra' (track 1)	5b, 5b, 5a	5b, 5b, 5a	5a
	8	'Nyere-nyere Lima Kaldja' (track 11)	5b, 5b, 5c	5b, 5b, 5c	5c
	9	'Nyere-nye Bangany Nyaye' (track 12)	5b, 5b, 5c, 5c	5b, 5b, 5c, 5c	5c
	12	'Yagarra Ye-yenenaya' (track 15)	5b, 5b, 5c	5b, 5b, 5c	5c
	13	'Naya Rradja Bangany Nye-ve' (tracks 16-19)	5c (Bandak) 5b, 5b, 5c (Barrtjap) 5b, 5c, 5c (Burrenjuck)	5c (Bandak) 5b, 5b, 5c (Barrtjap) 5b, 5c, 5c (Burrenjuck)	5c
	14	'Yagarra Nedja Tjine Rak-pe' (track 20)	5b, 5b, 5c	5b, 5b, 5c	5c

Table 4.2 Rhythmic modes used in Barrtjap's repertoire (coda is bold when different). VS = vocal section, IIS = internal instrumental section. Commas indicate successive vocal or instrumental sections in sequence through the song, where these are different. Plus signs indicate sequences of rhythmic modes occurring within a section. Names of performers in brackets.

Barrtjap is the only *wangga* singer to use quintuple metre (rhythmic mode 4d). He uses a gapped quintuple beating pattern (♩ ♩ 𝄾 ♩ 𝄾) in two of his three songs in the moderate tempo band: 'Yagarra Nga-bindja-ng Nga-mi-ngaye' (chapter 4, track 2) and 'Yagarra Tjüt Balk-nga-me Nga-mi' (chapter 4, track 22), and it also appears in the coda of the third song in that tempo band. The fast tempo song 'Be Bangany-nyaya' (song 7, chapter 4, track 10) is also in quintuple metre, though here it is the vocal rhythm rather than the stick beating that articulates the metre (see further in Marett, 2005, pp 172–74). It is clear that Barrtjap's favorite rhythmic modes were fast (twelve of his songs are entirely in this tempo band). He had a particular liking for songs in the fast uneven quadruple rhythmic mode 5c (♩ ♩ ♩ 𝄾) and it can be seen from the table that nine songs (almost half the repertory) are sung wholly or partly in this mode.

While fast songs are associated with a happy celebratory mood, by contrast the songs with unmeasured vocal sections (rhythmic mode 1), or vocal sections sung with slow beating (rhythmic mode 2) have a certain weight to them, and it is these songs that are performed at particularly serious parts of ceremonies. Three of these songs—'Ya[garra] Nga-bindja-ng Nga-mi' (chapter 4, track 7), 'Yagarra Tjine Rak-pe' (chapter 4, track 23) and 'Yagarra Delhi Nye-bindja-ng-barra-ngarrka' (chapter 4, track 24) are rarely, if ever, performed today.

Presenting the same text in different rhythmic modes in different vocal sections within an item

All six songs with vocal sections in rhythmic mode 5b change in their last vocal section to a different fast rhythmic mode; the fast even rhythmic mode 5a in the case of 'Ya Bangany-nyung Nga-bindja Yagarra' (track 1) and the fast uneven quadruple rhythmic mode 5c for the remaining five songs (the so-called *lerri* 'happy' songs—see further below): 'Nyere-nyere Lima Kaldja' (track 11), 'Nyere-nye Bangany Nyaya' (track 12); 'Yagarra Ye-yenenaya' (track 15); 'Naya Rradja Bangany Nye-ve ' (tracks 18-19) and 'Yagarra Nedja Tjine Rak-pe' (track 20). In all cases the instrumental sections (and the coda) take their rhythmic mode from the immediately preceding vocal section.

The five lerri 'happy' songs have the following characteristics in common with *lerri* songs in other Belyuen repertories (Mandji and Muluk):
- Fast tempo;
- Largely or totally isorhythmic texts, with some variability in the end point of the isorhythmic cycle;
- A high proportion of vocables ('ghost language') in the song texts.

Barrtjap's group of *lerri* songs shares the following additional characteristics:
- The first one or two vocal sections are sung in rhythmic mode 5b (fast doubled) and the final one or two in rhythmic mode 5c (fast uneven quadruple);
- Metre is always compound, that is, with triple subdivisions of the main beats;
- The instrumental sections continue the rhythmic mode of the preceding vocal section, except when a new rhythmic mode is to be taken up in the following vocal section. In these cases, the new rhythmic mode may be introduced at the very end of the preceding instrumental section.

Distribution of rhythmic mode between vocal sections and instrumental sections

Songs in the moderate and fast tempo bands remain in the same tempo band throughout, and some —namely those that use rhythmic modes 4d, 5c and 5a in their vocal sections—remain in the same rhythmic mode throughout all sections of the song, including the coda (the only example of a song in rhythmic mode 4a maintains that mode in the instrumental sections but changes to 4d for the coda).

By contrast, songs with vocal sections in the unmeasured and slow tempo bands change tempo band and rhythmic mode between vocal and instrumental sections. Songs in the slow even rhythmic mode 2 maintain that mode in the instrumental sections, but change to a fast tempo for the coda, while songs with vocal sections in the unmeasured rhythmic mode 1 tend to use fast tempo rhythmic modes both in instrumental sections and in the coda.

Mixing of rhythmic modes within a vocal section

The slow tempo songs 'Kanga Rinyala Nga-ve Bangany-nyung' (track 6) and 'Yagarra Delhi Nya-ngadja-barra-ngarrka' (track 24) are the only ones to exhibit any variability in rhythmic mode within a vocal section, hère depending on whether or not parts of the song are sung with the suspended form of slow beating (rhythmic mode 2b).

Mixing of rhythmic modes within an instrumental section

In one case, 'Ya[garra] Nga-bindja-ng Nga-mi' (chapter 4, track 7), Barrtjap uses a series of different rhythmic modes for the first instrumental section of the first item (5b+5a+2) but then settles on the fast uneven triple rhythmic mode (rhythmic mode 5d) for the remaining instrumental sections. See also further notes on 'Karra Ngadja-maka Nga-bindja-ng Ngami' below.

Melodic mode overview

Every one of Barrtjap's songs has a different melody, but the repertory is given melodic cohesion by the fact that all but one song are in the same (dorian) melodic mode. The exception is 'Yagarra Delhi Nya-ngadja-barra-ngarrka' (chapter 4, track 24). Perhaps its different (major) mode is attributable to the fact that it refers to a local Larrakiya Dreaming (the Hairy Cheeky Yam, Wilha), while the remainder of the repertory is associated with Barrtjap's own Wadjiginy traditional country south of the Cox Peninsula. Given that there is traditionally a close relationship between the melody of songs and the Dreamings of those who perform them, Barrtjap may have felt obliged to use a different melody in order to avoid any appearance of appropriating another group's cultural property.

Further notes on selected tracks

Here we provide some additional analytical notes on musical features of seven songs (tracks 1, 10, 12, 13, 18, 21 and 24).

Track 1 'Ya Bangany-nyung Nga-bindja Yagarra'

In other recordings of this song (Moy68-05-s01 and Mar88-04-s10 and s11) all vocal sections are sung with fast even beating (rhythmic mode 5a). This version is a little more varied in that it uses fast doubled beating (rhythmic mode 5b) for the first two vocal sections and reserves fast even beating for the third and final vocal section. The instrumental sections, as is always the case with fast even and fast doubled beating, maintains the rhythmic mode of the previous vocal section, but the change of rhythmic mode from 5b (fast doubled) to 5a (fast even) occurs towards the end of instrumental section 2. The coda, too, is in the same metre as the preceding vocal and instrumental section and uses the didjeridu mouth-sound pattern 'yit ngayi ngayi' typical of fast even beating. It is in the coda that the most vigorous and most formalised dancing occurs.

Track 10 'Be Bangany-nyaya'

Text phrases are realised as a two- or three-beat rhythmic cells, which at first follow each other in an irregular configuration but then settle into pairs that articulate a regular 5/4 metre (see musical transcription in example 7.4 in Marett, 2005, p 173). The conventions that determine the relationships between text phrases and rhythmic cells in this song are set out in detail in Marett, 2005, pp 172–74.

While the instrumental sections and coda maintain the fast even beating of the vocal sections (rhythmic mode 5a), the quintuple grouping of the sung text is reflected in Barrtjap's use in the coda of a quintuple form of didjeridu mouth sound: 'yit ngayi yit ngayi ngayi yit ngayi ngayi.'

Track 13 'Karra Ngadja-maka Nga-bindja-ng Ngami'

The instrumental sections of this song are unusual in a number of ways: first, they employ a number of rhythmic modes (fast even beating, followed by slow even beating, followed by one cycle of fast uneven triple); secondly, as elsewhere occurs only in codas, they are accompanied by didjeridu mouthsounds from the songman. Perhaps for this reason there is no instrumental section following vocal section 3. The singer proceeds directly to the coda, which is in the rhythmic mode hinted at at the end of each instrumental section, namely, rhythmic mode 5d (fast uneven triple).

Track 21 'Ya Rembe Ngaya Lima Ngaya'

A similar juxtaposition of duple and triple elements, as described on page 138 for the beginning of melodic sections 1 and 2, also occurs in melodic section 2, text phrase 7, where *yagarra yine nga-bindja-ya* ('what am I singing?'), is set to four beats, but the partial repetition in text phrase 8 is set to three beats. This juxtaposition of text elements set to two- (or four-) beat and three-beat rhythmic cells reminds us of song 7 'Be Bangany-nyaya' (track 10). That the metrical irregularity is intentional is confirmed in the coda, where Barrtjap explicitly adopts a quintuple beating pattern coupled with the didjeridu pattern used for quintuple beating.

Chapter 5
MULUK'S REPERTORY

Jimmy Muluk (born c. 1925, died sometime before 1986) was one of the great *wangga* songmen. In Muluk's performances we see the art of the *wangga* songman at its height. His musical virtuosity is matched by no other singer.[1] A Mendheyangal man, his traditional country lay around the Cape Ford area south of the Daly River mouth, but he lived most of his life in and around Belyuen on the Cox Peninsula. For many years he led a dance troupe presenting performances for tourists at Mica Beach and later Mandorah[2] (both on the Cox Peninsula, on the southern shores of Darwin Harbour), where he was recorded by Alice Moyle in 1968.

Figure 5.1 Jimmy Muluk performing for tourists at Mica Beach, early 1970s. Northern Territory Library, Mike Foley collection, photo PH0051/0009, reproduced with the permission of Belyuen community.

By the time Marett first visited Belyuen in 1988, Muluk had already passed away, so we are fortunate to have access to a significant body of archival recordings made by Alice Moyle in the 1960s, which represent the bulk of Jimmy Muluk's repertory discussed in this chapter. While the main themes of Jimmy Muluk's songs are ghosts and totemic beings, our understanding of these songs is more limited than for other *wangga* repertories. Even though Muluk gave Alice Moyle quite detailed prose texts for some songs (reproduced below), these spoken texts do not necessarily enlighten us as to the deeper meanings of songs. The song that the small remaining number of Mendhe speakers contributed most

---

1 As argued in chapter 2, Muluk's songs provided models for the development of the Walakandha *wangga* at Wadeye in the 1960s and 1970s (chapter 8), where performers for a time followed Muluk's practice with regard to flexible forms and the use of multiple rhythmic mode (Marett, 2007, pp 70–72). For a complex set of reasons, however, these practices fell out of use at Wadeye by the 1980s (Marett, 2007).

2 Marett's 2006 recording of Muluk's relative Robert Gordon singing some of the same songs at a tourist corroboree at the Mandorah hotel attests to the long tradition of Belyuen people performing for tourists.

Muluk's repertory • 155

Figure 5.2 Jimmy Muluk demonstrates the breadth of his musical interests, playing with Johnny Singh's band at Mica Beach, early 1970s. Northern Territory Library, Mike Foley collection, photo PH0008/0023, reproduced with the permission of Belyuen community.

additional detail on was 'Puliki', but even here, Muluk's prose explanation remains relatively opaque. Lysbeth Ford (2007) has previously published linguistic analysis and texts of two Muluk songs.

Although the track-by-track commentary may be somewhat shorter for this repertory, the musical analysis section at the end of the chapter is considerably longer than average, due to Muluk's love of variation and mastery of his craft. Musically, his repertory is by far the most diverse.

Notes on the recording sample

Table 5.1 summarises the songs from the Muluk repertory discussed in this chapter. We are relying largely on only two of Alice Moyle's recordings, a *burnim-rag* ceremony at the Bagot community in Darwin in 1962 (Moy62-26); a 1968 tourist corroboree held at Mandorah, on the Cox Peninsula near Belyuen (performers included Billy Mandji), and a second 1968 performance at Delissaville elicited for dance research (Moy68-1; Moy68-2). Moyle also recorded Muluk at the Darwin eisteddfod in 1964 (Moy64-10; Moy64-36) but the recordings are of such poor quality (being recorded inside at a distance from the singers) that we decided not to include them in the present collection. Moyle's recording of several young boys singing at the 1962 Darwin eisteddfod under Muluk's direction is, however, of sufficient quality to warrant inclusion (Moy62-27) (track 3). Muluk's songs have also been widely performed by other singers, some of whom are included here for comparative purposes. These include Muluk's contemporary Billy Mandji (recorded by Alice Moyle in 1968, track 2), his late grandson, Kenny Burrenjuck (recorded by Marett in 1997 and Furlan in 2002, track 18), and other relatives: Colin Worumbu Ferguson (recorded by Marett in 1997 and 2006) (tracks 4 and 6), Thomas Gordon (recorded by Marett and Barwick in 1997) and Robert Gordon (recorded by Marett and Barwick in 1997 and by Marett in 2006)[3]. Worumbu, Thomas Gordon and Robert Gordon are three of the young boys that Jimmy Muluk had trained up to perform at the 1962 and 1964 Darwin eisteddfods.

---

3   We have not included here any of the later recordings by Thomas and Robert Gordon.

Track	Song #	Title	Singer	Recording
Track 01	1	'Puliki' (Buffalo)	Muluk	Moy68-02-s05
Track 02		'Puliki' (Buffalo)	Mandji	Moy68-01-s04
Track 03		'Puliki' (Buffalo)	Worumbu, T & R Gordon	Moy62-27-s05
Track 04		'Puliki' (Buffalo)	Worumbu	Mar97-13A-s05
Track 05	2	'Tjinbarambara' (Seagull)	Muluk	Moy68-02-s02
Track 06		'Tjinbarambara' (Seagull)	Worumbu	Mar97-13A-s04
Track 07	3	'Wak' (Crow)	Muluk	Moy68-02-s03
Track 08	4	'Wörörö' (Crab)	Muluk	Moy68-02-s04
Track 09	5	'Pumandjin' (Place name: a hill)	Muluk	Moy62-26-s21
Track 10	6	'Piyamen.ga' (Shady Tree) Two items	Muluk	Moy62-26-s15_16
Track 11		'Piyamen.ga' (Shady Tree)	Muluk	Moy62-26-s17
Track 12		'Piyamen.ga' (Shady Tree) Two items	Muluk	Moy62-26-s18_19
Track 13	7	'Lame Fella'	Muluk	Moy62-26-s06
Track 14		'Lame Fella'	Muluk	Moy62-26-s09
Track 15	8	'Rtadi-thawara' (Walking on the Mangroves)	Muluk	Moy62-26-s10
Track 16		'Rtadi-thawara' (Walking on the Mangroves)	Muluk	Moy62-26-s11_12
Track 17		'Rtadi-thawara' (Walking on the Mangroves)	Muluk	Moy62-26-s13_14
Track 18		'Rtadi-thawara' (Walking on the Mangroves)	Burrenjuck	AF2002-03-s03
Track 19	9	'Lerri' (Happy Dance)	Muluk	Moy62-26-s22_23
Track 20		'Lerri' (Happy Dance)	Muluk	Moy62-26-s24

Table 5.1 Songs from Jimmy Muluk's repertory discussed in this chapter.

As already pointed out in chapter 2, an important characteristic of Muluk's performance is the use of highly flexible forms and multiple rhythmic modes, and for this reason we have included multiple versions of a number of his songs. When we have only one recording of a particular version of a song, we have included it even if there are technical problems: track 8, for example, is included even though it suffers from wind noise, and track 20 suffers from fluctuating tape speeds owing to failing batteries.

TRACK 1 (Moy68-02-s5)

Song 1: Puliki

Sung text	Free translation
rimili dje the raga mele dje	Rimili dje the raga mele dje
rimili dje the raga mele dje	Rimili dje the raga mele dje
rimili dja da raga mele dja	Rimili dja da raga mele dja
nga-ni-purr-mbele ngayi-nö alawa mari-pinindjela	I will always dance for you at Mari-pinindjela [Mica Beach]
rimili dja da raga mele dja	Rimili dja da raga mele dja

Jimmy Muluk's song 'Puliki' (Buffalo) is one of the best known of all *wangga*. It is widely sung, even today. Recordings have been made as far away as Mowanjum in the western Kimberley (Various artists, 1991, track 3). Alice Moyle published two recordings of this song in *Songs from the Northern Territory, volume 1* (AM Moyle, 1967a, track 13).

Figure 5.3 Buffalo dance at the tourist corroboree, Mica Beach, September 1972. Photograph by Allan Laurence, with permission of Belyuen community.

Figure 5.4 The 'Buffalo' chases a dancer up a tree at the tourist corroboree, Mica Beach, September 1972. Photograph by Allan Laurence, reproduced with the permission of Belyuen community.

The song describes a Buffalo *ngutj* (ancestral spirit)[4] who has swum from Matpil (a favourite camping place near Mandorah) across to Mica Beach, where he dances. The song text consists of a section in 'ghost language,' followed by a section in Mendhe, in which the ghostly Buffalo sings that he will always dance at Mica Beach. In some performances only the ghost language section is sung. In more public performances, such as tourist corroborees, the deeper meaning of the song is concealed, so that the song is interpreted as being not about a ghostly Buffalo, but rather a buffalo hunt. The dancing in tourist corroborees plays out this more mundane interpretation.

Two stories about 'Puliki' have been translated and discussed by Lysbeth Ford. The first was given by Jimmy Muluk himself, recorded by Alice Moyle in 1968:

> *Pitj alawa ngany ngandhi, mari pinindjila. Yuwana gamengwulhayi. Yiya yuwananganayi. Nganamutharriya. Puliki ngaden gumbu. Wangga ganapurr ganeneyi. Wanggangani ganapurr ganamörögumbu. kakdjen gana. Ganayi. merrangarr gamayi. Gananganayi. Ganapirrwuda. Madjelanganayi , Midjili gami. Ganawulhaga yiinhdha garru.*

There's a certain beach belonging to me, a curving beach on the peninsula (Mica Beach). That [old] man over there told me to come back. It was from him, away from here. I was packing up, with my back to him. I saw buffalo tracks. He was dancing. He was dancing for me till daybreak. Then he went away. He walked. He stood in the jungle. He walked from there. He swims. From Madjelaba he came out at Midjili. He deliberately comes back right here. (Ford, 2007, p 80)

The second was told to Ford in Mendhe twenty years later by Alice Jorrock:

> *Wel wulmen gaya, puliki ganapirrwudayi mari ngandhi, la pinindjila. Puliki ganapurr, wulmen wadjet gaya. Ginmenerre wulmen. inmenerre. Gaden awa puliki wangga ganapurr gaya. Ganapirrwudayi. Wangga ganapurr gaya buliki. Wulmen manhdha gamen. Gameneyi manhdha. Garrungatj.*

Well, the old man lies down there on the peninsula, where the buffalo had swum, over the other side of the creek. The buffalo dances, the old man lies there and watches. The old man wakes up, he wakes up. He watches the buffalo who is always dancing *wangga*. He had swam there. The buffalo always dances *wangga*. The old man picks up the song. He picked up the song. He hides. That's all. (Ford, 2007, p 80)

In track 1 we hear a recording of Jimmy Muluk himself, recorded by Alice Moyle in 1968 during a tourist corroboree held at the Mandorah hotel. Somewhat distractingly, in all songs recorded by Moyle on this occasion a whistle is blown intermittently; this was intended to assist the later synching of the audio tape with a silent film of the dancing taken at the same time.

Three further performances of 'Puliki' are included in this chapter. In track 2, Jimmy Muluk's contemporary, Billy Mandji sings his own, slightly different version of the song. On track 3 we hear an even earlier recording made by Alice Moyle in 1964 of four boys from Delissaville (Belyuen) singing at the Darwin eisteddfod. Two of these, Colin Worumbu Ferguson and Robert Gordon (see above), are still singing the song today. Track 4 is a recording of Colin Ferguson singing in 1998, also at Mandorah. See the notes for tracks 2–4 below for further details.

See the musical analysis section at the end of this chapter for detailed discussion of Muluk's use of rhythmic modes in this song.

---

4   *Ngutj* is the Emmi-Mendhe word for ancestral spirit, cognate with the Batjamalh word *wunymalang*.

SONG STRUCTURE SUMMARY

VOCAL SECTION 1

Melodic section 1

Text phrases 1–3

Rhythmic mode 2a (slow even)
rimili dje the raga mele dje
rimili dje the raga mele dje
rimili dja da raga mele dja

Melodic section 2

Text phrase 4

Rhythmic mode 2b (slow even, stick beating suspended)

nga	-ni	-purr	-mbele	ngayi	-nö	alawa	mari-pinindjela
1MIN.S.IR	walk	dance	2MIN.BEN	1MIN.S.IR lie	PURP	beach	place name

I will always dance for you at Mari-pinindjela [Mica Beach]

Text phrase 5

Rhythmic mode 2b (slow even, stick beating suspended)
rimili dja da raga mele dja

INSTRUMENTAL SECTION 1

Rhythmic mode 2a (slow even)

VOCAL SECTION 2

Melodic section 1

Text phrases 1–3

Rhythmic mode 2a (slow even)
rimili dje the raga mele dje
rimili dje the raga mele dje
rimili dja da raga mele dja

Melodic section 2

Text phrase 4

Rhythmic mode 2b (slow even, stick beating suspended)

nga	**-ni**	**-purr**	**-mbele**	**ngayi**	**-nö**	**alawa**	**mari-pinindjela**
1MIN.S.IR	walk	dance-	2MIN.BEN	1MIN.S.IR lie	PURP	beach	place name

I will always dance for you at Mari-pinindjela (Mica Beach)

Text phrase 5

Rhythmic mode 2b (slow even, stick beating suspended)
rimili dja da raga mele dja

INSTRUMENTAL SECTION 2

Rhythmic mode 4a (moderate even)

VOCAL SECTION 3

Melodic section 1

Text phrases 1–3

Rhythmic mode 2a (slow even)
rimili dje the raga mele dje
rimili dje the raga mele dje
rimili dja da raga mele dja

Melodic section 2

Text phrase 4

Rhythmic mode 2b (slow even, stick beating suspended)

nga	**-ni**	**-purr-**	**-mbele**	**ngayi**	**-nö**	**alawa**	**mari-pinindjela**
1MIN.S.IR	walk	dance-	2MIN.BEN	1MIN.S.IR lie	PURP	beach	place name

I will always dance for you at Mari-pinindjela (Mica Beach)

Text phrase 5

Rhythmic mode 2b (slow even, stick beating suspended)
rimili dja da raga mele dja

INSTRUMENTAL SECTION 3

Rhythmic mode 2a (slow even)

VOCAL SECTION 4

Melodic section 1

Text phrases 1–3
Rhythmic mode 2a (slow even)
rimili dje the raga mele dje
rimili dje the raga mele dje
rimili dja da raga mele dja

Melodic section 2

Text phrase 4
Rhythmic mode 2b (slow even, stick beating suspended)

nga	**-ni**	**-purr-**	**-mbele**	**ngayi**	**-nö**	**alawa**	**mari-pinindjela**
1MIN.S.IR	walk	dance-	2MIN.BEN	1MIN.S.IR lie	PURP	beach	place name

I will always dance for you at Mari-pinindjela (Mica Beach)

Text phrase 5
Rhythmic mode 2b (slow even, stick beating suspended)
rimili dja da raga mele dja

VOCAL SECTION 5

Melodic section 1

Text phrases 1–3
Rhythmic mode 2a (slow even)
rimili dje the raga mele dje
rimili dje the raga mele dje
rimili dja da raga mele dja

Melodic section 2

Text phrase 4
Rhythmic mode 2b (slow even, stick beating suspended)

nga	**-ni**	**-purr-**	**-mbele**	**ngayi**	**-nö**	**alawa**	**mari-pinindjela**
1MIN.S.IR	walk	dance-	2MIN.BEN	1MIN.S.IR lie	PURP	beach	place name

I will always dance for you at Mari-pinindjela (Mica Beach)

Text phrase 5
Rhythmic mode 2b (slow even, stick beating suspended)
rimili dja da raga mele dja

INSTRUMENTAL SECTION 4

Rhythmic mode 2a (slow even)

VOCAL SECTION 6

Melodic section 1

Text phrases 1–3

Rhythmic mode 2a (slow even)
rimili dje the raga mele dje
rimili dje the raga mele dje
rimili dja da raga mele dja

Melodic section 2

Text phrase 4

Rhythmic mode 2b (slow even, stick beating suspended)

nga	**-ni**	**-purr-**	**-mbele**	**ngayi**	**-nö**	**alawa**	**mari-pinindjela**
1MIN.S.IR	walk	dance-	2MIN.BEN	1MIN.S.IR lie	PURP	beach	place name

I will always dance for you at Mari-pinindjela (Mica Beach)

Text phrase 5

Rhythmic mode 2b (slow even, stick beating suspended)
rimili dja da raga mele dja

VOCAL SECTION 7

Melodic section 1

Text phrases 1–3

Rhythmic mode 2b (slow even, stick beating suspended)
rimili dje the raga mele dje
rimili dje the raga mele dje
rimili dja da raga mele dja

INSTRUMENTAL SECTION 5

Rhythmic mode 4e (moderate doubled)

TRACK 2 (Moy68-01-s04)

Song 1: Puliki

Around the same time that she recorded Jimmy Muluk's version, Alice Moyle recorded 'Puliki' in an even longer version by Muluk's contemporary, Billy Mandji (see chapter 6 for discussion of Mandji's own repertory). Mandji's version of the ghost language text is slightly different, and the text phrase in Mendhe omits the word *alawa* (beach). *Alawa* is in fact redundant to meaning, because a local Mendhe-speaking audience would already know that *mari-pinindjela* is a beach. The slow even beating used in the first nine vocal sections is said to represent the Buffalo swimming, and the fast beating in the final eight vocal sections his dancing on the beach (see the music analysis section at the end of the chapter for further details).

TRACK 3 (Moy62-27-s05)

Song 1: Puliki

In 1962 Alice Moyle recorded four boys from Delissaville (Belyuen), Colin Worumbu Ferguson, Robert Gordon, Thomas Gordon and James Gumbuduk singing 'Puliki' at the Darwin eisteddfod. As discussed more fully in the musical analysis section, the boys' performance shows some confusion in the text performance, and in the second half of the song uses a type of clapstick accompaniment that Muluk himself was never recorded using with this song. This example shows clearly the perils that flexible structures pose for inexperienced performers, and helps to explain why songs tend to become more stable and simple in structure over time—particularly when they are not performed by the original composer.

TRACK 4 (Mar97-13A-s05)

Song 1: Puliki

In this elicited performance, recorded by Marett on the beach at Mandorah in 1997, Colin Worumbu Ferguson, now a mature man in his late 40s, sings the same song. Here he structures the item in a similar way to that adopted by his relative Billy Mandji in track 2 above (see the music analysis section at the end of this chapter for more details). Given that Worumbu is Billy Mandji's brother's son and one of the inheritors of his songs, it is not surprising that this performance adopts these characteristics of Mandji's style. The similarity even extends to imitation of Mandji's voice quality. Marett has pointed out that at Belyuen, the imitation of the voice of a deceased singer is important for the efficacy of mortuary ceremonies (Marett, 2005, pp 68–69).

TRACK 5 (Moy68-02-s02)

Song 2: Tjinbarambara

Sung text	Free translation
aa karra tjinbarambara kala-nö dirr	Ah, seagull is closing its beak [going to die]
nganggu-ga kaya yawa-ndha	Our [seagull] is truly always there

Alice Moyle recorded Jimmy Muluk singing 'Tjinbarambara' (Seagull) in 1968, at the same tourist corroborree as 'Puliki'. Like 'Puliki,' this song survives to the present day. As recently as 2006, Marett heard it sung by Colin Worumbu Ferguson and Robert Gordon, both of whom were recorded singing Jimmy Muluk songs as boys in the 1960s (see track 3). The Emmi-Mendhe word *tjinbarambara* 'seagull' appears to be cognate with the Marri Tjavin word *tjinmel* (chapter 8, track 39), and here refers to the Seagull totemic ancestor. Our consultants explained the significance of 'closing the beak' as an image of death.[5] 'Tjinbarambara' has a through-composed couplet text whose linguistic form remains identical throughout the song. In this track, however, Muluk presents part of the text in an unusual musical form: there is a strong vocal diminuendo throughout text phrase 2, to the point where it is almost inaudible by the end. Nobody today is able to explain why Muluk sang text phrase 2 in this way. The same phrase is presented at a normal volume in Colin Worumbu Ferguson's performance of the same song (track 6). When Muluk spoke this text for Alice Moyle (Moy68-07), he clearly enunciated both text phrases, with no corresponding diminuendo.

It is perhaps significant that text phrase 2 is the element of the song that makes it clear that Seagull is a totemic ancestor. We may speculate that Muluk uses diminuendo here in order to obscure the totemic significance of the song, just as the Buffalo dance performed for tourists suppresses the interpretation of 'Puliki' as totemic Buffalo ancestor. Alice Moyle did not elicit a Seagull story to explain this song, and we have not been able to either. Perhaps the story is no longer known, or perhaps there is some sensitivity about it.

SONG STRUCTURE SUMMARY

VOCAL SECTIONS 1–10

Melodic section 1

Text phrase 1

Rhythmic mode 5c (fast uneven quadruple)

aa	**karra**	**tjinbarambara**	**kala**	**-nö**	**dirr**
ah	SW	seagull	3MIN.A.R bite	PURP	tooth

Ah, seagull is closing its beak [going to die]

Text phrase 2 (practically inaudible)

Rhythmic mode 5c (fast uneven quadruple)

nganggu	**-ga**	**kaya**	**yawa**	**-ndha**
1/2PRO	TOP	3MIN.S.R lie	3MIN.ANAPH.DEIC	really

Our [seagull] is truly always there

INSTRUMENTAL SECTIONS 1–10

Rhythmic mode 5c (fast uneven quadruple)

---

5 The idea of 'closing the mouth' as a metaphor for death is an ancient one, widely encountered in Asia. The images of the two Kongorikishi (Japanese Nio, Chinese Er Jiang, Korean Guengang) that stand at the entrance gates of Buddhist temples exemplify this. The right-hand statue has his mouth open, representing the vocalisation of the first grapheme of the Devanagari script which is pronounced 'a'. The left statue has his mouth closed, representing the vocalisation of the last grapheme of the Devanagari script, which is pronounced 'hu'. These two characters together symbolise the birth and death of all things. Humans are supposedly born speaking the 'a' sound with mouths open and die speaking a 'hu' with mouths closed.

TRACK 6 (Mar97-13A-s04)

Song 2: Tjinbarambara

Sung text	Free translation
aa karra tjinbarambara kala-nö dirr	Ah, seagull is closing its beak [going to die]
nganggu-ga kaya yawa-ndha	Our [seagull] is truly always there
[inaudible text]	[inaudible text]

In this version of the song, recorded by Marett in 1997, Colin Worumbu Ferguson sings the version of the text given by Jimmy Muluk to Alice Moyle without significant vocal diminuendo, but he then adds some additional (inaudible) text, which is not transcribed. As in all other recorded versions, rhythmic mode 5c (fast uneven quadruple) is used, but somewhat unusually—since songs in rhythmic mode 5c usually stay in this mode from beginning to end—Ferguson changes to fast even beating (rhythmic mode 5a) for the final instrumental section.

SONG STRUCTURE SUMMARY

VOCAL SECTIONS 1–3

Melodic section 1

Text phrase 1

Rhythmic mode 5c (fast uneven quadruple)

aa	karra	tjinbarambara	kala	-nö	dirr
ah	SW	seagull	3MIN.A.R bite	PURP	tooth

Ah, seagull is closing its beak [going to die]

Text phrase 2

Rhythmic mode 5c (fast uneven quadruple)

nganggu	-ga	kaya	yawa	-ndha
½PRO	TOP	3MIN.S.R lie	3MIN.ANAPH.DEIC	really

Our [seagull] is truly always there

Text phrase 3 (text inaudible)

Rhythmic mode 5c (fast uneven quadruple)

INSTRUMENTAL SECTIONS 1–2

Rhythmic mode 5c (fast uneven quadruple)

INSTRUMENTAL SECTION 3

Rhythmic mode 5a (fast even)

TRACK 7 (Moy68-02-s03)

Song 3: Wak

Sung text	Free translation
aa karra kana-kalkal rtadi nganggu-ga kaya yawa-ndha	Ah, he is always climbing on top of our stuff there
aa karra wak kana-kalkal rtadi nganggu-ga kaya yawa-ndha	Ah, Crow is always climbing on top of our stuff there
aa karra wak-ngana-yi	Ah, it was because of Crow
kana-kalkal rtadi nganggu-ga kaya yawa-ndha	Who is always climbing on top of our stuff there
aa karra wak-ngana-yi	Ah, it was because of Crow
kana-kalkal rtadi nganggu-ga kaya yawa-ndha	Who is always climbing on top of our stuff there
aa karra wak-ngana-yi	Ah, it was because of Crow
kana-putput rtadi nganggu-ga kaya yawa-ndha	Who is always walking on top of our stuff there
aa karra wak-ngana-yi	Ah, it was because of Crow
kana-putput rtadi nganggu-ga kaya yawa-ndha	Who is always walking on top of our stuff there
aa karra wak-ngana-yi	Ah, it was because of Crow
kana-kalkal rtadi nganggu-ga kaya yawa-ndha	Who is always climbing on top of our stuff there
aa karra wak-ngana-yi	Ah, it was because of Crow
kana-putput rtadi nganggu-ga kaya yawa-ndha	Who is always walking on top of our stuff there
aa karra wak-ngana-yi	Ah, it was because of Crow
kana-putput rtadi nganggu-ga kaya yawa-ndha	Who is always walking on top of our stuff there
aa karra wak-ngana-yi	Ah, it was because of Crow
kana-putput rtadi nganggu-ga kaya yawa-ndha	Who is always walking on top of our stuff there

This performance by Jimmy Muluk was recorded at the same tourist corroboree as 'Puliki' (track 1) and 'Tjinbarambara' (track 5). The dancers' calls of *wak* (Crow) mingle with the words of the song. The song text comprises two minimally different forms of a closely related text phrase. The first, which uses *kalkal* (climb) as the main verb, means 'he is always climbing on top of our stuff'. The second, which uses *putput* (walk) as the main verb, means 'he is always walking on top of our stuff'. The use of the co-verb *kaya* 'lie', like the use of the cognate co-verb *kavulh* in Marri Tjavin and Marri Ammu *wangga*, implies ancestral action, and that the Crow here is totemic.

Jimmy Muluk also told the following story about Crow. Ford discusses this text and the text of the *wangga* song (Ford, 2007, pp 78–80).

Miya wakngana gilanggala gaya yawandha. Tjanggurrinyya miya gilanggala yene gana. na ganyavanayinö awak gilanganggala miya. Ganakalalka rtedi. Yuwa ganakalalkrtediya wakngana miya. Kayilana wakga miya gilaninya. Wut palat vunidjenda.wak kak ganivulhut. nganyamörögumbuninya. Wina yu! wak kak gana ganavil.

'Crow is always eating our tucker there in that place we know. It's our tucker that he keeps walking on and eating with his back to us. He would have spoilt it all. Crow eats our tucker. He climbs on top with his back to us. It's all Crow's fault; he's climbing on top of the tucker over there with his back to us. Don't let crow eat it all. They should walk again on the earth outside now. Crow ought to let go of the tucker. I should sing all night for that stuff. Satisfied, Crow goes away, flies away.'

SONG STRUCTURE SUMMARY

VOCAL SECTION 1

Melodic section 1

Text phrase 1

Rhythmic mode 1 (without clapsticks)

aa	karra	kana	-kalkal	rtadi	nganggu	-ga	kaya	yawa	-ndha
SW	SW	3MIN.S.R walk	climb	on top	1/2MIN.PRO	TOP	3MIN.S.R lie	3MIN.ANAPH DEIC	really

Ah, he is always climbing on top of our stuff there

Melodic section 2

Text phrase 2

Rhythmic mode 1 (without clapsticks)

aa	karra	wak	kana	-kalkal	rtadi	nganggu	-ga	kaya	yawa	-ndha
SW	SW	crow	3MIN.S.R walk	-climb	on top	1/2MIN.PRO	TOP	3MIN.S.R lie	3MIN. ANAPH.DEIC	really

Ah, Crow is always climbing on top of our stuff there

INSTRUMENTAL SECTION 1

Rhythmic mode 2 (slow even)

VOCAL SECTION 2

Melodic section 1

Text phrase 1

Rhythmic mode 1 (without clapsticks)

aa	karra	wak	-ngana	-yi
SW	SW	crow	from	PERF

Ah, it was because of Crow

kana	-kalkal	rtadi	nganggu	-ga	kaya	yawa	-ndha
3MIN.S.R walk	climb-	on top	1/2MIN.PRO	TOP	3MIN.S.Rlie	3MIN.ANAPH DEIC	really

who is always climbing on top of our stuff there

INSTRUMENTAL SECTION 2

Rhythmic mode 4a (moderate even)

VOCAL SECTION 3

Melodic section 1

Text phrase 1

Rhythmic mode 1 (without clapsticks)

aa	karra	wak	-ngana	-yi
SW	SW	crow	from	PERF

Ah, it was because of Crow

kana	-kalkal	rtadi	nganggu	-ga	kaya	yawa	-ndha
3MIN.S.R walk	climb-	on top	½MIN.PRO	TOP	3MIN.S.R lie	3MIN.ANAPH DEIC	really

who is always climbing on top of our stuff there

INSTRUMENTAL SECTION 3

Rhythmic mode 2 (slow even)

VOCAL SECTION 4

Melodic section 1

Text phrase 1

Rhythmic mode 1 (without clapsticks)

aa	karra	wak	-ngana	-yi
SW	SW	crow	from	PERF

Ah, it was because of Crow

kana	-putput	rtadi	nganggu	-ga	kaya	yawa	-ndha
3MIN.S.R walk-	walk	on top	½MIN.PRO	TOP	3MIN.S.R lie	3MIN.ANAPH DEIC	really

who is always walking on top of our stuff there

INSTRUMENTAL SECTION 4

Rhythmic mode 4a (moderate even)

VOCAL SECTION 5

Melodic section 1

Text phrase 1

Rhythmic mode 1 (without clapsticks)

aa	karra	wak	-ngana	-yi
SW	SW	crow	from	PERF

Ah, it was because of Crow

kana	-putput	rtadi	nganggu	-ga	kaya	yawa	-ndha
3MIN.S.R walk-	walk	on top	½MIN.PRO	TOP	3MIN.S.R lie	3MIN.ANAPH DEIC	really

who is always walking on top of our stuff there

Melodic section 2

Text phrase 2

Rhythmic mode 1 (without clapsticks)

aa	karra	wak	-ngana	-yi
SW	SW	crow	from	PERF

Ah, it was because of Crow

kana	-kalkal	rtadi	nganggu	-ga	kaya	yawa	-ndha
3MIN.S.R walk	climb-	on top	½MIN.PRO	TOP	3MIN.S.Rlie	3MIN.ANAPH DEIC	really

who is always climbing on top of our stuff there

INSTRUMENTAL SECTION 5

Rhythmic mode 4a (moderate even)

VOCAL SECTION 6

Melodic section 1

Text phrase 1

Rhythmic mode 1 (without clapsticks)

aa	karra	wak	-ngana	-yi
SW	SW	crow	from	PERF

Ah, it was because of Crow

kana	-putput	rtadi	nganggu	-ga	kaya	yawa	-ndha
3MIN.S.R walk-	walk	on top	½MIN.PRO	TOP	3MIN.S.R lie	3MIN.ANAPH DEIC	really

who is always walking on top of our stuff there

INSTRUMENTAL SECTION 6

Rhythmic mode 4a (moderate even)

VOCAL SECTION 7

Melodic section 1

Text phrase 1

Rhythmic mode 1 (without clapsticks)

aa	karra	wak	-ngana	-yi
SW	SW	crow	from	PERF

Ah, it was because of Crow

kana	-putput	rtadi	nganggu	-ga	kaya	yawa	-ndha
3MIN.S.R walk-	Walk	on top	½MIN.PRO	TOP	3MIN.S.R lie	3MIN.ANAPH DEIC	really

who is always walking on top of our stuff there

Melodic section 2

Text phrase 2

Rhythmic mode 1 (without clapsticks)

aa	karra	wak	-ngana	-yi
SW	SW	crow	from	PERF

Ah, it was because of Crow

kana	-kalkal	rtadi	nganggu	-ga	kaya	yawa	-ndha
3MIN.S.R walk	climb-	on top	½MIN.PRO	TOP	3MIN.S.Rlie	3MIN.ANAPH DEIC	really

who is always walking on top of our stuff there

INSTRUMENTAL SECTION 7

Rhythmic mode 4e (moderate doubled)

TRACK 8 (Moy68-02-s04)

Song 4: Wörörö

Sung text	Free translation
karra ngany-ngana-yi	This was from me
karra nganya-rtadi-mbele thawara ngayi	Let me always walk on top of the mangrove for you
karra ngany-ngana-yi	This was from me
karra nganya-rtadi-mbele thawara ngayi-nö	I will always walk on top of the mangrove for you
ö	Ö

Like 'Wak,' this song about *Wörörö* (Crab) Dreaming shows Muluk's love of minimal textual variation. The two couplets, 'This was from me/Let me always walk on top of the mangrove for you' and 'This was from me/I will always walk on top of the mangrove for you' are almost identical. The only difference in the original Mendhe is that the second couplet ends with *-nö*, a morpheme that is not present at the end of the first couplet.

At the beginning of each couplet, the song-giving ghost states: 'this'—that is, the song—'is from me.' The association of this text with 'Crab' comes from the second text phrase, reflecting the fact that people have to walk on the sharp mangrove spikes when crabbing. The significance of the song is no longer fully understood. Perhaps the speaker is getting crabs for a sweetheart, but we can assume that, as with other *wangga*, there is also a deeper significance relating to death.[6]

Muluk gave Alice Moyle the following spoken text about Crab, which, together with the sung text, has been discussed elsewhere in more detail by Ford (2007, p 78).

> *Awa wörörör kaknganawandhinö wörörör. Pörrme karrabidjendan. Tjinbilirr nganiyulhuk. Awanö nganyanöve. Ngaden kaneneyi wörörör yene yeri. Nganalhukngungaya. Kanangalhat. Ngarragumbudirr. Ngundanma yene beyik. Nganaya ngandan nganyadut. Nganyanöve. Ngundanma yene beyik. Ngandhivelhe kakdjen nganakal.*

'I will always go away and follow crab. The tide is out again. I go into the mangrove swamp. I'll always sing for [crab]. I saw crab sitting in a hole. I'm entering the hole, facing away from me, against my will. It bites me, I grab the claw. I put it into the bag. I walk away, I hang up the bag, I find a crab. I'll always sing for [the creature]. I put it into the bag. I got it for you and I'm climbing up [out of the mangrove swamp].'

Here, as in the other songs recorded at the Mandorah tourist corroboree in 1968 (tracks 1, 5 and 7), there are many vocal sections—nine in all. As Marett has observed elsewhere (Marett, 2005, p 88), danced performances—particularly those for tourists—tend to have a greater number of vocal sections than non-danced performances.

---

6   In his discussion of the Murinbata (Murriny Patha) myth of Old Crow and Old Crab, Stanner reports that the Murinbata (Murriny Patha) 'maintained that crabs did not die if left unmolested. When they grew old they changed their shells and renewed their youth and strength' (Stanner, 1989 (1963), p 155). It is intriguing that Muluk performed his Crow and Crab songs consecutively.

SONG STRUCTURE SUMMARY

VOCAL SECTIONS 1–9

Melodic section 1

Text phrase 1

Rhythmic mode 1 (without clapsticks)

karra	ngany	-ngana	-yi
SW	1MIN.PRO	from	PERF

This was from me

Text phrase 2

Rhythmic mode 1 (without clapsticks)

karra	nganya	-rtadi	-mbele	thawara	ngayi
SW	1MIN.S.IR walk	back	2MIN.BEN	mangrove	1MIN.S.IR lie

Let me always walk on top of the mangrove for you

Text phrase 3

Rhythmic mode 1 (without clapsticks)

karra	ngany	-ngana	-yi
SW	1MIN.PRO	from	PERF

This was from me

Text phrase 4

Rhythmic mode 1 (without clapsticks)

karra	nganya	-rtadi	-mbele	thawara	ngayi	-nö
SW	1MIN.S.IR walk	back	2MIN.BEN	mangrove	1MIN.S.IR lie	PURP

I will always walk on top of the mangrove for you

Text phrase 5

Rhythmic mode 1 (without clapsticks)

ö
SW

Ö

INSTRUMENTAL SECTIONS 1–2

Rhythmic mode 2 (slow even)

INSTRUMENTAL SECTION 3

Rhythmic mode 4a (moderate even)

INSTRUMENTAL SECTIONS 4–8

Rhythmic mode 2 (slow even)

INSTRUMENTAL SECTION 9

Rhythmic mode 4e (moderate doubled)

TRACK 9 (Moy62-26-21)

Song 5: Pumandjin

Sung text	Free translation
ee	Ee
karra kana-nga-mu-viye karru	She [Numbali] is dancing [making a deliberate movement of her hands above her head]
viye pumandjin yakarre	On top of Pumandjin, yakarre!
ee	Ee
karra kama-ngana-yi	It [the song] came from she [Numbali] who is standing
kana-nga-mu-viye karru viye pumandjin yakarre	Dancing [making a deliberate movement of her hands above head] on top of Pumandjin, yakarre!
ee	Ee
karra kama-ngana-yi	It [the song] came from she [Numbali] who is standing Dancing
kana nga-mu-viye	[making a movement of her hands above head]
karra kama-ngana-yi	It [the song] came from she [Numbali] who is standing
kana-nga-mu-viye karru yawa-ndha	dancing [making a deliberate movement of her hands above head], truly there
ee	Ee

This song, recorded by Alice Moyle at Bagot in 1962, is about Jimmy Muluk's deceased sister, Numbali (not explicitly named in the song), who is dancing on the top of Pumandjin, a hill behind Mica Beach (Muluk's long-time place of residence, previously mentioned in the text of 'Puliki' [track 1]). Although his ancestral country lay far away, to the south of the Daly River, Jimmy Muluk had a particularly strong association with this local area, now known as Talc Head, which in the 1960s and 1970s was also the site of a camp for tourists for whom Muluk regularly performed his *wangga*. The text states that the song comes from 'her', that is his sister, and precisely describes her dancing movements—a particular movement of the hands above the head that is characteristic of women's dancing in this area.

In its playful variation of text, melody and rhythm, this song is typical of Jimmy Muluk's corpus.

Figure 5.5 In 2011, relatives of Jimmy Muluk in Belyuen identified this dancer as his sister Numbali, dancing at the tourist corroboree, Mica Beach, September 1972. Photograph by Allan Laurence.

SONG STRUCTURE SUMMARY

VOCAL SECTION 1

Melodic section 1

Text phrase 1

Rhythmic mode 1 (without clapsticks)

ee
SW

Ee

Melodic section 2

Text phrase 2

Rhythmic mode 1 (without clapsticks)

karra	kana	-nga	-mu	-viye	karru
SW	3MIN.S.R walk	3MIN.F.REFL	do	head	3MIN.S.R travel

She [Numbali] is dancing [making a deliberate movement of her hands above her head]

Muluk's repertory • 175

viye	pumandjin	yakarre
head	place-name	EXCL

on top of Pumandjin, *yakarre*!

INSTRUMENTAL SECTION 1

Rhythmic mode 4a (moderate even)

VOCAL SECTION 2

Melodic section 1

Text phrase 1

Rhythmic mode 1 (without clapsticks)

ee
SW

Ee

Melodic section 2

Text phrase 2

Rhythmic mode 1 (without clapsticks)

karra	kama	-ngana	-yi
SW	3MIN.S.R.stand	from	PERF

It [the song] came from she [Numbali] who is standing

kana	-nga	-mu	-viye	karru	viye	pumandjin	yakarre
3MIN.S.R walk	3MIN.F.REFL	do	head	3MIN.S.R travel	head	place-name	EXCL

dancing [making a deliberate movement of her hands above head] on top of Pumandjin, *yakarre*!

INSTRUMENTAL SECTION 2

Rhythmic mode 4a (moderate even)

VOCAL SECTION 3

Melodic section 1

Text phrase 1

Rhythmic mode 1 (without clapsticks)

ee
SW

Ee

Text phrase 2

Rhythmic mode 4a (moderate even)

karra	**kama**	**-ngana**	**-yi**
SW	3MIN.S.R.stand	from	PERF

It [the song] came from she [Numbali] who is standing

kana	**nga**	**-mu**	**-viye**
3MIN.S.R walk	3MIN.F.REFL	do	head

dancing [making a movement of her hands above head]

INSTRUMENTAL SECTION 3

Rhythmic mode 4a (moderate even)

VOCAL SECTION 4

Melodic section 1

Text phrase 1

Rhythmic mode 1 (without clapsticks)

karra	**kama**	**-ngana**	**-yi**
SW	3MIN.S.R.stand	from	PERF

It [the song] came from she [Numbali] who is standing

kana	**-nga**	**-mu**	**-viye**	**karru**	**yawa**	**-ndha**
3MIN.S.R walk	3MIN.F.REFL	do	head	3MIN.S.R travel	3MIN.ANAPH DEIC	really

dancing [making a deliberate movement of her hands above head], truly there

Melodic section 2

Text phrase 2

Rhythmic mode 4a (moderate even)

ee
SW

Ee

INSTRUMENTAL SECTION 4

Rhythmic mode 4a (moderate even)

TRACKS 10–12 A General Introduction

Song 6: Piyamen.ga

Five consecutive items (tracks 10–12), of 'Piyamen.ga' (Shady Tree) were recorded at a *burnim-rag* ceremony at Bagot by Alice Moyle in 1962. Tracks 10 and 12 each contain two inseparable items, with the didjeridu stopping and immediately restarting before the final instrumental section of the first item of each pair is completed. Each of the five items in the set comprises a number of vocal sections, which combine text elements and rhythmic modes in a variety of different ways. For more detail, see the musical analysis section at the end of this chapter. Vocal sections in this song comprise 1, 2 or rarely 3 melodic sections.

In this performance of 'Piyamen.ga' Muluk uses three different texts, which he combines in various ways, always to create a three-phrase melodic section. When Muluk fragments these texts and re-combines elements from one text with those from another to form a new melodic or vocal section, we see him ringing the changes on his text as nowhere else in his repertory.

Sung text	Free translation
Text A	
karra yenetpi yenetpiwe yenetpirrang	karra yenetpi yenetpiwe yenetpirran
karra yenetpi yenetpiwe yenetpirrang	karra yenetpi yenetpiwe yenetpirrang
karra yenetpirrang	karra yenetpirrang
Text B	
karra kana-nga-lhumbu kaya yawa-ndha	She [a ngutj] is always lying in number four leg truly there
Text C	
karra ngany-ngana-yi ngula-pit-kumbu ngiya ö	This song is from me, who always cleans the ground with my foot
karra piyamen.ga ngani-gurriny	Under my shady tree
karra ngiya-pit dörr	I always clean the ground

Text A is entirely in ghost language and represents an untranslated utterance by the song-giving ghost *(ngutj)*. Text B is in Mendhe and describes the song-giving ghost lying in 'number four leg,' that is, with one foot crossed over the knee of the other leg—a posture often adopted by song-giving ghosts and by songmen when receiving songs from ghosts.[7] Text C, which is also in Mendhe, represents the song-giving ghost's own description of herself sweeping the ground with her foot under her shady tree. This sweeping movement is used by women dancers in this song.

Muluk presents these texts in full, but he also fragments and recombines elements of them (see the notes for each track below, and the musical analysis section of this chapter for further analysis).

---

7   The pose is also mentioned in songs in most other *wangga* repertories (see chapters 6-9), the exception being Barrtjap (chapter 4).

Figure 5.6 Henry Jorrock performing a standing version of the number four leg pose, Belyuen, 1997. Photograph by Linda Barwick, reproduced with the permission of Belyuen community.

TRACK 10 (Moy62-26-s15_16)
Song 6: Piyamen.ga

Sung text	Free translation
Item 1	
karra yenetpi yenetpiwe yenetpirrang	Karra yenetpi yenetpiwe yenetpirrang
karra yenetpi yenetpiwe yenetpirrang	Karra yenetpi yenetpiwe yenetpirrang
karra yenetpirrang	Karra yenetpirrang
karra yenetpi yenetpiwe yenetpirrang	Karra yenetpi yenetpiwe yenetpirrang
karra yenetpi yenetpiwe yenetpirrang	Karra yenetpi yenetpiwe yenetpirrang
karra yenetpirrang	Karra yenetpirrang
karra yenetpi yenetpiwe yenetpirrang	Karra yenetpi yenetpiwe yenetpirrang
karra yenetpi yenetpiwe yenetpirrang	Karra yenetpi yenetpiwe yenetpirrang
karra yenetpirrang	Karra yenetpirrang
karra yenetpi yenetpiwe yenetpirrang	Karra yenetpi yenetpiwe yenetpirrang
karra yenetpi yenetpiwe yenetpirrang	Karra yenetpi yenetpiwe yenetpirrang
karra yenetpirrang	Karra yenetpirrang
Item 2	
karra yenetpi yenetpiwe yenetpirrang	Karra yenetpi yenetpiwe yenetpirrang
karra yenetpi yenetpiwe yenetpirrang	Karra yenetpi yenetpiwe yenetpirrang
karra yenetpirrang	Karra yenetpirrang
karra yenetpi yenetpiwe yenetpirrang	Karra yenetpi yenetpiwe yenetpirrang
karra yenetpi yenetpiwe yenetpirrang	Karra yenetpi yenetpiwe yenetpirrang
karra yenetpirrang	Karra yenetpirrang
karra kana-nga-lhumbu kaya yawa-ndha	She [a ngutj] is always lying in number four leg truly there
karra kana-nga-lhumbu kaya yawa-ndha	She [a ngutj] is always lying in number four leg truly there
karra yenetpirrang	Karra yenetpirrang
karra yenetpi yenetpiwe yenetpirrang	Karra yenetpi yenetpiwe yenetpirrang
karra yenetpi yenetpiwe yenetpirrang	Karra yenetpi yenetpiwe yenetpirrang
karra yenetpirrang	Karra yenetpirrang

As mentioned in the general introduction to 'Piyamen.ga,' item 1 and three of the four vocal sections of item 2 consist only of Text A. Text B is introduced in vocal section 3 of item 2 where it is repeated and then followed by a fragment (the last text phrase) of Text A. The variant form of rhythmic mode 4a is used in vocal sections 2 and 3 of both item 1 and 2.

SONG STRUCTURE SUMMARY

Item 1 (Moy62-26-s15)

VOCAL SECTION 1

Melodic section 1

Text phrases 1–3

Rhythmic mode 4a (moderate even)

karra yenetpi yenetpiwe yenetpirrang
karra yenetpi yenetpiwe yenetpirrang
karra yenetpirrang

Melodic section 2

Text phrases 4–6

Rhythmic mode 4a (moderate even)

karra yenetpi yenetpiwe yenetpirrang
karra yenetpi yenetpiwe yenetpirrang
karra yenetpirrang

INSTRUMENTAL SECTION 1

Rhythmic mode 4a

VOCAL SECTION 2

Melodic section 1

Text phrases 1–3

Rhythmic mode 4a (var) (moderate even, with beating initially very quiet then crescendo throughout text phrase 3)

karra yenetpi yenetpiwe yenetpirrang
karra yenetpi yenetpiwe yenetpirrang
karra yenetpirrang

INSTRUMENTAL SECTION 2

Rhythmic mode 4a (moderate even)

VOCAL SECTION 3

Melodic section 1

Text phrases 1–3

Rhythmic mode 4a (var) (moderate even, with beating initially very quiet then crescendo throughout text phrase 3)

karra yenetpi yenetpiwe yenetpirrang
karra yenetpi yenetpiwe yenetpirrang
karra yenetpirrang

INSTRUMENTAL SECTION 3

Rhythmic mode 4a (moderate even)

Item 2 (Moy62-26-s16)

VOCAL SECTION 1

Melodic section 1

Text phrases 1–3

Rhythmic mode 4a (moderate even)
karra yenetpi yenetpiwe yenetpirrang
karra yenetpi yenetpiwe yenetpirrang
karra yenetpirrang

INSTRUMENTAL SECTION 1

Rhythmic mode 4a (moderate even)

VOCAL SECTION 2

Melodic section 1

Text phrases 1–3

Rhythmic mode 4a (var) (moderate even, with beating initially very quiet then crescendo throughout text phrase 3)

karra yenetpi yenetpiwe yenetpirrang
karra yenetpi yenetpiwe yenetpirrang
karra yenetpirrang

Melodic section 2

Text phrases 4

Rhythmic mode 4a (moderate even)

karra	kana	-nga	-lhumbu	kaya	yawa	-ndha
SW	3MIN.S.R walk	3MIN.F.REFL	thigh	3MIN.S.R lie	3MIN.ANAPH DEIC	really

She [a *ngutj*] is always lying in number four leg truly there

Text phrases 5

Rhythmic mode 4a (moderate even)

karra	kana	-nga	-lhumbu	kaya	yawa	-ndha
SW	3MIN.S.R walk	3MIN.F.REFL	thigh	3MIN.S.R lie	3MIN.ANAPH DEIC	really

She [a *ngutj*] is always lying in number four leg truly there

Text phrase 6

Rhythmic mode 4a (moderate even)

karra yenetpirrang

INSTRUMENTAL SECTION 2

Rhythmic mode 4a (moderate even)

VOCAL SECTION 3

Melodic section 1

Text phrases 1–3

Rhythmic mode 4a (var) (moderate even, with beating initially very quiet then crescendo throughout text phrase 3)

karra yenetpi yenetpiwe yenetpirrang
karra yenetpi yenetpiwe yenetpirrang
karra yenetpirrang

INSTRUMENTAL SECTION 3

Rhythmic mode 4a (moderate even)

TRACK 11 (Moy62-26-s17)

Song 6: Piyamen.ga

Sung text	Free translation
Item 3	
karra yenetpi yenetpiwe ngiya-pit dörr	Karra yenetpi yenetpiwe; I always clean the ground.
karra yenetpi yenetpiwe ngiya-pit dörr	Karra yenetpi yenetpiwe; I always clean the ground.
karra yenet-pit dörr	I always clean the ground.
karra yenetpi yenetpiwe ngiya-pit dörr	Karra yenetpi yenetpiwe ngiya-pit dörr
karra yenetpi yenetpiwe ngiya-pit dörr	Karra yenetpi yenetpiwe ngiya-pit dörr
karra yenet-pit dörr	Karra yenet-pit dörr
karra kana-nga-lhumbu kaya yawa-ndha	She [a *ngutj*] is always lying in number four leg truly there
karra kana-nga-lhumbu kaya yawa-ndha	She [a *ngutj*] is always lying in number four leg truly there
karra ngiya-pit dörr	I always clean the ground
karra yenetpi yenetpiwe ngiya-pit dörr	Karra yenetpi yenetpiwe I always clean the ground.
karra yenetpi yenetpiwe ngiya-pit dörr	Karra yenetpi yenetpiwe I always clean the ground.
karra ngiya-pit dörr	I always clean the ground.
karra yenetpi yenetpiwe ngiya-pit dörr	Karra yenetpi yenetpiwe I always clean the ground.
karra yenetpi yenetpiwe ngiya-pit dörr	Karra yenetpi yenetpiwe I always clean the ground.
karra ngiya-pit dörr	I always clean the ground.
karra ngany-ngana-yi ngula-pit-kumbu ngiya ö	It [the song] is from me, who always cleans it [the ground] with my foot ö.
karra piyamen.ga ngani-gurriny	[Under] my shady tree.
karra ngiya-pit dörr	I always clean the ground.
karra yenetpi yenetpiwe ngiya-pit dörr	Karra yenetpi yenetpiwe I always clean the ground.
karra yenetpi yenetpiwe ngiya-pit dörr	Karra yenetpi yenetpiwe I always clean the ground.
karra ngiya-pit dörr	I always clean the ground.

At the end of vocal section 3 of item 3, Muluk introduces Text 3 for the first time. But even before he does this, he takes the fragment of this text (the last text phrase, '[karra] ngiya-it dörr') that he combined with Text B in the following item, and now combines it with a fragment of Text A 'Karra yenetpi yenitpiwe' to create the text seen in melodic section 1 of vocal section 1 as well as in a number of later melodic sections. In the third melodic section of vocal section 1 he once again combines this Text C fragment with Text B.

SONG STRUCTURE SUMMARY

Item 3 (Moy62-26-s17)

VOCAL SECTION 1

Melodic section 1

Text phrases 1–3

Rhythmic mode 4a (moderate even)
karra yenetpi yenetpiwe ngiya-pit dörr
karra yenetpi yenetpiwe ngiya-pit dörr
karra ngiya-pit dörr

Melodic section 2

Text phrases 3–5

Rhythmic mode 4a (moderate even)
karra yenetpi yenetpiwe ngiya-pit dörr
karra yenetpi yenetpiwe ngiya-pit dörr
karra ngiya-pit dörr

Melodic section 3

Text phrases 6

Rhythmic mode 4a (moderate even)

karra	**kana**	**-nga**	**-lhumbu**	**kaya**	**yawa**	**-ndha**
SW	3MIN.S.R walk	3MIN.F.REFL	thigh	3MIN.S.R lie	3MIN.ANAPH DEIC	really

She [a *ngutj*] is always lying in number four leg truly there

Text phrases 7

Rhythmic mode 4a (moderate even)

karra	**kana**	**-nga**	**-lhumbu**	**kaya**	**yawa**	**-ndha**
SW	3MIN.S.R walk	3MIN.F.REFL	thigh	3MIN.S.R lie	3MIN.ANAPH DEIC	really

She [a *ngutj*] is always lying in number four leg truly there

Text phrase 8

Rhythmic mode 4a (moderate even)
Karra ngiya-pit dörr

INSTRUMENTAL SECTION 1

Rhythmic mode 4a (moderate even)

VOCAL SECTION 2

Melodic section 1

Text phrases 1–3

Rhythmic mode 4a (var) (moderate even, with beating initially very quiet then crescendo throughout text phrase 3)

karra yenetpi yenetpiwe ngiya-pit dörr
karra yenetpi yenetpiwe ngiya-pit dörr
karra ngiya-pit dörr

INSTRUMENTAL SECTION 2

Rhythmic mode 4a (moderate even)

VOCAL SECTION 3

Melodic section 1

Text phrases 1–3

Rhythmic mode 4a (var) (moderate even, with beating initially suspended then crescendo throughout)
karra yenetpi yenetpiwe ngiya-pit dörr
karra yenetpi yenetpiwe ngiya-pit dörr
karra ngiya-pit dörr

Melodic section 2

Text phrase 4

Rhythmic mode 4a (moderate even)

karra	ngany	-ngana	-yi	ngula	-pit	-kumbu	ngiya	ö
SW	1MIN.PRO	from	PERF	1MIN.finger	clean	foot	1MIN.S.R lie	SW

It [the song] is from me, who always cleans it [the ground] with my foot.

Text phrase 5

Rhythmic mode 4a (moderate even)

karra	piyamen.ga	ngani	-gurriny
SW	tree sp.	1MIN.PRO	POSS

[Under] my shady tree.

Text phrase 6

Rhythmic mode 4a (moderate even)

karra	ngiya	-pit	dörr
SW	1.MIN.S.R lie	clean	ground

I always clean the ground.

INSTRUMENTAL SECTION 3

Rhythmic mode 4a (moderate even)

VOCAL SECTION 4

Melodic section 1

Text phrases 1–3

Rhythmic mode 4a (var) (moderate even, with beating initially suspended then crescendo throughout)
karra yenetpi yenetpiwe ngiya-pit dörr
karra yenetpi yenetpiwe ngiya-pit dörr
karra ngiya-pit dörr

INSTRUMENTAL SECTION 4

Rhythmic mode 4a (moderate even)

TRACK 12 (Moy62-26-s18_19)

Song 6: Piyamen.ga

Sung text	Free translation
Item 4	
karra yenetpi yenetpiwe ngiya-pit dörr	Karra yenetpi yenetpiwe I always clean the ground
karra yenetpi yenetpiwe ngiya-pit dörr	Karra yenetpi yenetpiwe I always clean the ground
karra ngiya-pit dörr	I always clean the ground
karra ngany-ngana-yi ngula-pit-kumbu ngiya ö	This song is from me, who always cleans the ground with my foot ö.
karra piyamen.ga ngani-gurriny	[Under] my shady tree.
karra ngiya-pit dörr	I always clean the ground.
karra yenetpi yenetpiwe ngiya-pit dörr	Karra yenetpi yenetpiwe I always clean the ground
karra yenetpi yenetpiwe ngiya-pit dörr	Karra yenetpi yenetpiwe I always clean the ground
karra ngiya-pit dörr	I always clean the ground
karra ngany-ngana-yi ngula-pit-kumbu ngiya ö	This song is from me, who always cleans the ground with my foot ö.
karra piyamen.ga ngani-gurriny	[Under] my shady tree.
karra ngiya-pit dörr	I always clean the ground.
Item 5	
karra yenetpi yenetpiwe ngiya-pit dörr	Karra yenetpi yenetpiwe I always clean the ground
karra yenetpi yenetpiwe ngiya-pit dörr	Karra yenetpi yenetpiwe I always clean the ground
karra ngiya-pit dörr	I always clean the ground
karra yenetpi yenetpiwe ngiya-pit dörr	Karra yenetpi yenetpiwe I always clean the ground
karra yenetpi yenetpiwe ngiya-pit dörr	Karra yenetpi yenetpiwe I always clean the ground
karra ngiya-pit dörr	I always clean the ground
karra ngany-ngana-yi ngula-pit-kumbu ngiya ö	This song is from me, who always cleans the ground with my foot ö.
karra piyamen.ga ngani-gurriny	[Under] my shady tree.
karra ngiya-pit dörr	I always clean the ground.

The melodic and vocal sections of items 4 and 5 comprise only two text forms: either the combined fragments of Texts A and C seen in the previous item, or one complete iteration of Text C.

SONG STRUCTURE SUMMARY

Item 4 (Moy62-26-s18)

VOCAL SECTION 1

Melodic section 1

Text phrases 1–2

Rhythmic mode 4a (moderate even)

karra yenetpi yenetpiwe ngiya-pit dörr
karra yenetpi yenetpiwe ngiya-pit dörr
karra ngiya-pit dörr

Melodic section 2

Text phrase 4

Rhythmic mode 4a (moderate even)

karra	**ngany**	**-ngana**	**-yi**	**ngula**	**-pit**	**-kumbu**	**ngiya**	**ö**
SW	1MIN.PRO	from	PERF	1MIN.finger	clean	foot	1MIN.S.R lie	SW

It [the song] is from me, who always cleans it [the ground] with my foot.

Text phrase 5

Rhythmic mode 4a (moderate even)

karra	**piyamen.ga**	**ngani**	**-gurriny**
SW	tree sp.	1MIN.PRO	POSS

[Under] my shady tree

Text phrase 6

Rhythmic mode 4a (moderate even)

karra	**ngiya**	**-pit**	**dörr**
SW	1.MIN.S.R lie	clean	ground

I always clean the ground.

INSTRUMENTAL SECTION 1

Rhythmic mode 4a (moderate even)

VOCAL SECTION 2

Melodic section 1

Text phrases 1–2

Rhythmic mode 4a (var) (moderate even, with beating initially suspended then crescendo throughout)

karra yenetpi yenetpiwe ngiya-pit dörr
karra yenetpi yenetpiwe ngiya-pit dörr
karra ngiya-pit dörr

Melodic section 2

Text phrase 4

Rhythmic mode 4a (moderate even)

karra	ngany	-ngana	-yi	ngula	-pit	-kumbu	ngiya	ö
SW	1MIN.PRO	from	PERF	1MIN.finger	clean	foot	1MIN.S.R lie	SW

It [the song] is from me, who always cleans it [the ground] with my foot.

Text phrase 5

Rhythmic mode 4a (moderate even)

karra	piyamen.ga	ngani	-gurriny
SW	tree sp.	1MIN.PRO	POSS

[Under] my shady tree.

Text phrase 6

Rhythmic mode 4a (moderate even)

karra	ngiya	-pit	dörr
SW	1.MIN.S.R lie	clean	ground

I always clean the ground.

INSTRUMENTAL SECTION 2

Rhythmic mode 4a (moderate even)

Item 5 (Moy62-26-s19)

VOCAL SECTION 1

Melodic section 1

Text phrases 1–2

Rhythmic mode 4a (moderate even)
karra yenetpi yenetpiwe ngiya-pit dörr
karra yenetpi yenetpiwe ngiya-pit dörr
karra ngiya-pit dörr

INSTRUMENTAL SECTION 1

Rhythmic mode 4a (moderate even)

VOCAL SECTION 2

Melodic section 1

Text phrases 1–2

Rhythmic mode 4a (var) (moderate even, with beating initially suspended then crescendo throughout)
karra yenetpi yenetpiwe ngiya-pit dörr
karra yenetpi yenetpiwe ngiya-pit dörr
karra ngiya-pit dörr

Melodic section 2

Text phrase 4

Rhythmic mode 4a (moderate even)

karra	ngany	-ngana	-yi	ngula	-pit	-kumbu	ngiya	ö
SW	1MIN.PRO	from	PERF	1MIN.finger	clean	foot	1MIN.S.R lie	SW

It [the song] is from me, who always clean it [the ground] with my foot.

Text phrase 5

Rhythmic mode 4a (moderate even)

karra	piyamen.ga	ngani	-gurriny
SW	tree sp.	1MIN.PRO	POSS

[Under] my shady tree.

Text phrase 6

Rhythmic mode 4a (moderate even)

karra	**ngiya**	**-pit**	**dörr**
SW	1.MIN.S.R lie	clean	ground

I always clean the ground.

INSTRUMENTAL SECTION 2

Rhythmic mode 4a (moderate even)

Figure 5.7 This picture from a tourist corroboree, Mica Beach, September 1972, may show the dance for 'Lame Fella' (song 7). Photograph by Allan Laurence, reproduced with the permission of Belyuen community.

TRACK 13 (Moy62-26-s06)

Song 7: Lame Fella (slow version)

Sung text	Free translation
yele mele delhe	Yele mele delhe
yele mele delhe	Yele mele delhe
yele mele delhe	Yele mele delhe
yele mele delhe	Yele mele delhe
karra kuman-na-dherr pöndör kaya yawa-ndha	He is always truly there propping his cheek on his hand with his elbow bent

At the beginning of this track, Wadjiginy songman Brian Enda is recorded giving the following explanation in Aboriginal English to Alice Moyle, saying that the song is about a lame man. Lameness is associated with the dead, and limping movements are often included in men's dancing. In the slow version (track 13), each vocal section comprises text in both ghost language and Mendhe. The text in Mendhe describes the 'lame fella' as being 'always truly there propping his cheek on his hand with his elbow bent.'

> What's the name? Old man, lame fella. That, down this way. Old man, lame fella. Im bin very lame, when im bin lay down, im bin you know cripple fella. This one corroboree, that's what they bin gettim.

> 'What's the name of the song? Lame man. That [comes from] down this way. This old lame man was very lame, he was lying down, he was a cripple. This is the corroboree song they received.'

Lying down leaning on one elbow and propping one's head on a hand is associated with receiving songs from ghosts, and is a posture occasionally adopted by old men in ritual dancing.

'Lame Fella' is performed using two contrasting tempi. In this track, the song is performed in a slow version, while on track 14 we hear a version with fast even beating (see further details in the musical analysis section of this chapter).

SONG STRUCTURE SUMMARY

VOCAL SECTION 1

Melodic section 1

Text phrases 1–4

Rhythmic mode 2b (slow even, stick beating suspended)

yele mele delhe
yele mele delhe
yele mele delhe
yele mele delhe

Text phrase 5

Rhythmic mode 2b (slow even, stick beating suspended)

karra	**kuman**	**-na**	**-dherr**	**pöndör**	**kaya**	**yawa**	**-ndha**
SW	3MIN.A.R poke	3MIN.M.REFL	cheek	elbow	3MIN.S.R lie	3MIN.ANAPH DEIC	really

He is always truly there propping his cheek on his hand with his elbow bent

INSTRUMENTAL SECTION 1

Rhythmic mode 4a (moderate even) with Walakandha wangga cueing pattern

VOCAL SECTIONS 2–4

Melodic section 1

Text phrases 1–4

Rhythmic mode 2a (slow even)

yele mele delhe
yele mele delhe
yele mele delhe
yele mele delhe

Text phrase 5

Rhythmic mode 2b (slow even, stick beating suspended)

karra	**kuman**	**-na**	**-dherr**	**pöndör**	**kaya**	**yawa**	**-ndha**
SW	3MIN.A.R poke	3MIN.M.REFL	cheek	elbow	3MIN.S.R lie	3MIN.ANAPH DEIC	really

He is always truly there propping his cheek on his hand with his elbow bent

INSTRUMENTAL SECTION 2

Rhythmic mode 4a (moderate even)

INSTRUMENTAL SECTION 3

Rhythmic mode 4* (moderate doubled followed by moderate even)

INSTRUMENTAL SECTION 4

Rhythmic mode 4e (moderate doubled)

TRACK 14 (Moy62-26-s09)

Song 7: Lame Fella (fast version)

Sung text	Free translation
yele mele dagaldja yawa-ndha mele dagaldja	Yele mele dagaldja truly there mele dagaldja
yele mele dagaldja yawa-ndha mele dagaldja	Yele mele dagaldja truly there mele dagaldja
yele mele dagaldja yawa-ndha mele dagaldja	Yele mele dagaldja truly there mele dagaldja
karra kana-ngana-yi kaya yawa-ndha	This [song] was from him who is always truly walking there
yele mele dagaldja yawa-ndha mele dagaldja	Yele mele dagaldja truly there mele dagaldja

The tune and the subject of track 14 are the same as for track 13. As in track 13, the text comprises text phrases in ghost language followed by a text phrase in Mendhe, but in track 14 the (largely) ghost language text and the (largely) Mendhe text are allocated to separate vocal sections. The Mendhe text asserts that this song 'was from him [that is, the "lame fella"] who is always truly walking there'. The use of the phrase 'always truly walking there' supports the idea that the 'lame fella' is some sort of totemic ghost.

Note that while the slow version accompanied the text about the ghost lying down, the fast version accompanies text in which the ghost is described as walking. We have previously encountered a similar use of tempo change to signify change in the activity of an ancestral ghost in Billy Mandji's version of 'Puliki' (track 2), where slow beating was associated with the ghostly Buffalo swimming, and fast beating with him dancing on Mica Beach.

SONG STRUCTURE SUMMARY

VOCAL SECTION 1

Melodic section 1

Text phrases 1–3

Rhythmic mode 5a (fast even)

yele	mele	dagaldja	yawa	-ndha	mele	dagaldja
SW	SW	SW	3MIN.ANAPH DEIC	really	SW	SW

Yele mele dagaldja truly there mele dagaldja

INSTRUMENTAL SECTION 1

Rhythmic mode 5a (fast even)

VOCAL SECTION 2

Melodic section 1

Text phrase 1

Rhythmic mode 5a (fast even)

karra	kana	-ngana	-yi	kaya	yawa	-ndha
SW	3MIN.S.R walk	from	PERF	3MIN.S.R lie	3MIN.ANAPH DEIC	really

This [song] was from him who is always truly walking there

Text phrase 2

Rhythmic mode 5a (fast even)

yele	mele	dagaldja	yawa	-ndha	mele	dagaldja
SW	SW	SW	3MIN.ANAPH DEIC	really	SW	SW

Yele mele dagaldja truly there mele dagaldja

INSTRUMENTAL SECTION 2

Rhythmic mode 5a (fast even)

VOCAL SECTION 3

Melodic section 1

Text phrases 1-3

Rhythmic mode 5a (fast even)

yele	mele	dagaldja	yawa	-ndha	mele	dagaldja
SW	SW	SW	3MIN.ANAPH DEIC	really	SW	SW

Yele mele dagaldja truly there mele dagaldja

INSTRUMENTAL SECTION 3

Rhythmic mode 5a (fast even)

VOCAL SECTION 4

Melodic section 1

Text phrase 1

Rhythmic mode 5a (fast even)

karra	kana	-ngana	-yi	kaya	yawa	-ndha
SW	3MIN.S.R.walk	from	PERF	3MIN.S.R lie	3MIN.ANAPH DEIC	really

This [song] was from him who is always truly walking there

Text phrase 2

Rhythmic mode 5a (fast even)

yele	mele	dagaldja	yawa	-ndha	mele	dagaldja
SW	SW	SW	3MIN.ANAPH DEIC	really	SW	SW

Yele mele dagaldja truly there mele dagaldja

INSTRUMENTAL SECTION 4

Rhythmic mode 5a (fast even)

TRACKS 15–17 A General Introduction

Song 8: Rtadi-thawara

It has not been possible to elicit very much information about the meaning of this song beyond what is presented in the Mendhe text, namely 'he always walks on the top of the mangroves.' In this case, 'he' is presumably some sort of totemic ghost, perhaps Crab (as in track 8). As is always the case when the singer himself is not available for consultation, there is some difficulty involved in transcribing the ghost language vocables. In the recording, the articulation of *dagele* is often so fast that it sounds at first like *dele*, though slowing down of the recording reveals the presence of the syllable *ge*.

Like 'Piyamen.ga' (tracks 10–12), this song consists of a number of items of the same song text. Here, as just seen for 'Lame Fella' (tracks 13 and 14), each item has a different rhythmic treatment of the text, although here the Mendhe text remains basically the same throughout, in each case describing the ghost 'walking'. The biggest contrast concerns rhythmic mode. This song is discussed in some detail in the musical analysis section at the end of this chapter.

TRACK 15 (Moy62-26-s10)

Song 8: Rtadi-thawara

Sung text	Free translation
Item 1	
rrene rrene rrene dagele dagele rrene	Rrene rrene rrene dagele dagele rrene
rrene rrene dagele dagele dagele rrene (twice)	Rrene rrene dagele dagele dagele rrene
karra kana-kumbu kaya rtadi thawara	He always walks on the top of the mangroves
rrene rrene rrene dagele dagele rrene	Rrene rrene rrene dagele dagele rrene
rrene rrene dagele dagele dagele rrene	Rrene rrene dagele dagele dagele rrene
ee	Ee
rrene rrene dagele dagele dagele rrene	Rrene rrene dagele dagele dagele rrene
rrene rrene rrene dagele dagele rrene	Rrene rrene rrene dagele dagele rrene
rrene rrene dagele dagele dagele rrene	Rrene rrene dagele dagele dagele rrene

SONG STRUCTURE SUMMARY

Item 1 (Moy62-26-s10)

VOCAL SECTION 1

Melodic section 1

Text phrases 1–2

Rhythmic mode 2b (slow even, stick beating suspended)
rrene rrene rrene dagele dagele rrene
rrene rrene dagele dagele dagele rrene

Melodic section 2

Text phrases 3–4

Rhythmic mode 2b (slow even, stick beating suspended)
rrene rrene rrene dagele dagele rrene
rrene rrene dagele dagele dagele rrene

Melodic section 3

Text phrase 5

Rhythmic mode 2b (slow even, stick beating suspended)

karra	kana	-kumbu	kaya	rtadi	thawara
SW	3MIN.S.R walk	foot	3MIN.S.R lie	on top	mangrove

He always walks on the top of the mangroves

INSTRUMENTAL SECTION 1

Rhythmic mode 4a (moderate even)

VOCAL SECTION 2

Melodic section

Text phrases 1–2

Rhythmic mode 2a (slow even)
rrene rrene rrene dagele dagele rrene
rrene rrene dagele dagele dagele rrene

Melodic section 2

Text phrases 3–4

Rhythmic mode 2b (slow even, stick beating suspended)
Ee
rrene rrene dagele dagele dagele rrene

INSTRUMENTAL SECTION 2

Rhythmic mode 4a (moderate even)

VOCAL SECTION 3

Melodic section 1

Text phrases 1–2

Rhythmic mode 2a (slow even)
rrene rrene rrene dagele dagele rrene
rrene rrene dagele dagele dagele rrene

INSTRUMENTAL SECTION 3

Rhythmic mode 4e (moderate doubled)

TRACK 16 (Moy62-26-s11_12)

Song 8: Rtadi-thawara

Sung text	Free translation
Item 2	
rrene rrene rrene dagele rrene	Rrene rrene rrene dagele rrene
rrene yelende dagele dagele rrene	Rrene yelende dagele dagele rrene
(twice)	
karra kana-kumbu kaya rtadi thawara yawa-ndha	He always walks on the top of the mangroves
rrene rrene rrene dagele rrene	Rrene rrene rrene dagele rrene
rrene yelende dagele dagele rrene	Rrene yelende dagele dagele rrene
karra kana-kumbu kaya rtadi thawara yawa-ndha	He always walks on the top of the mangroves
Item 3	
rrene rrene rrene dagele rrene	Rrene rrene rrene dagele rrene
rrene yelende dagele dagele rrene	Rrene yelende dagele dagele rrene
karra kana-kumbu kaya rtadi thawara yawa-ndha	He always walks on the top of the mangroves
(twice)	

SONG STRUCTURE SUMMARY

Item 2 (Moy62-26-s11)

VOCAL SECTION 1

Melodic section 1

Text phrases 1–2

Rhythmic mode 5c (fast uneven quadruple)
rrene rrene rrene dagele rrene
rrene yelende dagele dagele rrene

Melodic section 2

Text phrases 3–4

Rhythmic mode 5c (fast uneven quadruple)
rrene rrene rrene dagele rrene
rrene yelende dagele dagele rrene

Melodic section 3

Text phrase 5

Rhythmic mode 5c (fast uneven quadruple)

karra	kana	-kumbu	kaya	rtadi	thawara	yawa	-ndha
SW	3MIN.S.R walk	foot	3MIN.S.R lie	on top	mangrove	3MIN.ANAPH DEIC	really

He always walks on the top of the mangroves

INSTRUMENTAL SECTION 1

Rhythmic mode 5c (fast uneven quadruple)

VOCAL SECTION 2

Melodic section 1

Text phrases 1–2

Rhythmic mode 5c (fast uneven quadruple)
rrene rrene rrene dagele rrene
rrene yelende dagele dagele rrene

Melodic section 2

Text phrase 3

Rhythmic mode 5c (fast uneven quadruple)

karra	kana	-kumbu	kaya	rtadi	thawara	yawa	-ndha
SW	3MIN.S.R walk	foot	3MIN.S.R lie	on top	mangrove	3MIN.ANAPH DEIC	really

He always walks on the top of the mangroves

INSTRUMENTAL SECTION 2

Rhythmic mode 5c (fast uneven quadruple)

Item 3 (Moy62-26-s12)

VOCAL SECTION 1

Melodic section 1

Text phrases 1–2

Rhythmic mode 5c (fast uneven quadruple)
rrene rrene rrene dagele rrene
rrene yelende dagele dagele rrene

Melodic section 2

Text phrase 3

Rhythmic mode 5c (fast uneven quadruple)

karra	kana	-kumbu	kaya	rtadi	thawara	yawa	-ndha
SW	3MIN.S.R walk	foot	3MIN.S.R lie	on top	mangrove	3MIN.ANAPH DEIC	really

He always walks on the top of the mangroves

INSTRUMENTAL SECTION 1

Rhythmic mode 5c (fast uneven quadruple)

VOCAL SECTION 2

Melodic section 1

Text phrases 1–2

Rhythmic mode 5c (fast uneven quadruple)
rrene rrene rrene dagele rrene
rrene yelende dagele dagele rrene

Melodic section 2

Text phrase 3

Rhythmic mode 5c (fast uneven quadruple)

karra	kana	-kumbu	kaya	rtadi	thawara	yawa	-ndha
SW	3MIN.S.R walk	foot	3MIN.S.R lie	on top	mangrove	3MIN.ANAPH DEIC	really

He always walks on the top of the mangroves

INSTRUMENTAL SECTION 2

Rhythmic mode 5c (fast uneven quadruple)

TRACK 17 (Moy62-26-s13_14)

Song 8: Rtadi-thawara

Sung text	Free translation
Item 4	
rrene yelende dagele dagele rrene	Rrene yelende dagele dagele rrene
rrene yelende dagele dagele rrene	Rrene yelende dagele dagele rrene
(twice)	
rrene yelende dagele dagele rrene	Rrene yelende dagele dagele rrene
rrene yelende dagele dagele rrene	Rrene yelende dagele dagele rrene
karra kana-kumbu kaya rtadi thawara yawa-ndha	He always walks on the top of the mangroves
rrene yelende dagele dagele rrene	Rrene yelende dagele dagele rrene
rrene yelende dagele dagele rrene	Rrene yelende dagele dagele rrene
Item 5	
rrene yelende dagele dagele rrene	Rrene yelende dagele dagele rrene
rrene yelende dagele dagele rrene	Rrene yelende dagele dagele rrene
rrene yelende dagele dagele rrene	Rrene yelende dagele dagele rrene
rrene yelende dagele dagele rrene	Rrene yelende dagele dagele rrene

SONG STRUCTURE SUMMARY

Item 4 (Moy62-26-s13)

VOCAL SECTION 1

Melodic section 1

Text phrases 1–2

Rhythmic mode 5b (fast doubled)
rrene rrene rrene dagele dagele rrene
rrene rrene rrene dagele dagele rrene

Melodic section 2

Text phrases 3–4

Rhythmic mode 5b (fast doubled)
rrene rrene rrene dagele dagele rrene
rrene rrene rrene dagele dagele rrene

INSTRUMENTAL SECTION 1

Rhythmic mode 5b (fast doubled)

VOCAL SECTION 2

Melodic section 1

Text phrases 1–2

Rhythmic mode 5b (fast doubled)
rrene rrene rrene dagele dagele rrene
rrene rrene rrene dagele dagele rrene

Melodic section 2

Text phrase 3

Rhythmic mode 5b (fast doubled)

karra	kana	-kumbu	kaya	rtadi	thawara	yawa	-ndha
SW	3MIN.S.R walk	foot	3MIN.S.R lie	on top	mangrove	3MIN.ANAPH DEIC	really

He always walks on the top of the mangroves

INSTRUMENTAL SECTION 2

Rhythmic mode 5b (fast doubled)

VOCAL SECTION 3

Melodic section 1

Text phrases 1–2

Rhythmic mode 5b (fast doubled)
rrene rrene rrene dagele dagele rrene
rrene rrene rrene dagele dagele rrene

INSTRUMENTAL SECTION 3

Rhythmic mode 5b (fast doubled)

Item 5 (Moy62-26-s14)

VOCAL SECTION 1

Melodic section 1

Text phrases 1–2

Rhythmic mode 5b (fast doubled)
rrene rrene rrene dagele dagele rrene
rrene rrene rrene dagele dagele rrene

INSTRUMENTAL SECTION 1

Rhythmic mode 5b (fast doubled)

VOCAL SECTION 2

Melodic section 1

Text phrases 1–2

Rhythmic mode 5b (fast doubled)
rrene rrene rrene dagele dagele rrene
rrene rrene rrene dagele dagele rrene

INSTRUMENTAL SECTION 2

Rhythmic mode 5b (fast doubled)

TRACK 18 (AF2002-03-s03)

Song 8: Rtadi-thawara

This version, sung by Jimmy Muluk's grandson, Kenny Burrenjuck, was performed at a ceremony held to mark two events: the opening of the Belyuen community Bangany *wangga* archive—a digital sound archive built by Linda Barwick and funded by the Northern Territory Library—and the launch of the CD *Rak Badjalarr*. Barwick had been playing Jimmy Muluk's recordings of 'Rtadi-thawara' to Burrenjuck prior to the ceremony. He remarked, 'Oh, I'd forgotten that one.' Two hours later he performed 'Rtadi-thawara' in a version similar to Muluk's version on track 16, that is the version in rhythmic mode 5c (fast uneven quadruple). Burrenjuck's performance is, however, substantially faster and he uses slightly different vocables. This performance attests to the power of local digital archives to assist songmen in remembering and retaining old songs.

TRACKS 19–20 A General Intoduction

Song 9: Lerri

Sung text	Free translation
Items 1, 2 and 3	
aa nyele nye nye nyele nye nye	Aa nyele nye nye nyele nye nye.
ade kani yelendaga dagane dagane	Ade kani yelendaga dagane dagane

Barrtjap (chapter 4) and Mandji (chapter 6) also performed *lerri*, 'happy', songs, typically entirely in ghost language and performed fast. Muluk performed his *lerri* song in three different tempi across three items. The first two items are dovetailed in track 19 while track 20 presents item 3. The recording of this track is damaged by fluctuating tape speed. Every effort has been made to correct this since this is the only recording of a *lerri* song performed in this rhythmic mode.

As always, there were difficulties in transcribing the ghost language vocables, and what is presented here is necessarily tentative.

SONG STRUCTURE SUMMARY

TRACK 19 (Moy62-26-s22_23)

Item 1 (Moy62-26-s22)

VOCAL SECTION 1

Melodic section 1

Text phrases 1–2

Rhythmic mode 2b (slow even, stick beating suspended)
aa nyele nye nye nyele nye nye
ade kani yelendaga dagane dagane

Melodic section 2

Text phrases 3–4

Rhythmic mode 2a (slow even)
aa nyele nye nye nyele nye nye
ade kani yelendaga dagane dagane

INSTRUMENTAL SECTION 1

Rhythmic mode 4a (moderate even)

VOCAL SECTION 2

Melodic section 1

Text phrases 1–2

Rhythmic mode 2a (slow even, stick beating suspended)
aa nyele nye nye nyele nye nye
ade kani yelendaga dagane dagane

INSTRUMENTAL SECTION 2

Rhythmic mode 4* (moderate doubled followed by moderate even)

VOCAL SECTION 3

Melodic section 1

Text phrases 1–2
Rhythmic mode 2a+2b (slow even followed by suspension of beating (in text phrase 2)
aa nyele nye nye nyele nye nye
ade kani yelendaga dagane dagane

INSTRUMENTAL SECTION 3

Rhythmic mode 4* (moderate doubled followed by moderate even)

VOCAL SECTION 4

Melodic section 1

Text phrases 1–2

Rhythmic mode 2a+2b (slow even followed by suspension of beating (in text phrase 2)
aa nyele nye nye nyele nye nye
ade kani yelendaga dagane dagane

INSTRUMENTAL SECTION 4

Rhythmic mode 4e (moderate doubled)

Item 2 (Moy62-26-s23)

VOCAL SECTION 1

Melodic section 1

Text phrases 1–2

Rhythmic mode 4a (moderate even)
aa nyele nye nye nyele nye nye
ade kani yelendaga dagane dagane

INSTRUMENTAL SECTION 1

Rhythmic mode 4a (moderate even).

VOCAL SECTION 2

Melodic section 1

Text phrases 1–2

Rhythmic mode 4a (moderate even)
aa nyele nye nye nyele nye nye
ade kani yelendaga dagane dagane

INSTRUMENTAL SECTION 2

Rhythmic mode 4a (moderate even)

VOCAL SECTION 3

Melodic section 1

Text phrases 1–2

Rhythmic mode 4a (moderate even)
aa nyele nye nye nyele nye nye
ade kani yelendaga dagane dagane

INSTRUMENTAL SECTION 3

Rhythmic mode 4a (moderate even)

TRACK 20 (Moy62-26-s24)

[Item 3]

VOCAL SECTIONS 1–3

Melodic section 1

Text phrases 1–2

Rhythmic mode 5b (fast doubled)
aa nyele nye nye nye nyele nye nye
karra kani yelendaga dagane dagane

INSTRUMENTAL SECTIONS 1–3

Rhythmic mode 5b (fast doubled)

MUSICAL ANALYSIS OF MULUK'S REPERTORY

Because this repertory was not analysed in *Songs, dreamings and ghosts,* and because of Muluk's great variety of musical variation, here we provide considerable additional detail on his musical style. This section of the chapter provides an overview of Muluk's use of song structure, textual variation, rhythmic mode and melodic mode across his repertory, as well as additional musical detail on some of the tracks.

Song structure overview

All Jimmy Muluk's songs comprise an introductory instrumental section and a number of vocal sections, each of which is usually followed by an instrumental section. Because the recording made by Alice Moyle in 1968 was of a tourist corroboree involving long dramatic dances, this corpus contains a number of very long songs. 'Wörörö' (track 8), for example, has nine vocal sections and Muluk's version of 'Puliki' (track 1) has seven. Another feature of Muluk's style, which we will deal with in more detail shortly, is the presentation of several items of a song using contrasting text structures and rhythmic modes.

Text structure overview

Structurally, the texts of Jimmy Muluk's songs may be classified into three broad groups: texts repeated exactly from vocal section to vocal section and from item to item of the same song (Group 1); texts repeated almost identically but incorporating small changes that subtly affect the meaning (Group 2); and texts whose forms change from vocal section to vocal section and even within a single vocal section (Group 3). We mentioned in chapter 2 that songs sung regularly in ceremony tend to have more stable texts, allowing clear unisonal singing and providing a clearer, less ambiguous focus than texts that are highly variable. In the case of Muluk's songs, however, text instability does not seem to have the same implications. His songs were regularly sung in ceremony as well as on more informal occasions. It is perhaps his ability to balance regularity in other aspects of form—rhythmic mode and melody in particular—with instability of text that allowed him a degree of freedom with regard to the stability of his texts. It is normally the case that when one element of form is varied others remain stable.

Group 1: stable texts. The three Jimmy Muluk songs in this category are: 'Tjinbarambara' (track 5), 'Lerri' (tracks 19 and 20) and 'Wörörö' (track 8). 'Tjinbarambara' takes the form of a couplet that is repeated in each vocal section of all recorded performances by Muluk. 'Lerri' contains only vocable text, which is repeated exactly across all three items (irrespective of its rhythmic setting) and in all vocal sections. While we have only one example of 'Wörörö' (track 8), and cannot therefore test the stability of this text over a large number of items, the text does remain entirely stable for each of the nine vocal sections of this long single performance. 'Wörörö' also reveals an important aspect of Muluk's poetics, namely his love of subtle shifts of meaning brought about by minute adjustments to the text. The first four text phrases of each of the nine vocal sections take the form of a pair of couplets, ABAB^1, where B^1 is an altered version of B produced by the addition of a final particle *nö*, which in turn produces a subtle shift of meaning.

A   This was from me
B   Let me always walk on top of the mangrove for you
A   This was from me
B^1 I will always walk on top of the mangrove for you

Group 2. Let us turn now to the three texts that exhibit subtle changes from vocal section to vocal section: 'Puliki' (Buffalo) (track 1), 'Wak' (Crow) (track 7), 'and 'Pumandjin' (track 9). Muluk's performance of the text of 'Puliki' is completely stable for the first six vocal sections, but truncated in the final vocal section, where he omits the final two text phrases (text phrases 4 and 5) (see further information below under rhythmic mode).

'Wak' is a somewhat more complex than 'Puliki' and exhibits the same love of subtle shifts of meaning brought about by small adjustments of the text as we found in 'Wororo'. Except for the first vocal section, which presents a looser, introductory version of the text, all vocal sections consist of one or both of the following two closely related text phrases:

> Ah, it was because of Crow, who is always climbing *(kalkal)* on top of our stuff there.

or

> Ah, it was because of Crow, who is always walking *(putput)* on top of our stuff there.

In the case of 'Pumandjin', each vocal section is made up of some or all of two text phrases, the first of which is sung on the vocable *e* and the second of which consists of variable text in Mendhe. While the form of the vocable text phrase is entirely stable, its placement is not: in vocal sections 1-3 it is the first text phrase, while in vocal section 4 it is the last. The fullest form of the text in Mendhe occurs in vocal section 2, thus:

> *karra kama-ngana-yi* 'It [the song] came from she [Numbali] who is standing'
> *kana-nga-mu-viye karru* 'dancing [making a deliberate movement of hands above her head]'
> *viye pumandjin yakerre* 'on top of Pumandjin, yakerre'

All vocal sections except vocal section 2 use only two of these three text phrases: thus, vocal section 1 uses the last two and vocal sections 3 and 4 use the first two. All four vocal sections thus contain the second text phrase.

Group 3. This consists of two songs which have much more variable text: 'Rtadi-thawara' (tracks 15–17) and 'Piyamen.ga' (tracks 10–12). Muluk sings five items of each song, with between two and five vocal sections in each. Both songs contain an evolving and complex mix of text in Mendhe and text in ghost language. A detailed analysis of precisely how Muluk develops the texts of these two songs is beyond the scope of the present discussion, though a fuller account is planned.

Rhythmic mode overview

Jimmy Muluk's use of rhythmic mode is the most complex encountered among the *wangga* repertories under consideration (see table 5.2).

Tempo band of vocal section	#	Song title	Rhythmic mode of VS	Rhythmic mode of IIS	Rhythmic mode of FIS
Unmeasured					
Without clapsticks	3	'Wak' (track 7)	1	2, 4a, 2, 4a, 4a, 4a	**4e**
	4	'Wörörö' (track 8)	1	2, 2, 4a, 2, 2, 2, 2, 2	**4e**
	5	'Pumandjin' (track 9)	1	4a	4a
Measured					
Slow (50–54bpm)	1	'Puliki' (tracks 1-4)	2a+2b, 2b (Muluk)	2a, 4a, 2a, Ø, 2a, Ø	**4e**
			2a (VS1-9), 5a (VS10-17) (Mandji)	Ø (1-9), 5a (10-16)	5a
			2a, 4b, 4b (boys)	Ø, 4b	4b
			2a, 2a, 5a, 5a (Worumbu)	2a, Ø, 5a	5a
	7	'Lame Fella' (item 1) (track 13)	2b, 2a+2b	4a, 4a, 4*	**4e**
	8	'Rtadi-thawara' (item 1) (track 15)	2b, 2a+2b, 2a	4a, 4a	**4e**
	9	'Lerri' (item 1) (track 19, item 1)	2b+2a, 2a, 2a+2b, 2a+2b	4a, 4*, 4*	**4e**
Moderate (110–13bpm)	9	'Lerri' (item 2) (track 19, item 2)	4a	4a	4a
	6	'Piyamen.ga' (5 items) (tracks 10–12)	4a + 4a, 4a (var), 4a (var)	4a	4a
			4a, 4a (var) + 4a, 4a (var)		
			4a+4a+4a, 4a (var), 4a (var) + 4a, 4a (var)		
			4a + 4a, 4a (var) + 4a		
			4a, 4a (var) + 4a		
Fast (126–40bpm)	7	'Lame Fella' (item 2) (track 14)	5a	5a	5a
	2	'Tjinbarambara' (tracks 5-6)	5c	5c	**5a**
	8	'Rtadi-thawara' (items 2 and 3) (tracks 16, 18)	5c	5c	5c
Fast doubled (244–80/122–40bpm)	8	'Rtadi-thawara' (items 4 and 5) (track 17)	5b	5b	5b
	9	'Lerri' (item 3) (track 20)	5b	5b	5b

Table 5.2 Rhythmic modes used in Jimmy Muluk's repertory (track references are to chapter 5). VS = vocal section, IIS = internal instrumental section, FIS = final instrumental section. FIS is bold when different. Commas indicate successive vocal or instrumental sections in sequence through the song, where these are different. Plus signs indicate sequences of rhythmic modes occurring within a section. Names of performers in brackets.

The following comments regard only performances by Muluk himself and not those of other singers of his songs, such as Billy Mandji or Colin Worumbu Ferguson.

Presenting the same text in different rhythmic modes in successive items

Table 5.2 shows that for three songs Muluk presents a number of successive items in different rhythmic modes: 'Lame Fella' is sung first with slow even beating (rhythmic mode 2, with the beating sometimes suspended) (track 13) and then with fast even beating (rhythmic mode 5a) (track 14); 'Lerri' is sung first with slow even beating (rhythmic mode 2, with the beating sometimes suspended), then with moderate even beating (rhythmic mode 4a) (items 1 and 2, track 19), and finally with fast doubled beating (rhythmic mode 5b (track 20); 'Rtadi-thawara' is sung first in rhythmic modes 2a (slow even beating) and 2b (suspended slow even beating) (track 15), then items 2 and 3 are in rhythmic mode 5c (fast uneven quadruple) (track 16), and items 4 and 5 are in rhythmic mode 5b (fast doubled) (track 17).[8]

Distribution of rhythmic mode between vocal sections and instrumental sections

As can be seen from Table 5.2 above, songs in the moderate, fast and fast doubled tempo bands tend to use the same tempo across the whole song.[9] Other *wangga* singers also tend to maintain the same rhythmic mode in both vocal and instrumental section for these tempo bands. In songs with vocal sections in the slow and unaccompanied rhythmic modes (1 and 2), however, Muluk's practice is particularly rich in the variety of rhythmic modal combinations between vocal sections and instrumental sections. As table 5.2 shows, in these cases it is the instrumental sections that exhibit the greatest variety of rhythmic mode.

In rhythmic mode 1, 'Pumandjin' uses only rhythmic mode 4a (moderate even) in all instrumental sections, while individual instrumental sections in the two other songs ('Wak' and 'Wörörö') are presented in two different tempo bands and three different rhythmic modes: rhythmic modes 2a (slow even), 4a (moderate even) and 4e (moderate doubled, used for the final instrumental section in each case). This means that the dancers would normally utilise three different styles of dancing in the course of the song (one for the unmeasured vocal sections, and two different forms of rhythmic movement for the slow and moderate tempo sections).[10]

The situation can be equally complex with songs whose vocal sections are in the slow even rhythmic mode 2. For example, in instrumental sections of Muluk's performances of 'Puliki' we find the same three different rhythmic modes (2a, 4a and 4e) as in 'Wak' and 'Wörörö', and a number of vocal sections even proceed one to another without any instrumental section (these are marked Ø in the table). 'Lame Fella' (item 1) and 'Lerri' (item 1) also use several different forms of the moderate rhythmic modes for their instrumental sections: rhythmic modes 4a (moderate even), 4* (a combination mixing rhythmic

---

8 The practice of presenting successive items of the same text in different rhythmic modes was probably not uncommon back in the 1960s and 1970s. The early Walakandha *wangga*, which Marett has argued elsewhere was influenced by Muluk's practice (Marett, 2007, pp 70–71), also display this characteristic, and we have noted a more limited use of the practice across vocal sections of a single item in Barrtjap's repertory (chapter 4). As pointed out by Barwick (2006), the Muyil *lirrga* repertory, sung alongside *wangga* in circumcision ceremonies at Wadeye, is also conspicuous in its use of different rhythmic modes across different items of the same song. (For a more detailed discussion of multiple rhythmic modes, see Marett, 2005, pp 203–10.)

9 There is some variation in rhythmic mode (but not tempo) in 'Piyamen.ga', which mixes suspended and normal versions of rhythmic mode 4a in the vocal section, and in Worumbu's performance of 'Tjinbarambara', which uses the fast even (5a) rather than the fast uneven (quadruple) rhythmic mode (5c) in its final instrumental section.

10 Because these performances were simultaneously recorded on audio tape and filmed on silent 8mm film, it may be possible in future to comment further about the relationship between dance and rhythmic modes. At present, however, the film and audio recordings remain unsynched.

modes 4e and 4a which will be discussed in more detail below), and 4e (moderate doubled), used for the final instrumental section.

Mixing of rhythmic modes within a vocal section

Another type of rhythmic modal complexity typical of Muluk songs is the presentation of different text phrases within a single vocal section in different rhythmic modes. In both slow and moderate tempo bands this occurs by suspending the clapstick beating for a portion of the vocal section. Note that in the absence of clapstick beating the same tempo is maintained by the didjeridu pulse.

Muluk's repertory exhibits numerous cases where slow beating is suspended in the clapsticks while the regular pulse is maintained in the didjeridu (rhythmic mode 2b), Examples of performances by Muluk that mix normal slow even beating (rhythmic mode 2a) with the suspended form may be found in the vocal sections of: 'Puliki', (track 1), 'Lame Fella' (item 1, track 13), 'Rtadi-thawara' (item 1, track 15) and 'Lerri' (item 1, track 19). In all these cases the didjeridu clearly articulates a regular pulse that marks the text at precisely the same point as the clapsticks do when these are present.[11] In some cases you can also hear handclapping reinforcing the slow even metre, even when the clapsticks are absent. Table 5.2 shows that Muluk always exerted the option of occasionally suspending beating in rhythmic mode 2.

Muluk also uses suspended moderate beating in parts of vocal sections otherwise using rhythmic mode 4a (this occurs in all five items of 'Piyamen.ga', tracks 10–12). We have applied the label 'rhythmic mode 4a (var)' to such instances. In all vocal sections except the first of each item, Muluk suspends the stick beating at the beginning of text phrase 1, then gradually introduces quiet stick beating in the course of the vocal section, increasing the volume after the last syllable of the final text phrase.[12] This seems analogous to the suspension of beating in rhythmic mode 2 just discussed.[13]

Mixing of rhythmic modes within an instrumental section

Another distinctive feature of Muluk's style is the mixing of rhythmic modes within a single instrumental section.[14] This occurs in two songs, 'Lame Fella' (item 1) (track 13) and 'Lerri' (item 1) (track 19) where in certain instrumental sections a sequence of moderate doubled clapstick beats (rhythmic mode 4e) is followed by a sequence of moderate even clapstick beats (rhythmic mode 4a), which in turn is followed

---

11 The repertories studied in *Songs, dreamings and ghosts* revealed a limited number of similar cases, all involving the apparent combination of rhythmic modes 1 and 2 (Marett, 2005, pp 164–67). On the basis of this rather small amount of evidence—five songs in all—Marett came to the tentative conclusion that 'when slow even beating is suspended but the metrical pulse is continued by the didjeridu … the piece remains in rhythmic mode 2. When, on the other hand there is no metrical alignment between the voice and didjeridu … the mode shifts to rhythmic mode 1' (Marett, 2005, p 167). Two Barrtjap songs, 'Kanga Rinyala Nga-ve Bangany-nyung' (chapter 4, track 6) and 'Yagarra Delhi Nya-ngadja-barra-ngarrka' (chapter 4, track 24) were cited by Marett as exemplifying the former case, while three songs from the Walakandha *wangga* group 2B—'Kubuwemi' (chapter 8, track 12), 'Yendili No. 1' (chapter 8, track 13), and 'Lhambumen' (chapter 8, track 31)—exemplify the latter.

12 Item 2 of Muluk's 'Lerri' follows a similar pattern to 'Piyamen.ga' in that rhythmic mode 4a is used for both the vocal and the instrumental section; the special practice of suspending, then introducing the beats in a gradual crescendo is not, however, used in this item.

13 In 'Walakandha No. 9a', one of the early Walakandha *wangga* songs (chapter 8, track 8), we find the beating in rhythmic mode 4a is suspended at the beginning of a text phrase and even though in this case there is no crescendo we have designated this too as 'rhythmic mode 4a (var)'. It seems likely that the early Walakandha *wangga* composers, whom we know to have been influenced by Muluk, borrowed this innovation from him. The only analogous practice elsewhere in the *wangga* corpus occurs in the first vocal section of 'Song for Anson Bay' in Billy Mandji's repertory (chapter 6, track 9), where a gradual crescendo is introduced in both voice and clapsticks through the first text phrase of the first vocal section.

14 This feature was carried over into the early Walakandha *wangga* (Marett, 2007, p 71).

by two iterations of a characteristic cueing pattern (see below). This combination of two rhythmic modes is classified as rhythmic mode 4* in table 5.2 and in the song structure summaries above.[15]

Cueing patterns in instrumental sections

Some instrumental sections in the moderate tempo band contain a cueing pattern typical of Jimmy Muluk's style, and significant for the history of *wangga*. This is the pattern ♫♩ ♫♩♩ 𝄾, which in *Songs, dreamings and ghosts* was labelled the 'Walakandha *wangga* cueing pattern'. In the Walakandha *wangga* this pattern signals the end of almost every instrumental section, which led Marett to regard it as distinctive of the Walakandha *wangga* (as indeed it is). The frequent use of the pattern in Muluk's historically earlier repertory shows that it is likely to have been adopted from here for use in the early Walakandha *wangga* by Stan Mullumbuk (Marett, 2007, p 71). As mentioned in chapter 1, we know that before the composition of the Walakandha *wangga*, Jimmy Muluk was one of the singers who used to visit Wadeye for ceremony.

Nonetheless, the way Muluk uses the cueing pattern differs from its use in the Walakandha *wangga*. While in the Walakandha repertory it is used for all fast instrumental sections irrespective of their position in the song, Muluk marks the end of final instrumental sections in 4a with the different pattern ♩♩♩ 𝄾 ♩ (in all other cases—that is, for all internal instrumental sections in the moderate rhythmic modes 4a and 4*, and for final instrumental sections in 4e—he uses the standard cueing pattern). These uses of the cueing pattern are noted in the song structure summaries above.

Melodic mode overview

Muluk's songs are relatively homogenous with regard to their melodic modal qualities, like Barrtjap's repertory (chapter 4). Six of Muluk's nine songs—'Puliki', 'Tjinbarambara', 'Wak', 'Piyamen.ga', 'Lame Fella', and 'Rtadi-thawara'—are in a major mode and all are either an octave or a ninth in range, with two of them, 'Tjinbarambara' and 'Wak', sharing the same melody. A further two songs—'Wörörö' and 'Lerri'—use a mixolydian series, and one—'Pumandjin'—has a particularly florid melody that includes a number of chromatic notes and a degree of melodic instability.[16] The significance of melodic modal differences is, like the opaque qualities of the text, difficult to interpret at this distance in time, though the fact that major modality is used in two-thirds of the songs suggests that these songs belong to the the corpus of a single composer or lineage.

Further notes on selected tracks

Here we provide some additional analytical notes on musical features of seven songs ('Puliki', 'Wak', 'Wörörö', 'Piyamen.ga', 'Lame Fella', 'Rtadi-thawara' and 'Lerri').

Tracks 1–4 'Puliki'

Here we provide additional detail on the musical differences between Muluk's performance (track 1) and the three other performances of this song (tracks 2–4).

'Puliki' as performed by Muluk (track 1)

All text phrases in Muluk's 1968 performance of 'Puliki' are in the slow tempo band. Melodic section 1, which comprises text phrases 1-3, is entirely in 'ghost language' and in vocal sections 1-6 is accompanied

---

15 Given the complementary distribution patterns, where 4* occurs only in internal instrumental sections, and 4e only occurs in final instrumental sections, it is possible to argue that 4* and 4e are allomorphs, that is, realisations of the same pattern in different environments.

16 This complex style of melody is found elsewhere in our corpus, for example in Lambudju's song, 'Bandawarra-ngalgin', but it is rare.

by slow even beating (rhythmic mode 2a), ending with the clapstick beating pattern ♫ ♩ followed by a period of undifferentiated solo didjeridu drone[17] before the next melodic section. Melodic section 2 comprises text phrase 4, which is in Mendhe, and text phrase 5, which is in ghost language. This melodic section is accompanied throughout by rhythmic mode 2b (slow with clapsticks suspended, though sometimes handclapping accompaniment can be heard).

Table 5.3 shows that the pattern is varied in the last vocal section (7), where Muluk instead performs melodic section 1 (text phrases 1-3) with suspended slow beating (rhythmic mode 2b) (instead of the previous slow even rhythmic mode 2a), and omits the second melodic section (text phrases 4-5), before performing the final instrumental section in rhythmic mode 4e (moderate doubled). Here Muluk uses a change of expected rhythmic mode to mark the final vocal section and instrumental section, and, within the vocal sections, to differentiate the two melodic sections (which are also differentiated by use of ghost language vs Mendhe). A similar correlation can be noted with regard to 'Piyamen.ga' (tracks 10–12).

Table 5.3 shows that the rhythmic modal structure of the instrumental sections is also complex. In three cases (vocal sections 1, 3 and 5) the rhythmic mode of the instrumental sections is the same as that of the following vocal section, namely rhythmic mode 2a. Vocal section 2, instead, is followed by an instrumental section in rhythmic mode 4a (moderate even). Two vocal sections (4 and 6) proceed directly to the next vocal section without an instrumental section, being separated only by the solo didjeridu drone that follows each melodic section. The final vocal section (7) is followed by an instrumental section in rhythmic mode 4e (moderate doubled beating).

VS #	MS1	MS2	IS
1	2a	2b	2a
2	2a	2b	4a
3	2a	2b	2a
4	2a	2b	(absent)
5	2a	2b	2a
6	2a	2b	(absent)
7	2b	(absent)	4e

Table 5.3 Rhythmic modes in Jimmy Muluk's performance of 'Puliki' (track 1). VS = vocal section, MS = melodic section, IS = instrumental section.

'Puliki' as performed by Mandji (track 2)

This is a very long performance, with 17 vocal sections. Only vocal sections 2, 4 and 8 include Muluk's second melodic section (text phrases 4 and 5); the remaining 14 vocal sections comprise a single melodic section (text phrases 1-3). Unlike Muluk's performance in track 1, Mandji's never suspends the clapstick beating (rhythmic mode 2b). In the first nine vocal sections (including those with two melodic sections) he performs every melodic section in the same way, with slow even stick beating (rhythmic mode 2a) ending with the ♫ ♩ clapstick pattern followed by a period of didjeridu solo, with no following instrumental section. For the final eight vocal sections (10-17), Mandji changes the

---

17 We have considered whether the solo didjeridu drone should perhaps be analysed as an instrumental section in rhythmic mode 1 (without clapsticks). Because this is the only song in the corpus with this feature, and because the extended solo didjeridu drones occur after each melodic section, rather than after the complete vocal section, we have considered these to be part of the vocal section, and accordingly have classified vocal sections 4 and 6 as lacking an instrumental section.

rhythmic mode to employ fast even stick beating (rhythmic mode 5a) for both vocal and instrumental sections.

'Puliki' as performed by the boys (track 3)

The boys performed two melodic sections with slow stick beating (rhythmic mode 2a), in the characteristic form for this song, with the usual concluding ♫ ♩ on the sticks followed by solo didjeridu, with no instrumental section. There was some evident uncertainty about the text of the second melodic section, which one or two of the boys began to sing with text phrases 4, while the remainder began with text phrase 1 (to form a new vocal section). Once the disagreement became apparent, they all quickly reverted to a truncated form of text phrases 2-3. The remaining two vocal sections (both in the single melodic section form) were accompanied by moderate uneven quadruple stick beating (rhythmic mode 4b), a rhythmic mode never used by Muluk in any recordings of this song that survive.

'Puliki' as performed by Worumbu (track 4)

Here Worumbu structures the item in a similar way to that adopted by Billy Mandji, contrasting the slow even beating (rhythmic mode 2a) of the first vocal sections with fast even beating (rhythmic mode 5a) in the last vocal section. Also like Mandji is the use of both the single and double melodic section forms of the slow text. This performance can be viewed as a compressed version of what Billy Mandji sang in track 2.[18]

Tracks 5–12 'Piyamen.ga'

Examples of text recombination are: item 1, which is made up entirely of repetitions of Text A; item 2, vocal section 3 where Muluk performs Text B twice in full; item 3, vocal section 3, melodic section 2 (track 12) where Text C is introduced in full for the first time.

In 'Piyamen.ga,' Muluk uses only one rhythmic mode, rhythmic mode 4a, but he presents it in two forms: normal moderate even beating, and in the variant form unique to him, which we label 'rhythmic mode 4a (var)'. In this special form Muluk suspends the beating, or beats very quietly, for the first two text phrases of the melodic section, then increases the volume in the course of the last text phrase (text phrase 3).

We can see in table 5.4 that Muluk uses the normal form of rhythmic mode 4a for the first vocal section of each item. For subsequent vocal sections, he always performs the first melodic section in the variant form (rhythmic mode 4a [var]), and any subsequent melodic sections in the normal form. The six melodic sections that are entirely in Mendhe text (marked in bold in table 5.4) each appear as the final melodic section in a vocal section, and are therefore always accompanied by the normal form of moderate even beating.[19] As in 'Puliki' (track 1), we can see a relationship between item structure (whether a vocal section is initial or non-initial in the item), text language (whether it is in ghost language or Mendhe) and rhythmic mode (whether it is the normal or variant form of rhythmic mode 4a).

---

18   Worumbu uses, like Muluk, a slightly slower tempo for the fast even beating of rhythmic mode 5 (here 130bpm, versus the 135bpm used by Mandji).

19   Conversely, the first melodic section of each vocal section is always wholly or partly in *ngutj* (ghost) language.

Item	VS #	MS1	MS2	MS3
1	1.VS1	4a	4a	
	1.VS2	4a (var)		
	1.VS3	4a (var)		
2	2.VS1	4a		
	2.VS2	4a (var)	4a	
	2.VS3	4a (var)		
3	3.VS1	4a	4a	4a
	3.VS2	4a (var)		
	3.VS3	4a (var)	4a	
	3.VS4	4a (var)		
4	4.VS1	4a	4a	
	4.VS2	4a (var)	4a	
5	5.VS1	4a		
	5.VS2	4a (var)	4a	

Table 5.4 **Rhythmic mode use within vocal sections of all five items of 'Piyamen.ga'. Bold** marks text entirely in Menhdhe.

Track 13–14 'Lame Fella'

In the slow version (track 13) Muluk performs the vocal sections in rhythmic mode 2a, that is with slow even beating, with the beating sometimes suspended (rhythmic mode 2b), and each vocal section comprises text in both ghost language and Mendhe. In the fast version (track 14) the vocal sections are performed with fast even (*merrguda*) clapstick beating throughout (rhythmic mode 5a), and vocal sections using ghost language alternate with vocal sections in Mendhe.

The instrumental sections of the slow version of 'Lame Fella' are particularly interesting. Instrumental sections 1 and 2 are in rhythmic mode 4a (moderate even beating) with 'Walakandha *wangga* cueing patterns'. In instrumental section 3, a sequence of moderate doubled beating (rhythmic mode 4e) is followed by a sequence of moderate even beating (rhythmic mode 4a), which concludes with the 'Walakandha *wangga*' cueing pattern ♫ ♩ ♫ ♩ ♩ 𝄽 (see further discussion of this cueing pattern above). The final instrumental section uses moderate doubled beating (rhythmic mode 4e).

Track 15–17 'Rtadi-thawara'

Item 1 (track 15) presents the text in rhythmic modes 2a (slow even beating), with the beating suspended for some text phrases (rhythmic mode 2b). In items 2 and 3 (track 16), which are dovetailed, the text is presented in the fast uneven quadruple mode (rhythmic mode 5c). In items 4 and 5, which are also dovetailed, the text is presented in the fast doubled rhythmic mode (rhythmic mode 5b).

Track 19–20 'Lerri'

Items 1 and 2 are dovetailed in track 19. Item 1 uses slow beating in rhythmic modes 2a and 2b for the vocal sections, while item 2 is sung with moderate even beating (rhythmic mode 4a) and item 3 (track 20) is sung to fast doubled beating (rhythmic mode 5b). A variety of moderate beating patterns are used for the instrumental sections of item 1. Item 3 is sung throughout in rhythmic mode 5b (fast doubled beating).

Figure 6.1 Tourist corroboree group at Mandorah, 1968, including Billy Mandji (holding clapsticks) and other Delissaville performers including Tommy Lippo, Bobby Lane, Jacky Woody (didjeridu), Alan Nama, Jimmy Muluk, Henry Jorrock, Boy Bickford, and Tommy Barrtjap. Photograph by Alice Moyle, Delissaville (Belyuen), 1968. Photograph by Alice Moyle, courtesy of Alice Moyle family and AIATSIS (Moyle.A3.Cs - 25033), reproduced with the permission of Belyuen community.

Figure 6.2 Billy Mandji's daughter, Marjorie Bilbil, helps Allan Marett and Lysbeth Ford to write down texts of Billy Mandji songs, Mandorah, 1997. Photograph by Linda Barwick, reproduced with the permission of Belyuen community.

Chapter 6
MANDJI'S REPERTORY

Billy Mandji was a prolific and popular Belyuen songman. He was first recorded by Alice Moyle in 1959 (and again in 1962, 1964 and 1968) (see *Songs from the Northern Territory*, AM Moyle, 1967a, for published examples of some of these recordings). He was last recorded by Allan Marett in 1988, shortly before his death. In discussing the musical conventions of Billy Mandji's repertory, we must remember that any generalisations made here are, as was the case with Muluk, made on the basis of a relatively limited sample of songs.

Although Marett met and recorded Mandji, he was never able to work with him on the documentation of his songs. All translations and interpretations presented here are the result of working with other speakers, especially his extremely knowledgeable 'daughter', Marjorie Bilbil.

In addition to composing songs of his own, Billy Mandji inherited songs from the Emmiyangal brothers Robert Man.guna, George Ahmat and 'Darkie' Appang Wanggigi. For this reason, several of his songs are in Emmi. Only one song recorded here has text in his own language, Marri Tjavin, and many that are attributed to him comprise only vocable texts (ghost language). This conspicuous use of vocable texts was perhaps a strategy for coping with the fact that he was living in a community, Belyuen, where Marri Tjavin was not widely spoken. Billy Mandji also sang the Mendhe songs of Jimmy Muluk (some recordings were included in chapter 5), and often took the role of backup singer to Muluk.

Notes on the recording sample

Mandji's repertory was probably substantially more extensive than the eleven songs that we have been able to include in this chapter. Songs by Billy Mandji have been performed by singers such as his 'sons' (brother's sons, or nephews according to western nomenclature) Colin Worumbu Ferguson and Les Kundjil, the Jaminjung singer Major Raymond, the Wadjiginy singer Kenny Burrenjuck, and Mandji's 'daughter' (brother's daughter) Marjorie Bilbil. There may still be unlocated recordings of Billy Mandji himself. The full documentation of these songs remains a task for the future.[1]

---

1   Known recorded performances by Billy Mandji of *wangga* songs include: Alice Moyle 59-03 (AIATSIS archive number A1243), 6/5/1959 at Bagot; Moyle 62-01 (A1370), 21/5/1962 at Bagot; Moyle 62-27 (A1379), 13/7/1962 at Bagot; Moyle 64-36-37, 64-10 (A2529B, A2530AB, 2531A), 11/7/64 at the Darwin Eisteddfod (with Jimmy Muluk); Moyle 68-01-2 (A1143), 2/6/1968 at Mandorah (tourist corroboree, with Jimmy Muluk); Moyle 68-02-4 (A1143), 3/7/1968 at Delissaville (with Jimmy Muluk); Moyle 68-07 (A2670), 4/6/1968 at Mandorah (song words, with Jimmy Muluk); Wadeye Aboriginal Sound Archive D004, presumably at Wadeye, pre-1976 (compilation tape 'Song and Dance 1'); Marett 88-40-42 (A1630-32), 11/9/1988 at Batchelor. Mandji (or possibly the Jaminjung singer Major Raymond) was recorded at Timber Creek in 1966 by John Cleverly (FT6, AIATSIS archive tape LA160). Major Raymond was also recorded by Alice Moyle at Kununurra in 1968 singing Billy Mandji's songs (Moyle 68-74 (A2699), 23/8/68). Mandji was also recorded by Alice Moyle at Delissaville singing djanba (a non-didjeridu-accompanied public dance-song genre originating at Wadeye), along with a singer identified by Moyle as Philip Mileru (Moyle 68-6 (A2670), 3/6/1968). Performances of Mandji's songs by his relatives include several by his 'son' Colin Ferguson and Kenny Burrenjuck (Marett AT97/8 (A16960), 30/7/1997 at Belyuen; Marett AT97/13 (A16974-5), 8/11/97 at Mandorah; by his 'son' Les Kundjil (Marett DAT98/7 (A17050-51), 21/9/98 at Wadeye; Marett DAT98/15 (A17070), 15/10/98 at Wadeye); by Burrenjuck alone (Furlan DAT2002-03, 6/8/2002 at Belyuen); by Ferguson alone (Barwick 20080817NRP, 17/8/2008 at Darwin); and by Ferguson's sister (Mandji's daughter) Marjorie Bilbil at Belyuen in 2006 (Barwick 20060713MB, 13/7/2006 at Belyuen).

Figure 6.3 One of Billy Mandji's relatives to have inherited rights to sing the repertory was the late Les Kundjil (pictured here in Wadeye, 1999), who, however, usually preferred to sing Walakandha *wangga* songs (see Chapter 8). Photograph by Allan Marett, reproduced with the permission of Wadeye community.

Figure 6.4 Colin Worumbu, son of Billy Mandji, teaches Allan Marett to sing one of his songs, at AIATSIS conference, Canberra, 2001. Photograph by Linda Barwick, with permission of Belyuen community.

The recorded sample under consideration here is therefore limited. Most of the tracks are taken from recordings made by Alice Moyle in 1959, 1962 and 1968 and by Marett in 1988 (see table 6.1). Other recordings exist, but for a variety of reasons we have not been able to include any tracks from these at this stage.[2] Future research on these, and on the recordings of Billy Mandji songs by Kundjil and Worumbu may lead us to modify some of the conclusions below.

Track	Song #	Title	Singer	Recording
Track 01	1	'Duwun'	Mandji	Moy62-27-s09
Track 02		'Duwun'	Mandji	Mar88-40-s12
Track 03	2	'Happy (*lerri*) Song No. 1'	Mandji	Moy68-01-s01
Track 04		'Happy (*lerri*) Song No. 1'	Mandji	Mar88-41-s04
Track 05	3	'Happy (*lerri*) Song No. 2'	Mandji	Moy68-01-s02
Track 06	4	'Happy (*lerri*) Song No. 3'	Mandji	Moy62-27-s10
Track 07	5	'Duwun Crab Song'	Mandji	Moy68-01-s03
Track 08	6	'Karra Mele Ngany-endheni-nö'	Mandji	Mar88-40-s13
Track 09	7	'Song from Anson Bay'	Mandji	Moy59-03-s03
Track 10		'Song from Anson Bay'	Mandji	Moy59-03-s04
Track 11	8	'Robert Man.guna's Song'	Mandji	Moy62-27-s08
Track 12	9	'Happy (lerri) Song No. 4'	Mandji	Mar88-40-s09
Track 13	10	'Happy (lerri) Song No. 5'	Mandji	Mar88-42-s04
Track 14	11	'Happy (lerri) Song No. 6'	Mandji	Mar88-42-s05

Table 6.1 Songs from Billy Mandji's repertory discussed in this chapter.

TRACK 1 (Moy62-27-s09)

Song 1: Duwun

Sung text	Free translation
dagan mele dagaldja dagan mele nele	Dagan mele dagaldja dagan mele nele
dagan mele dagaldja dagan mele nele	Dagan mele dagaldja dagan mele nele
ee	Ee
karra duwun-ngana-yi	This came from Duwun
gidji-djedjet-mandha-ya	Where he sat down and sang out that song
karra ka-me-yi	That's what he sang

This song, which was composed by Robert Man.guna (an Emmiyangal songman who lived in the first half of the twentieth century), belongs to a series about *pörrme* (Mendhe 'sea') made by Man.guna's brother 'Darkie' Appang Wanggigi and was first recorded by Alice Moyle in 1962 at Bagot (Darwin). It is about Duwun, the island off the west coast of the Cox Peninsula known in English as 'Indian Island.'

---

2 John Cleverly, for example, recorded Mandji (or possibly the Jaminjung singer Major Raymond) at Timber Creek in 1966 but the recording suffers from serious technical flaws. In the last years of his life, the late Les Kundjil was never in good enough health to work on his Mandji songs. We hope in future, however, to be able to work more extensively with Colin Worumbu Ferguson, who is now the sole inheritor of Billy Mandji's repertory.

Melodic section 1 comprises untranslated ghost language (this melodic section is presented twice in vocal section 1, but only once in later vocal sections). Melodic section 2 comprises text in Emmi, which explains that the preceding ghost language came from Duwun, where 'he' (that is, the song-giving ghost) sat down and sang it. Note that the composer is here describing his dream vision. Speaking to Alice Moyle 1968, Billy Mandji said, 'I sat down and sang the song from Duwun' (*nginen-djedjet-manhdha duwun-ngana-yi*).

After every second vocal section there is an instrumental section using fast uneven quadruple beating (rhythmic mode 5c).

SONG STRUCTURE SUMMARY

VOCAL SECTIONS 1–4

Melodic section 1 (repeated in vocal section 1)

Text phrases 1–2

Rhythmic mode 2 (slow even)

dagan mele dagaldja dagan mele nele
dagan mele dagaldja dagan mele nele

Text phrase 3

Rhythmic mode 1 (without clapsticks)

ee

Melodic section 2

Text phrase 4

Rhythmic mode 2 (slow even)

karra	**duwun**	**-ngana**	**-yi**
SW	place name	-from	-PERF

This came from Duwun,

gidji	**-djedjet**	**-mandha**	**-ya**
3MIN.S.R use arms	-sit down	-song	-away from speaker

where he sat down and sang out that song

Text phrase 5

Rhythmic Mode 1 (without clapsticks)

karra	**ka-me**	**-yi**
SW	3MIN.A.R say	PERF

That's what he sang

INSTRUMENTAL SECTION 1 (follows vocal section 2)

Rhythmic mode 5c (fast uneven quadruple)

INSTRUMENTAL SECTION 2 (follows vocal section 4)

Rhythmic mode 5c (fast uneven quadruple)

TRACK 2 (Mar88-40-s12)

Song 1: Duwun

This recording was made at a *burnim-rag* (rag-burning) ceremony at Batchelor in 1988. It was the one and only time Marett recorded Mandji, who was already advanced in years. We are able to compare this version with track 1, recorded over a quarter of a century earlier by Alice Moyle.

It is remarkable how little 'Duwun' has changed over the course of 26 years. The two vocal sections present the same text, to the same melody, using the same rhythmic modes as the first two vocal sections of the 1968 performance, right down to the repetition of melodic section 1 in vocal section 1. The most striking differences between this version and the version in track 1 lie in the instrumental sections.

First, in the 1988 performance, instrumental sections follow each of the two vocal sections, whereas in 1962 instrumental sections occurred only after every second vocal section. Secondly, Mandji used different beating patterns in the instrumental sections (see further details in the music analysis section at the end of this chapter). The reason for these changes is that in 1962 he was performing the song at Bagot for Belyuen dancers, whereas in 1988 he was performing for a group of dancers from Peppimenarti, where the Walakandha *wangga* is used for all public ceremonies. In order to make the performances work, Mandji chose to adopt the form of stick beating that his dancers were familiar with, thus displaying his command of the *wangga* style as performed across the whole Daly region.

TRACK 3 (Moy68-01-s01)

Song 2: Happy (*lerri*) Song No. 1

Sung text	Free translation
nye nye nyelene nye nye nye nye	Nye nye nyelene nye nye nye nye
nye nye nyelene nye nye nye nye	Nye nye nyelene nye nye nye nye
ngammanya-mu-viye ngammiya	Let's both always keep dancing (with our hands above our heads)
ngandhi mandha na-gurriny yakarre	That song of his, yakarre

This 'happy' (*lerri*) dance song was recorded by Alice Moyle at a tourist corroborree at Mandorah in 1968. Track 4 has a version of the same song recorded at a *burnim-rag* ceremony at Batchelor in 1988. As is often the case with *lerri* dances, the tempo is fast and the song comprises a high proportion of vocables (see previous discussion in chapters 4 and 5).

Here, the section in Mendhe (text phrase 3) is an exhortation to dance to the section in vocables (text phrases 1 and 2) that precedes it. Dancing with hands above head is a characteristic of women's dancing and was mentioned in Muluk's song 'Pumandjin' (chapter 5, track 9). The sounds of dance-calls and the dancers' feet beating on the ground can be heard during the instrumental sections on this recording.

Figure 6.5 Billy Mandji's grandson Ian Bilbil plays *kenbi* (didjeridu) for Kenny Burrenjuck at Belyuen, 2006. ABC2006-02-32. Photograph by Gretchen Miller, ABC Radio National, reproduced with the permission of Belyuen community.

SONG STRUCTURE SUMMARY

VOCAL SECTIONS 1–5

Melodic section 1

Text phrases 1–2

Rhythmic mode 5a (fast even)[beating wholly or partially suspended in vocal sections 3, 4 and 5 (rhythmic mode 5a [var])

nye nye nyelene nye nye nye nye

nye nye nyelene nye nye nye nye

Text phrase 3

Rhythmic mode 5a (fast even beating)

ngammanya	**-mu**	**-viye**	**ngammiya**
1/2.MIN.R walk	-do	-head	1/2.MIN.R lie

Let's both always keep dancing (with our hands above our heads)

ngandhi	**mandha**	**na**	**-gurriny**	**yakarre**
a certain	song	3MIN.M.PRO	-POSS	alas

that song of his, yakarre

224 • For the sake of a song

INSTRUMENTAL SECTIONS 1–5

Rhythmic mode 5a (fast even beating)

TRACK 4 (Mar88-41-s04)

Song 2: Happy (*lerri*) Song No. 1

In this short ceremonial performance of the song, which follows that of 1968 in all major respects (including the suspension of beating for the first text phrase of the second vocal section), the sounds of dancing and/or mourning relatives can be heard. The 1988 performance is, however, slightly faster in tempo (141bpm) than the 1968 performance (138bpm). This may be because it is danced in a ceremonial context.

TRACK 5 (Moy68-01-s02)

Song 3: Happy (*lerri*) Song No. 2

Sung text	Free translation
da ribene ribene ana anarra	Da ribene ribene ana anarra
da ribene ribene ana anarra	Da ribene ribene ana anarra
at bwat bwane ribene yenet di	At bwat bwane ribene yenet di

Like 'Happy Song No. 1,' Billy Mandji's second happy (*lerri*) song is in rhythmic mode 5a (fast even beating) although the beating is suspended in vocal section 1 (which has no following instrumental section). Like many happy songs, it consists entirely of unglossable 'ghost language,' that is, it is made of entirely of vocables. Like the track 3 performance of 'Happy Song No.1,' it was recorded by Alice Moyle in 1968 at Mandorah.

Later that year, Moyle returned and had Billy Mandji speak the words of the song for her. Although there is no exact correspondence between the sung version and his spoken text—which is given in disjointed fragments and includes some text not actually in the song—there is enough for us to transcribe what is sung with some confidence, although the performance of the vocable 'word' *ribene* seems to be frequently elided to *rene*. Note that text phrases 1 and 2, which repeat the vocable text 'da ribene ribene ana anarra,' are performed with a strong nasal timbre, contrasting with the throatier and smoother timbre of text phrase 3 'at bwat bwane ribene yenet di'. This gives the effect of two alternating voices, as in a conversation.

This long danced performance comprises ten repetitions of the vocal section, with an instrumental section following each vocal section except the first.

SONG STRUCTURE SUMMARY

VOCAL SECTIONS 1–10

Melodic section 1

Text phrases 1–2

Rhythmic mode 5a (fast even) (beating is suspended (rhythmic mode 5a [var]) for text phrase 1 in vocal section 1)

da ribene ribene ana anarra

da ribene ribene ana anarra

Text phrase 3

Rhythmic mode 5a (fast even)

at bwat bwane ribene yenet di

INSTRUMENTAL SECTIONS 1–9 (there is no instrumental section after vocal section 1)

Rhythmic mode 5a (fast even)

TRACK 6 (Moy62-27-s10)

Song 4: Happy (*lerri*) Song No. 3

Happy (*lerri*) Song No. 3 was recorded by Alice Moyle at Bagot in 1962.[3] Like the preceding happy songs, this performance is fast (in rhythmic mode 5a [fast even beating]) and predominantly in 'ghost language' (vocable text), though in vocal section 5, melodic section 1 bears the following text in Emmi: *karra ka-me-ngana-yi gidji-djedjet-mandha-ya* 'This [i.e., the vocable text] is what he sang when he gave me this song'.[4] Despite many hours working with native speakers, we have not been able to arrive at a reliable version of the text, so have decided not to include a text transcription here, but can make some statements about the form (see further details in music analysis section).

TRACK 7 (Moy68-01-s03)

Song 5: Duwun Crab Song

Sung text	Free translation
yene ne yene ne	Yene ne yene ne
yene ne yene ne	Yene ne yene ne
karra ka-me-ngana-yi kaya	This song came from the one who is always singing this

---

3   This song was titled 'Song from Anson Bay' in the published version (track 11(a), *Songs from the Northern Territory*, volume 1). Note that the same title was used by Moyle for the quite different Billy Mandji song recorded by her in 1959 (see tracks 9 and 10). It seems likely that Mandji could have applied this description to many of his songs, since the ancestral country of Emmiyangal and Mendheyangal people, from whom he inherited much of his repertory, lies on the shores of Anson Bay, in the Daly region to the south of Darwin.

4   See track 1 for glossing of *karra ka-me-ngana-yi*, and track 7 for glossing of *gidji-djedjet-mandha-ya*.

As in the preceding track, the text in Emmi (text phrase 2) explains that the preceding section in ghost language (text phrase 1) came from a ghost, that is, 'the one who is always singing this.'

This long performance—comprising twelve vocal sections—was recorded by Alice Moyle in 1968 at a tourist corroborree at Mandorah (Jimmy Muluk was also recorded on this occasion, see chapter 5). It accompanies the Crab dance, which continued to be performed at tourist corroborees at the Mandorah Hotel into the 1990s and beyond (albeit to a different song). The text has no direct relationship to the subject matter of the dance, during which the dancers mime hunting for and catching a crab (the dancers can be heard occasionally in the background). Unusually, there is only one instrumental section in this performance, which occurs after the final vocal section. Here the dancers, having caught the crab, perform the stamping movements typical of *wangga*.

VOCAL SECTIONS 1–12

Melodic section 1

Text phrase 1

Rhythmic mode 2 (slow even)

yene ne yene ne

yene ne yene ne

Text phrase 2

Rhythmic mode 1 (without clapsticks)

karra	ka	-me	-ngana	-yi	kaya
SW	3MIN.A.R	say	from	PERF	3MIN.S.R.lie

This song came from the one who is always singing this

INSTRUMENTAL SECTION 1 (after final vocal section)

Rhythmic mode 4e (moderate doubled)

TRACK 8 (Mar88-40-s13)

Song 6: Karra Mele Ngany-endheni-nö

Sung text	Free translation
nyele nye nyele nye	Nyele nye nye nyele nye
nyele nye nyele nye	Nyele nye nye nyele nye
karra mele ngany-endheni-nö	This is for my brother now
ngawanya-bet-mörö-gumbu ngayi ya	let me always sing it for him all night long
nyele nye nyele nye	Nyele nye nyele nye
nyele nye nyele nye	Nyele nye nyele nye
karra mana ngindivelh-ni-bik-mi-ni	You have to always look out for my brother,
kan-djen-ndja-wurri	who is really here now singing to us
kani-gulukguluk	and who keeps coughing
kinyi-ni-venggi-tit-ngangga-wurri kani	and who keeps appearing in number four leg and singing to us whether we like it or not
nyele nye nyele nye	Nyele nye nyele nye
nyele nye nyele nye	Nyele nye nye nyele nye
karra mele ka-me-nganila-ngana-yi	This is from my brother who sang this for me now
ngany-endheni-nö nganya-bet-mörö-gumbu ngayi ya	let me always sing it for him all night long
nyele nye nyele nye	Nyele nye nyele nye
nyele nye nyele nye	Nyele nye nye nyele nye
karra mana ngindivelh-ni-bik-mi-ni	You have to always look out for my brother
kan-djen-ndja-wurri	who is really here now singing to me
kin-verri-wut-wurri kani ya	and he keeps walking towards me

Marett recorded this at the same 1988 *burnim-rag* as track 4. Vocal sections 1 and 3 are in Mendhe, while vocal sections 2 and 4 are in Marri Tjavin (Mandji's ancestral language). It is rare for songs to mix languages in this way; we may speculate that this song might have been formed from two previously independent songs, which here have been interleaved. Instrumental sections occur after every two vocal sections, that is, following the Marri Tjavin vocal sections 2 and 4.

Although there is still a great deal that we do not understand about this song—including the reason for the combination of these particular two languages—the subject matter of the two pairs of vocal sections is clearly a totemic song-giving ghost. The word for 'brother' (*mele* in Mendhe or *mana* in Marri Tjavin) is the relationship term used in these languages and other *wangga* songs to address totemic ghosts (Marett, 2005, p 114), and the reference to 'number four leg' evokes a characteristic of song-giving ghosts that is mentioned often in *wangga* songs (see, for example Muluk's song 'Piyamen. ga' chapter 5, tracks 10–12).

It may be noted that there seems to be some instability in the form of the vocable text that begins each vocal section. The Mendhe expression *mörö-gumbu*, literally 'buttock-foot', is an idiom meaning 'from top to bottom' or 'right through,' which here means 'all night long.'

SONG STRUCTURE SUMMARY

VOCAL SECTION 1 (Mendhe)

Melodic section 1

Text phrase 1
Rhythmic mode 2 (slow even)
nyele nye nyele nye
nyele nye nyele nye

Text phrase 2
Rhythmic mode 1 (without clapsticks)

karra	**mele**	**ngany**	**-endheni**	**-nö**
SW	brother	1MIN.PRO	now	DAT

This is for my brother now

ngawanya	**-bet**	**-mörö**	**-gumbu**	**ngayi**	**ya**
1MIN.A.IR.make	open	buttocks	foot	1MIN.S.IR lie	SW

Let me always sing it for him all night long

VOCAL SECTION 2 (Marri Tjavin)

Melodic section 1

Text phrase 1
Rhythmic mode 2 (slow even)
nyele nye nyele nye
nyele nye nyele nye

Text phrase 2
Rhythmic mode 1 (without clapsticks)

karra	**mana**	**ngindivelh**	**-ni**	**-bik**	**-mi**	**-ni**
SW	brother	2.MIN.IR lie	3.MIN.M.IO	look-	eye	PURP

You have to always look out for my brother,

kan	**-djen**	**-ndja**	**-wurri**
near DEIC	now	really	toward speaker

who is really here now singing to us,

kani	**-gulukguluk**
3MIN.S.R.move	cough

and who keeps coughing

kinyi	-ni	-venggi	-tit	-ngangga	-wurri	kani
3MIN.S.R.make	3MIN.M.REFL	knee	bend	1/2.ADVERS	toward speaker	3MIN.S.R walk

and who keeps appearing in number 4 leg and singing to us whether we like it or not

INSTRUMENTAL SECTION 1

Rhythmic mode 4a (moderate even)

VOCAL SECTION 3 (Mendhe)

Melodic section 1

Text phrase 1

Rhythmic mode 2 (slow even)

nyele nye nyele nye
nyele nye nyele nye

Text phrase 2

Rhythmic mode 1 (without clapsticks)

karra	mele	ka	-me	-nganila	-ngana	-yi
SW	brother	3MIN.A.R	say	1MIN.BEN	from	PERF

This is from my brother who sang this for me now

ngany	-endheni	-nö	ngawanya	-bet	-mörö	-gumbu	ngayi	ya
1MIN.PRO	now	DAT	1MIN.A.IR.make	open	buttocks	foot	1MIN.S.IR lie	SW

Let me always sing it for him all night long

VOCAL SECTION 4 (Marri Tjavin)

Melodic section 1

Text phrase 1

Rhythmic mode 2 (slow even)

nyele nye nyele nye
nyele nye nyele nye

Text phrase 2

Rhythmic mode 1 (without clapsticks)

karra	mana	ngindivelh	-ni	-bik	-mi	-ni
SW	brother	2.MIN.IR lie	3.MIN.M.IO	look-	eye	PURP

You have to always look out for my brother,

kan	-djen	-ndja	-wurri		
near DEIC	now	really	toward speaker		

who is really here now singing to me

kin	-verri-	-wut	-wurri	kani	ya
3MIN.S.R.make	foot	walk	toward speaker	3MIN.S.R walk	SW

and he keeps walking towards me

INSTRUMENTAL SECTION 2

Rhythmic mode 4e (moderate doubled) with Walakandha wangga cueing patterns

TRACK 9 (Moy59-03-s03)

Song 7: Song from Anson Bay

Sung text	Free translation
Item 1	
ne rrene ne ne rrene ne	Ne rrene ne ne rrene ne
ne rrene ne ne rrene ne	Ne rrene ne ne rrene ne
ee ö	Ee ö

Tracks 9 and 10 were recorded by Alice Moyle at Bagot in 1959. This song, which Moyle titled 'Song from Anson Bay', is entirely in the language of a ghost (*ngutj*), that is, it comprises entirely untranslatable vocables, the transcription of which is only approximate.

The first item (track 9) begins with wordless melody, from which the vocable text and the clapstick beating gradually emerge (see the music analysis section for further details).[5] The text as given is repeated with little change in the three subsequent vocal sections. Note that a final clapstick beat that might have been expected at the end of track 9 (compare with the end of track 10) was missing from Moyle's original recording of this item.

SONG STRUCTURE SUMMARY

VOCAL SECTION 1

Melodic section 1

Text Phrase 1

Rhythmic mode 4b (var) (moderate uneven quadruple, suspended initially, then 4b emerges gradually)
mm mm ne rrene ne
ne rrene ne ne rrene ne
ee ö

---

5   This suspended form of rhythmic mode 4b is designated as 'rhythmic mode 4b (var)' in the song structure summary.

VOCAL SECTIONS 2–4

Melodic section 1

Text Phrase 1

Rhythmic mode 4b (moderate uneven quadruple)

ne rrene ne ne rrene ne

ne rrene ne ne rrene ne

ee ö

INSTRUMENTAL SECTIONS 1–4

Rhythmic mode 4b (moderate uneven quadruple)

TRACK 10 (Moy59-3-s04)

Song 7: Song from Anson Bay

Sung text	Free translation
Item 2	
rrene rrene ne ne rrene ne	Rrene rrene ne ne rrene ne
rrene rrene ne ne rrene ne	Rrene rrene ne ne rrene ne
ee ö	Ee ö

In item 2 (track 10) a slightly but consistently different version of the text can be heard throughout.

VOCAL SECTIONS 1–4

Melodic section 1

Text Phrase 1

Rhythmic mode 4b (moderate uneven quadruple)

rrene rrene ne ne rrene ne

rrene rrene ne ne rrene ne

ee ö

INSTRUMENTAL SECTIONS 1–4

Rhythmic mode 4b (moderate uneven quadruple)

TRACK 11 (Moy62-27-s08)
Song 8: Robert Man.guna's Song

This song was composed by the Emmiyangal songman Robert Man.guna, who was also the composer of Duwun (tracks 1 and 2). Various features suggest that this may be another 'happy' song (see the music analysis section for further details). As in tracks 9 and 10, the text comprises untranslatable ghost language, but here each vocal section begins with wordless melody. Once again, it has proven impossible to obtain a reliable transcription of the vocables, and therefore no text is given here.

TRACK 12 (Mar88-40-s09)
Song 9: Happy (*lerri*) Song No. 4

Tracks 12–14 were recorded by Marett at the same *burnim-rag* as tracks 2, 4 and 8. We have identified all three as 'happy songs' based on their musical and textual characteristics. All have unglossable and unstable vocable texts, which we do not include here.

Track 12 is in moderate tempo, slower than most happy songs.

TRACK 13 (Mar88-42-s04)
Song 10: Happy (*lerri*) Song No. 5

As one expects of performances at the height of ceremony, the tempo is at the high end of the fast tempo band (about 140 beats per minute). This performance begins with a ritual call, or *malh*, by the dancers. This and the following track 14 were recorded from amongst the dancers, so the singing is somewhat distant; we have decided to include them here, however, because they give a sense of the lively atmosphere at a ceremony.

TRACK 14 (Mar88-42-s05)
Song 11: Happy (*lerri*) Song No. 6

Like the preceding track, this song has a purely vocable text and is performed at faster tempo than usual, although here the beating is in the uneven quadruple rhythmic mode (5c).

MUSICAL ANALYSIS OF MANDJI'S REPERTORY

Because this repertory was not analysed in *Songs, dreamings and ghosts* we provide here additional detail on Mandji's musical style. This section of the chapter provides an overview of Mandji's use of song structure, textual variation, rhythmic mode and melodic mode across his repertory, as well as additional musical detail on some of the tracks.

Song structure overview

Like most *wangga* songs, those of Billy Mandji alternate vocal and instrumental sections. Some of his performances, particularly those recorded by Alice Moyle at the tourist corroboree in 1968, have, like those of Muluk recorded on the same occasion, a particularly large number of vocal sections, for example, 'Happy Song No. 2' (track 5) has 10 vocal sections, 'Duwun Crab Song' (track 7) has 12, and Mandji's version of Muluk's 'Puliki' (chapter 4, track 2) has 17.

Text structure overview

Overall, the majority of Mandji's text phrases are in non-human language. Since he did not live in the country of his Marri Tjavin ancestors, Mandji would not have been in a position to receive songs from them on a regular basis, since, as noted in chapter 4 with regard to Barrtjap, song-giving ancestors do not travel far from their country-based sites. Except for the mixed Mendhe and Marri Tjavin in 'Karra Mele Ngany-endheni-nö' and some Mendhe text in 'Happy (*lerri*) Song No. 1' (track 3), all the human language text in Mandji's songs is in Emmi. We know that Mandji inherited songs from the Emmiyangal songmen, Robert Man.guna and his brothers, and we might reasonably assume that the songs with text in Emmi came from them. The predominance of vocable text phrases in Mandji's own songs might result from the fact that Mandji could neither receive texts in the language of his ancestors, nor translate them into the languages local to the area around Belyuen, where he had chosen to live. On the other hand, songs with vocable texts that are opaque to all participants in ritual may serve a useful function in a multilingual environment precisely because they do not privilege the language of any one group, as Barwick has observed with regard to songs in Western Arnhem Land, (Manmurulu, et al., 2008). Belyuen was, at the time Mandji was composing his songs, just such a multilingual environment.

Texts that comprise three text phrases, the first two of which are identical and the third different, are common in the songs of Billy Mandji; indeed all six songs for which we have obtained texts conform to this pattern. Three—'Happy Song No. 1', (track 3), 'Duwun Crab Song' (track 7) and 'Karra Mele Ngany-endheni-nö' (track 8)—have text in the form aaB, that is, a pair of text phrases in vocables (ghost language, indicated by lower case) followed by a text phrase in human language (indicated by upper case). In the first two songs the human language is in Emmi or Mendhe, but in 'Karra Mele Ngany-endheni-nö' Mandji alternates between Mendhe and Marri Tjavin in successive vocal sections, and in this song the text phrase in human language is unusually long. In 'Duwun' a pair of text phrases in ghost language are followed by a second pair in Emmi (aaBC). Two further songs, 'Happy Song No. 2', (track 5) and 'Song from Anson Bay' (tracks 9 and 10) have text phrases that are entirely in vocables in the form aab, and 'Happy Song No. 5', (track 13), although not transcribed, also clearly conforms to the aab form.

This common structure in Mandji's repertory is comparable to that labelled Group 2 in the Walakandha *wangga* repertory (Marett, 2005, p 122). Here each vocal section comprises three text phrases, the first two of which are identical and the third different. The form of these Walakandha *wangga* Group 2B songs can be represented as AAb, where upper case letters represent text in human language (Marri Tjavin) and lower case represents text using vocables (ghost language).

It may not be entirely coincidental that Billy Mandji's song texts conform to a pattern that is also prominent in the principal Marri Tjavin repertory, the Walakandha *wangga*. Let us not forget that although he lived much of his life at Belyuen, Mandji was Marri Tjavin and maintained links with his Marri Tjavin kin living at Wadeye and its associated outstations. On the other hand, since two of the three Mandji texts with the form aaB have Emmi as the language of the human language text phrase, we cannot tie this form exclusively to Marri Tjavin precedents, or see it as strongly marking Mandji's Marri Tjavin heritage.

Rhythmic mode overview

None of Billy Mandji's vocal sections are entirely without clapstick beating (rhythmic mode 1). Neither are any songs entirely in rhythmic mode 2 (slow even). Rather, three songs use a combination of rhythmic modes 1 and 2 (without clapsticks and slow even beating respectively) for their vocal sections (see table 6.2).

Tempo band of vocal section	#	Song title	Rhythmic mode of VS	Rhythmic mode of IIS	Rhythmic mode of FIS
Unmeasured/measured					
Without clapsticks/Slow (46–48bpm)	1	'Duwun' (Indian Island) (tracks 1–2)	2+1	5c (Belyuen) 5a (Peppi)	5c (Belyuen) **5b** (Peppi)
	5	'Duwun Crab Song' (track 7)	2+1	Ø	**4e**
	6	'Karra Mele Ngany-endheni-nö' (track 8)	2+1	4a	**4e**
Measured					
Moderate (110–16bpm)	7	'Song from Anson Bay' (tracks 9–10)	4b (var), 4b 4b	4b 4b	4b 4b
	9	'Happy Song No. 4' (track 12)	4c (VS1), 4a (VS2-4)	4c, 4a	4a
Fast (130–40bpm)	2	'Happy Song No. 1' (tracks 3-4)	5a (VS1-2), 5a (var)+5a (VS3-5)	5a	5a
	3	'Happy Song No. 2' (track 5)	5a (var)+5a, 5a	5a	5a
	4	'Happy Song No. 3' (track 6)	5a	5a	5a
	8	'Robert Man.guna's Song' (track 11)	5a	5a	5a
	10	'Happy Song No. 5' (track 13)	5a	5a	5a
	11	'Happy Song No. 6' (track 14)	5c	5c	5c

Table 6.2 Rhythmic modes in Billy Mandji's repertory. VS = vocal section, IIS = internal instrumental section, FIS = final instrumental section. FIS is bold when different. Commas indicate successive vocal or instrumental sections in sequence through the song, where these are different. Plus signs indicate sequences of rhythmic modes occurring within a section. Names of performers in brackets.

Distribution of rhythmic mode between vocal sections and instrumental sections

All songs in the fast and moderate tempo band use the same tempo (and usually the same rhythmic mode) for both the vocal and instrumental sections and have texts that are by and large stable and predictable. They are wonderful vehicles for vigorous and often ostentatious dancing, and are for this reason are very popular. The repertory contains a large number of 'happy' (*lerri*) songs, that is, lively songs with texts that comprise mostly vocables. These are mostly in the fast tempo band, but one ('Happy Song No. 4', track 12) is in the moderate tempo band.

As we observed in Barrtjap's repertory, a high proportion of songs have vocal sections in the fast tempo band. In Mandji's repertory, the majority are in the fast even rhythmic mode (5a), while only one, 'Happy Song No. 6', (track 14) uses the fast uneven (quadruple) rhythmic mode (rhythmic mode 5c) preferred in Barrtjap's repertory.

Presenting the same text in different rhythmic modes in different vocal sections within an item

Both moderate tempo songs show variation across vocal sections within an item in their use of rhythmic mode. 'Happy Song No. 4', (track 12) uses the unusual moderate uneven (triple) beating (rhythmic mode 4c) for vocal section 1 and the following instrumental section, and then moderate even beating (rhythmic mode 4a) for the remaining vocal and instrumental sections, while the first item of 'Song from Anson Bay' (tracks 9), uses an unusual suspended form of rhythmic mode 4b (var) in the first vocal section only, with rhythmic mode 4b (moderate uneven quadruple) being used for the rest of the item and throughout the following item (track 10).

Variation in rhythmic mode between vocal sections according to their position within an item can also be found in 'Happy Song No. 1' (tracks 3–4), where the initial vocal sections use rhythmic mode 5a (fast even), whereas the later vocal sections begin with a suspended form of this pattern (rhythmic mode 5a [var]). In 'Happy Song No. 2' (track 5), the reverse applies, where the suspended form is used in the first vocal section, while the later ones use the normal form of beating (see further below).

Mixing of rhythmic modes within a vocal section

Mandji's repertory has a number of instances of the use of different rhythmic modes within a vocal section.

As mentioned above, the three slow songs in Mandji's repertory each use a combination of rhythmic modes 2 and 1 (slow even beating and without clapsticks respectively) for their vocal sections (see table 6.2).[6] In each case the vocal section is made up of one or more melodic sections that begin with slow even beating for the first text phrases and then change to unmeasured style for the final text phrases in the melodic section. In two cases the two rhythmic modes are used in an interesting relationship with the textual contrast between ghost language and human language.[7] In 'Duwun Crab Song' (track 7) and 'Karra mele ngany-endheni-nö' (track 8), rhythmic mode 2 (slow even) is used for the text in ghost language (vocables) while rhythmic mode 1 (without clapsticks) is used for text in human language (Emmi).[8]

---

6   Note that in these songs of Mandji, the portions of the vocal section without clapsticks are unmeasured, with the didjeridu patterning bearing little relationship to the unmeasured vocal rhythm. This is different from suspended form of rhythmic mode 2b used by Jimmy Muluk and others, in which the didjeridu keeps the metre while clapsticks are suspended.

7   In 'Duwun' (tracks 1 and 2) ghost language and human language are contrasted by presentation over the same tune in successive melodic sections.

8   A similar use of rhythmic mode to underscore the contrast between human and ghostly language can also be found in the songs of Jimmy Muluk, see for example in all vocal sections but the last of 'Puliki' (chapter 5, track 1) and in 'Lame

Mandji also unusually suspends the fast even stickbeating (rhythmic mode 5a) in the ghost language text phrases (1-2) of the last three vocal sections of 'Happy Song No. 1' (track 3), with the normal form employed for text phrase 3, which is in human language. The same effect is employed in 'Happy Song No. 2' (track 5), but here, instead of being in human language, text phrase 3 is also performed in ghost language, but with a very different vocal timbre and with different vocables from those used in text phrases 1-2. This seems to confirm that Mandji deliberately used variation in rhythmic mode to set off different 'voices' in his song texts.

Another possible instance of mixing rhythmic modes within a single vocal section occurs in Mandji's performance of the first item of 'Song from Anson Bay' (chapter 6, track 9), where he begins singing wordless melody very quietly. As the volume increases through the first vocal section, the vocable text and the clapstick beating (in moderate uneven quadruple rhythmic mode 4b) gradually emerge. This is the only instance across the whole corpus of this use of crescendo in stickbeating accompaniment, though Jimmy Muluk's 'Piyamen.ga' contains numerous instances of suspended beating, sometimes with a crescendo in the course of a text phrase, in rhythmic mode 4a (var) (see for example chapter 5, track 12). Since this is a single instance that is not repeated in any other songs in Mandji's recorded repertory, we are not certain whether this variant of rhythmic mode 4b was used systematically within the rhythmic modal system. On the other hand, it seems likely that recordings capture only a small part of Mandji's whole repertory, so we have included this variant form as rhythmic mode 4b (var) in the table of rhythmic modes in chapter 2 (table 2.1).

Variation in rhythmic mode of instrumental sections across items

When Mandji performed 'Duwun' (track 1) in 1962, his dancers were from Delissaville (Belyuen) and for this reason he adopted for the instrumental section rhythmic mode 5c (fast uneven quadruple), which provides the best vehicle for the style of dancing favoured at Belyuen. When he performed the same song in 1988 at a *burnim-rag* ceremony at Batchelor, however, the dancers were from Wadeye and Peppimenarti. For this occasion Mandji performed the instrumental sections of 'Duwun' (track 2) in the form commonly used in the Walakandha *wangga*, that is, using rhythmic mode 5a (fast even) beating plus Walakandha *wangga* cueing patterns for the non-final instrumental sections, and rhythmic mode 5b (fast doubled) plus Walakandha *wangga* cueing pattern for the final instrumental section. The dancers were thus able to perform in the style most familiar to them, thus ensuring the success of the ceremonial dancing on this occasion.

Melodic mode overview

Turning now to the question of melody, the vast majority of Billy Mandji's songs are, like those of Jimmy Muluk, sung in a major mode. It is difficult to interpret this as marking Mandji's Marri Tjavin identity, however, since the majority of Walakandha *wangga* songs and Ma-yawa *wangga* songs are in the dorian mode, a mode that Mandji does not employ at all. True, both repertories do have a small number of songs in the major mode, for example Philip Mullumbuk's Walakandha *wangga* songs, but they can hardly be regarded as representative. It is more likely perhaps, given the closeness of the Emmi and Mendhe languages (see chapter 3), and Mandji's use of Emmi for most text phrases in human language, that they reflect some sort of joint Emmi-Mendhe identity: after all. Mandji both received songs from Emmi songmen and sang regularly with the Mendhe songman, Jimmy Muluk. The fact that the only song that is not in the major mode is 'Robert Man.guna's Song', however, presents some problems for this theory.

Fella' (item 1) (chapter 5, track 13), where in vocal sections 2–4 the slow even beating used for text phrases in ghost language is suspended when text in Mendhe is being sung.

Further notes on selected tracks

Here we provide some additional analytical notes on musical features of six songs ('Happy Song No. 1', 'Happy Song No. 3', 'Karra Mele Ngany-endheni-nö', 'Song for Anson Bay', 'Robert Man.guna's Song' and 'Happy Song No. 4').

Track 3 'Happy song No. 1'

Somewhat unusually, in the later part of the item, Mandji sometimes suspends the beating during text phrases 1 (VS 3 and 4) or 1-2 (VS 5). This feature is also found in vocal section 1 of 'Happy Song No. 2' in track 5.

Track 6 'Happy Song No. 3'

Each vocal section consists of two melodic sections, separated by a breath. In vocal sections 1, 2, 4 and 6, the same vocable text phrase is repeated four times: twice over each melodic section (AA'AA). In vocal sections 3 and 7 the first two repetitions of the vocable text are replaced by wordless melisma over the melodic section 1 ([melisma]'AA).

It is clear that for this song, while varying the text and to some extent the melodic contour for melodic section 1, Mandji keeps the second melodic section relatively stable. This systematic variation in presentation of text over the same melody is reminiscent of Jimmy Muluk's compositional procedures discussed in chapter 5.

Track 8 'Karra Mele Ngany-endheni-nö'

In his use of moderate even beating with Walakandha *wangga* beating patterns for instrumental section 1, Mandji appears to follow a pattern established by Jimmy Muluk whereby vocal sections in rhythmic modes 1 and 2 (both are used here) are followed by this pattern. The final pattern too follows Muluk's pattern in that it uses doubled beating in the moderate tempo band (rhythmic mode 4e).

Track 9 'Song from Anson Bay'

The use of rhythmic mode 4b (moderate uneven quadruple) is relatively unusual in the corpus. Of the singers included in this study, only Mandji and Lambudju use this mode: in Lambudju's case for one song only (Marett, 2005, p. 196), while for Mandji there is a second example at track 12. This is the only instance of rhythmic mode 4b (var).

Track 11 'Robert Man.guna's Song'

The use of rhythmic mode 5a (fast even), together with vocable text, suggests that this might be another 'happy song.' Somewhat unusually this is in a Lydian mode (C D E F sharp G A B). Bobby Lambudju Lane provides the only other example of this modal practice in the corpus (Marett, 2005, 194).

Track 12 'Happy song No. 4'

This song begins in rhythmic mode 4c (moderate uneven triple) for the first vocal and instrumental sections, and moves in the second vocal section to rhythmic mode 4a (moderate even beating). Note that the ending is fairly messy, with relatively unsynchronised handclapping in the coda, perhaps because the audience members clapping along were unfamiliar with the song. It is slower than most happy songs, but the first two items of Muluk's 'Lerri' song (chapter 5, track 19) also use moderate tempo.

Chapter 7
LAMBUDJU'S REPERTORY

Bobby Lambudju Lane (1941–1993) was one of the two leading songmen at Belyuen in the late 1980s and early 1990s (the other being Barrtjap, see chapter 4). The character of his songs stands, however, in marked contrast to those of Barrtjap. Whereas Barrtjap's repertory is marked by an economy of form, Lambudju's songs were more varied: his texts use a richer variety of forms and lexicon, and even mix two languages, Batjamalh and Emmi; his melodies are diverse and use an array of different modes. Lambudju's extensive use of sung vocables during instrumental sections is another distinctive feature.

The key to this diversity is the fact that Lambudju's repertory came from a number of different sources: apart from those that he composed himself, he inherited songs from his two Wadjiginy 'fathers' Aguk Malvak and Alalk, from his Emmiyangal adoptive father, Mun.gi, as well as from other members of the family.

Three of Lambudju's father's brothers, Aguk Malvak, Alalk and Tjulatji, were leading songmen in the first half of the twentieth century. Because Lambudju was too young to learn these songs before they died, his father, Jack Lambudju, asked his sister's daughter's Emmiyangal husband, Nym Mun.gi, to hold the songs in trust until such time as Lambudju came of age. In our two earliest recordings, from 1959 and 1962 respectively, we hear a very young Lambudju singing alongside Mun.gi's son Rusty Benmele Moreen, who at that time was undoubtedly the more accomplished singer. Benmele, however, died young, and by the time that Marett arrived in Belyuen in 1986, Lambudju was the undisputed master of this tradition, singing songs inherited from the upper generations alongside many of his own composition.

Figure 7.1 Bobby Lambudju Lane at Indian Island, 1989. Photograph by Adrienne Haritos, reproduced with the permission of Belyuen community.

Figure 7.2 Tourist corroboree performers at Mandorah, 1987. Bobby Lane Lambudju is second from left (rear). Roger (Rossy) Yarrowin is second from right (kneeling). Tommy Barrtjap is the singer seated on the right. Photograph by John N. Doyle, reproduced with the permission of Belyuen community.

The texts of many of Lambudju's songs concern his country to the north of the Daly River and in particular Rak Badjalarr (North Peron Island), the place to which people from Belyuen return after their death. Many of his songs, for example 'Rak Badjalarr' (tracks 1–6), 'Bandawarra-ngalgin' (tracks 7–9), 'Karra Balhak Malvak' (track 10) and 'Karra-ve Kanya-verver' (tracks 11 and 12) contain the words of wunymalang ghosts, singing as they return to Rak Badjalarr and its surrounding country. Other songs, for example 'Benmele' (track 13), 'Tjerrendet' (track 15) and 'Tjendabalhatj' (track 16) concern specific individuals, while others, for example 'Bangany Nye-bindja-ng' (track 17) are about the act of singing and dancing itself. There are also a number of songs—for example 'Lima Rak-pe' (track 24), 'Bende Ribene' (track 28) and 'Limila Karrawala' (track 29)—that are entirely, or largely in ghost language (vocables).

Notes on the recording sample

Because Lambudju's life was cut short at a relatively young age, the corpus of recordings is not large, although it does have an intriguing historical depth (see table 7.1).

Track	Song #	Title	Singer	Recording
Track 01	1	'Rak Badjalarr'	Lambudju	Mar86-04-s07
Track 02		'Rak Badjalarr'	Lambudju	Moy62-01-s01
Track 03		'Rak Badjalarr'	Wurrpen	Wes61-s15
Track 04		'Rak Badjalarr'	Benmele	Wes61-s25
Track 05		'Rak Badjalarr'	Worumbu	Mar97-13-s13
Track 06		'Rak Badjalarr'	Worumbu	Tre08-01-s26
Track 07	2	'Bandawarra-ngalgin'	Lambudju	Mar86-04-s02
Track 08		'Bandawarra-ngalgin'	Lambudju	Mar86-04-s03
Track 09		'Bandawarra-ngalgin'	Lambudju	Mar86-04-s04
Track 10	3	'Karra Balhak Malvak'	Lambudju	Mar86-04-s09
Track 11	4	'Karra-ve Kanya-verver'	Lambudju	Mar86-04-s01
Track 12		'Karra-ve Kanya-verver'	Lambudju and Rankin	Moy62-01-s02
Track 13	5	'Benmele'	Lambudju	Mar86-04-s10
Track 14	6	'Winmedje'	Lambudju	Mar86-04-s06
Track 15	7	'Tjerrendet'	Lambudju	Mar86-04-s05
Track 16	8	'Tjendabalhatj'	Lambudju	Mar86-04-s11
Track 17	9	'Bangany Nye-bindja-ng'	Lambudju	Mar91-04-s04
Track 18	10	'Walingave'	Lambudju	Mar91-04-s05
Track 19	11	'Djappana'	Lambudju	Mar91-05-s04
Track 20		'Djappana'	Lambudju	Mar91-05-s05
Track 21		'Djappana'	Lambudju	Mar91-05-s06
Track 22		'Djappana'	Lambudju	Mar91-05-s07
Track 23	12	'Karra Balhak-ve'	Lambudju and Benmele	Moy59-03-s01_02
Track 24	13	'Lima Rak-pe'	Lambudju and Benmele	Moy62-01-s03
Track 25	14	'Mubagandi'	Yarrowin	Mar97-05-s01
Track 26		'Mubagandi'	Yarrowin	Mar97-05-s02
Track 27		'Mubagandi'	Yarrowin	Mar97-05-s03
Track 28	15	'Bende Ribene'	Worumbu and Yarrowin	Tre08-01-s08
Track 29	16	'Limila Karrawala'	Worumbu and Yarrowin	Tre08-01-s14

Table 7.1 Songs from Lambudju's repertory discussed in this chapter.

In all, sixteen songs have been recorded over a fifty-year period from 1959 to the present.[1] The earliest recording, from 1959, was made by Alice Moyle when Lambudju was only in his late teens. In 1962, Moyle again recorded Lambudju, now about twenty, singing four songs, including the song with which he is most strongly associated, 'Rak Badjalarr' (track 1–6). Lambudju was also recorded by Marett in 1986 and 1991. Lambudju's adoptive brother, Rusty Benmele Moreen, was recorded singing with Lambudju by Alice Moyle in 1959, and later recorded solo by LaMont West at Beswick Creek (Barunga) in 1961. Colin Worumbu Ferguson, who took over Lambudju's repertory after his death, was recorded on a number of occasions by Marett in 1997 and by Treloyn in 2008. Worumbu's brother, Les Kundjil, also sang Lambudju's songs on occasion, and Roger Yarrowin, Lambudju's brother-in-law, also received some of his songs. In 2008, Worumbu was at particular pains to fill in any gaps in our knowledge of the various Belyuen repertories.

TRACK 1 (Mar86-04-s07)
Song 1: Rak Badjalarr

Sung text	Free translation
rak badjalarr-maka bangany-nyung (repeated)	[I am singing] for the sake of a song for my ancestral country, North Peron Island
ii winmedje ngan-dji-nyene	I am [sitting] eating oysters

Badjalarr is North Peron Island, the ancestral country (*rak*) to which Lambudju inherited rights through his father. It lies to the north of the mouth of the Daly River. It is regarded as dangerous to all but senior traditional owners and those properly introduced to the country by them, for it is the land of the dead for the Wadjiginy and others living at Belyuen. It is inhabited by *wunymalang* ghosts, who can come from Badjalarr to Belyuen to give songs to songmen. This dangerous aspect of the song is reflected in the rhythmic setting of its text (see below).

The opening text phrase, *rak badjalarr-maka bangany-nyung* ('for the sake of a song for my ancestral country, North Peron Island') contains an ellipsis, which was clarified by Lambudju when he spoke the text and added the words, *nga-bindjan-ng* ('I am singing') to provide the meaning, 'I am singing for the sake of a song for my ancestral country, North Peron Island'. And yet the meaning is still not clear until one understands that we are hearing the words of a *wunymalang*, and that 'for the sake of' means, 'for the sake of [giving you] a song for my ancestral country, North Peron Island.' Sung in ceremony, however, we hear the voice of the living singer declaring that he is singing for the sake of providing the participants with a song about his country, North Peron Island. Badjalarr is one of several sites in the Daly region mentioned by name in Lambudju's songs. The dangerous aspect of Badjalarr is reflected in the fact that the rhythmitic setting disguises the words 'Rak Badjalarr' by setting them as if they were, 'Rakba djala.' When sung, *rakba* sounds like *rak-pe*, which has been glossed elsewhere as 'eternal country.' So dangerous is Badjalarr that its name cannot be spoken for fear of calling the ancestral ghosts back into the realm of the living. Even Lambudju himself disguised the name when he spoke about it: '*Rak badjalarr bangany, bangany-nyung nga-bindja-ng*, which means that's the name of the place, *djalarr*'.

---

[1] Note that this is two more than were published on the CD *Rak Badjalarr: Wangga songs from North Peron Island* by Bobby Lane (Marett, Barwick and Ford, 2001), and one more than was published in *Songs Dreamings and Ghosts* (Marett, 2005).

The text phrase about eating oysters refers to the fact that Badjalarr provides food for its children, and oysters are abundant there. Oysters also abound around the Cox Peninsula where Lambudju and most other Wadjiginy live, thus providing a link between their ancestral country and their current place of residence. This text phrase also contains an ellipsis: the final word *ngami* ('I sit') is supplied in the spoken version, but is not sung. This song and its significance are discussed in greater detail in Marett's book *Songs, dreamings and ghosts* (2005).

This chapter includes six versions of 'Rak Badjalarr', two sung by Lambudju himself (from 1986 and 1962), one by his adoptive brother, Rusty Benmele Moreen (from 1961), one by Lawrence Wurrpen (1961) and two by Colin Worumbu Ferguson (from 1997 and 2008), the singer who has inherited Lambudju's songs. These provide insights into how a song can develop over time and as it is passed from songman to songman. Note that all of these singers apart from Wurrpen—who was not a central member of the lineage—use the conspicuous vocalisations in the instrumental section so typical of Lambudju's own performances. See the music analysis section of this chapter for detailed discussion of the musical changes in these six versions.

SONG STRUCTURE SUMMARY

VOCAL SECTIONS 1–2

Melodic section 1

Text phrases 1–5

Rhythmic mode 5d (fast uneven triple)

rak	**badjalarr**	**-maka**	**bangany**	**-nyung**
father's country	place name	for	song	DAT

[I am singing] for the sake of a song for my ancestral country, North Peron Island

Melodic section 2

Text phrase 6

Rhythmic mode 5d (fast uneven triple)

ii	**winmedje**	**ngan**	**-dji**	**-nyene**
SW	oyster	1MIN.A/3AUG.O	eat	R

I am [sitting] eating oysters

INSTRUMENTAL SECTIONS 1–2

Rhythmic mode 5d (fast uneven triple)

TRACK 2 (Moy62-01-s01)

Song 1: Rak Badjalarr

Sung text	Free translation
rak badjalarr bangany nye-bindja-ng (repeated)	You sing a song for my ancestral country, North Peron Island
ii winmedje ngan-dji-nyene	I am [sitting] eating oysters

This is our earliest recording of 'Rak Badjalarr,' recorded by Alice Moyle in 1962. Although the quality of the recording is less than ideal owing to its having been originally recorded at a very low level, it has been included here because it gives us a chance to hear Bobby Lane singing while he was still a young man of about twenty.

There are a number of textual and musical differences between this version and the 1986 version on track 1 (see discussion below in the music analysis section of the chapter).

SONG STRUCTURE SUMMARY

VOCAL SECTIONS 1–2

Melodic section 1

Text phrases 1–5

Rhythmic mode 5a (fast even)

rak	badjalarr	bangany	nye	-bindja	-ng
father's country	place name	song	2MIN.S.IR	sing	SIM

You sing a song for my ancestral country, North Peron Island

Melodic section 2

Text phrase 6

Rhythmic mode 5a (fast even)

ii	winmedje	ngan	-dji	-nyene
SW	oyster	1MIN.A/3AUG.O	eat	R

I am [sitting] eating oysters

INSTRUMENTAL SECTIONS 1-2 [Various vocables are sung during these sections]

Rhythmic mode 5a (fast even)

TRACK 3 (Wes61-s15)

Song 1: Rak Badjalarr

Sung text	Free translation
rak badjalarr-maka bangany [-nyung] (repeated)	[I am singing] [for the sake of] a song for my ancestral country, North Peron Island
ii winmedje ngan-dji-nyene	I am [sitting] eating oysters

This performance was recorded by the linguist LaMont West at Beswick Creek (now Barunga) in 1961, that is, a year before the performance on track 2. The singer is Lawrence Wurrpen, a man from Delissaville (Belyuen) who had moved to Beswick Creek, where his wife's family lived. Wurrpen apparently brought with him various Belyuen repertories: in chapter 4 (track 17), Wurrpen can also be heard singing a song by Tommy Barrtjap. Other performances by Wurrpen are discussed in Marett, 2005, pp 212-16. See further details of Wurrpen's performance in the music analysis section of this chapter.

TRACK 4 (Wes61-s25)

Song 1: Rak Badjalarr

Sung text	Free translation
rak badjalarr-maka bangany-nyung (repeated)	[I am singing] for the sake of a song for my ancestral country, North Peron Island
ii winmedje ngan-dji-nyene	I am [sitting] eating oysters

This version is sung by Rusty Benmele Moreen, the son of Mun.gi, Lambudju's adoptive father and teacher, and hence Lambudju's adoptive elder brother. Benmele, who died at a tragically young age in the early 1980s (see further with regard to the song, 'Benmele' [track 13]), was senior to Lambudju. What we hear in this recording is an accomplished singer at the height of his powers.

While the text, text rhythm and melody are very similar to the version heard in track 1, Benmele's treatment of rhythmic mode is more complex (see further details in the music analysis section of this chapter). This performance is discussed in more detail in Marett, 2005, pp 189–91.

SONG STRUCTURE SUMMARY

VOCAL SECTION 1

Melodic section 1

Text phrases 1–5

Rhythmic mode 5a (var) (fast even with beating suspended)

rak	badjalarr	-maka	bangany	-nyung
father's country	place name	CAUS	song	DAT

[I am singing] for the sake of a song for my ancestral country, North Peron Island

[beating in rhythmic mode 5b (fast doubled) begins between melodic sections 1 and 2]

Melodic section 2

Text phrase 6

Rhythmic mode 5b (fast doubled)

ii	winmedje	ngan	-dji	-nyene
SW	oyster	1MIN.A/3AUG.O	eat	R

I am [sitting] eating oysters

INSTRUMENTAL SECTION 1

Rhythmic mode 5b (fast doubled)

VOCAL SECTION 2 AND 3

Melodic section 1

Text phrases 1–5

Rhythmic mode 5b (fast doubled)

rak	badjalarr	-maka	bangany	-nyung
father's country	place name	CAUS	song	DAT

[I am singing] for the sake of a song for my ancestral country, North Peron Island

Melodic section 2

Text phrase 6

Rhythmic mode 5b (fast doubled)

ii	winmedje	ngan	-dji	-nyene
SW	oyster	1MIN.A/3AUG.O	eat	R

I am [sitting] eating oysters

INSTRUMENTAL SECTIONS 2 AND 3

Rhythmic mode 5b (fast doubled)

VOCAL SECTION 4

Melodic section 1

Text phrases 1–5

Rhythmic mode 5e (fast uneven sextuple)

rak	badjalarr	-maka	bangany	-nyung
father's country	place name	CAUS	song	DAT

[I am singing] for the sake of a song for my ancestral country, North Peron Island

Melodic section 2

Text phrase 6

Rhythmic mode 5e (fast uneven sextuple)

ii	winmedje	ngan-dji	-nyene
SW	oyster	1MIN.A/AUG.O eat	R

I am [sitting] eating oysters

INSTRUMENTAL SECTION 4

Rhythmic mode 5e (fast uneven sextuple)

TRACK 5 (Mar97-13-s13)

Song 1: Rak Badjalarr

Following Lambudju's death in 1993, Colin Worumbu Ferguson took over singing his songs. Although Worumbu is from another language group (Marri Tjavin), his family has lived in Belyuen for many years. Worumbu divides his time between Belyuen and his wife's country near Wadeye.[2]

This performance of 'Rak Badjalarr' shows the influence of both Lambudju and Benmele (see further discussion in music analysis section). This performance, recorded by Marett on the beach one night at Mandorah, was so powerful that it called into our presence the ghost of Lambudju himself (see further Marett, 2005, p 191). The ritual call (*malh*) that can be heard at the end of the track is an indicator of the spiritual power of this performance.

---

[2] As discussed in chapter 1, Worumbu now has rights to sing a wide range of song repertories: from Belyuen, songs of Lambudju, Billy Mandji (Worumbu's father's brother), Jimmy Muluk and (to a lesser extent) Barrtjap. He also sings songs from the Wadeye area: not only the Walakandha *wangga* repertory that belongs to his own Marri Tjavin language group, but also some songs from the Ma-yawa *wangga*.

Figure 7.3 Colin Worumbu singing 'Rak Badjalarr' at Mandorah, 1997. Photograph by Allan Marett, reproduced with the permission of Belyuen community.

TRACK 6 (Tre08-01-s26)

Song 1: Rak Badjalarr

This performance was recorded by Sally Treloyn at Lee Point, Darwin. The performer is once again Colin Worumbu Ferguson. On this occasion Worumbu introduced several innovations to the text. One striking feature of this performance is its use of only two instead of three repetitions of the main text phrase in melodic section 1. As in Worumbu's 1997 performance, text phrase 1 is repeated at the end of melodic section 2 (vocal section 1); but in vocal sections 2 and 3 melodic section 2 is omitted altogether. Various features, including the fast doubled beating and some textual variation, remind us of Wurrpen's 1961 performance (track 3). By this time, the CD *Rak Badjalarr: Wangga songs for North Peron Island by Bobby Lane* (Marett, Barwick, & Ford, 2001), which contained the Wurrpen performance, had been in circulation for seven years and Worumbu was very familiar with it. He is quite candid about the fact that he learns songs from CDs and thus it is that modern technological media aid the transmission and maintenance of these traditions. Marett (2003) discusses the role of recordings in sustaining tradition, and the fact that in terms of local epistemology, recordings are regarded as being intrinsically identical to ghosts.

TRACK 7 (Mar86-04-s02)

Song 2: Bandawarra-ngalgin

Sung text	Free translation
bandawarra-ngalgin ka-djen-mene	It [the tide] is coming in at Bandawarra-ngalgin
bandawarra-ngalgin ka-djen-mene	It [the tide] is coming in at Bandawarra-ngalgin
bandawarra-ngalgin	Bandawarra-ngalgin

Bandawarra-ngalgin is the name given to a deep and dangerous hole in the ocean floor. It lies between the mouth of the Daly River and South Peron Island and forms part of Lambudju's ancestral country.

There are a number of interesting formal features of this song. The first is the oscillating glide that begins each melodic section. Glides of this sort can be heard in some of the oldest archival recordings of *wangga* but are rarely heard today. The second is the variability in ordering of the three text phrases, *bandawarra-ngalgin ka-djen-mene* ('It [the tide] is coming in at Bandawarra-ngalgin'), *nya-muy-ang nye-djang-nganggung* ('Stand up and dance woman, for us both') and *ngala-viyitj nya-mu-nganggung* ('Sit and clap hands for us both'). This variability can be observed not only across the three items presented here (tracks 7, 8 and 9) but also between vocal sections within each item. The third notable feature is the genre self-reference in the text phrases that refer to dancing and hand clapping. Here the singer is calling on the wider community to participate fully in the performance.

SONG STRUCTURE SUMMARY

VOCAL SECTION 1

Melodic sections 1–2

Text phrases 1–2

Rhythmic mode 1 (without clapsticks)

bandawarra-ngalgin	ka	-djen	-mene
placename	3MIN.S	come in	R

It [the tide] is coming in at Bandawarra-ngalgin

INSTRUMENTAL SECTION 1

Rhythmic mode 4a (moderate even)

VOCAL SECTION 2

Melodic section 1

Text phrase 1

Rhythmic mode 1 (without clapsticks)

bandawarra-ngalgin
placename

Bandawarra-ngalgin

INSTRUMENTAL SECTION 2

Rhythmic mode 5b (fast doubled)

TRACK 8 (Mar86-04-s03)

Song 2: Bandawarra-ngalgin

Sung text	Free translation
bandawarra-ngalgin ka-djen-mene	It [the tide] is coming in at Bandawarra-ngalgin
nya-muy-ang nye-djang-nganggung	Stand up and dance woman, for us both
bandawarra-ngalgin ka-djen-mene	It [the tide] is coming in at Bandawarra-ngalgin
ngala-viyitj nya-mu-nganggung	Sit and clap hands for us both

SONG STRUCTURE SUMMARY

VOCAL SECTION 1

Melodic section 1

Text phrase 1

Rhythmic mode 1 (without clapsticks)

bandawarra-ngalgin	**ka**	**-djen**	**-mene**
placename	3MIN.S	come in	R

It [the tide] is coming in at Bandawarra-ngalgin

Melodic section 2

Text phrase 2

Rhythmic mode 1 (without clapsticks)

nya	**-muy**	**-ang**	**nye**	**-djang**	**-nganggung**
2MIN.S.IR	sway	IR	2MIN.S.IR	stand	1/2MIN.IO

Stand up and dance woman, for us both

INSTRUMENTAL SECTION 1

Rhythmic mode 4a (moderate even)

VOCAL SECTION 2

Melodic section 1

Text phrase 1

Rhythmic mode 1 (without clapsticks)

bandawarra-ngalgin	**ka**	**-djen**	**-mene**
placename	3MIN.S	come in	R

It [the tide] is coming in at Bandawarra-ngalgin

Melodic section 2

Text phrase 2

Rhythmic mode 1 (without clapsticks)

ngala	**-viyitj**	**nya**	**-mu**	**-nganggung**
hand	clap	2MIN.S.IR	sit.IR	1MIN.IO

Sit and clap hands for us both

INSTRUMENTAL SECTION 2

Rhythmic mode 4a (moderate even)

TRACK 9 (Mar86-04-s04)

Song 2: Bandawarra-ngalgin

Sung text	Free translation
bandawarra-ngalgin ka-djen-mene	It [the tide] is coming in at Bandawarra-ngalgin
ngala-viyitj nya-mu-nganggung	Sit and clap hands for us both
bandawarra-ngalgin ka-djen-mene	It [the tide] is coming in at Bandawarra-ngalgin
nya-muy-ang nye-djang-nganggung	Stand up and dance woman, for us both
bandawarra-ngalgin ka-djen-mene	It [the tide] is coming in at Bandawarra-ngalgin
nya-muy-ang nye-djang-nganggung	Stand up and dance woman, for us both

SONG STRUCTURE SUMMARY

VOCAL SECTION 1

Melodic section 1

Text phrase 1

Rhythmic mode 1 (without clapsticks)

bandawarra-ngalgin	**ka**	**-djen**	**-mene**
placename	3MIN.S	come in	R

It [the tide] is coming in at Bandawarra-ngalgin

Melodic section 2

Text phrase 2

Rhythmic mode 1 (without clapsticks)

ngala	**-viyitj**	**nya**	**-mu**	**-nganggung**
hand	clap	2MIN.S.IR	sit.IR	1MIN.IO

Sit and clap hands for us both

INSTRUMENTAL SECTION 1

Rhythmic mode 4a (moderate even)

VOCAL SECTIONS 2–3

Melodic section 1

Text phrase 1

Rhythmic mode 1 (without clapsticks)

bandawarra-ngalgin	**ka**	**-djen**	**-mene**
placename	3MIN.S	come in	R

It [the tide] is coming in at Bandawarra-ngalgin

Melodic section 2

Text phrase 2

Rhythmic mode 1 (without clapsticks)

nya	**-muy**	**-ang**	**nye**	**-djang**	**-nganggung**
2MIN.S.IR	sway	IR	2MIN.S.IR	stand	1/2MIN.IO

Stand up and dance woman, for us both

INSTRUMENTAL SECTION 2

Rhythmic mode 4a (moderate even)

INSTRUMENTAL SECTION 3

Rhythmic mode 5b (fast doubled)

TRACK 10 (Mar86-04-s09)
Song 3: Karra Balhak Malvak

Sung text	Free translation
[ka] (second time only)	Ka
karra balhak malvak-karrang-maka ngarn-rdut-mene-ng ka-bara	Brother Malbak has gone and left me behind
bandawarra-ngalgin-bende nguk ka-maridje-ng ka-yeve	At Bandawarra-ngalgin now he is lying with one knee bent over the other
karra balhak werret-bende müng ya-mara nya-buring munguyil-malang	Quick now, brother, catch him up, fast-paddling one!
ngawardina ngawardina-djene-nung-bende	With a floating log

This song is addressed to the ghost of Lambudju's father's brother Aguk Malvak, one of the singers whose repertory Lambudju inherited. Malvak died some time after 1959, when he appears in the *Northern Territory Register of Wards* (1957, p 106) as 'Argog', tribal name 'Mauwot'; his birth date is given as 1895. The reason that Malvak is addressed as older brother (*balhak*) is because the composer of this song was, according to Lambudju, one of Malvak's younger brothers—the most likely candidates are Alalk or Tjulatji, both of whom were songmen. Ewers records Malvak as being one of the two main songmen at Delissaville in 1947 (the other was Barrtjap's 'father' Jimmy Bandak) (Ewers, 1954, p 25). This song describes Malvak's ghost lying at Bandawarra-ngalgin in one of the poses associated with the dead (one knee bent over the other, or 'number four leg' as this pose is commonly called),[3] and urges him to paddle across to Badjalarr (North Peron Island), the island of the dead to which all Wadjiginy people return.

---

3 See other references to 'number four leg' in the repertories of Jimmy Muluk (chapter 5), Billy Mandji (chapter 6), the Walakandha *wangga* (chapter 8), and the Ma-Yawa *wangga* (chapter 9).

SONG STRUCTURE SUMMARY

VOCAL SECTIONS 1–2

Melodic section 1

Text phrase 1a (vocal section 2 only)

Rhythmic mode 1 (without clapsticks)

ka
SW

Ka

Text phrase 1b

Rhythmic mode 1 (without clapsticks)

karra	**balhak**	**malvak**	**-karrang**	**-maka**
SW	older brother	person's name	ERG	PERF

Brother Malbak

ngarn	**-rdut**	**-mene**	**-ng**	**ka**	**-bara**
3MIN.A.1MIN.O	leave	R	SIM	3MIN.S	goR

has gone and left me behind

Text phrase 2

Rhythmic mode 1 (without clapsticks)

bandawarra-ngalgin	**-bende**
placename	now

At Bandawarra-ngalgin now

nguk	**ka**	**-maridje**	**-ng**	**ka**	**-yeve**
knee	3MIN.S	bend	SIM	3MIN.S	lie

he is lying with one knee bent over the other

Melodic section 2

Text phrase 3

Rhythmic mode 1 (without clapsticks)

karra	**balhak**	**werret**	**-bende**
SW	older brother	quickly	now

Quick now, brother,

müng	ya	-mara	nya	-buring	munguyil	-malang
arse	2MIN.A/3MIN.M.O.IR	kick	2MIN.S.IR	travel	paddle	FUL

catch him up, fast-paddling one!

Melodic section 3 (lower octave)

Text phrase 4

Rhythmic mode 1 (without clapsticks)

ngawardina	ngawardina	-djene	-nung	-bende
floating log	REDUP	with	PURP	now

with a floating log

INSTRUMENTAL SECTION 1

Rhythmic mode 4a (moderate even)

INSTRUMENTAL SECTION 2

Rhythmic mode 5b (fast doubled)

TRACK 11 (Mar86-04-s01)

Song 4: Karra-ve Kanya-verver

Sung text	Free translation
karra-ve kanya-verver-rtedi kay[a-ndhi]	It [a breeze] is forever cooling my back
karra-ve kak-ung-bende badjalarr	Away now to Badjalarr forever
ribene ribene ribene ribene ribene ribene …	Ribene ribene, ribene ribene, ribene ribene …
ii aa ü	ii, aa, ü
karra-ve kanya-verver-rtedi kaya-ndhi	It [a breeze] is forever cooling my back

Here a ghost sings about its journey to Badjalarr, the Wadjiginy island of the dead. Feeling the wind on your back is a sign of the presence of a ghost. Lambudju described getting this song from a Wumymalang ghost as follows: 'the wind's blowing and I'm lying down here. I slept and dreamt and a *maruy* (*wunymalang*) spirit came and sang the song. I got that picture and I sang that song' (Marett, Barwick and Ford, 2001, pp 13–14).

The song is in a mixture of Batjamalh and Emmi: text phrase 1 (*karra-ve kanya-verver-rtedi kay[a-ndhi]*) is in Emmi, while text phrase 2 (*karra-ve kak-ung-bende badjalarr*) is in Batjamalh. Such mixing of languages is unusual in *wangga* songs, but Lambudju is said to have frequently mixed the two languages in everyday conversation, perhaps because he was brought up in an Emmi-speaking family though his own ancestral language was Batjamalh. Despite Lambudju's claim to have composed this song himself, Marett has suggested that it is entirely possibly that this song is older, being one of the songs originally in Batjamalh transmitted to him from his father's generation via his adoptive father, Mun.gi, whose mother tongue was Emmi (Marett, 2005, p 195). This may be another explanation for the macaronic nature of the text.

Fluent speakers of Emmi assured us that text phrase 1 should end with the enclitic –*ndhi* (towards speaker), which would give the meaning, 'it [the wind] is always blowing on my back,' but it is not present in this performance, although careful listening suggests it is present when the text phrase is repeated at the end of the song. It can also be heard in the performance of this song that follows (track 12).

SONG STRUCTURE SUMMARY

VOCAL SECTION 1

Melodic section 1

Text phrase 1

Rhythmic mode 4c (moderate uneven triple)

karra	**-ve**	**kanya**	**-verver**	**-rtedi**	**kay[a**	**-ndhi]**
SW	forever	3MIN.A.IR.make	cool	back	3MIN.S.IR.lie	towards speaker

It [a breeze] is forever cooling my back

Text phrase 2

Rhythmic mode 4c (moderate uneven triple)

karra	**-ve**	**kak**	**-ung**	**-bende**	**badjalarr**
SW	forever	away	PURP	now	place name

Away now to Badjalarr forever

Text Phrase 3

Rhythmic mode 4c (mocerate uneven triple)

ribene	**ribene**	**ribene**	**ribene**	**ribene**	**ribene**	**ribene**	**rib**
SW	SW	SW	SW	SW	SW	SW	SW

ribene ribene, ribene ribene, ribene ribene …

Melodic section 2

Text phrase 4

Rhythmic mode 4c (moderate uneven triple)

ii	**aa**	**ü**
SW	SW	SW

ii, aa, ü

Melodic section 2

Text phrase 5

Rhythmic mode 4c (moderate uneven triple)

karra	-ve	kanya	-verver	-rtedi	kay[a	-ndhi]
SW	forever	3MIN.A.IR.make	cool	back	3MIN.S.IR.lie	towards speaker

It [a breeze] is forever cooling my back

INSTRUMENTAL SECTION 1

Rhythmic mode 4c (moderate uneven triple)

TRACK 12 (Moy62-01-s02)

Song 4: Karra-ve Kanya-verver

Sung text	Free translation
karra-ve kanya-verver-rtedi kaya-ndhi	It [a breeze] is forever cooling my back
karra-ve kak-ung-bende badjalarr	Away now to Badjalarr forever
ribene ribene ribene ribene ribene ribene …	Ribene ribene, ribene ribene, ribene ribene
ii aa ü	ii, aa, ü
ii aa ü	ii, aa, ü
karra-ve kak-ung-bende badjalarr	Away now to Badjalarr forever
ribene ribene ribene ribene	Ribene ribene, ribene ribene
ya ya, ya ya	Ya ya, ya ya

Track 12 is a performance of 'Karra-ve Kanya-verver' recorded by Alice Moyle in 1962. Here, the singers Lambudju and Douglas Rankin, structure the song slightly differently. While the melody, text and rhythmic mode are essentially the same as Lambuju's 1986 performance (track 11), this performance repeats text phrase 3 and in melodic section 2 replaces a repeat of text phrase 1—*karra-ve kanya-verver-rtedi kaya-ndhi*—with a repeat of text phrase 2—*karra-ve kak-ung-bende badjalarr*. Careful listening suggests that the full form of text phrase 1 was sung on this occasion.

SONG STRUCTURE SUMMARY

VOCAL SECTIONS 1–3

Melodic section 1

Text phrase 1

Rhythmic mode 4c (moderate uneven triple)

karra	-ve	kanya	-verver	-rtedi	kaya	-ndhi
SW	forever	3MIN.A.IR.make	cool	back	3MIN.S.IR.lie	towards speaker

It [a breeze] is forever cooling my back

Text phrase 2

Rhythmic mode 4c (moderate uneven triple)

karra	**-ve**	**kak**	**-ung**	**-bende**	**badjalarr**
SW	forever	away	PURP	now	place name

Away now to Badjalarr forever

Text phrase 3

Rhythmic mode 4c (moderate uneven triple)

ribene	**ribene**	**ribene**	**ribene**	**ribene**	**ribene**	**ribene**	**ribe**
SW	SW	SW	SW	SW	SW	SW	SW

ribene ribene, ribene ribene, ribene ribene

Melodic section 2

Text phrases 4–5

Rhythmic mode 4c (moderate uneven triple)

ii	**aa**	**ü**
SW	SW	SW

ii, aa, ü

Text phrase 6

Rhythmic mode 4c (moderate uneven triple)

karra	**-ve**	**kak**	**-ung**	**-bende**	**badjalarr**
SW	forever	away	PURP	now	place name

Away now to Badjalarr forever

Text phrase 7

Rhythmic mode 4c (moderate uneven triple)

ribene	**ribene**	**ribene**	**ribene**
SW	SW	SW	SW

ribene ribene, ribene ribene

Text phrase 8

Rhythmic mode 4c (moderate uneven triple)

ya	**ya**	**ya**	**ya**
SW	SW	SW	SW

ya ya, ya ya

INSTRUMENTAL SECTIONS 1–3

Rhythmic mode 4c (moderate uneven triple)

TRACK 13 (Mar86-04-s10)

Song 5: Benmele

Sung text	Free translation
benmele-maka kurratjkurratj ka-bindja nüng (repeated)	Benmele! Cuckoo! He sang for him
ii aa mm	ii, aa, mm

'Benmele' was composed in reaction to the death of Rusty Benmele Moreen in the early 1980s. Benmele was the adoptive elder brother of Lambudju, and at the time he was the senior singer in this tradition (Benmele can be heard singing on track 4). His death was a major loss to the community. The song describes the channel-billed cuckoo singing to Benmele to call him away to death. The significance of this is that any death announced by a channel-billed cuckoo is seen as a natural death, that is, a death not occasioned by sorcery. The song is essentially a denial of the involvement of any sorcery in Benmele's death. When this song is explained to children or outsiders, *kurratjkurratj* is usually glossed as 'kookaburra' so as to disguise this more serious meaning. A more detailed account of the various layers of interpretation associated with this song is given in Marett, 2005, pp 192–94.

Vocal sections 1–4 are sung isorhythmically (that is, with the same text syllables set to exactly the same rhythm each time). Lambudju takes a breath at the end of text phrases 2 and 4 leading to a truncation of the text phrase.

SONG STRUCTURE SUMMARY

VOCAL SECTIONS 1–3

Melodic section 1

Text phrases 1–4

Rhythmic mode 2 (slow even)

benmele	-maka	kurratjkurratj	ka	-bindja	nüng
benmele	PERF	channel-billed cuckoo	3MIN.S.R	sing	3MIN.IO

Benmele! Cuckoo! He sang for him

Melodic section 2

Text phrase 5

Rhythmic mode 2 (slow even)

ii	aa	mm
SW	SW	SW

ii, aa, mm

INSTRUMENTAL SECTIONS 1–3

Rhythmic mode 2 (slow even)

TRACK 14 (Mar86-04-s06)

Song 6: Winmedje

Sung text	Free translation
winmedje ngan-dji nyene nga-mi mm	I am sitting eating oysters
aa ee ü	aa, ee, ü

The Batjamalh words of text phrase 1 also appear as the final text phrase of 'Rak Badjalarr' (tracks 1–6). As explained in the notes to track 1, the reference to oysters links Lambudju's ancestral country on North Peron Island to his adoptive country at Belyuen on the Cox Peninsula. In 'Rak Badjalarr', a song-giving ghost is sitting on North Peron Island eating the oysters provided by that country; in dreaming 'Winmedje', Lambudju dreamt of his 'daughter' Audrey Lippo eating oysters at Two Fella Creek near Belyuen (in later discussions with our consultants, the composition was attributed to Lippo herself). In *Songs, dreamings and ghosts*, Marett explains in more detail how the two songs, 'Rak Badjalarr' and 'Winmedje' are related melodically, textually and in the details of their composition (2005, pp 186-87).

SONG STRUCTURE SUMMARY

VOCAL SECTIONS 1–2

Melodic section 1

Text phrase 1

Rhythmic mode 5c (fast uneven quadruple)

winmedje	ngan	-dji	nyene	nga	-mi	mm
oyster	1MIN.A/3AUG.O	eat	R	1MIN.S	sit	SW

I am sitting eating oysters

Melodic section 2

Text phrase 2

Rhythmic mode 5c (fast uneven quadruple)

aa	ee	ü
SW	SW	SW

aa, ee, ü

INSTRUMENTAL SECTIONS 1–2

Rhythmic mode 5c (fast uneven quadruple)

TRACK 15 (Mar86-04-s05)

Song 7: Tjerrendet

Sung text	Free translation
tjerrendet-maka ka-ngadja tjidja-nde bangany ka-bindja (repeated)	Tjerrendet has gone back it's this man's turn to sing a song

'Tjerrendet,' which means a traditional loincloth or 'cockrag,' was the nickname of Roy Mardi Bigfoot, who was an active performer at the time that Alice Moyle was recording performances at Mandorah at 1968. He had outstations both at Balgal opposite the Peron Islands and at Dum-in-Mirrie Island. Lambudju told us that he made this song one day when he saw Tjerrendet walking past his camp.

Lambudju's explanation of the song was:

> Tjerrendet means, like a person's name and this is what I'm singing about. Every time I repeat this *budjebudje yangbangga nitj* [I repeatedly call his name] he goes away and sings *kudja kabararrang bangany kabindja* [this man is singing a song] *kabindjeng kabara* [he sings as he goes], that means he goes out and repeating that song all the time, singing to himself.

Given that *wangga* are so often concerned with the activities of song-giving ghosts, we cannot but wonder whether this song in fact describes a visitation of Tjerrendet's ghost to the songman, Lambudju, whose turn it is now to sing the song.

SONG STRUCTURE SUMMARY

VOCAL SECTIONS 1–2

Melodic section 1

Text phrase 1–4

Rhythmic mode 3a (slow moderate even)

tjerrendet	**-maka**	**ka**	**-ngadja**
person'name	PERF	3MIN.S.R	go back.

Tjerrendet has gone back

tjidja	**-nde**	**bangany**	**ka**	**-bindja**
3MIN.M.DEIC	now	song	3MIN.S.R	sing

It's this man's turn to sing a song

INSTRUMENTAL SECTIONS 1–2

Rhythmic mode 3a (slow moderate even)

TRACK 16 (Mar86-04-s11)

Song 8: Tjendabalhatj

Sung text	Free translation
tjendabalhatj mive-maka nyen-ne-ne kanye-djanga (repeated)	Tjendabalhatj they saw you standing there

Tjendabalhatj was the Aboriginal name of Charlie Alliung, otherwise known as 'old Elliyong'. Lambudju explained this song as follows:

> *Tjendabalhatj makany mive nyinnene kanyedjanga*, that means this old Tjendabalhatj, Old Elliyong, went to visit this young person. *Mive nyenne nanggany kanyedjanga*, which means like he go visit him nearly every day.

There is clearly a more complex story lying behind this rather pithy explanation, which adds little to what is already in the song text. Lambudju told us that Tjendabalhatj was a *dawarrabörak* or sorceror, and as we have seen from 'Benmele,' stories about sorcery are often hidden from outsiders. Indeed, Alliung was one of two *dawarraböraks* who performed at a rag burning (*kapuk/karaboga*) ceremony recorded at Delissaville (the old name for Belyuen) in 1948 by the ABC journalist Colin Simpson (Barwick & Marett, 2011; Simpson, 1948, 1951).

SONG STRUCTURE SUMMARY

VOCAL SECTIONS 1–3

Melodic section 1

Text phrases 1–4

Rhythmic mode 5c (fast uneven quadruple)

tjendabalhatj	mive	-maka	nyen	-ne	-ne	kanye	-djanga
tjendabalhatj	eye	PERF	3AUG.A/2MIN.O	see	R	2MIN.S.R	stand

Tjendabalhatj they saw you standing there

INSTRUMENTAL SECTIONS 1–3

Rhythmic mode 5c (fast uneven quadruple)

TRACK 17 (Mar91-04-s04)

Song 9: Bangany Nye-bindja-ng [two items]

Sung text	Free translation
Item 1	
bangany nye-bindja-ng nya-mu-ngarrka ya-mara	Sit and sing a song for me, dance, man!
bangany nye-bindja-ng nya-mu-ngarrka ya-mara	Sit and sing a song for me, dance, man!
nya-muy-ang nye-djang-nganggung bangany-e ya-mara	Stand up and dance, woman, for us two Song. Dance, man!
ee nya-muy-ang nye-djang-nganggung bangany-e ya-mara	Ee, stand up and dance, woman, for us two. Song! Dance, man!
karra ee	Karra ee
Item 2	
bangany nye-bindja-ng nya-mu-ngarrka ya-mara	Sit and sing a song for me, dance, man!
bangany nye-bindja-ng nya-mu-ngarrka ya-mara	Sit and sing a song for me, dance, man!
nya-muy-ang nye-djang-nganggung bangany-e ya-mara	Stand up and dance, woman, for us two. Song! Dance, man!
ee nya-muy-ang nye-djang-nganggung bangany-e ya-mara	Ee, stand up and dance, woman, for us two. Song! Dance, man!
karra nya-mu nye-djang	Stand up and dance, woman.

Track 17 contains two items of 'Bangany nye-bindja-ng.' There is only the shortest of breaks between the two. This performance was recorded at the Belyuen waterhole one morning after a night of partying, hence the rather exuberant calls and comments from the dancers. For this occasion Lambudju used a pair of beer cans in place of clapsticks.

Lambudju said of this song:

> This spirit tells me to repeat that song what I been singing now. I got to repeat that song every now and then when I sing it. It says, 'sing me a song' and that's what it is, just like I said. I just keep on repeating that same word, *bangany nye-bindja-ng nya-mu*.

Lambudju's articulation of the self-reflexive nature of the song text—that the act of singing is the fulfillment of the song-giving ghost's sung command—is striking: 'It says, 'sing me a song' and that's what it is.'

One interesting self-referential feature of the song is that it refers to both men and women's accompanying dance. *Ya-mara* (literally, 'you kick') refers to men's dancing, and *nya-muya* (literally, 'you sway') to women's dancing. Presumably the 'us two' signified by the pronoun *-nganggung* refers to the singer and his didjeridu accompanist. In different performances of this song, Lambudju may substitute one of these terms for the other, depending who is dancing. In this elicited performance he showed off both forms.

We, and our Batjamalh-speaking consultants, have found it difficult to hear precisely what Lambudju is singing at the ends of text phrases 3 and 4 of both items. There seems to be additional text at the end of these text phrases in item 2, perhaps a partial repetition of *bangany nye-bindja-ng nya-mu*.

In the final instrumental sections, Lambudju rather playfully sings *di digidi di di* rather than his normal *di di di*.

SONG STRUCTURE SUMMARY

Item 1 (Mar91-04-s04)

VOCAL SECTION 1

Melodic section 1

Text phrases 1–2

Rhythmic mode 4b (moderate uneven quadruple)

bangany	nye	-bindja	-ng	nya	-mu	-ngarrka	ya	-mara
song	2MIN.S.IR	sing	SIM	2MIN.S.IR	sit.IR	1MIN.IO	2MIN.A.IR/3MIN.O	kick

Sit and sing a song for me, dance, man!

Text phrase 3

Rhythmic mode 4b (moderate uneven quadruple)

nya	-muy	-ang	nye	-djang	-nganggung	bangany	-e	ya	-mara
2MIN.S.IR	sway	IR	2MIN.S.IR	stand	1/2MIN.IO	song	SW	2MIN.A.IR 3MIN.O	kick

Stand up and dance, woman, for us two. Song! Dance, man!

Melodic section 2

Text phrase 4

Rhythmic mode 4b (moderate uneven quadruple)

ee	nya	-muy	-ang	nye	-djang	-nganggung	bangany	-e	ya	-mara
SW	2MIN.S.IR	sway	IR	2MIN.S.IR	stand	1/2MIN.IO	song	SW	2MIN.A.IR 3MIN.O	kick

Ee, stand up and dance, woman, for us two. Song! Dance, man!

Melodic section 3

Text phrase 5

Rhythmic mode 4b (moderate uneven quadruple)

karra	ee
SW	SW

Karra ee

INSTRUMENTAL SECTION 1

Rhythmic mode 4b (moderate uneven quadruple)

Item 2

VOCAL SECTION 1

Melodic section 1

Text phrases 1–2

Rhythmic mode 4b (moderate uneven quadruple)

bangany	**nye**	**-bindja**	**-ng**	**nya**	**-mu**	**-ngarrka**	**ya**	**-mara**
song	2MIN.S.IR	sing	SIM	2MIN.S.IR	sit.IR	1MIN.IO	2MIN.A.IR 3MIN.O	kick

Sit and sing a song for me, dance, man!

Text phrase 3

Rhythmic mode 4b (moderate uneven quadruple)

nya	**-muy**	**-ang**	**nye**	**-djang**	**-nganggung**	**bangany**	**-e**	**ya**	**-mara**
2MIN.S.IR	sway	IR	2MIN.S.IR	stand	1/2MIN.IO	song	SW	2MIN.A.IR 3MIN.O	kick

Stand up and dance, woman, for us two. Song! Dance, man!

Figure 7.4 Women at Belyuen, including Lambudju's daughters, dancing at the launch of Allan Marett's book, Belyuen, 2006. Photograph by Gretchen Miller, ABC Radio National, reproduced with the permission of Belyuen community.

Melodic section 2

Text phrase 4

Rhythmic mode 4b (moderate uneven quadruple)

ee	nya	-muy	-ang	nye	-djang	-nganggung	bangany	-e	ya	-mara
SW	2MIN.S.IR	sway	IR	2MIN.S.IR	stand	1/2MIN.IO	song	SW	2MIN.A.IR	3MIN.O kick

Ee, stand up and dance, woman, for us two. Song! Dance, man!

Melodic section 3

Text phrase 5

Rhythmic mode 4b (moderate uneven quadruple)

karra	nya	-mu	nye	-djang
SW	2MIN.S.IR	sit.IR	2MIN.S.IR	stand

Stand up and dance, woman

INSTRUMENTAL SECTION 1

Rhythmic mode 4b (moderate uneven quadruple)

TRACK 18 (Mar91-04-s05)

Song 10: Walingave

Sung text	Free translation
walingave-maka bangany nye-bindja-ng (repeated)	Sing a song for Walingave
ii aa walingave-maka bangany nye-bindja-ng walingave-maka bangany nye-bindja-ng	ii, aa Sing a song for Walingave Sing a song for Walingave

Lambudju explains, 'Now this song is about a place called Wali. Walingave. It's near Peron Island there somewhere, and what I'm singing there is, I just repeat that same old word: Wali, Walingave.' It is unclear precisely where Walingave is located.

In 1979 Brian Enda explained the song as follows (Marett, Barwick and Ford, 2001):

> Wally, that's the name of the Toyota at Port Keats when I was working up there. They call that Toyota 'Wally.' He had an accident somewhere near Daly River, you know that crossing? My 'father' Bobby Lane [asked] what time they're going to fix it. My father said [sings] '*wali muvu-maka*—like what time you going to move?' You know, he was [at] the garage. Well my old man said [sings] '*wali muvu-maka-yi bangany ney-bindja*—what time you going to move again?' My old man made that song you see, that's the one we're singing now.

It is possible that this explanation is what Ellis called 'a false front,' that is, an version of events that hides the true, deeper meaning (CJ Ellis, 1985, p 124), and that Lambudju's explanation, with its reference to a dimly remembered place in the ancestral country that he had never visited was true, but a matter of some sensitivity. It is also possible to argue, on the basis of the melody of this song (which is the same as 'Karra Balhak Malvak' [track 10]), that this was one of the older songs in Lambudju's repertory, perhaps composed by one of the songmen of his father's generation, who would have been better acquainted with country around North Peron Island (Marett, 2005, p 195). Interestingly, in 2008 Colin Worumbu Ferguson strongly asserted that Brian Enda's explanation was the correct one and that there was no such place as Walingave (personal communication, Allan Marett).

SONG STRUCTURE SUMMARY

VOCAL SECTIONS 1–2

Melodic section 1

Text phrases 1–6

Rhythmic mode 3b (slow moderate uneven triple)

walingave	**-maka**	**bangany**	**nye**	**-bindja**	**-ng**
place name	for	song	2MIN.S.IR	sing	SIM

Sing a song for Walingave

Melodic section 2

Text phrase 7

Rhythmic mode 3b (slow moderate uneven triple)

ii	**aa**
SW	SW

ii, aa

Text phrases 8–9

Rhythmic mode 3b (slow moderate uneven triple)

walingave	**-maka**	**bangany**	**nye**	**-bindja**	**-ng**
place name	for	song	2MIN.S.IR	sing	SIM

Sing a song for Walingave

INSTRUMENTAL SECTIONS 1–2

Rhythmic mode 3b (slow moderate uneven triple)

TRACKS 19–22 (Mar91-05-s04)

Song 11: Djappana

Sung text	Free translation
djappana rdinyale rdinyale djappana (repeated)	Djappana rdinyale rdinyale Djappana
ya	ya

Lambudju's comments are as follows: 'I just said that's the name of the place, Djappana. Djappana is near *tjine rakje* ['what's that place?'] the mouth of the Daly River, that Djappana, that's the name of the place. I just keep on repeating it, same word all the way.' Ruby Yarrowin, an Emmi speaker, told us that Djappana is to the north of the Daly River.

Lambudju sings the song almost identically on all four tracks, except that on track 22 he adds a third vocal and instrumental section.

SONG STRUCTURE SUMMARY

VOCAL SECTIONS 1–2

Melodic section 1

Text phrases 1–4

Rhythmic mode 5a (fast even)

djappana	**rdinyale**	**rdinyale**	**djappana**
place name	SW	SW	place name

Djappana rdinyale rdinyale Djappana

Text phrase 5

Rhythmic mode 5a (fast even)

ya
SW

ya

INSTRUMENTAL SECTIONS 1–2

Rhythmic mode 5a (fast even)

TRACK 23 (Moy59-03-s01 and s02)
Song 12: Karra Balhak-ve (two items)

Sung text	Free translation
karra balhak-ve bangany nga-bindja-ye (repeated)	Older brother I am forever singing a song
ii	ii

This song, recorded by Alice Moyle at Bagot in 1959, is noted in her fieldnotes as a 'song for Peron Island.' This is not only the earliest recording we have of Lambudju, but it is also one of the few recordings of him singing with Rusty Benmele Moreen. It is unlikely that this song was composed by Lambudju, indeed the minor mode quality of its melody suggest that it probably derived from the upper generation of singers that included Lambudju's father's brothers, Aguk Malvak, Alalk and Tjulatji (Marett, 2005, p 195).

In the notes to the CD recording, *Rak Badjalarr: Wangga songs from Peron Island by Bobby Lane* (Marett, Barwick & Ford, 2001, pp 29–30), we were misled by a spoken version of the text given to Alice Moyle in 1962 and mistakenly identified this as a song about the brolga. Our consultants, and indeed our own ears, confirm, however, that the penultimate word is *bangany* (song), not *belleny* (brolga). The song is, however, addressed to 'older brother,' a term used to address Dreamings as well as actual kin. Could this have been the Brolga Dreaming?

There are two dovetailed items.

SONG STRUCTURE SUMMARY

Item 1 (Moy59-02-s01)

VOCAL SECTIONS 1–3

Melodic section 1

Text phrases 1–3

Rhythmic mode 4a (moderate even)

karra	**balhak**	**-ve**	**bangany**	**nga**	**-bindja**	**-ye**
SW	older brother	forever	song	1MIN.S	sing	SW

Older brother I am forever singing a song

Melodic section 2

Text phrase 4

Rhythmic mode 4a (moderate even)

ii
SW

ii

INSTRUMENTAL SECTIONS 1–3

Rhythmic mode 4a (moderate even)

Item 2 (Moy59-03-s02)

VOCAL SECTIONS 1–2

Melodic section 1

Text phrases 1–3

Rhythmic mode 4a (moderate even)

karra	balhak	-ve	bangany	nga	-bindja	-ye
SW	older brother	forever	song	1MIN.S	sing	SW

Older brother I am forever singing a song

Melodic section 2

Text phrase 4

Rhythmic mode 4a (moderate even)

ii

SW

ii

INSTRUMENTAL SECTIONS 1–2

Rhythmic mode 4a (moderate even)

TRACK 24 (Moy62-01-s03)

Song 13: Lima Rak-pe

Sung text	Free translation
Lima rak-pe lima rak-pe (repeated)	*Lima* eternal country! *Lima* eternal country!
ya ya ya ya	ya ya ya ya

Once again we hear Lambudju singing with Rusty Benmele Moreen, this time in a recording made by Alice Moyle in 1962. Some consultants say that the words of this song have no meaning and are 'just for song,' but we have encountered the expression 'rak-pe' in too many songs, including a hint of it in 'Rak Badjalarr' (see notes to track 1), to take this at face value. It occurs in three of Barrtjap's songs: 'Yagarra Nedja Tjine Rak-pe' (Yagarra! Son, where is my camp/eternal country?) (chapter 4, track 20); 'Yagarra Rak Tjine Rak-pe' (Yagarra! Where is my eternal country?) (chapter 4, track 23); and 'Nyere-nye Bangany Nyaye' (chapter 4, track 12), where the second text phrase is *lima rak-pe ngadja ngaye* (*lima* my eternal country *ngaye*). Since in each of these cases *rak-pe* has been glossed as 'eternal country,' we have adopted that translation here.

The minor mode feeling of the melody, together with the early recording date, suggests too that this is an old song that may have been composed by one of Lambudju's 'fathers.'

SONG STRUCTURE SUMMARY

VOCAL SECTIONS 1–4

Melodic section 1

Text phrases 1–4

Rhythmic mode 4a (moderate even)

lima	**rak**	**-pe**	**lima**	**rak**	**-pe**
SW	country	forever	SW	country	forever

Lima eternal country! *Lima* eternal country!

Text phrase 5

Rhythmic mode 4a (moderate even)

ya	**ya**	**ya**	**ya**
SW	SW	SW	SW

ya ya, ya ya

INSTRUMENTAL SECTIONS 1–4

Rhythmic mode 4a (moderate even)

TRACK 25 (Mar97-05-s01)

Song 14: Mubagandi

Sung text	Free translation
a karra mubagandi ye-me-ngadja-nganggung-bende mm	Tell him to come back for you and me now, poor bugger
karra ye-me-ngadja-nganggung mm	Tell him to come back for you and me
ye-me-ngadja-nganggung ye-me-ngadja-nganggung-bende mm	Tell him to come back for you and me, tell him to come back for you and me now
karra ye-me-ngadja-nganggung mm	Tell him to come back for you and me

This performance was recorded in 1997, not long after the death of Lambudju. According to its Emmiyangal singer Roger Yarrowin, the song was composed by Lambudju and given to Yarrowin just prior to Lambudju's death (Marett and Barwick field tape DAT97/10). Because of various linguistic errors in the song text, some of our consultants have suggested that Yarrowin himself must have composed the song, which therefore must have been given to him by Lambudju in a dream after Lambudju's death. Given the liminal role of *wangga* songs within the interstices between the living and the dead, it is not surprising that people wish to sustain this mystery.[4]

According to fluent speakers of Batjamalh, the text of the song contains grammatical mistakes that a fluent speaker like Lambudju would not have made. *Ka-ngadja* is a simple verb meaning 'he returns.' While in Emmi it is possible to split off *-ngadja* ('return') and use it as a coverb with the inflected auxiliary *-me* ('do, say, tell'), as Yarrowin does, you cannot do this in Batjamalh. Perhaps this grammatical inconsistency points to Yarrowin's imperfect recall of Lambudju's text. Grammar aside, this would most easily translate as 'Tell him to come back to you and me.' In broad terms, the singer seems to be singing to a recently deceased relative, appealing to him to come back.

A second aspect of the song that may point to creative intervention by Yarrowin is the unusual melodic structure. While Lambudju often sang vocables and occasionally fragments of meaningful text in the lower octave, this usually occurred during the instrumental section. Here the lower octave melodic sections (2 and 4) are integral to the song. A possible model for this practice might be 'Karra Balhak Malvak' (track 10), where melodic section 3 contains text sung in the lower octave. The latter is an old song, however, from Lambudju's fathers' generation, not a song composed by Lambudju himself. See the music analysis section of this chapter for further discussion of musical features of this song.

SONG STRUCTURE SUMMARY

VOCAL SECTIONS 1–2

Melodic section 1

Text phrase 1

Rhythmic mode 5c (fast uneven quadruple)

a	karra	mubagandi	ye	-me	-ngadja	-nganggung	-bende	mm
SW	SW	poor bugger	3MIN.S.IR	do	come back	1/2MIN.IO	now	SW

Tell him to come back for you and me now, poor bugger

Melodic section 2 (lower octave)

Text phrase 2

Rhythmic mode 5c (fast uneven quadruple)

karra	ye	-me	-ngadja	-nganggung	mm
SW	3MIN.I.R	do	come back	1/2MIN.IO	SW

Tell him to come back for you and me

---

4   According to Marett's fieldnotes of 14 September 1998, several knowledgeable singers at Wadeye (including Les Kundjil, who had longstanding Belyuen connections, and Stephen Bunduck) affirmed that they had heard Lambudju himself sing 'Mubagandi', which seems to confirm its origin with Lambudju rather than Yarrowin.

Figure 7.5 Roger Yarrowin (wearing decorated belt) leads the dancing at Belyuen to celebrate the 2006 launch of Allan Marett's book *Songs, dreamings and ghosts*. Photograph by Gretchen Miller, ABC Radio National, reproduced with the permission of Belyuen community.

Melodic section 3

Text phrase 3

Rhythmic mode 5c (fast uneven quadruple)

ye	-me	-ngadja	-nganggung	ye	-me	-ngadja	-nganggung	-bende	mm
3MIN.I.R	do	come back	1/2MIN.IO -	3MIN.I.R	do	come back	1/2MIN.IO	now	SW

Tell him to come back for you and me, tell him to come back for you and me now

Melodic section 4

Text phrase 4

Rhythmic mode 5c (fast uneven quadruple)

karra	yeme	-ngadja	-nganggung	mm
SW	3MIN.I.R do	come back	1/2MIN.IO	SW

Tell him to come back for you and me

INSTRUMENTAL SECTIONS 1–2

Rhythmic mode 5c (fast uneven quadruple)

Lambudju's repertory • 273

TRACK 26 (Mar97-05-s02)

Song 14: Mubagandi (two items)

This track contains two dovetailed items of 'Mubagandi' (the didjeridu begins the second item before the first is finished). The text and musical structure of each item is the same as the version on track 25. The performance contains a number of ritual calls (*malh*), which the performer said were calls to the ghost of Lambudju.

TRACK 27 (Mar97-05-s03)

Song 14: Mubagandi

The text and musical structure of this item are the same as the previous three, except for one factor. In vocal section 2, Yarrowin suspends the stick beating. This is a powerful device, but one rarely heard (see music analysis section for more details).

TRACK 28 (Tre08-01-s08)

Song 15: Bende Ribene

Sung text	Free translation
bende ribene ribe (repeated)	Bende ribene ribe
yakerre balhak malvak-maka ka-bindja-ng ka-mi	Yakerre! He is singing for brother Malvak

This recording of a song composed by Lambudju, which he was never recorded singing himself, was made during an elicited session in 2008. In the course of the session Colin Worumbu Ferguson, to whom Marett had given draft CD copies for this and other chapters, filled in gaps in the repertory, giving us previously unrecorded, or rarely recorded, songs. Although we already had a recording of 'Bende Ribene' from 1991 (in which Worumbu performed with Les Kundjil), there were problems with the recording. This is a striking example of a consultant intervening in the production of this record of his culture. See the music analysis section for comments on musical features of this performance.

SONG STRUCTURE SUMMARY

VOCAL SECTIONS 1–2

Melodic section 1

Text phrases 1–4

Rhythmic mode 4a (moderate even)

bende	**ribene**	**ribe**
SW	SW	SW

Bende ribene ribe

Figure 7.6 Bobby Lane and Rusty Benmele Moreen singing *wangga* at Belyuen in 1979, with Les Kundjil in audience (with child in lap). Photograph by Adrienne Haritos, reproduced with the permission of Belyuen community.

Melodic section 2

Text phrase 5

Rhythmic mode 4a (moderate even) (quiet)

yakerre	balhak	malvak	-maka	ka	-bindja	-ng	ka	-mi
EXCL	brother	person	for	3MIN.S	sing	SIM	3MIN.S	Sit.R

Yakerre! He is singing for brother Malvak

INSTRUMENTAL SECTIONS 1–2

Rhythmic mode 4a (moderate even)

TRACK 29 (Tre08-01-s14)

Song 16: Limila Karrawala

This was another song of Lambudju's that we had previously failed to record or locate on archive copies. As for the previous track, Colin Worumbu Ferguson sang it for Marett in 2008 to complete the record of Lambudju's songs. It has the same melodic contour as 'Rak Badjalarr.' No song text is currently available for this track, but we do know that the word *karrawala* means 'hill.' See the music analysis section for further comments on this song.

MUSICAL ANALYSIS OF LAMBUDJU'S REPERTORY

Lambudju's repertory is significant because it exhibits a wide range of forms in every dimension of performance, text, melody and rhythmic mode.

Song structure summary

The structure of three of Lambudju's performances, 'Karra-ve Kanya-verver' (track 11) and the two items of 'Bangany Nye-bindja-ng' (track 17), is somewhat unusual in that they have only one vocal section followed by a single instrumental section (this is very unusual for any *wangga* song). Most of his other performances have two vocal sections and two instrumental sections. The largest number of vocal sections are contained in Rusty Benmele Moreen's performance of 'Rak Badjalarr' (track 4) and Lambudju's performance of 'Lima Rak-pe' (track 21), which each have four vocal and instrumental sections.

Text structure overview

Structurally the texts of Lambudju's songs take a variety of forms. Most, including songs such as 'Rak Badjalarr', 'Benmele' and 'Tjerrendet', have cyclical texts that are set isorhythmically, while some, including songs such as 'Bandawarra-ngalgin' and 'Karra-ve Kanya-verver', have through-composed texts. Some texts are entirely in human language, some in a mixture of ghost language and some entirely in ghost language. Most of Lambudju's song texts are stable from performance to performance. Notable exceptions to this are 'Bandawarra-ngalgin' (tracks 7–9), whose text is quite variable from item to item and from vocal section to vocal section, and there are several different versions of the text of 'Rak Badjalarr' (see further below).

A distinctive feature of Lambudju's style was his practice of singing vocables during instrumental sections on the 5th and 6th degrees of the scale (in the lower octave), rising to the tonic in the final instrumental section. This is reproduced by some singers, for example Colin Worumbu Ferguson, when they take up Lambudju's songs, but not all (see for example Laurence Wurrpen's performance of 'Rak Badjalarr' on track 3).

Rhythmic mode overview

Table 7.2 summarises Lambudju's practice with regard to rhythmic mode. He is the only singer to use the slow moderate tempo band, and his fast tempo band is slower than that of most other singers (typically 120–26bpm), which is partly why his repertory has a rather laid back feel to it. Note that Lambudju only uses the fast doubled rhythmic mode (5b) as the final instrumental section of his unmeasured songs, and never uses it in combination with fast tempo vocal sections.

Lambudju's songs use a relatively large number of rhythmic modes (very few share a rhythmic modal profile), which Marett has suggested appears to reflect the high degree of variety found in other aspects of Lambudju's repertory, such as melody (see below) (Marett, 2005).

Distribution of rhythmic mode between vocal sections and instrumental sections

One feature of Lambudju's practice that immediately leaps out is how often he uses the same rhythmic modes for both vocal and instrumental sections (the same cannot be said for others performing his songs, see tables 7.2, 7.4 and 7.5). This is the case for every song apart from the two songs in rhythmic mode 1 (which by definition must have a different rhythmic mode in the instrumental sections). Other singers tended to maintain the same rhythmic mode for songs in the moderate and fast tempo bands, but Lambudju extended this practice to the slow moderate and slow songs.

Tempo band of vocal section	#	Song title	Rhythmic mode of VS	Rhythmic mode of IIS	Rhythmic mode of FIS
Unmeasured					
Without clapsticks	2	Bandawarra-ngalgin (tracks 7-9)	1	4a	**5b** or 4a
	12	Karra Balhak Malvak (track 10)	1	4a	**5b**
Measured					
Slow (64–69bpm)	5	Benmele (track 13)	2	2	2
Slow Moderate (c. 99–107bpm)	7	Tjerrendet (track 17)	3a	3a	3a
	10	Walingave (track 18)	3b	3b	3b
Moderate (116bpm)	12	Karra Balhak-ve (track 23)	4a	4a	4a
	13	Lima Rak-pe (track 24)	4a	4a	4a
	9	Bangany Nye-bindja-ng[5] (track 17)	4b	4b	4b
	4	Karra-ve Kanya-verver (track 11 and 12)	4c	4c	4c
Fast (119–22bpm)	11	Djappana (tracks 19–22)	5a	5a	5a
	1	Rak Badjalarr (track 1)	5d	5d	5d
	1	Rak Badjalarr (track 2)	5a	5a	5a
	6	Winmedje (track 14)	5c	5c	5c
	16	Tjendabalhatj (track 16)	5c	5c	5c

Table 7.2 Rhythmic modes performed by Lambudju (track references are to chapter 7) VS= vocal section, IIS= internal instrumental section, FIS= final instrumental section, bold when different.

Presenting the same text in different rhythmic modes in different vocal sections within an item

This does not occur in Lambudju's own practice, but see the discussion below regarding performances of Lambudju songs by Benmele, Worumbu and Yarrowin.

Mixing of rhythmic modes within a vocal section

This does not happen in Lambudju's own practice or in that of others performing his songs apart from a couple of instances where the beating is suspended.

Variation in rhythmic mode of instrumental sections across items

This happens only in 'Bandawarra-ngalgin' (tracks 7–9) where the first performance uses rhythmic mode 5b (fast doubled) for the final instrumental section, while the second and third items use the same moderate even rhythmic mode 4a as found in the internal instrumental sections. Perhaps Lambudju initially followed the same pattern as used for 'Karra Balhak Malvak' (the other song in rhythmic mode 1) before deciding that the song should be performed in the second way.

Melodic mode overview

We have already mentioned that because of its complex pattern of transmission, Lambudju's repertory contains the widest variety of melodic modes. These are set out in table 7.3. In the top part of the table

---

5 In Marett 2005, this was erroneously allocated to Rhythmic mode 5c (fast uneven quadruple).

are songs that use either the lydian, chromatic or major modes. It can be seen that a number of these are attributed to Lambudju, sometimes alone, and sometimes in combination with other singers. In the lower part of the table are songs that use the dorian mode. Because none of the songs known to have been composed by Lambudju use this mode, and because those in the dorian mode have qualities that suggest that they are old—either by attribution to a composer of Lambudju's father's generation (Aguk Malvak), or because they were recorded when Lambudju was very young, or because they refer to places such as Djappana and Walingave about which Lambudju himself had little or no knowledge—it seems plausible to suggest that songs that use a lydian, major or chromatic series were probably composed by Lambudju himself, while those that use the dorian series are perhaps those that he inherited from his father's brothers.

Song	Pitch series	Attribution
'Tjerrendet'	A–G–F-sharp–D–C	
'Tjendabalhatj'	A–G–F-sharp–F–E–D–C	Lambudju
'Mubagandi'	A–G–F-sharp–F–C	Lambudju
'Bandawarra-ngalgin'	chromatic D to C	Lambudju
'Benmele'	chromatic E to C	Lambudju
'Winmedje'	E–D–C–A–G–E–D–C	Lambudju/Benmele/Audrey Lippo
'Rak Badjalarr'	A–G–E–D–C	Lambudju/Audrey Lippo
'Limila Karrawala'	A–G–E–D–C	Lambudju
'Bangany Nye-bindja-ng'	G-F-D-D-C	Lambudju
'Karra Balhak Malvak'	C–B-flat–A–G–F–E-flat–D–C	Attributed to Aguk Malvak
'Walingave'	C–B-flat–A–G–F–E-flat–D–C	
'Djappana'	B-flat–A–G–F–E-flat–D–C	
'Bende Ribene'	C–B-flat–G–F–E-flat –C	
'Karra Balhak-ve'	C–B-flat–A-flat–G–F–E-flat–D–C	Recorded in 1959
'Lima Rak-pe'	C–B-flat–A-flat–G–F–E-flat–D–C	Recorded in 1962
'Karra-ve Kanya-verver'	C–B-flat–A-flat–G–F–E–E-flat–D–C	Recorded in 1962

Table 7.3 Melodic modes and attributions of songs

Songs that share a melody

Only 'Rak Badjalarr' and 'Limila Karrawala' share a melody.

Further notes on selected tracks

Here we provide some additional analytical notes on musical features of several songs ('Rak Badjalarr', 'Bandawarra-ngalgin', 'Mubagandi', 'Bende Ribene' and 'Limila Karrawala').

Tracks 1–6 'Rak Badjalarr'

It is interesting to contrast Lambudju's use of rhythmic mode with the performances of his songs by other singers. Table 7.4 sets out the rhythmic modes used in all six performances of 'Rak Badjalarr' (tracks 1–6). Wurrpen's performance uses rhythmic mode 5b (fast doubled beating) throughout, which as we have noted was never used in this fashion by Lambudju himself; it is, however, not uncommon in other Belyuen song repertories. Benmele's version of the song uses a number of different rhythmic modal settings: the first vocal section is unaccompanied by clapsticks, but has a definite didjeridu pulse in synchrony with the vocal rhythm, so is probably to be counted as a suspended form of one of the fast rhythmic modes (we have classified it as 5a [var]). Fast doubled beating (5b) follows this and continues throughout vocal sections 2 and 3 and their following vocal sections, before the clapsticks change for the final vocal and instrumental sections to an unusual pattern unique in the *wangga* corpus: fast uneven sextuple rhythmic mode 5e, consisting of five crotchet beats followed by a crotchet rest. Note that both Wurrpen and Benmele remain within Lambudju's usual relaxed tempo range for fast songs (120–26bpm).

The final two performances, by Worumbu, are noteworthy in a number of respects. Like Benmele, both Worumbu's performances change rhythmic mode in the course of the song item, with the final item in a different rhythmic mode (the change is from 4c [moderate uneven triple] to 5a [fast even] in track 5, and from 5b [fast doubled] to 5d [fast uneven triple] in track 6). It is in tempo that we find the most interesting developments. We have already noted that Lambudju's fast tempo is performed with a more relaxed tempo than other singers. Worumbu's 1997 performance is so relaxed indeed that the fast uneven triple rhythmic mode 5d used in Lambudju's performances (at about 122bpm) becomes what can only be interpreted as a moderate tempo uneven triple rhythmic mode 4c (performed by Worumbu at 116bpm, the same tempo as used by Lambudju for 'Karra-ve Kanya-verver'). The final vocal section in fast even beating (rhythmic mode 5a) returns to Lambudju's preferred tempo (123bpm). In 2008, Worumbu performs the first two vocal sections with fast doubled beating (reminding us of Wurrpen's performance on track 3), finishing with Lambudju's characteristic rhythmic mode 5d. Remarkably, however, this song is performed throughout at approximately 130bpm, much faster than any of the other performances, but within the range commonly used by Worumbu's father, Billy Mandji, for fast songs (see table 2.4 in chapter 2).

Tempo band of first vocal section	#	Song title	Rhythmic mode of VS	Rhythmic mode of IIS	Rhythmic mode of FIS
Fast	1	'Rak Badjalarr' (track 1)	5d	5d	5d
	1	'Rak Badjalarr' (track 2)	5a	5a	5a
	1	'Rak Badjalarr' (Wurrpen) (track 3)	5b	5b	5b
	1	'Rak Badjalarr' (Benmele) (track 4)	5a (var), 5b, 5b, 5e	5b	**5e**
Moderate	1	'Rak Badjalarr' (Worumbu 1997) (track 5)	4c, 4c, 5a	4c	**5a**
Fast	1	'Rak Badjalarr' (Worumbu 2008) (track 6)	5b, 5b, 5d	5b	**5d**

Table 7.4 Rhythmic mode in six versions of Lambudju's song 'Rak Badjalarr'. Lambudju's two performances are shaded.

There are also small but significant textual differences between the various performances. Even in Lambudju's own performances, the text of the opening text phrases is slightly different. As we have seen, the text of the first version is '[I am singing] for the sake of a song for my ancestral country, North Peron Island'). In Lambudju's second version, the song-giving ancestral ghost simply issues his orders to the song-man: 'you sing a song for my ancestral country, North Peron Island.'

Wurrpen (track 3) often truncates the text of the opening text phrase. For most text phrases he simply sings *rak badjalarr-maka bangany* ('A song for my ancestral country North Peron Island'), sometimes extending this to *rak badjalarr-maka bangany-nyung* ('for the sake of a song for my ancestral country North Peron Island'). Wurrpen does not use Lambudju's distinctive vocalisation during instrumental sections, instead adding a coda of the type found in Barrtjap's repertory. This is a rare case of a singer mixing aspects of the two singers' styles. Benmele's practice in instrumental sections is similar to Lambudju's, where he sings similar vocables moving from the 6th to the 5th degree in non-final instrumental sections, resolving to the tonic in the final instrumental section.

Worumbu's performance in 1997 (track 5) uses the same text phrase 1 as used by Lambudju on track 2, *rak badjalarr bangany nye-bindja-ng* ('You sing a song for my ancestral country, North Peron Island'), but Worumbu puts his own stamp on the song by introducing an additional repeat of this text phrase at the end of melodic section 2. In the 2008 performance Worumbu consistently sings the elliptical text *rak badjalarr bangany-nyung* (as did Wurrpen) while his back up singer, Roger Yarrowin, caught unawares, appears to sing the full line.

Tracks 7–9 'Bandawarra-ngalgin'

The occurrence of both moderate and fast tempo bands within an item, as in the instrumental sections of tracks 7 and 9, is relatively unusual in *wangga*. While using moderate tempo (rhythmic mode 4a) for non-final instrumental sections, in the final instrumental sections of these tracks Lambudju uses fast doubled beating (rhythmic mode 5b) (see also Worumbu's 1997 performance of 'Rak Badjalarr' and Lambudju's performance of 'Karra Balhak Malvak').

Tracks 14–16 'Mubagandi', 'Bende Ribene' and 'Limila Karrawala'

Table 7.5 shows the use of rhythmic modes in the three Lambudju songs performed only by others.

Tempo band of first vocal section	#	Song title	Rhythmic mode of VS	Rhythmic mode of IIS	Rhythmic mode of FIS
Fast	14	'Mubagandi' (tracks 25-26) (Yarrowin)	5c	5c	5c
	14	'Mubagandi' (track 27) (Yarrowin)	5c+5c (var)	5c	5c
Moderate	15	'Bende Ribene' (track 28)	4a	4a	4a
	16	'Limila Karrawala' (track 29)	4c	4c	4c

Table 7.5 Rhythmic mode in four modern performances of Lambudju's songs 'Mubagandi', 'Bende Ribene', and 'Limila Karrawala'.

'Mubagandi' (tracks 25–27) is performed by Yarrowin in fast uneven quadruple rhythmic mode 5c (the same mode as used in 'Winmedje' and 'Tjendabalhatj' as performed by Lambudju). He performs the song at a much faster tempo than anything by Lambudju himself: 133bpm, which is a similar tempo to that used in the other *wangga* repertories for this rhythmic mode. In track 27, Yarrowin suspends the clapstick beating, though audience members and the didjeridu player Nicky Jorrock maintain the beat.

'Bende Ribene' (track 28) and 'Limila Karrawala' (track 29) were both performed by Worumbu in 2008. They are both performed at about 117bpm, closer to the usual range for Lambudju's moderate tempo songs (110–16bpm) than to his fast songs (120–26bpm). In Lambudju's own performances, he uses rhythmic mode 4a (moderate even) for 'Karra Balhak-ve' and rhythmic mode 4c (moderate uneven triple) for 'Karra-ve Kanya-verver'. Note that 'Limila karrawala' shares a melody with 'Rak Badjalarr', which Worumbu likewise performed in 1997 using rhythmic mode 4d at about the same tempo for 2 out of 3 vocal sections (see comments above).

Chapter 8
THE WALAKANDHA *WANGGA* REPERTORY

For the last thirty years or so, the Walakandha *wangga*, a repertory composed by Wadeye-based Marri Tjavin singers, has been the most prominent *wangga* repertory performed there. Initiated at Wadeye in the late 1960s by Stan Mullumbuk (1937–1980), the Walakandha *wangga* repertory has come to function as one arm of the tripartite ceremonial system organising ceremonial life at Wadeye, in complementary relationship with its sister repertories *djanba* and the *muyil lirrga*. As discussed in chapter 1, one striking common feature of these three new repertories is their high proportion of text in normal human language: Marri Tjavin in the case of the Walakandha *wangga*, Marri Ngarr in the case of the Muyil *lirrga* and Murriny Patha in the case of *djanba*.

The dominant themes of the Walakandha *wangga* repertory are related to the Walakandha—the Marri Tjavin ancestral dead—and their activities as givers of *wangga* songs and custodians of the living descendants. Several specific ancestors, the deceased kin of living Marri Tjavin involved in creation and performance of the repertory, are named in songs. These include Munggum, Berrida, Wutjelli, Munggumurri and Tjagawala, as well as an oblique reference in 'Yendili No. 5' (track 29) to the mother of Frank Dumoo, the recently deceased Marri Tjavin ritual leader. Songs refer, often by metaphorical means, to death, which is likened to the going out of the tide or to being hit by a breaker (this oft-used metaphor can also symbolise more general misfortune). In 'Karra Yeri-ngina' (track 34), the song-giving Walakandha expresses his sadness at leaving his children behind as he goes back to his totemic home at Pumut. There are also numerous references to ceremony, one of the most explicit of which occurs in 'Yenmilhi No. 1 (track 20). One song, 'Nginimb-andja' (track 4) also refers to the role that Walakandha play in keeping their descendants safe from strangers.

Figure 8.1 Large group of Walakandha *wangga* dancers including Les Kundjil, Maurice Ngulkur Warrigal Kungiung and Philip Mullumbuk. Photograph by Mark Crocombe, reproduced with the permission of Wadeye community.

Longing for return to Marri Tjavin ancestral country, which lies to the north of Wadeye, is another common theme. Many songs contain the expression *nidin-ngina* 'my dear country'. Many specific places are named. Foremost amongst these is the important hill, Yendili. Other songs name the Marri Tjavin outstation Nadirri, located at Kubuwemi, and various coastal places nearby, such as Truwu beach, the headland Rtidim, the mouth of the Moyle River at Dhenggi-diyerri and the Kinyirr Dreaming site at the end of the airstrip. Inland sites near another Marri Tjavin outstation at Perrederr include: Yenmungirini (the Pumut (Headache) Dreaming site); the hill Yenmilhi where Walakandha ancestors dwell; the billabongs at Lhambumen; the ceremonial grounds at Pelhi and Ngumali and so on. There is even mention of one Marri Ammu site, Pumurriyi (song 24), underlining the fact that although the Marri Tjavin compose these songs, the Marri Ammu form company with and dance alongside their Marri Tjavin countrymen in ceremony.

Notes on the recording sample

The tracks included in this chapter contains the texts of all known Walakandha *wangga* songs and are set out in table 8.1.[1] At least one performance of each song is included on the CD; where songs exist in a number of versions (for example with different rhythmic modes or with different melodies), each version is included. While there must have been other songs that were never recorded, particularly in the 1970s and early 1980s, what survives here is a substantial and important corpus of thirty-four song compositions. Most of the songs set out in table 8.1 have been discussed in earlier publications: the early and transitional *wangga* were discussed in Marett (2007) while many of those from the golden age to the present were discussed in *Songs, dreamings and ghosts* (Marett, 2005).

We divide our discussion of the Walakandha *wangga* repertory into five parts:

A: the early period songs, composed by Stan Mullumbuk (1937–c. 1980) in the period from the early 1960s to about 1980;

B: a performance by Thomas Kungiung (1934–1993) which we consider as transitional, containing four Stan Mullumbuk songs and two early compositions of his own;

C: the main body of Walakandha *wangga* songs, created by a number of different composers during a 'golden age' that spanned the years between 1986–1996;

D: a body of songs composed by Philip Mullumbuk and Les Kundjil that came to the fore after Kungiung's death in 1993; and

E: two miscellaneous songs that have a somewhat tangential relationship to the Walakandha *wangga* tradition.

Track	Song #	Title	Recording	Composer
A: Early period (Stan Mullumbuk's songs)				
Track 01	i	Walakandha No. 8	Kof86-03-s07	S. Mullumbuk
Track 02	ii	Walakandha No. 6	Rei74-01-s15	S. Mullumbuk
Track 03	iii	Wutjelli No. 2	Rei74-01-s16	S. Mullumbuk
Track 04	iv	Nginimb-andja (2 items)	Rei74-01-s19	S. Mullumbuk
Track 05	v	Walakandha No. 7	Mar99-04-s18	S. Mullumbuk

---

1 Because of the discovery of new recordings, and this volume's chronological ordering of recordings, the sequence of numbering for this repertory previously established in *Songs, dreamings and ghosts* (Marett, 2005, pp 238-241) has been substantially modified here. All songs from the early and transition period have been allocated numbers in Roman numerals, and the Arabic numeral sequence used for more recently composed songs has been adjusted to allow for the new songs from Kofod's 1986 recordings. Equivalences to the original numbering in Marett, 2005 have been indicated in footnotes to the relevant tracks.

Track	Song #	Title	Recording	Composer
B: Transition from the early period				
Track 06	i-a	Walakandha No. 8a (RM 5c)	?Hodd82-s01	S. Mullumbuk
Track 07	i-b	Walakandha No. 8b (RM 4a)	?Hodd82-s04	S. Mullumbuk
Track 08	vi-a	Walakandha No. 9a (RM 1+4a)	?Hodd82-s02	S. Mullumbuk
Track 09	vi-b	Walakandha No. 9b (RM1)	?Hodd82-s03	S. Mullumbuk
Track 10	vii	Yendili No. 6	?Hodd82-s06	T. Kungiung
Track 11	viii	Yenmilhi No. 2	?Hodd82-s08	T. Kungiung
C: Golden age (1986–1996)				
Track 12	1	Kubuwemi	Mar88-23-s02	W. Dumoo
Track 13	2	Yendili No. 1	Mar88-23-s03	W. Dumoo
Track 14	3	Yendili No. 2	Mar88-23-s08	M. Dumoo
Track 15	4	Walakandha No. 1	Mar88-24-s02	Unknown
Track 16	5a	Truwu [Truwu A melody]	Mar88-39-s02	T. Kungiung
Track 17	5b	Truwu [Truwu B melody]	Mar99-02-s14	L. Kundjil
Track 18	5c	Truwu [Truwu A/B melody]	Eni92-s08	T. Kungiung & L. Kundjil
Track 19	6	Nadirri	Mar88-30-s15	Unknown
Track 20	7	Yenmilhi No. 1	Mar88-54-s03	J. Dumoo
Track 21	8	Mirrwana	Mar88-40-s11	T. Kungiung
Track 22	9	Wutjelli No. 1	Eni92-s11	T. Kungiung
Track 23	10	Walakandha No. 2	Eni92-s06	T. Kungiung & T. Dumoo
Track 24	11	Pumurriyi (2 items)	Kof86-01/2-s15	T. Kungiung
Track 25	12	Thidha nany (2 items)	Kof86-01/2-s11	T. Kungiung
Track 26	13	Dhembedi-ndjen	Kof86-01/2-s12	M. Kungiung
Track 27	14	Tjagawala	Kof86-03/4-s10	W. Dumoo
Track 28	15	Karra	Kof86-03/4-s09	Unknown
Track 29	16	Yendili No. 5	WASA23-s06	W. Dumoo
D: Later period (Les Kundjil and Philip Mullumbuk's songs)				
Track 30	17	Yendili No. 3	Mar98-15-s06	L. Kundjil
Track 31	18	Lhambumen	Mar99-04-s16	L. Kundjil
Track 32	19	Yendili No. 4	Eni92-s24	P. Mullumbuk
Track 33	20	Walakandha No. 3	Mar99-04-s07	P. Mullumbuk
Track 34	21	Karra Yeri-ngina	Mar99-04-s08	P. Mullumbuk
Track 35	22	Walakandha No. 4	Mar99-04-s10	P. Mullumbuk
Track 36	23	Walakandha No. 5	Mar98-15-s21	P. Mullumbuk
Track 37	24	Kinyirr	Mar99-04-s21	P. Mullumbuk

Track	Song #	Title	Recording	Composer
E: Miscellaneous songs				
Track 38	25	Wedjiwurang	Croc04-01-s01	P. Mullumbuk
Track 39	26	Tjinmel	Mar98-07-s11	A. Piarlum

Table 8.1 Songs from the Walakandha *wangga* repertory discussed in this chapter, showing the five groupings adopted in the discussion.

We should point out that there are some important differences in the corpus discussed in this chapter compared to the songs used as the basis for Marett's previously published discussions of Walakandha *wangga* songs (Marett, 2005, 2007). First, Marett's discussion of the early and transitional *wangga* included eight versions of the song 'Yene yene' (each in a different rhythmic mode) recorded by Michael Walsh in 1972 (Marett, 2007). Unfortunately the quality of these recordings was too poor to warrant their publication and these performances are therefore not included in our analysis below; the interested reader can consult the publication. Secondly, the group of 'golden age' songs discussed here includes five more songs than were analysed in *Songs, dreamings and ghosts* (Marett, 2005, chapter 5). The five additional songs from this period (tracks 24–28) come from a 1986 recording by Frances Kofod that was not available at the time that *Songs, dreamings and ghosts* was written.[2] Thirdly, for the sake of completeness we have included two miscellaneous songs 'Wedjiwurang' (track 38) and 'Tjinmel' (track 39), but because of their marginal status within the Walakandha *wangga* tradition (to be explained further below), neither will be included in the music analysis section at the end of the chapter.

Performance and recording history of the Walakandha *wangga*

In this chapter, we have organised the track-by-track notes into the five groupings discussed above, with additional notes on each grouping preceding discussion of the relevant tracks.

A: The Early Period. Stan Mullumbuk's repertory (tracks 1–5)

It was during the mid- to late-1960s that Stan Mullumbuk composed the first Walakandha *wangga* songs (Marett, 2007, p 65). The earliest recordings of Stan Mullumbuk's corpus were made in 1972 by Michael Walsh and in 1974 by Lesley Reilly (Marett, 2007, p 66). In addition, Frances Kofod recorded Thomas Kungiung and others singing one of the songs from this period, 'Walakandha No. 8,' in 1986. By 1988 none of Stan Mullumbuk's songs were still being sung ceremonially, though a video made by SBS in 1994 of a Roman Catholic baptismal ceremony recorded on Airforce Hill near Wadeye shows Martin Warrigal Kungiung singing some of the older songs (Wadeye Aboriginal Video Archive WAVA236). In 1999, Allan Marett recorded Ambrose Piarlum singing one of Stan Mullumbuk's songs (track 5) for the purpose of documentation.

Four additional Stan Mullumbuk songs sung by Thomas Kungiung on tracks 6–9 are discussed together with two of Kungiung's own early compositions below under section B.

---

2   None of these five songs substantially alters the analysis previously set out by Marett (Marett, 2005, chapter 5).

TRACK 1 (Kof86-03-s07)

Song i: Walakandha No. 8[3]

Sung text	Free translation
karra walakandha kimi-nginanga-wurri kavulh-a	The Walakandha has always sung to me and I can't stop him

According to Frank Dumoo, this was the first Walakandha *wangga* song ever composed, probably sometime in the late 1960s (see chapter 1). Like most songs from this period, the text asserts that songmen have always received songs from Walakandha, and—since the Walakandha appear unbidden in their dreams—that there is no way for them to resist this. The songman's lack of agency in this process is indicated by the adversative pronominal, *-nginanga* (see chapter 3). There is nonetheless considerable evidence that once a living songman has been given the germ of a song, he does a significant amount of compositional work in order to render it suitable for the ceremonies of the living (Marett, 2005, p 45).

We do not have a recording of Stan Mullumbuk himself singing this song. The performance on track 1 is by Thomas Kungiung and others, and was recorded by Frances Kofod in 1986. This performance uses beating accompaniment that shows influence from Belyuen singers (see music analysis section for further details). Marett (2007, pp 70–72) has suggested that a number of stylistic features of the early Walakandha *wangga* can be traced back to the songs of Muluk in particular (chapter 5). Two earlier recordings of this song by Kungiung are included below at tracks 6 and 7 (see further discussion there).

SONG STRUCTURE SUMMARY

VOCAL SECTIONS 1–4

Melodic section 1

Text phrase 1

Rhythmic mode 5c (fast uneven quadruple)

karra	walakandha	kimi	-nginanga	-wurri	kavulh	-a
SW	walakandha	3MIN.S.R do	1MIN.ADVERS	towards speaker	3MIN.S.R lie[1]	PERF

The Walakandha has always sung to me and I can't stop him

INSTRUMENTAL SECTIONS 1–4

Rhythmic mode 5c (fast uneven quadruple)

---

3 Classified as Song 24 in Marett, 2005, p 241.

TRACK 2 (Rei74-01-s15)

Song ii: Walakandha No. 6[4]

Sung text	Free translation
aa yene yene	Aa yene yene
aa karra walakandha ki-nyi-ni venggi-tit -nginanga-wurri kavulh marzi mungirini	Aa, the Walakandha always manifests himself, lying down with one knee bent over the other and singing to me (or facing me) in the jungle

Like 'Walakandha No. 8', this song underlines the fact that songmen have no say in whether they receive songs or not. Lying with one leg crossed over another in 'number four leg' is a posture associated with song-creation.[5] The 'jungle' mentioned in the song lies behind Truwu beach near the Nadirri outstation. The part of speech '-*wurri*' simply means 'toward the speaker.' It is sometimes glossed as '[singing] to me' and sometimes as '[facing] towards me.' The vocable text in text phrase 1—*yene yene*—reproduces the sung utterances of the Walakandha. Spirit-language texts that contain very similar vocables occur not only in other Mullumbuk songs but also in Belyuen singer Billy Mandji's 'Duwun Crab Song' (chapter 6, track 7). Some rhythmic characteristics of this song resemble the stylistic practice of Jimmy Muluk (see further details in the music analysis section).

This is the first of three songs sung at a circumcision ceremony at Wadeye in 1974, recorded by the lay missionary, Lesley Reilly (née Rourke).

SONG STRUCTURE SUMMARY

VOCAL SECTIONS 1–4

Melodic section 1

Text phrase 1

Rhythmic mode 1 (without clapsticks)

aa	**yene**	**yene**
SW	SW	SW

Aa yene yene

Melodic section 2

Text phrase 2

Rhythmic mode 1 (without clapsticks)

aa	**karra**	**walakandha**	**ki**	**-nyi**	**-ni**
SW	SW	walakandha	3MIN.A.R	make	3MIN.REFL

Aa, the Walakandha always manifests himself

---

4 Classified as Song 20 in Marett, 2005, p 241.

5 See similar references to 'number four leg' poses in the songs of Jimmy Muluk (chapter 5), Billy Mandji (chapter 6), Lambudju (chapter 7) and the Ma-Yawa *wangga* (chapter 9).

venggi	-tit	-nginanga	-wurri	kavulh	marzi	mungirini
knee	bend	1MIN.M.ADVERS	towards speaker	3MIN.S.R lie	inside	jungle

lying down with one knee bent over the other and singing to me (or facing me) in the jungle

INSTRUMENTAL SECTIONS 1–3 (non-final)

Rhythmic mode 5*

INSTRUMENTAL SECTION 4 (final)

Rhythmic mode 5b (fast doubled)

TRACK 3 (Rei74-1-s16)

Song iii: Wutjelli No. 2[6]

Sung text	Free translation
yene yene yene yene yene yene yene yene yene yene yene yene (number of repetitions varies)	Yene, yene, yene, yene, yene, yene, yene, yene, yene, yene, yene, yene (number of repetitions varies)
karra wutjelli ki-nyi-ni venggi-tit-nginanga-wurri kavulh marzi mungirini	Wutjelli always manifests himself, lying down with one knee bent over the other and singing to me (or facing me) in the jungle

Wutjelli, a 'grandfather' of Philip and Stan Mullumbuk (Marett, 2005, p 47), is mentioned in a number of Walakandha *wangga* songs. Here he appears as a Walakandha, lying down in 'number four leg' position, a pose associated with song-giving.

The text of this song is closely related to that of 'Walakandha No. 6' (track 2), with the word 'Walakandha' being replaced by 'Wutjelli' in text phrase 2. The substitution of one text phrase or word for another within a textual template is a time-honoured compositional means for generating new songs, and is found frequently in the Walakandha *wangga* repertory. Here despite the textual similarity, and as if to underline the innovation, we find that the musical treatment, in particular the rhythmic mode, differs significantly from 'Walakandha No. 6' (see further details in the music analysis section). The precise number of repetitions of the vocable *yene* sung in text phrase 1 varies.

SONG STRUCTURE SUMMARY

VOCAL SECTIONS 1–5

Melodic section 1

Text phrase 1

Rhythmic mode 2 (slow even)

yene	**yene**	**yene**	**yene**	**yene**	**yene**	**yene**	**yene**	**yene**	**yene**	**yene**	**yene**
SW	SW	SW	SW	SW	SW	SW	SW	SW	SW	SW	SW

Yene, yene, yene, yene, yene, yene, yene, yene, yene, yene, yene, yene (number of repetitions varies)

---

6 Classified as Song 21 in Marett, 2005, p 241.

Text phrase 2

Rhythmic mode 2 (slow even)

karra	**wutjelli**	**ki**	**-nyi**	**-ni**
SW	wutjelli	3MIN.A.R	make	3MIN.REFL

Wutjelli always manifests himself,

venggi	**-tit**	**-nginanga**	**-wurri**	**kavulh**	**marzi**	**mungirini**
knee	bend	1MIN.M.ADVERS	towards speaker	3MIN.S.R lie	inside	jungle

lying down with one knee bent over the other and singing to me (or facing me) in the jungle

INSTRUMENTAL SECTIONS 1-5

Rhythmic mode 5a (fast even)

Figure 8.2 Edward Nemarluk, Tommy Moyle and John Chula dancing as suspicious Walakandha, Wadeye, 1988 (see Marett, 2005, p 99). Photograph by Mark Crocombe, reproduced with the permission of the Wadeye community.

TRACK 4 (Rei74-01-s19)

Song iv: Nginimb-andja[7] *(Two items)*

Sung text	Free translation
aa yene yene	Aa yene, yene
aa karra nginimb-andja kudinggi meri ngindji-nginanga-wurri kuniny kan-gu	Aa, who are these strangers who keep staring at me and don't recognise me?

In this song, a Walakandha expresses suspicion about an approaching stranger. One of the duties of the Walakandha dead is to protect their living descendants, and they are notoriously hostile to outsiders who have not been properly introduced to them or their country. Interlopers are likely to be physically or sexually assaulted, or to have unfortunate accidents visited upon them.

In this track two items are dovetailed, that is, the didjeridu begins item 2 before the stick beating for item 1 has been completed. The non-final instrumental sections have the same form as in 'Walakandha No. 6' (track 2).

SONG STRUCTURE SUMMARY

Item 1

VOCAL SECTIONS 1–4

Melodic section 1

Text phrase 1

Rhythmic mode 1 (without clapsticks)

aa	**yene**	**yene**
SW	SW	SW

Aa yene, yene

Melodic section 2

Text phrase 2

Rhythmic mode 1 (without clapsticks)

aa
SW

Aa

---

7   Classified as Song 22 and written as 'Niminbandja' in Marett, 2005, p 241.

karra	nginimb-andja	kudinggi	meri	ngindji	-nginanga	-wurri	kuniny	kan	-gu
SW	who-true	3AUG.S.R look	person	another	1MIN. ADVERS	towards speaker	3AUG.S.R walk	near DEIC	DTOP

Who are these strangers who keep staring at me and don't recognise me?

INSTRUMENTAL SECTIONS 1–3 (non-final)

Rhythmic mode 5*

INSTRUMENTAL SECTION 4 (final)

Rhythmic mode 5b (fast doubled)

Item 2

VOCAL SECTIONS 1–3

Melodic section 1

Text phrase 1

Rhythmic mode 1 (without clapsticks)

aa	yene	yene
SW	SW	SW

Aa Yene, yene

Melodic section 2

Text phrase 2

Rhythmic mode 1 (without clapsticks)

aa
SW

Aa

karra	nginimb-andja	kudinggi	meri	ngindji	-nginanga	-wurri
SW	who-true	3AUG.S.R look	person	another	1MIN.ADVERS	towards speaker

Who are these strangers who keep staring at me

kuniny	kan	-gu
3AUG.S.R walk	near DEIC	DTOP

and don't recognise me?

INSTRUMENTAL SECTIONS 1–2 (non-final)

*Rhythmic mode 5**

INSTRUMENTAL SECTION 3 (final)

Rhythmic mode 5b (fast doubled)

TRACK 5 (Mar99-04-s18)

Song v: Walakandha No. 7[8]

Sung text	Free translation
yene yene yene yene yene yene yene	Yene, yene, yene, yene, yene, yene, yene
karra walakandha	Karra walakandha
karra	Karra

This song by Stan Mullumbuk was sung to Marett by Ambrose Piarlum in 1999, explicitly as a historical curiosity rather than an item in the current repertory. In a subsequent rendition (not included here), a number of singers added text to the second text phrase, but in a rather chaotic and unsatisfactory manner. One of the versions of text phrase 2 is *karra walakandha kiminy-ga kavulh*, which means 'Walakandha always sing like this.' Frank Dumoo suggested that this is the correct form of the text, and that the form sung here is an abbreviation.

SONG STRUCTURE SUMMARY

VOCAL SECTIONS 1–3

Melodic section 1

Text phrase 1

Rhythmic mode 5c (fast uneven quadruple)

yene	**yene**	**yene**	**yene**	**yene**	**yene**	**yene**
SW	SW	SW	SW	SW	SW	SW

Yene, yene, yene, yene, yene, yene, yene

Text phrase 2

Rhythmic mode 5c (fast uneven quadruple)

karra	**walakandha**
SW	walakandha

Walakandha

---

8   Classified as Song 23 in Marett, 2005, p 241.

Melodic section 2

Text phrase 3

Rhythmic mode 5c (fast uneven quadruple)

karra
SW

Karra

INSTRUMENTAL SECTIONS 1–3

Rhythmic mode 5c (fast uneven quadruple)

B: The transition from the early period to the golden age (tracks 10–11)

In 1998, Gemma Ngunbe, the daughter of John Dumoo, gave Allan Marett a cassette tape that she had found in a storeroom at the Wadeye school. Marett (2007, pp 67, 73 [footnote 15]) has concluded that it probably belongs to a collection of recordings recorded by Bill Hoddinott in 1982.[9] The singer is Thomas Kungiung. Several of the songs (tracks 6–9) are early period compositions by Stan Mullumbuk, and others (tracks 10 and 11) are early compositions by Thomas Kungiung himself. The recording appears to document the transition from the early period, in which Mullumbuk was the dominant songman, to the golden age, when Kungiung emerged as the pre-eminent songman. In this recording Thomas Kungiung contrasts two approaches to rhythmic mode, the first typical of Stan Mullumbuk's practice, the second of his own. Juxtaposing consecutive song items with minimal variation is a strategy deployed by singers in many different Australian song traditions to draw attention to particular facets of song meaning and structure. Barwick has suggested that this approach to structuring a song performance fosters the development of inductive modes of musical learning (Barwick, 2005, 2006).

Kungiung begins by presenting Mullumbuk's practice of singing a song in a number of different rhythmic modes, which may have been a feature borrowed by Mullumbuk from the Belyuen singer Jimmy Muluk (see chapter 5). Kungiung first sings two versions of Mullumbuk's 'Walakandha No. 8' (see also track 1) in two different rhythmic modes.[10] He then sings two versions of another Mullumbuk song 'Walakandha No. 9', again contrasting rhythmic modal treatment,[11] and also introducing a contrast in melody between the two versions. Kungiung's presentation of two different Mullumbuk songs given contrasting musical treatments draws attention firmly to that aspect of their musical structure.

Kungiung then presents two of his own compositions, 'Yendili No. 6' and 'Yenmilhi No. 2' (tracks 10 and 11), consistently singing each vocal section in one, and only one, rhythmic mode. It seems that the practice of always singing songs in a single rhythmic mode was an important innovation introduced when Kungiung took over from Mullumbuk as the main Walakandha songman. Marett has concluded that Kungiung deliberately simplified rhythmic modal practice in this way in order to facilitate the participation of a greater number of dancers from a wider range of language groups (Marett, 2007).

Neither of these Kungiung compositions ('Yendili No. 6' and 'Yenmilhi No. 2') survived into the golden age (1986–1996). We may assume therefore that these are early compositions, and the closeness

---

9   It seems that this particular recording is not amongst others by Hoddinott deposited at AIATSIS, and no speech is recorded on the tape, so the identification of the recordist is necessarily tentative.

10   In the first, the vocal section is in rhythmic mode 5c (fast uneven quadruple)—the same rhythmic mode as was used for this song in track 1; in the second, it is in rhythmic mode 4a (moderate even).

11   In the first, the vocal section is in a combination of rhythmic mode 1 (without clapsticks) and rhythmic mode 4a (moderate even beating); in the second, it is in rhythmic mode 1 alone.

of their structure to those of the Mullumbuk songs supports this (see further discussion on this point below). One feature of these songs not found in the later Kungiung repertory is a small degree of text instability. Perhaps this is because the songs had not yet been subjected to the rigours of ceremonial performance, which usually requires the texts of songs to become fixed.

TRACK 6 (?Hodd82-s01)

Song i-a: Walakandha No. 8a[12]

Sung text	Free translation
karra walakandha kimi-nginanga-wurri kavulh-a	The Walakandha has always sung to me and I can't stop him
karra walakandha	Karra walakandha

Here Thomas Kungiung performs the text of 'Walakandha No. 8' (see also track 1) in the first of two different rhythmic modes—the songs are thus labelled 8a and 8b. The listener can easily perceive the differences in tempo and organisation of clapstick beating between the two songs presented here and in track 7 (see further details in the music analysis section of this chapter).

In both tracks 6 and 7, renditions of text phrase 2 descend into the lower octave. This is another feature typical of Kungiung's style of performance here and into the golden age.

SONG STRUCTURE SUMMARY

VOCAL SECTIONS 1–3

Melodic section 1

Text phrase 1

Rhythmic mode 5c (fast uneven quadruple)

karra	walakandha	kimi	-nginanga	-wurri	kavulh	-a
SW	walakandha	3MIN.S.R do	1MIN.ADVERS	towards speaker	3MIN.S.R lie	PERF

The Walakandha has always sung to me and I can't stop him

Melodic section 2 (descends to lower octave)

Text phrase 2

Rhythmic mode 5c (fast uneven quadruple)

karra	walakandha
SW	walakandha

Walakandha!

INSTRUMENTAL SECTONS 1–3

Rhythmic mode 5c (fast uneven quadruple)

---

12 Classified as Song 24 in Marett, 2005, p 241.

TRACK 7 (?Hodd82-s04)

Song i-b: Walakandha No. 8b

Sung text	Free translation
karra walakandha kimi-nginanga-wurri kavulh-a-gu	This is what the Walakandha has always sung to me and I can't stop him
karra walakandha	Karra walakandha

In this version of 'Walakandha No. 8' the text is very slightly modified by the addition of a final focus marker -*gu*, which slightly shifts the meaning from 'the Walakandha has always sung …' to 'this is what the Walakandha has always sung …'. We saw similar subtle shifts of meaning brought about by minute adjustments to the text in consecutive couplets of Jimmy Muluk's song 'Wörörö' (see chapter 5).

SONG STRUCTURE SUMMARY

VOCAL SECTIONS 1–3

Melodic section 1

Text phrase 1

Rhythmic mode 4a (moderate even)

karra	**walakandha**	**kimi**	**-nginanga**	**-wurri**	**kavulh**	**-a**	**-gu**
SW	walakandha	3MIN.S.R do	1MIN.ADVERS	towards speaker	3MIN.S.R lie	PERF	TOP

This is what the Walakandha has always sung to me and I can't stop him

Melodic section 2 (descends to lower octave)

Text phrase 2

Rhythmic mode 4a (moderate even)

karra	**walakandha**
SW	walakandha

Walakandha!

INSTRUMENTAL SECTIONS 1-3

Rhythmic mode 4a (moderate even)

TRACK 8 (?Hodd82-s02)

Song vi-a: Walakandha No. 9a[13]

Sung text	Free translation
karra walakandha kimi-wurri kavulh-a	He [a Walakandha] has always sung 'Walakandha' to me
karra walakandha	Karra walakandha!

In tracks 8 and 9 Kungiung performs the text of 'Walakandha No. 9' in two different rhythmic treatments (the two versions of the text being thus labelled 9a and 9b), and with two different melodies. The melody of track 8 is shared with Kungiung's own song 'Yendili No. 6' (track 10).

SONG STRUCTURE SUMMARY

VOCAL SECTIONS 1–3

Melodic section 1

Text phrase 1

Rhythmic mode 4a (var) (moderate even with beating initially suspended)

karra	**walakandha**	**kimi**	**-wurri**	**kavulh**	**-a**
SW	walakandha	3MIN.S.R say/sang	towards speaker	3MIN.S.R lie	PERF

He [a Walakandha] has always sung 'Walakandha' to me

Melodic section 2 (descends to lower octave)

Text phrase 2 (lower octave)

Rhythmic mode 4a (moderate even)

karra	**walakandha**
SW	walakandha

Walakandha!

INSTRUMENTAL SECTIONS 1–3

Rhythmic mode 4a (moderate even)

---

13 Not included in the list of Walakandha *wangga* songs in Marett, 2005, p 241.

VOCAL SECTION 4

Melodic section 1

Text phrase 1

Rhythmic mode 1 (without clapsticks)

karra	**walakandha**	**kimi**	**-wurri**	**kavulh**	**-a**
SW	walakandha	3MIN.S.R say/sang	towards speaker	3MIN.S.R lie	PERF

He [a Walakandha] has always sung 'Walakandha' to me

Melodic section 2 (descends to lower octave)

Text phrase 2 (lower octave)

Rhythmic mode 1 (without clapsticks)

karra	**walakandha**
SW	walakandha

Walakandha!

INSTRUMENTAL SECTION 4

Rhythmic mode 5b (fast doubled)

TRACK 9 (?Hodd82-s03)

Song vi-b: Walakandha No. 9b

Sung text	Free translation
karra	Karra
karra walakandha kimi-wurri kavulh-a	Karra, he [a Walakandha] has always sung 'Walakandha' to me
Karra walakandha	Karra walakandha!

Reflecting its different melody, the text here is preceded by an additional text phrase consisting of the sole untranslatable song-word *karra* (see chapter 3).

SONG STRUCTURE SUMMARY

VOCAL SECTIONS 1–3

Melodic section 1

Text phrase 1

Rhythmic mode 1 (without clapsticks)

karra
SW

Karra

Text phrase 2

Rhythmic mode 1 (without clapsticks)

karra	walakandha	kimi	-wurri	kavulh	-a
SW	walakandha	3MIN.S.R say/sing	towards speaker	3MIN.S.R lie	PERF

He [a Walakandha] has always sung 'Walakandha' to me

Melodic section 2 (descends to lower octave)

Text phrase 3 (lower octave)

Rhythmic mode 1 (without clapsticks)

karra	walakandha
SW	walakandha

Walakandha!

INSTRUMENTAL SECTIONS 1–2

Rhythmic mode 5*

INSTRUMENTAL SECTION 3

Rhythmic mode 5b (fast doubled)

TRACK 10 (?Hodd82-s06)

Song vii: Yendili No. 6[14]

Sung text	Free translation
karra yendili kimi-wurri kavulh-a	He [a Walakandha] has always sung 'Yendili' to me
karra yendili kimi-wurri kavulh-a	He [a Walakandha] has always sung 'Yendili' to me
aa	Aa
karra yendili kimi-wurri kavulh-a	He [a Walakandha] has always sung 'Yendili' to me
karra yendili kimi-wurri kavulh-a	He [a Walakandha] has always sung 'Yendili' to me
karra walakandha kimi-wurri kavulh-a	He [a Walakandha] has always sung 'Walakandha' to me
karra yendili kimi-wurri kavulh-a	He [a Walakandha] has always sung 'Yendili' to me
karra yendili kimi-wurri kavulh-a	He [a Walakandha] has always sung 'Yendili' to me
aa	Aa

This is one of Thomas Kungiung's early compositions. The text is clearly based on the model established by Stan Mullumbuk, but it is restructured into an AAB pattern in which the final B text phrase is often a vocable sung to a melisma.[15] At this early stage, Kungiung sometimes used Marri Tjavin, rather than vocable text for the final text phrase (see vocal section 2).

---

14 Classified as Song 25 in Marett, 2005, p 241.
15 Texts using this pattern proved very popular in the golden age (1986-96) and into the subsequent decade. Songs

Here Kungiung uses the same melody as used for Stan Mullumbuk's song 'Walakandha No. 9a' (track 8). When the other three composers (Wagon Dumoo, Les Kundjil and Philip Mullumbuk) later took up the AAB form, each adopted a new melody of his own. The instrumental sections of this song follow a pattern of beating that typifies the Walakandha *wangga* to this day, and differ in key respects from the pattern usually followed by Stan Mullumbuk (see the music analysis section for more details).

SONG STRUCTURE SUMMARY

VOCAL SECTION 1

Melodic section 1

Text phrases 1–2

Rhythmic mode 1 (without clapsticks)

karra	**yendili**	**kimi**	**-wurri**	**kavulh**	**-a**
SW	place name	3MIN.S.R say/sing	towards speaker	3MIN.S.R lie	PERF

He [a Walakandha] has always sung 'Yendili' to me

Text phrase 3

Rhythmic mode 1 (without clapsticks)

aa
SW

Aa

INSTRUMENTAL SECTION 1

Rhythmic mode 5a (fast even)

VOCAL SECTION 2

Melodic section 1

Text phrases 1--2

Rhythmic mode 1 (without clapsticks)

karra	**yendili**	**kimi**	**-wurri**	**kavulh**	**-a**
SW	place name	3MIN.S.R say/sing	towards speaker	3MIN.S.R lie	PERF

He [a Walakandha] has always sung 'Yendili' to me

---

that use this form include: 'Kubuwemi' (track 12), 'Yendili No. 1' (track 13) and 'Tjagawala' (track 27) (all composed by Wagon Dumoo); 'Dhembedi-ndjen' (track 26) (composed by Martin Warrigal Kungiung); 'Yendili No. 3' (track 30) (composed by Les Kundjil) and 'Yendili No. 4' (track 32) (composed by Philip Mullumbuk).

Text phrase 3

Rhythmic mode 1 (without clapsticks)

karra	walakandha	kimi	-wurri	kavulh	-a
SW	walakandha	3MIN.S.R say/sing	towards speaker	3MIN.S.R lie	PERF

He [a Walakandha] has always sung 'Walakandha' to me

INSTRUMENTAL SECTION 2

Rhythmic mode 5a (fast even)

VOCAL SECTION 3

Melodic section 1

Text phrases 1–2

Rhythmic mode 1 (without clapsticks)

karra	yendili	kimi	-wurri	kavulh	-a
SW	place name	3MIN.S.R say/sing	towards speaker	3MIN.S.R lie	PERF

He [a Walakandha] has always sung 'Yendili' to me

Text phrase 3

Rhythmic mode 1 (without clapsticks)

aa

SW

Aa

INSTRUMENTAL SECTION 3

Rhythmic mode 5b (fast doubled)

TRACK 11 (?Hodd82-s08)

Song viii: Yenmilhi No. 2[16]

Sung text	Free translation
karra yenmilhi kimi-wurri kavulh-a	He [a Walakandha] has always sung 'Yenmilhi' to me
karra yenmilhi kimi-wurri kavulh-a	He [a Walakandha] has always sung 'Yenmilhi' to me
karra wutjelli kimi-wurri kavulh-a	He [a Walakandha] has always sung 'Wutjelli' to me
karra yenmilhi kimi-wurri kavulh-a	He [a Walakandha] has always sung 'Yenmilhi' to me
karra yenmilhi kimi-wurri kavulh-a	He [a Walakandha] has always sung 'Yenmilhi' to me
karra walakandha kimi-wurri kavulh-a	He [a Walakandha] has always sung 'Walakandha' to me
karra yenmilhi kimi-wurri kavulh-a	He [a Walakandha] has always sung 'Yenmilhi' to me
karra yenmilhi kimi-wurri kavulh-a	He [a Walakandha] has always sung 'Yenmilhi' to me
karra wutjelli kimi-wurri kavulh-a	He [a Walakandha] has always sung 'Wutjelli' to me

This is the second of Thomas Kungiung's early compositions contained on the recordings attributed to Hoddinott, and like 'Yendili No. 6' it uses the AAB form. Here there is some variability in the last text phrase of each vocal section, where the singer switches between 'Wutjelli' (the name of an ancestor of Stan Mullumbuk) and 'Walakandha.'

Here the beating pattern adopted for the instrumental sections is the same as used in Mullumbuk's songs in the same rhythmic mode and differs from the pattern adopted in the Kungiung's own song 'Yendili No. 6' on the preceding track (see music analysis section for more details).

SONG STRUCTURE SUMMARY

VOCAL SECTION 1

Melodic section 1

Text phrases 1–2

Rhythmic mode 1 (without clapsticks)

karra	**yenmilhi**	**kimi**	**-wurri**	**kavulh**	**-a**
SW	place name	3MIN.S.R say/sing	towards speaker	3MIN.S.R lie	PERF

He [a Walakandha] has always sung 'Yenmilhi' to me

Text phrase 3

Rhythmic mode 1 (without clapsticks)

karra	**wutjelli**	**kimi**	**-wurri**	**kavulh**	**-a**
SW	person's name	3MIN.S.R say/sing	towards speaker	3MIN.S.R lie	PERF

He [a Walakandha] has always sung 'Wutjelli' to me

---

16 Classified as Song 26 in Marett, 2005, p 241.

INSTRUMENTAL SECTION 1

Rhythmic mode 5*

VOCAL SECTION 2

Melodic section 1

Text phrases 1–2

Rhythmic mode 1 (without clapsticks)

karra	yenmilhi	kimi	-wurri	kavulh	-a
SW	place name	3MIN.S.R say/sing	towards speaker	3MIN.S.R lie	PERF

He [a Walakandha] has always sung 'Yenmilhi' to me

Text phrase 3

Rhythmic mode 1 (without clapsticks)

karra	walakandha	kimi	-wurri	kavulh	-a
SW	walakandha	3MIN.S.R say/sing	towards speaker	3MIN.S.R lie	PERF

He [a Walakandha] has always sung 'Walakandha' to me

INSTRUMENTAL SECTION 2

Rhythmic mode 5*

VOCAL SECTION 3

Melodic section 1

Text phrases 1–2

Rhythmic mode 1 (without clapsticks)

karra	yenmilhi	kimi	-wurri	kavulh	-a
SW	place name	3MIN.S.R say/sing	towards speaker	3MIN.S.R lie	PERF

He [a Walakandha] has always sung 'Yenmilhi' to me

Text phrase 3

Rhythmic mode 1 (without clapsticks)

karra	wutjelli	kimi	-wurri	kavulh	-a
SW	person's name	3MIN.S.R say/sing	towards speaker	3MIN.S.R lie	PERF

He [a Walakandha] has always sung 'Wutjelli' to me

INSTRUMENTAL SECTION 3

Rhythmic mode 5b (fast doubled)

C: The golden age of the Walakandha *wangga* (tracks 12–29)

The decade from 1986 to 1996, now looked back on as a 'golden age', is a period in which there were a large number of active songmen, all of whom composed. These included Thomas Kungiung (1934–1993), Wagon Dumoo (1926–c. 1990), Martin Warrigal Kungiung (1935–c. 1997), Les Kundjil (1935–2009) and Philip Mullumbuk (1947–2008). There was also a strong body of dancers, many from other Marri language clans—who included Frank Dumoo (Marri Tjavin), Ambrose Piarlum (Marri Ngarr), John Chula (Matige), Edward Nemarluk (Marri Ammu) and Maurice Ngulkur (Marri Ammu)—and several excellent didjeridu players, foremost amongst whom was John Dumoo (1922–1997).

Figure 8.3 Some of the main contributors to the 'golden age' of the Walakanda *wangga*: Ambrose Piarlum, Frank Dumoo (playing didjeridu), Maurice Ngulkur, John Dumoo, Thomas Kungiung, and Les Kundjil singing *wangga* at a circumcision ceremony, Wadeye, 1988. Photograph by Mark Crocombe, reproduced with the permission of Wadeye community.

During this period the Walakandha *wangga* tradition was at its peak. Marett made recordings in 1988 and further recordings in the collection of the Wadeye Aboriginal Sound Archive were made by Michael Enilane, who was a teacher at the school from 1992 (tracks 12–23).[17] The earliest recordings for this period were made by Frances Kofod in 1986 (tracks 24–28), including five songs that by 1988 had apparently fallen out of the repertory: Stan Mullumbuk's first song 'Walakandha No. 8' (track 1),[18] 'Pumurriyi' (track 24), 'Thidha nany' (track 25), 'Dhembedi-ndjen' (track 26), 'Tjagawala' (track 27) and 'Karra' (track 28). Although Kofod's recording includes many songs that were also recorded by Marett in 1988 (including 'Kubuwemi', 'Yendili No. 1', 'Walakandha No. 1' and 'Nadirri'), only Marett's recordings of these songs are included here. There is also a single recording (track 29) that was discovered in the Wadeye Aboriginal Language Centre archive. Although the recording is undated, with no information as to who made it, the style of performance suggests that this song also belongs to the golden age.

---

17 For comparative purposes, this group of tracks also includes a recording of 'Truwu' (melody B) made by Allan Marett in 1999 (track 17).

18 Two performances of 'Walakandha No. 8' by Thomas Kungiung were also recorded by an unknown recordist, perhaps Hoddinot, c.1982 (see tracks 6 and 7).

TRACK 12 (Mar88-23-s02)

Song 1: Kubuwemi[19]

Sung text	Free translation
karra kubuwemi kimi-wurri kavulh[-a]	He [a Walakandha] has always sung 'Kubuwemi' to me
karra kubuwemi kimi-wurri kavulh[-a]	He [a Walakandha] has always sung 'Kubuwemi' to me
aa	Aa

Wagon Dumoo composed this song about Kubuwemi, the site on which the outstation of Nadirri now stands. Like a number of other songs, it asserts that Walakandha are an eternal source of songs about country (see also Marett, 2005, p 127). The recording, like those of the following three tracks, was made by Allan Marett at a circumcision ceremony at Wadeye on 17 May 1988 and the excitement surrounding the ceremony is palpable in the performance.

The text as given is the standard spoken form, and the same construction appears in earlier songs (tracks 10 and 11). Here the sung version seems to consistently omit the final syllable (whereby the perfective suffix '-*a*' is added to '*kavulh*'). In everyday speech, this omission would change the meaning from 'he has always sung' to 'he always sings', but our consultants always included the -*a* in their explanations of this song. Marett has argued that the sung text is a truncated form of the standard spoken text (Marett, 2005, pp 146–47). The next track, 'Yendili No. 1' (track 13), using a parallel construction, also omits the suffix.

Figure 8.4 Wagon Dumoo, composer of 'Kubuwemi', sings at a circumcision ceremony in Wadeye in 1988. Photograph by Mark Crocombe, reproduced with the permission of the Dumoo family.

---

19 Classified as Song 1 in Marett, 2005, p 238.

SONG STRUCTURE SUMMARY

VOCAL SECTIONS 1–4

Melodic section 1

Text phrases 1–2

Rhythmic mode 2 (slow even beating)

karra	kubuwemi	kimi	-wurri	kavulh	[-a]
SW	place name	3MIN.S.R say/sing	towards speaker	3MIN.S.R lie	[PERF]

He [a Walakandha] has always sung 'Kubuwemi' to me

Text phrase 3

Rhythmic mode 1 (without clapsticks)

aa
SW

Aa

INSTRUMENTAL SECTIONS 1–3

Rhythmic mode 5a (fast even)

INSTRUMENTAL SECTION 4

Rhythmic mode 5b (fast doubled)

TRACK 13 (Mar88-23-s03)

Song 2: Yendili No. 1[20]

Sung text	Free translation
karra yendili kimi-wurri kavulh[-a]	He [a Walakandha] has always sung 'Yendili' to me
karra yendili kimi-wurri kavulh[-a]	He [a Walakandha] has always sung 'Yendili' to me
aa	Aa

Wagon Dumoo composed this song, which is clearly modeled on 'Kubuwemi.' In this case the song is the topic is Yendili, an iconic hill where there are a number of important Marri Tjavin Dreaming sites.

---

20 Classified as Song 2 in Marett, 2005, p 238.

SONG STRUCTURE SUMMARY

VOCAL SECTIONS 1–4

Melodic section 1

Text phrases 1–2

Rhythmic mode 2 (slow even beating)

karra	**yendili**	**kimi**	**-wurri**	**kavulh**	**[-a]**
SW	place name	3MIN.S.R say/sing	towards speaker	3MIN.S.R lie	[PERF

He [a Walakandha] has always sung 'Yendili' to me

Text phrase 3

Rhythmic mode 1 (without clapsticks)

aa
SW

Aa

INSTRUMENTAL SECTIONS 1–3

Rhythmic mode 5a (fast even)

INSTRUMENTAL SECTION 4

Rhythmic mode 5b (fast doubled)

TRACK 14 (Mar88-23-s08)

Song 3: Yendili No. 2[21]

Sung text	Free translation
karra yendili yendili arr-girrit-ni	Yendili! Yendili! Look after it!
karra yendili yendili arr-girrit-ni	Yendili! Yendili! Look after it!
aa ye-ngin-a	Aa, my dear children/my dear descendants

This song was composed by Maudie Attaying Dumoo, who gave it to her husband Wagon Dumoo to perform. Because Attaying is Marri Ngarr, not Marri Tjavin, the text is in Marri Ngarr language. This is a rare example of a *wangga* song composed by a woman.

The most common explanation of this song is that the words of the text were originally spoken by the song's composer to her children as she and her husband were leaving their house at Nadirri to go back to Wadeye. A second, deeper meaning is that the song is a call from the ancestral dead to their living descendants urging them to look after their country (see further discussion of this song in Marett, 2005, p 66). The melody is shared with 'Yendili No. 3' by Les Kundjil and 'Yendili No. 4' by Philip Mullumbuk.

---

21 Classified as Song 3 in Marett, 2005, p 239.

SONG STRUCTURE SUMMARY

VOCAL SECTIONS 1–4

Melodic sections 1–2

Text phrases 1–2

Rhythmic mode 1 (without clapsticks)

karra	**yendili**	**yendili**	**arr**	**-girrit**	**-ni**
SW	place name	place name	2MIN.A.IR. use hands	hold	PURP

Yendili! Yendili! Look after it!

Melodic section 3

Text phrase 3

Rhythmic mode 1 (without clapsticks)

aa	**ye**	**-ngin**	**-a**
SW	child/descendant	1MIN.O	PERF

Aa, my dear children/my dear descendants

INSTRUMENTAL SECTIONS 1–3

Rhythmic mode 5a (fast even)

INSTRUMENTAL SECTION 4

Rhythmic mode 5b (fast doubled)

TRACK 15 (Mar88-24-s02)

Song 4: Walakandha No. 1[22]

Sung text	Free translation
karra walakandha	Walakandha!

Nobody can remember who made this song, or of two other songs using the same melody, 'Nadirri' (track 19) and 'Karra' (track 28).

Even in so simple a text, the communicative function is complex. Because of reciprocal use of the term 'Walakandha' by the dead to call the living, and by the living to call the dead, the vocative text *karra walakanda* simultaneously constitutes a call from the dead to living Walakandha in the act of song creation, and, when sung in ceremony, a call of the living to dead Walakandha. The reciprocal use of the term articulates and enacts themes of intimacy between the two orders of being, so that the song functions as two-way communication—from the dead to the living, and from the living to the dead (see further discussion of this song in Marett, 2005, p 65).

---

22 Classified as Song 6 in Marett, 2005, p 239.

SONG STRUCTURE SUMMARY

VOCAL SECTIONS 1–3

Melodic section 1

Text phrase 1

Rhythmic mode 1 (without clapsticks)

karra	**walakandha**
SW	walakandha

Walakandha!

INSTRUMENTAL SECTIONS 1–3

Rhythmic mode 5a (fast even)

INSTRUMENTAL SECTION 4

Rhythmic mode 5b (fast doubled)

TRACK 16 (Mar88-39-s02)

Song 5a: Truwu [Truwu A melody][23]

Sung text	Free translation
karra walakandha purangang kuwa-vapa-winyanga truwu nidin-ngin-a walakandha	Walakandha! The waves are crashing on them Truwu! My dear country! Walakandha!
karra munggum kimelha kuwa karrivirrilhyi truwu nidin-ngin-a walakandha	Munggum! He stands behind a beach hibiscus and peeps out Truwu! My dear country! Walakandha!
karra walakandha	Walakandha!

This most popular and enduring song of the Walakandha *wangga* repertory was composed by Thomas Kungiung. It refers to a specific Walakandha, a deceased ancestor called Munggum (the father of Bruno Munggum Berrida), who flourished around the turn of the twentieth century (also mentioned in 'Walakandha No. 4' [track 35]). Here Munggum stands behind a beach hibiscus (*Hibiscus tiliaceus*) at Truwu beach and regards his descendants—whom he refers to as 'Walakandha' (see the notes to the previous track)—being battered by the waves. Waves in this case stand for the exigencies of life. When sung in the context of a mortuary ritual the song stands as an expression of ancestral sympathy for the pain being suffered by the living as they mourn a dead relative. This performance was recorded by Allan Marett at a *burnim-rag* ceremony held at Nadirri on 19 June 1988, and is discussed in detail in *Songs, dreamings and ghosts* (Marett, 2005, pp 112–16).

The text of 'Truwu' is sung to three different but related melodies. Marri Tjavin people whose traditional estates lie at the coast (such as Thomas Kungiung, heard here) perform the song to the

---

[23] Classified as Song 7a in Marett, 2005, p 239.

Truwu A melody. This was the most frequently used melody for this song during the golden age (see further Marett, 2005, pp 117–20). The other two melodies, Truwu B and Truwu A/B, can be heard in tracks 17 and 18 respectively.

SONG STRUCTURE SUMMARY

VOCAL SECTIONS 1–3

Melodic section 1

Text phrase 1

Rhythmic mode 1 (without clapsticks)

karra	**walakandha**	**purangang**	**kuwa**	**-vapa**	**-winyanga**
SW	walakandha	sea	3MIN.S.R stand	crash	3AUG.ADVERS

Walakandha! The waves are crashing on them

truwu	**nidin**	**-ngin**	**-a**	**walakandha**
place name	country	1MIN.O	PERF	walakandha

Truwu! My dear country! Walakandha!

Melodic section 2

Text phrase 2

Rhythmic mode 1 (without clapsticks)

karra	**munggum**	**kimelha**	**kuwa**	**karrivirrilhyi**
SW	person's name	3MIN.peep out	3MIN.S.R stand	beach hibiscus

Munggum! He stands behind a beach hibiscus and peeps out

truwu	**nidin**	**-ngin**	**-a**	**walakandha**
place name	country	1MIN.O	PERF	walakandha

Truwu! My dear country! Walakandha!

Melodic section 3 (lower octave; vocal section 1 only)

Text phrase 3

Rhythmic mode 1 (without clapsticks)

karra	**walakandha**
SW	walakandha

Walakandha!

INSTRUMENTAL SECTIONS 1-2

Rhythmic mode 5a (fast even)

INSTRUMENTAL SECTION 3
Rhythmic mode 5b (fast doubled)

TRACK 17 (Mar99-02-s14)
Song 5b: Truwu [Truwu B melody][24]

The text is the same as for track 16, but here 'Truwu' is sung to the Truwu B melody. This melody is used by Marri Tjavin people (such as Les Kundjil, heard here) whose country lies inland. It is not unusual in Aboriginal music for melodies to represent an association to particular tracts of country and their associated Dreamings. Just as the people who live near the coast are closely related to those who live immediately inland, so too are the melodies. Marett argues that this close relationship is symbolised in the fact that the different pentatonic scales used for Truwu A and Truwu B both derive from a common heptatonic series in the dorian melodic mode (see further Marett, 2005, pp 117-20).

Although strictly speaking this performance by Les Kundjil lies outside the golden age (having been recorded by Allan Marett during a procession at a funeral at Wadeye on 9 July 1999), there can be little doubt that this melody was also performed during earlier times.

TRACK 18 (Eni92-s08)
Song 5c: Truwu [Truwu A/B melody][25]

This performance of Truwu, sung by Thomas Kungiung, Les Kundjil and Philip Mullumbuk, was recorded by a local schoolteacher, Michael Enilane, during a circumcision ceremony at Wadeye in 1992. Here 'Truwu' is set to the Truwu A/B melody, which takes the notes of the pentatonic Truwu A melody (as sung by Kungiung in track 16) and combines them with those of the pentatonic Truwu B melody (as sung by Kundjil in track 17) so as to produce the heptatonic melody in dorian mode that underlies them both. This version emphasises the commonalities, rather than the distinctions, between inland and coastal Marri Tjavin people.

TRACK 19 (Mar88-30-s15)
Song 6: Nadirri[26]

Sung text	Free translation
karra walakandha nadirri ka-rri-tik-nginanga-ya	Brother Walakandha! The tide has gone out at Nadirri and I couldn't stop it [I couldn't stop him dying]
aa nadirri ka-rri-tik-nyinanga-ya	Aa, the tide has gone out at Nadirri and I couldn't stop it
(aa nadirri ka-rri-tik-nyinanga-ya)	(Aa, the tide has gone out at Nadirri and I couldn't stop it)

For the Marri Tjavin, tide is a metaphor for the cycle of birth, death and rebirth. Here the ebbing tide symbolises death, as a song-giving Walakandha sings of the death of one of his descendants.

---

24 Classified as Song 7c in Marett, 2005, p 240.
25 Classified as Song 7b in Marett, 2005, p 239.
26 Classified as Song 8 in Marett, 2005, p 240.

This song, by an unknown composer, is performed by Martin Warrigal Kungiung in an elicited performance recorded by Allan Marett at Peppimenarti on 6 June 1988. The backup singers included Warrigal's 'father' (father's brother) Thomas Kungiung, and the didjeridu player is Raphael Thardim. The tune is shared with two other songs by unknown composers, 'Walakandha No. 1' (track 15) and 'Karra' (track 28).

SONG STRUCTURE SUMMARY

VOCAL SECTIONS 1–3

Melodic section 1

Text phrase 1

Rhythmic mode 1 (without clapsticks)

karra	walakandha	nadirri	ka	-rri	-tik	-nginanga	-ya
SW	walakandha	place name	3MIN.S.R	use hands	ebb	1MIN.ADVERS	PERF

Brother Walakandha! The tide has gone out at Nadirri and I couldn't stop it [I couldn't stop him dying]

Melodic section 2

Text phrase 2

Rhythmic mode 1 (without clapsticks)

aa	nadirri	ka	-rri	-tik	-nyinanga	-ya
SW	place name	3MIN.S.R	use hands	ebb	1MIN.ADVERS	PERF

Ah, the tide has gone out at Nadirri and I couldn't stop it

Melodic section 3 (optional; vocal section 1 only)

Text phrase 3

Rhythmic mode 1 (without clapsticks)

aa	nadirri	ka	-rri	-tik	-nyinanga	-ya
SW	place name	3MIN.S.R	use hands	ebb	1MIN.ADVERS	PERF

Ah, the tide has gone out at Nadirri and I couldn't stop it

INSTRUMENTAL SECTIONS 1-2

Rhythmic mode 5a (fast even)

INSTRUMENTAL SECTION 3

Rhythmic mode 5b (fast doubled)

TRACK 20 (Mar88-54-s03)

Song 7: Yenmilhi No. 1[27]

Sung text	Free translation
karra mana	Brother!
ngumbun-nim djeni ngumbun-nim djeni	Let's all go now; let's all go now
pelhi yidha wandhi yidha yidha yenmilhi	Pelhi is there, there behind Yenmilhi Hill
mana tittil kuwa ngangga-nim	Brother, there are clapsticks for all of us
djindja-wurri	Come with us!
ee	Ee

This song was composed by John Dumoo. The story goes that John Dumoo was crossing the Moyle floodplain and got lost. He lay down and went to sleep and then heard this song, in which the Walakandha dead invited him to accompany them to a ceremony at the ceremony ground at the site Pelhi. This elicited performance by Martin Warrigal Kungiung and others was recorded by Allan Marett at Peppimenarti on 20 November 1988.

Unusually for the Walakandha *wangga* of the golden age, the song uses fast even beating (rhythmic mode 5a) throughout. Today most men at Wadeye do not know how to perform the dance for this song.

SONG STRUCTURE SUMMARY

VOCAL SECTIONS 1–4

Melodic section 1

Text phrase 1

Rhythmic mode 5a (fast even beating)

karra	**mana**
SW	brother

Brother!

Text phrase 2

Rhythmic mode 5a (fast even beating)

ngumbun	**-nim**	**djeni**	**ngumbun**	**-nim**	**djeni**
1/2AUG.S.IR.go	AUG	now	1/2AUG.S.IR.go	AUG	now

Let's all go now; let's all go now

---

27 Classified as Song 9 in Marett, 2005, p 240.

Text phrase 3

Rhythmic mode 5a (fast even beating)

pelhi	**yidha**	**wandhi**	**yidha**	**yidha**	**yenmilhi**
place name	there	behind	there	there	place name

Pelhi is there, there behind Yenmilhi Hill

Text phrase 4

Rhythmic mode 5a (fast even beating)

mana	**tittil**	**kuwa**	**ngangga**	**-nim**
brother	clapsticks	3MIN.S.R stand	1/2AUG.DAT	AUG

Brother, there are clapsticks for all of us

Text phrase 5

Rhythmic mode 5a (fast even beating)

djindja	**-wurri**
here	towards speaker

Come with us!

Melodic section 2

Text phrase 6

Rhythmic mode 5a (fast even beating)

ee
SW

Ee

INSTRUMENTAL SECTIONS 1–4

Rhythmic mode 5a (fast even beating)

TRACK 21 (Marett88-40-s11)

Song 8: Mirrwana[28]

Sung text	Free translation
karra	Karra
karra walakandha mirrwana kavulh-ni verri ngangga-ya	A [living] Walakandha has laid himself down at the foot of a cabbage palm tree and there is nothing that you and I can do about it
karra	Karra
karra walakandha kimi-wurri kavulh	The [dead] Walakandha always sings to me
aa	Aa
karra walakandha mirrwana kavulh-ni verri ngangga-ya	A [living] Walakandha has laid himself down at the foot of a cabbage palm tree and there is nothing that you and I can do about it
karra walakandha kimi-wurri kavulh	The [dead] Walakandha always sings to me

This song was composed by Martin Warrigal Kungiung, who performs it here. The first three text phrases of this song contain an utterance by a ghost: one of the Walakandha dead notices a living descendant lying under a cabbage palm and seizes this opportunity to give him a song. In the final text phrase, performed in the lower octave, the focus seems to switch to an observation added by the singer.

The text phrase structure differs significantly in the two vocal sections, though the two Marri Tjavin text phrases appear in each. This elicited performance was recorded by Allan Marett at a *burnim-rag* ceremony at Batchelor on 11 September 1988.

SONG STRUCTURE SUMMARY

VOCAL SECTION 1

Melodic section 1

Text phrase 1

Rhythmic mode 1 (without clapsticks)

karra
SW

Karra

---

28 Classified as Song 10 in Marett, 2005, p 240.

Melodic section 2

Text phrase 2

Rhythmic mode 1 (without clapsticks)

karra	**walakandha**	**mirrwana**	**kavulh**	**-ni**	**verri**	**ngangga**	**-ya**
SW	walakandha	cabbage palm	3MIN.S.R lies	PURP	foot	1/2ADVERS	PERF

A [living] Walakandha has laid himself down at the foot of a cabbage palm tree and there is nothing that you and I can do about it

Melodic section 3

Text phrase 3

Rhythmic mode 1 (without clapsticks)

karra
SW

Karra

Melodic section 4 (lower octave)

Text phrase 4

Rhythmic mode 1 (without clapsticks)

karra	**walakandha**	**kimi**	**-wurri**	**kavulh**
karra	walakandha	3MIN.S.R say/sang	towards speaker	3MIN.S.R lies

The [dead] Walakandha always sings to me

INSTRUMENTAL SECTION 1

Rhythmic mode 5a (fast even)

VOCAL SECTION 2

Melodic section 1

Text phrase 1

Rhythmic mode 1 (without clapsticks)

aa
SW

Aa

Melodic section 2

Text phrase 2

Rhythmic mode 1 (without clapsticks)

karra	walakandha	mirrwana	kavulh	-ni	verri	ngangga	-ya
SW	walakandha	cabbage palm	3MIN.S.R lies	PURP	foot	1/2ADVERS	PERF

A [living] Walakandha has laid himself down at the foot of a cabbage palm tree and there is nothing that you and I can do about it

Melodic section 3 (lower octave)

Text phrase 3

Rhythmic mode 1 (without clapsticks)

karra	walakandha	kimi	-wurri	kavulh
karra	walakandha	3MIN.S.R say/sang	towards speaker	3MIN.S.R lies

The [dead] Walakandha always sings to me

INSTRUMENTAL SECTION 2

Rhythmic mode 5b (fast doubled)

TRACK 22 (Eni92-s11)

Song 9: Wutjelli No. 1[29]

Sung text	Free translation
mana wutjelli ka-ni-put-puwa kuwa rtidim nidin-ngin-a	Wutjelli is standing with one leg crossed over the other, Rtidim! My dear country!
karra walakandha purangang devin kuwa-vapa-winyanga truwu nidin-ngin-a	Walakandha! The lonely waves are crashing on them, Truwu! My dear country!
(karra walakandha purangang)	(Walakandha! Waves)

This song was composed by Thomas Kungiung. Wutjelli, mentioned also in 'Wutjelli No. 2' (track 3) and 'Yenmilhi No. 2' (track 11), was a 'grandfather' (grandfather's brother) of Philip and Stan Mullumbuk (Marett, 2005, p 47). Here he stands in the number four leg pose marking him as one of the dead, watching the waves crashing down on his descendants from his vantage point at Rtidim, the headland to the north of Truwu beach. As in 'Truwu' (tracks 16-18), the waves here are a metaphor for the exigencies of life.

This performance was recorded by Michael Enilane at a circumcision ceremony at Wadeye in 1992, where the singers included Thomas Kungiung and Les Kundjil. As he often does, Kungiung sometimes repeats the beginning of text phrase 2 at the lower octave before moving to the instrumental section.

---

29 Classified as Song 11 in Marett, 2005, p 240.

SONG STRUCTURE SUMMARY

VOCAL SECTIONS 1–3

Melodic section 1

Text phrase 1

Rhythmic mode 1 (without clapsticks)

mana	**wutjelli**	**ka**	**-ni**	**-put**	**-puwa**	**kuwa**	**rtidim**	**nidin**	**-ngin**	**-a**
brother	person's name	3MIN.S.R	walk	bends	leg	3MIN.S.R stand	place name	country	1MIN.O	PERF

Wultjelli is standing with one leg crossed over the other Rtidim! My dear country!

Melodic section 2

Text phrase 2

Rhythmic mode 1 (without clapsticks)

karra	**walakandha**	**purangang**	**devin**	**kuwa**	**-vapa**	**-winyanga**	**truwu**	**nidin**	**-ngin**	**-a**
karra	walakandha	sea	alone	3MIN.S.R stand	crash	3AUG. ADVERS	place name	country	1MIN.O	PERF

Walakandha! The lonely waves are crashing on them Truwu! My dear country!

Melodic section 3 (lower octave; vocal section 1 only)

Text phrase 2

Rhythmic mode 1 (without clapsticks)

karra	**walakandha**	**purangang**
karra	walakandha	sea

Walakandha! Waves

INSTRUMENTAL SECTIONS 1–2

Rhythmic mode 5a (fast even)

INSTRUMENTAL SECTION 3

Rhythmic mode 5b (fast doubled)

TRACK 23 (Eni92-s06)

Song 10: Walakandha No. 2[30]

Sung text	Free translation
karra walakandha ngindji kiny warri kurzi kubuwemi nidin-ngin-a	A certain Walakandha is living there for a whole year, Kubuwemi! My dear country!
karra ngatha devin bugim rtadi-nanga kuwa kubuwemi nidin-ngin-a	There is a solitary house with a white roof there, Kubuwemi! My dear country!

This song, composed by Thomas Kungiung, is about Terence Dumoo living alone at Kubuwemi for a whole year following his move from Wadeye (Port Keats) to an outstation on his traditional country. The song-giving Walakandha uses the expressions 'a certain Walakandha' to refer to Terence; as mentioned previously, 'Walakandha' is used reciprocally by the dead to refer to the living and by the living to refer to the dead. The song is said to have been received in dream by Terence Dumoo and Thomas Kungiung simultaneously.

As in the preceding track, Kungiung sometimes repeats the beginning of text phrase 2 at the lower octave before moving to the instrumental section. This performance was recorded by Michael Enilane at a circumcision ceremony at Wadeye in 1992. A version of this song, re-composed by Maurice Ngulkur, is also included in the Ma-yawa *wangga* repertory (chapter 9, tracks 1 and 2).

SONG STRUCTURE SUMMARY

VOCAL SECTIONS 1–2

Melodic section 1

Text phrase 1

Rhythmic mode 1 (without clapsticks)

karra	**walakandha**	**ngindji**	**kiny**	**warri**	**kurzi**	**kubuwemi**	**nidin**	**-ngin**	**-a**
SW	walakandha	one	whole	wet season	3MIN.S.R sit	place name	country	1MIN.O	PERF

A certain Walakandha is living there for a whole year, Kubuwemi! My dear country!

Melodic section 2

Text phrase 2

Rhythmic mode 1 (without clapsticks)

karra	**ngatha**	**devin**	**bugim**	**rtadi**	**-nanga**	**kuwa**	**kubuwemi**	**nidin**	**-ngin**	**-a**
SW	house	solitary	white	roof	3MIN.S.M. ADVERS	3MIN.S.R stand	place name	country	1MIN.O	PERF

There is a solitary house with a white roof there, Kubuwemi! My dear country!

---

30 Classified as Song 12 in Marett, 2005, p 240.

INSTRUMENTAL SECTION 1

Rhythmic mode 5a (fast even)

INSTRUMENTAL SECTION 2

Rhythmic mode 5b (fast doubled)

TRACK 24 (Kof86-01/2-s15)

Song 11: Pumurriyi[31] *(Two items)*

Sung text	Free translation
mana walakandha pumurriyi kin-kurr-nginanga-ya	Brother Walakandha, it [a breaker] hit me at Pumurriyi and I couldn't stop it
ee mana pumurriyi kin-kurr-nginanga-ya	Ee brother, it [a breaker] hit me at Pumurriyi and I couldn't stop it
ee mana pumurriyi kin-kurr-nginanga-ya	Ee brother, it [a breaker] hit me at Pumurriyi and I couldn't stop it

Pumurriyi is an important and well known site of the Marri Ammu people[32] and the performance of a song about Pumurriyi acknowledges that the Marri Ammu are also participants in the Walakandha *wangga* repertory. Here the impact of death on the singer is likened to being hit by a breaker.

Two items, the first with four vocal sections and the second with three, are sung without a break. Because the text is stable from performance to performance, only the first item is included in the song structure summary. The arhythmic stickbeating at the very end of the track is a signal that a performance session has concluded.

This and the following four tracks were recorded by Frances Kofod at Wadeye on 16 June 1986. This song—one of those that seem to have fallen out of use by 1988—is sung to the same melody as 'Mirrwana' (track 19).

SONG STRUCTURE SUMMARY

VOCAL SECTIONS 1–4

Melodic section 1

Text phrase 1

Rhythmic mode 1 (without clapsticks)

mana	walakandha	pumurriyi	kin	-kurr	-nginanga	-ya
brother	walakandha	place	3MIN.S.R move	-hit	1.MIN.ADVERS	PERF

Brother Walakandha, it [a breaker] hit me at Pumurriyi and I couldn't stop it

---

31 This song was not listed in Marett, 2005, pp 238–41.

32 Pumurriyi is also mentioned in explanations of the Ma-yawa *wangga* song 'Wulumen Tulh' (chapter 9, track 28).

Melodic sections 2–3

Text phrases 2–3

Rhythmic mode 1 (without clapsticks)

ee	mana	pumurriyi	kin	-kurr	-nginanga	-ya
eh	brother	place	3MIN.S.R move	-hit	1.MIN.ADVERS	PERF

Ee brother, it [a breaker] hit me at Pumurriyi and I couldn't stop it

INSTRUMENTAL SECTIONS 1–3

Rhythmic mode 5a (fast even)

INSTRUMENTAL SECTION 4

Rhythmic mode 5b (fast doubled)

TRACK 25 (Kof86-01/2-s11)

Song 12: Thidha nany[1] *(Two items)*

Sung text	Free translation
karra walakandha ambi thidha nany devin	Walakandha, your father is not alone
yigin kangi-da-rzan walakandha	I am sitting facing him
karra walakandha	Walakandha!

Here a Walakandha is comforting the bereaved, whom he addresses as 'Walakandha,' by asserting that his or her deceased father is not alone but in the company of deceased relatives.

This song, probably composed by Thomas Kungiung, is sung to the Truwu A melody and presumably predates Kungiung's later composition, 'Truwu.' Once again we have two items sung without a break, the first with four vocal sections and the second with three. Only the first item is included in the song structure summary.

SONG STRUCTURE SUMMARY

VOCAL SECTIONS 1–4

Melodic section 1

Text phrase 1

Rhythmic mode 1 (without clapsticks)

karra	walakandha	ambi	thidha	nany	devin
karra	walakandha	NEG	father	2MIN.PRO	alone

Walakandha, your father is not alone

---

1 This song was not listed in Marett, 2005, pp 238–41.

Melodic section 1

Text phrase 2

Rhythmic mode 1 (without clapsticks)

yigin	**kangi**	**-da**	**-rzan**	**walakandha**
1MIN.PRO	1MIN.S.R sit	-beside	towards	walakandha

I am sitting facing him

Melodic section 2

Text phrase (lower octave)

Rhythmic mode 1 (without clapsticks)

karra	**walakandha**
karra	walakandha

Walakandha!

INSTRUMENTAL SECTIONS 1–3

Rhythmic mode 5a (fast even)

INSTRUMENTAL SECTION 4

Rhythmic mode 5b (fast doubled)

TRACK 26 (Kof86-01/2-s12)

Song 13: Dhembedi-ndjen[2]

Sung text	Free translation
karra walakandha dhembedi-ndjen ngumbu-vup-nim	Walakandha, let's all get going now
karra walakandha dhembedi-ndjen ngumbu-vup-nim	Walakandha, let's all get going now
aa	Aa

A Walakandha, in the course of giving Martin Warrigal Kungiung this song, tells him that both the living and the dead now need to bring the song into the world (by rendering it as a *wangga* song fit to be performed in ceremony). This is a perfect description of how the living and the dead collaborate to produce songs.

---

2   This song was not listed in Marett, 2005, pp 238–41.

SONG STRUCTURE SUMMARY

VOCAL SECTIONS 1–3

Melodic section 1

Text phrases 1–2

Rhythmic mode 1 (without clapsticks)

karra	walakandha	dhembedi	-ndjen	ngumbu	-vup	-nim
SW	walakandha	walk	now	1/2AUG.S.IR.go	set off	AUG

Walakandha, let's all get going now

Text phrase 3

Rhythmic mode 1 (without clapsticks)

aa
SW

Aa

INSTRUMENTAL SECTIONS 1–2

Rhythmic mode 5a (fast even)

INSTRUMENTAL SECTION 3

Rhythmic mode 5b (fast doubled)

TRACK 27 (Kof86-03/4-s10)

Song 14: Tjagawala[3]

Sung text	Free translation
karra tjagawala wumburli ki-nyi-ng-kurr[-a]	Tjagawala! A breaker has hit me
karra tjagawala wumburli ki-nyi-ng-kurr[-a]	Tjagawala! A breaker has hit me
angga wakai ki-nyi-ng-kurr[-a]	Grandson! Dead! It's hit me

Wagon Dumoo made this song for his deceased grandson, Tjagawala, whose name means 'frigate bird.' As in Pumurriyi, death is likened to being hit by a breaker. This is vividly confirmed by the final text phrase, 'Grandson! Dead! It's hit me.'

---

3 This song was not listed in Marett, 2005, pp 238-41.

SONG STRUCTURE SUMMARY

VOCAL SECTIONS 1–3

Melodic section

Text phrases 1-2

Rhythmic mode 2 (slow even)

karra	**tjagawala**	**wumburli**	**ki**	**-nyi**	**-ng**	**-kurr**	**[-a]**
SW	frigate bird/person's name	breaker	3MIN.A.R	make	1MIN.O	hit	[PERF]

Tjagawala! A breaker has hit me

Text phrase 3

Rhythmic mode 1 (without clapsticks)

angga	**wakai**	**ki**	**-nyi**	**-ng**	**-kurr**	**[-a]**
grandson	finished	3MIN.A.R	make	1MIN.O	hit	[PERF]

Grandson! Dead! It's hit me

INSTRUMENTAL SECTIONS 1–2

Rhythmic mode 5a (fast even)

INSTRUMENTAL SECTION 3

Rhythmic mode 5b (fast doubled)

TRACK 28 (Kof86-03/4-s09)

Song 15: Karra[4]

This text, by an unknown composer, consists simply of the word '*karra*' sung to the same tune as 'Nadirri' (track 19) and 'Walakandha No. 1' (track 15). Another point of similarity to the latter song is the economy of its text, which in the case of 'Walakandha No. 1' consists only of the words '*karra walakandha*.'

---

4   This song was not listed in Marett, 2005, pp 238-41.

TRACK 29 (WASA23-s06)

Song 16: Yendili No. 5[5]

Sung text	Free translation
yendili yendili yendili yendili	Yendili, Yendili, Yendili, Yendili!
karra karrila karrila yendili	Hill, Yendili Hill!
ngatja windjeni ngumunit-nginyanga-ndjen	My child, I have to tell you something bad
wudi yendili ngil-dim-mi-nginanga-ndjen	I have to close down the spring at Yendili

This song is about the death of Honorata Ngenawurda, the mother of Frank, Wagon, Terence, Claver and John Dumoo, all of whom are or were key figures in the Walakandha *wangga* tradition. Here, her spirit appears in a dream to her son, Wagon Dumoo, announcing that because of her death, she has to close down a particular Dreaming waterhole at Yendili, causing it to dry up. As in 'Walakandha No. 4' (track 34), we see the country itself responding to death.

The date, occasion and recordist of this performance, which is in the collection of the Wadeye Aboriginal Sound Archive, are unknown.

SONG STRUCTURE SUMMARY

VOCAL SECTIONS 1–2

Melodic section 1

Text phrase 1

Rhythmic mode 1 (without clapsticks)

yendili	**yendili**	**yendili**	**yendili**
place name	place name	place name	place name

Yendili, Yendili, Yendili, Yendili!

Text phrase 2

Rhythmic mode 1 (without clapsticks)

karra	**karrila**	**karrila**	**yendili**
SW	hill	hill	place name

Hill, Yendili Hill!

Text phrase 3

Rhythmic mode 1 (without clapsticks)

ngatja	**windjeni**	**ngumunit**	**-nginyanga**	**-ndjen**
child	bad	1MIN.A.R pick up	1MIN.ADVERS	now

My child, I have to tell you something bad

---

5   Classified as Song 19 in Marett, 2005, p 241.

Text phrase 4

Rhythmic mode 1 (without clapsticks)

wudi	**yendili**	**ngil**	**-dim**	**-mi**	**-nginyanga**	**-ndjen**
water	place name	1MIN.A.cut	sink	spring	2MIN.ADVERS	now

I have to close down the spring at Yendili

INSTRUMENTAL SECTION 1

Rhythmic mode 5a (fast even)

INSTRUMENTAL SECTION 2

Rhythmic mode 5b (fast doubled)

D: The Walakandha *wangga* in the decade 1996 to 2006 (tracks 30–37)

By the mid-to-late 1990s, the singer/composers Thomas Kungiung, Wagon Dumoo and Martin Warrigal Kungiung, as well as many of the dancers and the didjeridu player John Dumoo, had either passed away or ceased to be ceremonially active. In the early part of this period, Les Kundjil, a singer who had played a key role both in the initial creation of the Walakandha *wangga* and its blossoming in the golden age, emerged as the senior songman, but he was already quite old and his powers were dwindling. Before long Philip Mullumbuk, the much younger brother of Stan Mullumbuk, eclipsed Kundjil as the most active songman, composing many complex and beautiful songs and taking on the main ceremonial role, which he continued until his death in 2008.

Figure 8.5 Philip Mullumbuk, Les Kundjil and Colin Worumbu sing Walakandha *wangga* for a circumcision ceremony at Wadeye, 1997. Photograph by Mark Crocombe, reproduced with the permission of Wadeye community.

Thomas Kungiung's son Charles is now emerging as the leading singer in this tradition. We have some recordings of him leading a ceremony in 2009 but have not yet had a chance to work on these with him.

Figure 8.6 Charles Kungiung, Wadeye, 1999. Photograph by Allan Marett, reproduced with the permission of Wadeye community.

TRACK 30 (Mar98-15-s06)
Song 17: Yendili No. 3[6]

Sung text	Free translation
karra yendili yendili karra mana nidin-ngin-a	Yendili! Yendili! Brother! My dear country!
karra yendili yendili karra mana nidin-ngin-a	Yendili! Yendili! Brother! My dear country!
ee karra mana nidin-ngin-a	Ee brother! My dear country!

This song was composed by Les Kundjil. While its text follows the AAB structure found in numerous Walakandha *wangga* songs, it is unusual in a number of ways: it contains no verbs— just exclamations— and the song word *karra*, which normally begins a text phrase, occurs both initially and in the middle of the text phrase (see further Marett, 2005, p 126). The melody is the same as Maudie Dumoo's song 'Yendili No. 2', which also shares several text elements.

This recording was elicited by Allan Marett at Wadeye on 15 October 1998.

---

6   Classified as Song 4 in Marett, 2005, p 239.

SONG STRUCTURE SUMMARY

VOCAL SECTIONS 1–3

Melodic sections 1–2

Text phrases 1-2

Rhythmic mode 1 (without clapsticks)

karra	**yendili**	**yendili**	**karra**	**mana**	**nidin**	**-ngin**	**-a**
SW	place name	place name	SW	brother	country	1MIN.O	PERF

Yendili! Yendili! Brother! My dear country!

Melodic section 3

Text phrase 3

Rhythmic mode 1 (without clapsticks)

ee	**karra**	**mana**	**nidin**	**-ngin**	**-a**
eh	SW	brother	country	1MIN.O	PERF

Ee brother! My dear country!

INSTRUMENTAL SECTIONS 1–2

Rhythmic mode 5a (fast even)

INSTRUMENTAL SECTION 3

Rhythmic mode 5b (fast doubled)

TRACK 31 (Mar99-04-s16)

Song 18: Lhambumen[7]

Sung text	Free translation
karra lhambumen lhambumen kimi-wurri kavulh[-a]	He [a Walakandha] has always sung 'Lhambumen' to me
karra lhambumen lhambumen kimi-wurri kavulh[-a]	He [a Walakandha] has always sung 'Lhambumen' to me
aa	Aa

This song by Les Kundjil (like Wagon Dumoo's songs 'Kubuwemi' (track 12) and 'Yendili No. 1' (track 13), with which it shares a melody and text structure) affirms that Walakandha ancestors are an eternal source of songs about country (see also Marett, 2005, p 127). Lhambumen is one of two billabongs on the Moyle floodplain (the other is Lhambudinbu). This is where the Wallaroo, Wedjiwurang, jumped to from Yederr when he was fighting with the Emu (see Philip Mullumbuk's song 'Wedjiwurang' on

---

7   Classified as song 18 in Marett, 2005, p 241.

track 38). The translation assumes that, as in previous songs, the final perfective marker is suppressed in text phrases 1 and 2.

SONG STRUCTURE SUMMARY

VOCAL SECTIONS 1–3

Melodic section 1

Text phrases 1–2

Rhythmic mode 1 (without clapsticks)

karra	**lhambumen**	**lhambumen**	**kimi**	**-wurri**	**kavulh**	**[-a]**
karra	lhambumen	lhambumen	3MIN.S.R say/sing	towards speaker	3MIN.S.R lie	[PERF]

He [a Walakandha] has always sung 'Lhambumen' to me

Text phrase 3

Rhythmic mode 1 (without clapsticks)

aa
SW

Aa

INSTRUMENTAL SECTIONS 1–2

Rhythmic mode 5a (fast even)

INSTRUMENTAL SECTION 3

Rhythmic mode 5b (fast doubled)

Figure 8.7 Les Kundjil singing Walakandha *wangga* for Allan Marett, Wadeye, 1998. Photograph by Allan Marett, reproduced with the permission of Wadeye community.

TRACK 32 (Eni92-s24)

Song 19: Yendili No. 4[8]

Sung text	Free translation
karra yendili yendili ngirrin-ni	We all have to walk to Yendili
karra yendili yendili ngirrin-ni	We all have to walk to Yendili
aa yeri-ngin-a	Aa, my dear children/descendants!

Philip Mullumbuk composed this song. While Philip himself regarded this as a discrete song, others argue that it is a version of Maudi Dumoo's 'Yendili No. 2' (track 14), on which it is clearly based (it also shares a melody and some text with Les Kundjil's 'Yendili No. 3' on track 30). This is the first time we hear Philip's uniquely delicate and flexible style of singing, in a recording made by Michael Enilane at a circumcision ceremony in 1992.

Figure 8.8 Philip Mullumbuk singing his *wangga* for Allan Marett, Wadeye, 1999. Photograph by Allan Marett, reproduced with the permission of Wadeye community.

SONG STRUCTURE SUMMARY

VOCAL SECTIONS 1–3

Melodic sections 1–2

Text phrases 1–2

Rhythmic mode 1 (without clapsticks)

karra	**yendili**	**yendili**	**ngirrin**	**-ni**
SW	place name	place name	1AUG.EXCL.IR.go	PURP

We all have to walk to Yendili

---

8   Classified as Song 5 in Marett, 2005, p 239.

Melodic section 3

Text phrase 3

Rhythmic mode 1 (without clapsticks)

aa	yeri	-ngin	-a
SW	child/descendant	1MIN.O	PERF

Aa, my dear children/descendants!

INSTRUMENTAL SECTIONS 1–2

Rhythmic mode 5a (fast even)

INSTRUMENTAL SECTION 3

Rhythmic mode 5b (fast doubled)

TRACK 33 (Mar99-04-s07)

Song 20: Walakandha No. 3[9]

Sung text	Free translation
karra walakandha-ga kiminy-gimi-vini kunya aven-andja	Walakandhas! They are saying, 'where has everyone gone?'
kan-gu kavulh-wuwu duwarr kubuwemi-gu	As for here, Kubuwemi is deserted
karra walakandha kudinggi-yirrir kuniny purangang ngindji ngandjen	The Walakandhas [i.e., Dumoo, Kundjil and Mullumbuk] are wandering around at a certain other coastal estate
kubuwemi nidin-ngin-a	Kubuwemi! My dear country!

In this song by Philip Mullumbuk, a group of Walakandhas (in this case, the ancestral dead) find Kubuwemi deserted and ask where everyone has gone. They are told that everyone (here 'Walakandha' refers to the living) has gone to another coastal estate. This song refers to an occasion on which Wagon Dumoo, Les Kundjil and Philip Mullumbuk went south to the estate of the Murriny Patha-speaking Yek Nangu clan, to perform ceremony. Perhaps this was the *burnim-rag* ceremony for Johnny Ninnal held in Nangu country sometime around 1990, which gave rise to a *djanba* song describing an encounter between performers of *wangga* and *wurltjirri* songs (Barwick, et al., 2010, djanba 65).[10]

Formally the song shows Philip Mullumbuk's love of long, grammatically elaborate text phrases, each of which is often sung to the same melody. We will see this pattern repeated in the following song.

---

9   Classified as Song 13 in Marett, 2005, p 240.

10 For the text of *djanba* song 65, see sydney.edu.au/wadeyesong/songtexts/158.

SONG STRUCTURE SUMMARY

VOCAL SECTIONS 1–2

Melodic section 1

Text phrase 1

Rhythmic mode 1 (without clapsticks)

karra	**walakandha**	**-ga**	**kiminy**	**-gimi**	**-vini**	**kunya**	**aven**	**-andja**
SW	walakandha	TOP	3AUG.A.R say	talking	UAUG	3AUG.S.R stand	where	true

Walakandhas! They are saying, 'where has everyone gone?

kan	**-gu**	**kavulh**	**-wuwu**	**duwarr**	**kubuwemi**	**-gu**
right here	TOP	MIN.S.R lie	empty	ground	place name	TOP

As for here, Kubuwemi is deserted'

Melodic section 2

Text phrase 2

Rhythmic mode 1 (without clapsticks)

karra	**walakandha**	**kudinggi**	**-yirrir**	**kuniny**	**purangang**	**ngindji**	**ngandjen**
SW	walakandha	3AUG.S.R look	go round	3AUG.S.R walk	sea	one	different

The Walakandhas [i.e., Dumoo, Kundjil and Mullumbuk] are wandering around at a certain other coastal estate

kubuwemi	**nidin**	**-ngin**	**-a**
place name	country	1MIN.O	PERF

Kubuwemi! My dear country!

INSTRUMENTAL SECTION 1

Rhythmic mode 5a (fast even)

INSTRUMENTAL SECTION 2

Rhythmic mode 5b (fast doubled)

TRACK 34 (Mar99-04-s08)

Song 21: Karra yeri-ngina[11]

Sung text	Free translation

karra yeri-ngin-a
    ka-rri-yitjip-wandhi-nginanga ka-ni dhenggi-diyerri
    nidin-ngin-a
	My dear children!
	They keep appearing in the distance behind me at the mouth of the Moyle River, my dear country!

karra yeri meri yigin-ga djindja-wurri kangi-nginanga yenmungirini na pumut pumut kurzi	You boys, come here I've got to stay here at Yenmungirini where the Headache Dreaming is

This song was given to its composer Philip Mullumbuk by the ghost of Wagon Dumoo following his death. Wagon's spirit has returned to Yenmungirini, the site of his Dreaming, Pumut (Headache), where he must remain. He can see his male descendants only faintly as they gather at the mouth of the Moyle River. At this time the Dumoo family were living in Philip Mullumbuk's country at Nadirri near the Moyle mouth, some distance away from their clan estate near Perrederr.

The recording was elicited by Allan Marett at Wadeye in 1999.

SONG STRUCTURE SUMMARY

VOCAL SECTIONS 1–3

Melodic section 1

Text phrase 1

Rhythmic mode 1 (without clapsticks)

karra	**yeri**	**-ngin**	**-a**
SW	child	1MIN.O	PERF

My dear children!

ka	-rri	-yitjip	-wandhi	-nginanga	ka	-ni	dhenggi-diyerri	nidin	-ngin	-a
3MIN.AR	use hands	appear faintly	behind	1MIN.ADVERS	3MIN.S.R	walk	place name	country	1MIN.O	PERF

They keep appearing in the distance behind me at the mouth of the Moyle River, my dear country!

---

11 Classified as Song 14 in Marett, 2005, p 241.

Melodic section 2

Text phrase 2

Rhythmic mode 1 (without clapsticks)

karra	**yeri**	**meri**	**yigin**	**-ga**	**djindja**	**-wurri**
SW	child	people	1MIN.PRO	TOP	here	towards speaker

You boys, come here

kangi	**-nginanga**	**yenmungirini**	**na**	**pumut**	**pumut**	**kurzi**
1MIN.SRsit	1MIN.ADVERS	place name	LOC	headache	headache	3MIN.SRsit

I've got to stay here at Yenmungirini where the Headache Dreaming is

INSTRUMENTAL SECTIONS 1–2

Rhythmic mode 5a (fast even)

INSTRUMENTAL SECTION 3

Rhythmic mode 5b (fast doubled)

TRACK 35 (Mar99-04-s10)

Song 22: Walakandha No. 4[12]

Sung text	Free translation
karra walakandha ngindji kimi-nginanga-wurri kavulh na karrivirrilhyi	A certain Walakandha is always singing to me beside the beach hibiscus and I can't stop him
karra berrida munggumurri kunya-nin-viyi-nginanga-vini-wurri	He says, 'Berrida and Munggumurri are both standing looking at the top of their hill [Yendili] and I can't stop them
karra wandhi wandhi kiminy-gimi-vini kunya	They are standing, looking behind them [over their shoulders]
karrila yendili kuwa-thet-viyi-ngangga-wurri mana	He says, '[The trees and grasses] on the top (head) of Yendili Hill are standing upright, brother'
purangang kavulh nginanga-wurri [mana]	The tide is always coming in on me, [brother]'

Here a Walakandha sings of two other Walakandha ancestors: Berrida (Bruno Munggum Berrida, the son of Munggum);[13] and Munggumurri, grandfather of Philip Mullumbuk, the composer of this song. They are looking over their shoulders at Yendili Hill, where the trees and grasses are standing up like hairs on the back of a dog in response to a death. The final text phrase affirms that like the tide, life and death are in constant flux.

---

12 Classified as Song 15 in Marett, 2005, p 241.

13 Berrida is also mentioned in the text of 'Truwu' (tracks 16–18).

Formally this is the most complex of Philip Mullumbuk's *wangga*. Text phrases 1 and 2 are sung to one melodic section, repeated for text phrases 3 and 4. The poignant final text phrase is set to its own melody.

SONG STRUCTURE SUMMARY

VOCAL SECTIONS 1–2

Melodic Section 1

Text phrase 1

Rhythmic mode 1 (without clapsticks)

karra	walakandha	ngindji	kimi	-nginanga	-wurri	kavulh	na	karrivirrilhyi
SW	walakandha	one	3MIN.A.R do	1MIN.ADVERS	towards speaker	MIN.S.R lie	LOC	beach hibiscus

A certain Walakandha is always singing to me beside the beach hibiscus and I can't stop him

Text phrase 2

Rhythmic mode 1 (without clapsticks)

karra	berrida	munggumurri	kunya	-nin	-viyi	-nginanga	-vini	-wurri
SW	person's name	person's name	3AUG.S.R stand	3MIN.O	head	1MIN.ADVERS	UAUG	towards speaker

He says, 'Berrida and Munggumurri are both standing looking at the top of their hill [Yendili] and I can't stop them

Melodic Section 2

Text phrase 3

Rhythmic mode 1 (without clapsticks)

karra	wandhi	wandhi	kiminy	-gimi	-vini	kunya
SW	behind	behind	3AUG.A.R say	look	UAUG	3AUG.S.R stand

They are standing, looking behind them [over their shoulders]

Text phrase 4

Rhythmic mode 1 (without clapsticks)

karrila	yendili	kuwa	-thet	-viyi	-ngangga	-wurri	mana
hill	place name	3MIN.S.R stand	upright	head	1/2MIN.DAT	towards speaker	brother

He says, '[The trees and grasses] on the top (head) of Yendili Hill are standing upright, brother'

Melodic Section 3

Text phrase 5

Rhythmic mode 1 (without clapsticks)

purangang	kavulh	nginanga	-wurri	[mana]
sea	3MIN.S.R lie	1MIN.ADVERS	towards speaker	[brother]

The tide is always coming in on me, [brother]'

INSTRUMENTAL SECTION 1

Rhythmic mode 5a (fast even)

INSTRUMENTAL SECTION 2

Rhythmic mode 5b (fast doubled)

TRACK 36 (Mar98-15-s21)

Song 23: Walakandha No. 5[14]

Sung text	Free translation
karra walakandha kakap kiminy-vini kuniny kurriny-rtadi-warambu-nganan-wurri-ya dhenggi-diyerri djanden-ni	The Walakandhas keep calling out as they came towards me from high in the inland country to there, at the Moyle River mouth
wuuu	'Wuuu!'
yakerre ngumali nidin-ngin-a	Oh, Ngumali, my dear country

In this song, another composed by Philip Mullumbuk, a Walakandha who is standing at Ngumali, the men's ceremonial ground near the mouth of the Moyle river, watches a group of Walakandha (probably living Marri Tjavin men) coming back from the high inland country to the northwest, calling out '*wuuu*' as they go.

SONG STRUCTURE SUMMARY

VOCAL SECTIONS 1–3

Melodic section 1

Text phrase 1

Rhythmic mode 1 (without clapsticks)

karra	walakandha	kakap	kiminy	-vini	kuniny
SW	walakandha	call out	3AUG.A.R say	UAUG	3AUG.S.R walk

The Walakandhas keep calling out

---

14 Classified as Song 16 in Marett, 2005, p 241.

kurriny	-rtadi	-warambu	-nganan	-wurri	-ya
3AUG.S.R go down	back	high inland country	ABL	towards speaker	PERF

as they came towards me from high in the inland country

dhenggi-diyerri	djanden	-ni
place name	there	DAT

to there, at the Moyle River mouth

Melodic section 2

Text phrase 2

Rhythmic mode 1 (without clapsticks)

wuuu
SW

'Wuuu!'

Melodic section 3

Text phrase 3

Rhythmic mode 1 (without clapsticks)

yakerre	ngumali	nidin	-ngin	-a
EXCL	place name	country	1MIN.O	PERF

Oh, Ngumali, my dear country

INSTRUMENTAL SECTIONS 1–2

*Rhythmic mode 5**

INSTRUMENTAL SECTION 3

Rhythmic mode 5b (fast doubled)

TRACK 37 (Mar99-04-s21)

Song 24: Kinyirr[15]

Sung text	Free translation
karra mana kinyirr waddi kunyininggi-mukurr-vini-ya	Look to Kinyirr brother, you should have told those two people to make it clear with the Dreaming
karra mana nidin-ngin-a	Brother, my dear country
kinyirr mana nidin-ngin-a	Kinyirr, brother, my dear country

---

15 Classified as Song 17 in Marett, 2005, p 241.

This song by Philip Mullumbuk is about the making of the airstrip for the Nadirri outstation, during which operation the Leech Dreaming site, Kinyirr, was damaged by a bulldozer.

SONG STRUCTURE SUMMARY

VOCAL SECTIONS 1–3

Melodic section 1

Text phrase 1

Rhythmic mode 1 (without clapsticks)

karra	**mana**	**kinyirr**	**waddi**	**kunyininggi**	**-mukurr**	**-vini**	**-ya**
SW	brother	place name	2MIN.A.IR look	3DL.S.R make	clear	UAUG	PERF

Look to Kinyirr brother, you should have told those two people [who are making the airstrip] to make it clear with the Dreaming [Kinyirr is a Leech Dreaming site]

karra	**mana**	**nidin**	**-ngin**	**-a**
SW	brother	country	1MIN.O	PERF

Brother, my dear country

Melodic section 2

Text phrase 2

Rhythmic mode 1 (without clapsticks)

kinyirr	**mana**	**nidin**	**-ngin**	**-a**
place name	brother	country	1MIN.O	PERF

Kinyirr, brother, my dear country

INSTRUMENTAL SECTIONS 1–2

Rhythmic mode 5a (fast even)

INSTRUMENTAL SECTION 3

Rhythmic mode 5b (fast doubled)

E. Miscellaneous songs (tracks 38–39)

For the sake of completeness, we decided to include in our corpus two songs that are somewhat peripheral to the Walakandha *wangga* repertory. Philip Mullumbuk's song about the ancestral Wallaro, Wedjiwurang, does not conform to the normal conventions of *wangga* and there is some question about whether it is really a *wangga* at all (Ford, 2007). Similarly, Ambrose Piarlum's song about the Seagull Dreaming, 'Tjinmel', is not, strictly speaking, a Walakandha *wangga*—since it was composed without the assistance of the ancestral dead—but it is included here because of his close association with the *thanggurralh* 'company' group of Walakandha *wangga* performers.

TRACK 38 (Croc04-01-s01)

Song 25: Wedjiwurang[1]

Sung text	Free translation
CHORUS:	CHORUS:
kurzi namadjawalh namadjawalh	He lives at Namadjawalh, Namadjawalh
(repeated)	(repeated)
awu kanyi-ngin	The animal is our totem
wedjiwurang-ga yivi-ndja kurru-kut-a-ga	It was the Wallaroo that went down there
yi kanbirrin devin-da	Alone again, to Kanbirrin over yonder,
CUE: ngadja-wurl-da-ni	CUE: I'm going back again
CHORUS: (repeated as above)	CHORUS: (repeated as above)
yimurdigi na-ndjen	Then at Yimurdigi
kimelh-a-wurri	He peeped out [from the bushes]
meri karru-tjip-wurri	A black man is coming towards him
CUE: ngadja-wurl-ni	CUE: I'm going to go back
CHORUS: (repeated as above)	CHORUS: (repeated as above)
ku-muyi-ni masri-ndjen ka-ni	Then, he kept coming out of the swamp to him (Emu)
yelhi-ndjen kundjiny-vini-ya	The two of them had a stick fight
nang-ga mutjirr-ga viyi	As for that fellow, Emu, his head [got hit by Wallaroo]
nang-ga ka-rri-birr-a vi-rtadi-gu ka-ni	Emu grabbed the same stick and hit Wallaroo on the top of the spine
CUE: ngadja-wurl	CUE: I'm going to go back
CHORUS: (repeated as above)	CHORUS: (repeated as above)
nang-ga wedjiwurang-ga	As for that fellow, Wallaroo,
kurzi-varrvatj-a	He was still jumping
lhambudinbu na-ndjen ka-ni-thung-mi-ya	At Lhambudinbu he cracked open the ground and made a waterhole
kuwa-wurl-a yivi-ndja	He went back yonder to that place
namadjawalh-dja nang-ga yivi-ndja	Namadjawalh, that place over yonder, which is his true place
ka-ni-wurr-a-gu	That is where he died

This song about the Marri Tjavin totemic Dreaming Wedjiwurang ('Wallaroo') is structurally quite unlike other Walakandha *wangga* songs. In its verse-and-chorus structure it is more like an English ballad (Ford, 2007, p 76). Vocal sections comprising narrative text about the activities of Wedjiwurang in the ancestral period alternate with a chorus that asserts over and over that the ancestral Wallaroo lives at Namadjawalh. This text phrase, 'He lives at Namadjawalh, Namadjawalh,' is repeated isorhythmically with a single melodic section. The text phrases on the vocal section are, in contrast, more like those of

---

1 This song was not listed in Marett, 2005, pp 238–41.

other Walakandha *wangga*. Each text phrase is sung to a melodic section comprising only two notes. Each move from a vocal section back to the chorus is cued by the sung phrase, 'I'm going back again' or 'I'm going back.'

Another unusual feature, also encountered in the songs of Jimmy Muluk, is that in some of the narrative vocal sections, the singer starts singing without clapstick beating, then introduces a very quiet tapping that gets gradually louder throughout the vocal section.[2] It is possible that Mullumbuk learnt this technique from recordings of Muluk that were circulating in the community.

Even though the quality of this recording is less than ideal, we have included it because it represents the only record we have of this extraordinary song. Despite a number of attempts, we were unable to make another recording before Philip Mullumbuk's unexpected death in 2008. Ford has written about this song in considerable detail elsewhere (Ford, 2007, pp 76–89).

SONG STRUCTURE SUMMARY

CHORUS

Melodic section 1

Text phrases 1–5

Rhythmic mode 5a (fast even)

kurzi	**namadjawalh**	**namadjawalh**
3MIN.S.R sit	place name	place name

He lives at Namadjawalh, Namadjawalh

VOCAL SECTION 1

Melodic section 1

Text phrase 1

Rhythmic mode 5a (var) (fast even, clapsticks getting louder)

awu	**kanyi**	**-ngin**
animal	totem	1MIN.O

The animal is our totem

Melodic section 2

Text phrase 2

Rhythmic mode 5a (var) (fast even, clapsticks getting louder)

wedjiwurang	**-ga**	**yivi**	**-ndja**	**kurru**	**-kut**	**-a**	**-ga**
wallaroo	TOP	far DEIC	true	3MIN.S.R go down	go down	PERF	TOP

It was the Wallaroo that went down there

---

2   We have classified this pattern as rhythmic mode 5a (var) in the song structure summary.

Melodic section 3

Text phrase 3

Rhythmic mode 5a (var) (fast even, clapsticks getting louder)

yi	**kanbirrin**	**devin**	**-da**
farDEIC	place name	alone	again

Alone again, to Kanbirrin over yonder,

CUE [sung on tonic]

Rhythmic mode 5a (fast even)

ngadja	**-wurl**	**-da**	**-ni**
1MIN.S.IR.walk	go back	again	PURP

I'm going back again

CHORUS

Melodic section 1

Text phrases 1–5

Rhythmic mode 5a (fast even)

kurzi	**namadjawalh**	**namadjawalh**
3MIN.S.R sit	place name	place name

He lives at Namadjawalh, Namadjawalh

VOCAL SECTION 2

Melodic section 1

Text phrase 1

Rhythmic mode 5a (var) (fast even, clapsticks getting louder)

yimurdigi	**na**	**-ndjen**
name	LOC	then

Then at Yimurdigi

Melodic section 2

Text phrase 2

Rhythmic mode 5a (var) (fast even, clapsticks getting louder)

kimelh	**-a**	**-wurri**
3MIN.S.Rpeep	PERF	towards speaker

He peeped out [from the bushes]

Melodic section 3

Text phrase 3

Rhythmic mode 5a (var) (fast even, clapsticks getting louder)

meri	**karru**	**-tjip**	**-wurri**
man	3MIN.S.R travel	be black	towards speaker

A black man is coming towards him

CUE [sung on tonic]

Rhythmic mode 5a (fast even)

ngadja	**-wurl**	**-ni**
1MIN.S.IR.walk	go back	PURP

I'm going to go back

CHORUS

Melodic section 1

Text phrases 1-5

Rhythmic mode 5a (fast even)

kurzi	**namadjawalh**	**namadjawalh**
3MIN.S.R sit	place name	place name

He lives at Namadjawalh, Namadjawalh

VOCAL SECTION 3

Melodic section 1

Text phrase 1

Rhythmic mode 5a (var) (fast even, clapsticks getting louder)

ku	**-muyi**	**-ni**	**masri**	**-ndjen**	**ka**	**-ni**
3MIN.S.R Ø	come out	3.MIN.M.IO	belly	then	3MIN.S.R	walk

Then, he kept coming out of the swamp to him (Emu)

Melodic section 2

Text phrase 2

Rhythmic mode 5a (var) (fast even, clapsticks getting louder)

yelhi	**-ndjen**	**kundjiny**	**-vini**	**-ya**
weapon	then	3AUG.A.R make	UAUG	PERF

The two of them had a stick fight

Melodic section 3

Text phrase 3

Rhythmic mode 5a (var) (fast even, clapsticks getting louder)

nang	**-ga**	**mutjirr**	**-ga**	**viyi**
3MIN.M.PRO	TOP	emu	TOP	head

As for that fellow, Emu, his head [got hit by Wallaroo]

Melodic section 4

Text phrase 4

Rhythmic mode 5a (var) (fast even, clapsticks getting louder)

nang	**-ga**	**ka**	**-rri**	**-birr**	**-a**	**vi**	**-rtadi**	**-gu**	**ka**	**-ni**
3MIN.M.PRO	TOP	3MIN.A.R	use hands	grab	PERF	head	back	DTOP	3MIN.S.R	walk

Emu grabbed the same stick and hit Wallaroo on the top of the spine

CUE [sung on tonic]

Rhythmic mode 5a (fast even)

ngadja	**-wurl**
1S.IR.walk	go back

I'm going to go back

CHORUS

Melodic section 1

Text phrases 1–5

Rhythmic mode 5a (fast even)

kurzi	**namadjawalh**	**namadjawalh**
3MIN.S.R sit	place name	place name

He lives at Namadjawalh, Namadjawalh

VOCAL SECTION 4

Text phrase 1

Rhythmic mode 5a (var) (fast even, clapsticks getting louder)

nang	**-ga**	**wedjiwurang**	**-ga**
3MIN.M.PRO	TOP	wallaroo	TOP

As for that fellow, Wallaroo,

Text phrase 2

Rhythmic mode 5a (var) (fast even, clapsticks getting louder)

kurzi	**-varrvatj**	**-a**
3MIN.S.R sit	jump	PERF

He was still jumping

lhambudinbu	**na**	**-ndjen**	**ka**	**-ni**	**-thung**	**-mi**	**-ya**
place name	LOC	then	3MIN.S.R	walk	crack open	eye	PERF

At Lhambudinbu he cracked open the ground and made a waterhole

Text phrase 3

Rhythmic mode 5a (var) (fast even, clapsticks getting louder)

kuwa	**-wurl**	**-a**	**yivi**	**-ndja**
3MIN.S.R stand	return	PERF	far DEIC	true

He went back yonder to that place

Text phrase 4

Rhythmic mode 5a (var) (fast even, clapsticks getting louder)

namadjawalh	**-dja.**	**nang**	**-ga**	**yivi**	**-ndja**
place name	really	3MIN.M.PRO	TOP	FarDEIC	true

That place Namadjawalh over yonder, which is his true place

Text phrase 5

Rhythmic mode 5a (var) (fast even, clapsticks getting louder)

ka	**-ni**	**-wurr**	**-a**	**-gu**
3MIN.S.R	walk	die	PERF	DTOP

That is where he died.

INSTRUMENTAL CODA

Rhythmic mode 5a (fast even)

Figure 8.9 Ambrose Piarlum singing 'Tjinmel' for Allan Marett, Wadeye, 1998. Photograph by Allan Marett, reproduced with the permission of Wadeye community.

TRACK 39 (Mar98-07-s11)

Tjinmel[3]

Sung text	Free translation
karra mm	Karra, mm
karra tjinmel devin rtadi-wunbirri ka-rri-wuwu rtadi ka-ni-ya	The solitary seagull kept soaring above Rtadi-wunbirri
karra mm	Karra, mm
aa rtadi-wunbirri tjinmel devin	Above Rtadi-wunbirri the solitary seagull is soaring
karra mm	Karra, mm
karra tjinmel devin ka-rri wuwu rtadi ka-ni-ya rtadi-wunbirri	The solitary seagull kept soaring above Rtadi-wunbirri
karra mm	Karra, mm
kagandja	Here!
karra mm	Karra, mm
karra mana kagandja rtadi-wunbirri devin ka-rri wuwu rtadi	Brother, right here above Rtadi-wunbirri he soars alone
karra mm	Karra, mm

Tjinmel ('Seagull') has its Dreaming site at a *wudi-pumininy* (freshwater spring) in the sea at Yederr in Matige country. Although this song is not strictly a Walakandha *wangga*, since it was composed by Ambrose Piarlum without spirit assistance, it has been included here because of Piarlum's close association with the group who sing Walakandha *wangga*.

---

3 This song was not listed in Marett, 2005, pp 238–41.

Because each vocal section is different—the text formulae are arranged in a different order from one vocal section to another—each is written out in full. The instrumental sections follow the patterns common for Walakandha *wangga* of the golden age.

SONG STRUCTURE SUMMARY

VOCAL SECTION 1

Melodic section

Text phrase 1
Rhythmic mode 1 (without clapsticks)

karra	**mm**
SW	SW

Karra, mm

Text phrase 2
Rhythmic mode 1 (without clapsticks)

karra	**tjinmel**	**devin**	**rtadi-wunbirri**	**ka**	**-rri**	**-wuwu**	**rtadi**	**ka**	**-ni**	**-ya**
SW	seagull	alone	place name	3MIN.AR	use hands	soar	on top	3MIN.S.R	walk	PERF

The solitary seagull kept soaring above Rtadi-wunbirri

Text phrase 3
Rhythmic mode 1 (without clapsticks)

karra	**mm**
SW	SW

Karra, mm

Melodic section 2

Text phrase 3
Rhythmic mode 1 (without clapsticks)

aa	**rtadi-wunbirri**	**tjinmel**	**devin**	**ka**	**-rri**	**-wuwu**	**rtadi**
SW	place name	seagull	alone	3MIN.AR	use hands	soar	back

Above Rtadi-wunbirri the solitary seagull is soaring

INSTRUMENTAL SECTION 1

Rhythmic mode 5a (fast even)

VOCAL SECTION 2

Melodic section 1

Text phrase 1
Rhythmic mode 1 (without clapsticks)

karra   **mm**
SW   SW

Karra, mm

Text phrase 2
Rhythmic mode 1 (without clapsticks)

karra	**tjinmel**	**devin**	**ka**	**-rri**	**wuwu**	**rtadi**	**ka**	**-ni**	**-ya**	**rtadi-wunbirri**
SW	seagull	alone	3MIN.AR	use hands	soar		on top	3MIN.S.R	walk	PERF	place name

The solitary seagull kept soaring above Rtadi-wunbirri

Text phrase 3
Rhythmic mode 1 (without clapsticks)

karra   **mm**
SW   SW

Karra, mm

CUE

kagandja
here

Here!

INSTRUMENTAL SECTION 2
Rhythmic mode 5a (fast even)

VOCAL SECTION 3

Melodic section 1

Text phrase 1
Rhythmic mode 1 (without clapsticks)

karra   **mm**
SW   SW

Karra, mm

Text phrase 2

Rhythmic mode 1 (without clapsticks)

karra	mana	kagandja	rtadi-wunbirri	devin	ka	-rri	wuwu	rtadi
SW	brother	right here	place name	alone	3MIN.AR	use hands	soar	on top

Brother, right here above Rtadi-wunbirri he soars alone

Text phrase 3

Rhythmic mode 1 (without clapsticks)

karra	mm
SW	SW

Karra, mm

INSTRUMENTAL SECTION 3

Rhythmic mode 5b (fast doubled)

MUSICAL ANALYSIS OF THE WALAKANDHA REPETORY

Song structure overview

The early and transitional Walakandha *wangga* follow the normal pattern for *wangga*: an introductory instrumental introduction is followed by a series of paired vocal and instrumental sections. The majority of songs have between three and four vocal and instrumental section pairs. None have fewer than three, and one song 'Wutjelli No. 2' (track 3) has five.

Text structure overview

Twenty-three of the thirty-four texts in the Walakandha *wangga* repertory are through-composed, with no repetition of text phrases within a vocal section (these are listed as group 1 in table 8.2). These include all of Stan Mullumbuk's repertory, and a substantial proportion of songs by other composers. The texts of most of Stan Mullumbuk's songs take one of two forms: they are comprised either of a single through-composed text phrase in Marri Tjavin, or of two text phrases, the first in ghost language and the second in human language (Marri Tjavin). Vocal sections of the second type are also found in the songs of Jimmy Muluk, which, as we have argued elsewhere, had a considerable influence on Mullumbuk's early songs.

Eleven songs have some repetition of text phrases within the vocal section (listed in group 2 in table 8.2). Ten of them have the text form AAB, in which two identical text phrases in Marri Tjavin are followed by a third, contrasting text phrase, which in many cases is in ghost language (see a more elaborate discussion of text form in this repertory in Marett, 2005, pp 125–27). Texts using this pattern proved very popular in the golden age (1986-96) and into the subsequent decade. The remaining song 'Pumurriyi' (track 24) has the text form ABB.

Group	Songs
1 (23 songs)	'Walakandha No. 8a', 'Walakandha No. 1', 'Walakandha No. 6', 'Wutjelli No. 2', 'Nginimb-andja', 'Walakandha No. 7', 'Walakandha No. 8a', 'Walakandha No. 8b', 'Walakandha No. 9a', 'Walakandha No. 9b', 'Truwu', 'Wutjelli No. 1', 'Walakandha No. 2', 'Walakandha No. 3', 'Walakandha No. 5', 'Kinyirr', 'Thidha nany', 'Karra Yeri-ngina', 'Walakandha No. 4', 'Mirrwana', 'Yendili No. 5', 'Nadirri', 'Yenmilhi No. 1', 'Karra'
2 (11 songs)	'Yenmilhi No. 2', 'Yendili No. 2', 'Yendili No. 3', 'Yendili No. 4', 'Tjagawala' AAB 'Yendili No. 6', 'Kubuwemi', 'Yendili No. 1', 'Lhambumen', ' 'Dhembedi-ndjen', 'Pumurriyi'

Table 8.2 The Walakandha *wangga* repertory subdivided on the basis of text structure. Vocal sections of group 1 songs have through-composed text, while group 2 songs have some internal repetition of text phrases.

Rhythmic mode

For comparative purposes, we discuss rhythmic mode in the early and transitional period songs separately from the later songs composed in the golden age and afterwards.

Early use of rhythmic mode in the Walakandha *wangga*

The early and transitional songs (tracks 1–11) are quite varied in rhythmic modal treatment, in ways that resemble the Muluk repertory in several respects (see table 8.3). Four different tempo bands were represented in this group of songs, although rhythmic mode 1 (without clapsticks) was the most commonly used for vocal sections.

Tempo band of vocal section		#	Song title	Rhythmic mode of VS	Rhythmic mode of IIS	Rhythmic mode of FIS
Unmeasured						
Without clapsticks		ii	'Walakandha No. 6' (track 2)	1	5*	**5b**
		iv	'Nginimb-andja' (track 4)	1	5*	5b
		vi-b	'Walakandha No. 9b' (track 9)	1	5*	**5b**
		viii	'Yenmilhi No. 2' (track 11)	1	5*	**5b**
		vii	'Yendili No. 6' (track 10)	1	5a	**5b**
Measured						
Slow (60–72bpm)		iii	'Wutjelli No. 2' (track 3)	2	5a	5a
Moderate (c. 112bpm)		i-b	'Walakandha No. 8b' (track 7)	4a	4a	4a
		vi-a	'Walakandha No. 9a' (track 8)	4a (var) + 4a, or 1 (VS4)	4a	**5b**
Fast (120–36bpm)		i	'Walakandha No. 8' (track 1)	5c	5c	5c
		i-a	'Walakandha No. 8a' (track 6)	5c	5c	5c
		v	'Walakandha No. 7'	5c	5c	5c

Table 8.3 Rhythmic modes in the early and transitional period Walakandha *wangga*. VS = vocal section, IIS = internal instrumental section, FIS = final instrumental section. FIS is bold when different.

Presenting the same text in different rhythmic modes in successive items

Two songs—'Walakanda No. 8' and 'Walakanda No. 9'—were performed in two modes. To this we can add the evidence from Walsh's recordings (not included here), which contain a performance of one song—'Yene yene'—in no fewer than seven different rhythmic modes (Marett, 2007, p 67).

Presenting the same text in different rhythmic modes in different vocal sections within an item

'Walakandha No. 9a' (track 8) is the only song in this group to present the same text in different rhythmic modes, with the first two vocal sections in moderate even (rhythmic mode 4a or 4a [var]), and the third vocal section in rhythmic mode 1. This has a flow-on effect into the following (final) instrumental section, which uses rhythmic mode 5b, in conformity with the practice adopted in the five songs with all vocal sections in rhythmic mode 1.

Distribution of rhythmic mode between vocal sections and instrumental sections

As in other *wangga* repertories, songs with vocal sections in the unaccompanied and slow tempo bands use moderate or fast tempi in their instrumental sections, while songs with vocal sections in the moderate and fast tempo bands tend to use the same tempo throughout the whole song.

Mixing of rhythmic modes within a vocal section

In 'Walakandha No. 9a' we see an unusual suspended form of rhythmic mode 4a (rhythmic mode 4a [var]) where the beating is suspended for the early part of the text phrase as in Muluk's 'Piyamen.ga' (tracks 10–12), except that here the clapsticks recommence in the middle of the text phrase rather than at the end.[1]

Mixing of rhythmic modes within an instrumental section

The majority of songs with vocal sections in rhythmic mode 1 use internal instrumental sections with the same complex beating pattern as was found in Jimmy Muluk's rhythmic mode 4* (that is a period of doubled beating is followed by a period of even beating which is followed by the Walakandha *wangga* cueing pattern), except that here the tempo is fast rather than moderate. Marett sees this as one of several pieces of evidence that indicate that in creating the new Walakandha *wangga* repertory, Mullumbuk was influenced by Muluk (Marett, 2007, pp 70–71).

Use of rhythmic mode in the later periods of the Walakandha *wangga*

In the golden age and the later period of the Walakandha *wangga*, almost all songs used the same rhythmic mode in their instrumental sections. Marett has speculated that this developed because the Walakandha *wangga* is performed by a wide range of language groups compared to most other repertories, so that simplifying the dancing (and therefore the system of rhythmic modes that underpins dancing) allowed for better and stronger unisonal dancing (Marett, 2007, p 72).

---

1   A similar effect occurs in some text phrases of Philip Mullumbuk's song 'Wedjiwurang' (track 38), where it occurs in the fast tempo band (rhythmic mode 5a [var]). Fast even stickbeating is initially suspended and then gradually enters in the course of the text phrase.

Tempo Band	Number of songs	Vocal Section	Instrumental Section	Final IS
Unmeasured				
	18	1	5a	5b
Measured				
Slow even	5	2, 1	5a	5b
Fast even	1	5a	5a	5a

Table 8.4 Rhythmic modes used in the later Walakandha *wangga* (1986–2000).

Distribution of rhythmic mode between vocal sections and instrumental sections

Despite the relative lack of measured songs in this sample, the principle still holds true that songs with vocal sections in the unaccompanied and slow tempo bands use moderate or fast tempi in their instrumental sections, while songs with vocal sections in the moderate and fast tempo bands tend to use the same tempo throughout the whole song. Table 8.4 shows that here most songs (18 out of 24) have vocal sections in rhythmic mode 1, with a further five songs in a combination of rhythmic mode 2 and rhythmic mode 1. All 23 of these songs use fast rhythmic modes in their instrumental sections (see further below). Only one song, 'Yenmilhi No. 1' (track 20) does not fit this model. It conforms to a pattern found quite often in other *wangga* repertories, namely, using fast even beating (rhythmic mode 5a) throughout, in both vocal and instrumental sections.

Mixing of rhythmic modes within a vocal section

As already mentioned, five songs use mixed rhythmic modes within the vocal section: they use rhythmic mode 2 for the first two text phrases (AA) of the vocal section and rhythmic mode 1 (without clapsticks) for the third (B).[2] All five songs use Wagon Dumoo's melody 'Kubuwemi' (see discussion of shared melodies below).

Distribution of rhythmic mode between internal and final instrumental sections

The twenty-three songs wholly or partly in rhythmic mode 1 have identical practice in their instrumental sections, namely that non-final instrumental sections are performed using rhythmic mode 5a, while final ones use rhythmic mode 5b. All use the Walakandha *wangga* cueing pattern (♫ ♩ ♫ ♩ ♩ 𝄽) to mark the ends of instrumental sections.

Melody overview

In *Songs, dreamings and ghosts*, Marett was able to show that all the Walakandha *wangga* melodies from the later period used one of two melodic modal series, dorian or major (Marett, 2005, p 118). In table 8.5 we have updated this analysis to include the additional songs in the present corpus.

---

2 In these cases the irregular didjeridu pulse and asynchronous vocal rhythm show that the section without clapsticks is clearly in rhythmic mode 1, and not the suspended form of rhythmic mode 2 (rhythmic mode 2b).

Song	Composer
Melodies using the dorian modal series	
Songs with a unique melody	
'Wutjelli No. 2'	Stan Mullumbuk
'Walakandha No. 7'	Stan Mullumbuk
'Walakandha No. 9b'	Stan Mullumbuk
'Yenmilhi No. 2'	Thomas Kungiung
'Wutjelli No. 1'	Thomas Kungiung
'Yenmilhi No. 1'	John Dumoo
'Yendili No. 5'	Wagon Dumoo
Songs that share a melody	
'Walakandha No. 6', 'Nginimb-andja'	Stan Mullumbuk
'Walakandha No. 8a', 'Walakandha No. 8b'	Stan Mullumbuk
'Walakandha No. 9a', 'Yendili No. 6'	Stan Mullumbuk, Thomas Kungiung
'Kubuwemi', 'Yendili No. 1', 'Tjagawala', 'Lhambumen' ('Dhembedi-ndjen')	Wagon Dumoo, Les Kundjil Martin Warrigal Kungiung
'Truwu', 'Thidha nany'	Thomas Kungiung
'Mirrwana', 'Pumurriyi'	Thomas Kungiung
Songs with two melodies	
'Mirrwana A' (not in recorded sample)	Thomas Kungiung
'Mirrwana B'	Martin Warrigal Kungiung
'Truwu A'	Thomas Kungiung
'Truwu B'	Les Kundjil
'Truwu A/B'	Thomas Kungiung, Philip Mullumbuk, Les Kundjil
Melodies using the major modal series	
Songs with a unique melody	
'Walakandha No. 2'	Thomas Kungiung/Terence Dumoo
'Walakandha No. 4'	Philip Mullumbuk
Songs that share a melody	
'Nadirri', 'Walakandha No. 1', 'Karra'	Unknown
'Yendili No. 2', 'Yendili No. 3', 'Yendili No. 4'	Maudie Dumoo, Les Kundjil, Philip Mullumbuk
'Karra Yeri-ngina', 'Walakandha No. 3', 'Walakandha No. 5', 'Kinyirr'	Philip Mullumbuk

Table 8.5 Melodies and modal series used in the vocal sections of Walakandha *wangga*.

Songs that share a melody

As can be seen from table 8.5, sharing melodies is quite common in the Walakandha *wangga* repertory. Only nine of the thirty-four songs have a unique melody, while twenty-five songs share their melody with at least one other.[3] A total of nine melodies are shared amongst these twenty-five songs. Although it

---

3   The proportion of shared melodies would be even greater if we were to group together all Stan Mullumbuk's melodies, which each involve a descent, with varying degrees of elaboration, from either C or B flat to the tonic an octave below. However, the melodies of two pairs of songs sound particularly close ('Walakandha No. 6' (track 2) and 'Nginimb-andja' (track 4) on the one hand, and 'Walakandha No. 8a' (track 6) and 'Walakandha No. 8b' (track 7), on the other), so these

is common for a melody to be re-used by its original composer, there are numerous instances in which a melody is shared across different composers. Two songs ('Mirrwana' and 'Truwu') are sung to more than one melody, adding a further three melodies to make a total of twenty-one melodies altogether.

Four songs use the dorian-mode Kubuwemi melody, which was almost certainly composed by Wagon Dumoo (with 'Dhembedi-ndjen', a potential fifth song in the group, placed in brackets), because it is perhaps to be classified as closely related rather than identical to the Kubuwemi melody). Another large group comprises the four songs using the major mode 'Karra Yeri-ngina' melody.

As mentioned, two songs, 'Truwu' and 'Mirrwana', are sung to more than one melody. Although we do not know the circumstances that gave rise to the use of two different melodies (A and B) for 'Mirrwana' by Thomas Kungiung and his 'son' Martin Warrigal Kungiung,[4] we do know that in the case of 'Truwu' the two melodies ('Truwu A' and 'Truwu B') represent different affiliation to country on the part of their singers (Marett has called the former the coastal melody and the latter the inland melody), and that 'Truwu A/B' was a compromise arrived at when singers with different affiliations sang together (Marett, 2005, pp 117–21).

Songs sharing a melodic mode

Two different melodic modal series, dorian and major are used in the repertory. There is a clear tendency for songs by a single composer to use the same melodic mode.

Dorian-mode melodies include all Stan Mullumbuk's early songs, all compositions by Wagon Dumoo (or his brother John) and most compositions by Thomas Kungiung (or his brother Martin Warrigal), together with one song by Les Kundjil.

Melodies using the major modal series include all of Philip Mullumbuk's known compositions, two other melodies by an unknown composer and by Maudie Dumoo (the latter borrowed by Les Kundjil and Philip Mullumbuk), and a joint composition by Thomas Kungiung and Terence Dumoo, 'Walakandha No. 2' (track 23).

Les Kundjil's compositional output, which uses both dorian and major modes, seems to constitute an apparent exception to the convention linking composer with melodic mode, until we realise that all three songs were closely based on models by other composers. The two dorian mode songs (a different melodic setting of Kungiung's song 'Truwu' [track 17] and 'Lhambumen' [track 31]) were based on melodies composed by Thomas Kungiung ('Truwu', track 16, identical also in text)[5] and Wagon Dumoo ('Kubuwemi' and 'Yendili No. 1', which share a melody and textual template with 'Lhambumen'). Kundjil's major mode song 'Yendili No. 3' shares melody, topic and some textual formulae with Maudie Dumoo's 'Yendili No. 2'.

The other apparent exception to the usual convention is 'Walakandha No. 2', the only major mode song attributed to Thomas Kungiung, but he is not the only composer, since the song is supposed to have been dreamed simultaneously by Kungiung and Terence Dumoo.

---

are the ones we have classified as sharing melodies.

4   Martin Warrigal Kungiung's father Ned Narjic Kungiung was a brother of Thomas Kungiung, so Martin would have called Thomas too by the kin-term 'father'. For technical reasons we have not been able to include a recording of Thomas Kungiung's 'Mirrwana A' melody.

5   Kundjil's 'Truwu B' (track 17) simply involves using a different pentatonic subset of the dorian modal series from that used by Kungiung in 'Truwu A' (track 16). 'Truwu A/B' (track 18) is a compromise form arrived at by reconciling the Truwu A and B melodies in performance (for more details see additional analytical notes to track 18 below and Marett, 2005, pp 117–121).

Further notes on selected tracks

Tracks 1,6 'Walakandha 8a'

This is one of only two songs in the entire Walakandha *wangga* repertory that uses rhythmic mode 5c (fast uneven quadruple)—the other is 'Walakandha No. 7' (track 5), which was also composed by Mullumbuk. This rhythmic mode is prominent in the repertories of the Belyuen singers, Jimmy Muluk and Tommy Barrtjap, who, according to Frank Dumoo, frequently performed at Wadeye in the period immediately before the establishment of the Walakandha *wangga* repertory.

Track 2 'Walakandha No. 6'

Non-final instrumental sections have a form that is peculiar to songs of the early period: a passage of fast doubled beating (rhythmic mode 5b) is followed by a passage of fast even beating (rhythmic mode 5a) which is in turn followed by the cueing pattern (♫ ♩ ♫ ♩ ♩ 𝄽) typical of the Walakandha *wangga*. We designate this 'rhythmic mode 5*'. The final instrumental section, as in all Walakandha *wangga* songs with vocal sections in rhythmic mode 1, comprises only fast doubled beating (rhythmic mode 5b) followed by Walakandha *wangga* cueing patterns (see further chapter 2).

Tracks 6–7 'Walakandha No. 8a' and '8b'

The performance in track 6 is in rhythmic mode 5c (fast uneven quadruple) (the same rhythmic mode used for this song in track 1), while the clapstick accompaniment in track 7 is in rhythmic mode 4a (moderate even). The different tempi for each track are easily perceived by the listener: track 6 has fast stick beating at a rate of 127 beats per minute, whilst track 7 has moderate tempo beating at 113 beats per minute. The different clapstick beating patterns are likewise easily perceived (uneven quadruple in the first track, even beating in the second).

Tracks 8–9 'Walakandha No. 9a' and '9b'

In track 8 the first three vocal sections are sung in rhythmic mode 4a (var), in which the stickbeating is suspended for the first part of each vocal section, with moderate even beating (117 beats per minute) normally beginning on the final melismatic syllable *-a* of text phrase 1.[6] Rhythmic mode 4a is then maintained throughout text phrase 2 (which is sung at the lower octave) and the instrumental section. The deployment of suspended beating at the beginning of vocal sections is also found in Jimmy Muluk's *wangga* (see for example Muluk's song 6 'Piyamen.ga'). In Kungiung's performance, the final vocal section is sung entirely in the unaccompanied rhythmic mode 1, and the final instrumental section is in rhythmic mode 5b (fast doubled beating).

In track 9 Kungiung sings the entire text in rhythmic mode 1 (without clapsticks), and using a different melody. As seems to be standard for Stan Mullumbuk's songs in this rhythmic mode, the non-final instrumental sections use rhythmic mode 5* (fast doubled moving to fast even beating, see also tracks 2 and 4), while the final instrumental section is entirely in rhythmic mode 5b.

Track 10 'Yendili No. 6' and track 11 'Yenmilhi No. 2'

These two compositions by Thomas Kungiung use different approaches in the internal (non-final) instrumental sections. In track 10 they are performed in rhythmic mode 5a (fast even beating) with final instrumental sections in 5b (fast doubled beating), both with the cueing patterns typical of the golden age. This is the pattern of beating that typifies the Walakandha *wangga* to this day.

---

[6] In vocal section 1 the text is truncated and finishes on *-wurri*.

In track 11, the beating used for the instrumental sections of 'Yenmilhi No. 2' is the same as used for Mullumbuk's songs in rhythmic mode 1 ('Walakandha No. 6', 'Nginimb-andja' and 'Walakandha No. 9b', tracks 2, 4 and 9), that is, rhythmic mode 5* in the internal instrumental sections, and rhythmic mode 5b (fast doubled) for the final.

Track 26 'Dhembedi-ndjen'

With its AAB text form, which we first encountered in 'Yendili No. 6' (track 10) and 'Yenmilhi No. 2' (track 11), this song is related to other songs from this period such as 'Kubuwemi' (track 12), 'Yendili No. 1' (track 13), 'Tjagawala' (track 27) and 'Lhambumen' (track 31) (see also Marett, 2005, pp 126-27). The melody is related but not identical to other songs from the golden age that use this form, but the rhythmic mode is different: whereas the four above-mentioned songs use rhythmic mode 2 (slow even) for the A text phrase and rhythmic mode 1 (without clapsticks) for the B text phrase, this song uses rhythmic mode 1 throughout the vocal section.

Track 27 'Tjagawala'

In terms of textual form, melody and rhythmic mode, this song is very similar to 'Kubuwemi' (track 12), 'Yendili No. 1' (track 13), 'Tjagawala' (track 27) and 'Lhambumen' (track 31). As in these songs, the final perfective marker is suppressed in text phrases 1 and 2 (see the notes to track 12).

Track 31 'Lhambumen'

Somewhat unusually for songs that take the AAB text form, Kundjil performed the first vocal section entirely without clapsticks, only adopting the slow even beating for vocal sections 2 and 3.

Track 36 'Walakandha No. 5'

Here Philip Mullumbuk uses for non-final instrumental sections the old fashioned form of beating (rhythmic mode 5*) favoured by his brother Stan Mullumbuk.

CHAPTER 9
THE MA-YAWA *WANGGA* REPERTORY

This chapter contains texts and recordings of all known Ma-yawa *wangga*, a repertory of songs given to songmen by the Marri Ammu ancestral ghosts known as Ma-yawa.[1] In the days before the advent of the tripartite ceremonial system at Wadeye (discussed in chapter 1), it seems that this repertory was frequently performed at Wadeye, but once the Marri Ammu adopted the Walakandha *wangga* as the repertory to be used for ceremonies for their kin—and all evidence suggests that this goes back to the 1960s at least—the use of the Ma-yawa *wangga* in the major ceremonies of *burnim-rag* and circumcision declined. We only ever heard the Ma-yawa *wangga* repertory performed for minor ceremonies such as graduations (at Batchelor College) or bravery awards, as when the Administrator of the Northern Territory presented such an award to a boy at Peppimenarti in 1998.

Figure 9.1 The originator of the Ma-yawa *wangga* repertory, Charlie Niwilhi Brinken (left) seated alongside the Walakandha *wangga* performance group at a circumcision ceremony at Wadeye, 1988. Singers are Thomas Kungiung and Les Kundjil, with John Dumoo playing kanbi (didjeridu). Photograph by Mark Crocombe, reproduced with the permission of Wadeye community.

All but one of the Ma-yawa *wangga* songs were composed by the senior Marri Ammu law man and artist Charlie Niwilhi Brinken (c. 1910–1993), but so far as we know, no recording was ever made of him singing. Maurice Tjakurl Ngulkur (Nyilco) (1940–2001), the Marri Ammu songman who inherited the repertory and added one of his own songs to it, passed away in November 2001, and since that time the songs have rarely been performed. To our knowledge no Marri Ammu singer has emerged to take over this repertory, but in recent years some of the songs seem to have been assimilated into the Walakandha *wangga* repertory. Two Marri Tjavin singers, Frank Dumoo and Colin Worumbu Ferguson, performed one of the songs for Marett in 2008; and another Marri Tjavin man, Ngulkur's son-in-law

---

1 Ma-yawa beings are to the Marri Ammu what Walakandha are to the Marri Tjavin.

Charles Kungiung, also performed a number of Ma-yawa songs alongside Walakandha *wangga* songs at a *burnim-rag* ceremony recorded by Barwick and Treloyn at Batchelor in 2009.

The Ma-yawa *wangga* repertory holds a unique place within the corpus. No other repertory focuses as strongly on the Dreamings (*ngirrwat*) and Dreaming sites (*kigatiya*) of the owning group. The repertory deploys a potent metaphor for the mixing of the living and dead in ceremony: this is the *wudi-pumininy*, a freshwater spring that flows into the salt water at high tide below the cliffs at Karri-ngindji in the north of Marri Ammu country. There are also songs about the Mayawa dead dancing on the top of the cliffs at Rtadi-wunbirri, and references to the specific Ma-yawa ancestor, Tulh.

Figure 9.2 A bark painting by Charlie Niwilhi Brinken, showing Ma-yawa dancing in ceremony. Note the women dancers on the left, and the didjeridu player and singer (Brinken himself) near the centre. Courtesy of Sotheby's Australia, reproduced with the permission of Wadeye community.

But in addition to these references to the Ma-yawa dead, there are many songs in the repertory that refer to other totemic ancestors. Here we have explicit and revealing statements about the actions of Dreamings (see for example 'Tjerri' (song 5, track 13)), and the incorporation into song of creation stories (see for example 'Wulumen Tulh' (song 12, tracks 28–29)). Five songs concern Marri Ammu Dreamings and four are about Dreaming sites (though the distinction may be a little forced in that it is impossible to refer to one without the other). The remaining three songs are about the human world rather than Dreamings, though in each case there is an association with ceremony or ghosts: 'Watjendanggi' (Dingo) (song 6) is probably about a boy being led away into seclusion prior to circumcision; 'Na-Pebel' (song 11) is about a particular sand bar that, according to Ngulkur, although not a Dreaming site *per se* is nevertheless a place where Ma-yawa congregate; and 'Walakandha Ngindji' (song 1) concerns Walakandha, the Marri Tjavin ancestral dead, who also manifest as Dreamings.

In another distinctive feature not found to this degree elsewhere in the *wangga* corpus, the singer articulates relationship to his country and its associated Dreamings and Dreaming sites by the use of melody. The Ma-yawa songs about Dreamings use only two melodies, which come to be emblematic of the Marri Ammu and their ancestors.[2]

---

2   In other parts of Australia, for example in Central Australia, melody is thought of as being the 'taste' or 'scent' of the ancestor (C Ellis, 1984, p 171; C Ellis, Ellis, Tur, & McCardell, 1978, p 74; RM Moyle, 1979, p 71). In north-eastern and central Arnhem Land, melodies are associated with specific groups of people and are regarded as a form of clan property (Anderson, 1992; Keen, 1994; Knopoff, 1992; Toner, 2003)

Figure 9.3 Maurice Tjakurl Ngulkur taking a break from performing *wangga* for Allan Marett, Wadeye, 1999. Photograph by Allan Marett, reproduced with the permission of Wadeye community.

Notes on the recording sample

Ngulkur's repertory comprised only twelve songs. These make up the total surviving repertory for the Ma-yawa *wangga* current at Wadeye in the period between 1998 and 2000.[3]

In all, we have access to five performances of the Ma-yawa *wangga*. The first was elicited by Marett at Wadeye in October 1998. The second was made the next day at Peppimenarti, in the context of a ceremony at which the Administrator of the Northern Territory conferred a bravery award on a boy from that community. In 1999 a third recording was made by Marett at Ngulkur's initiative in order to add another song, 'Na-Pebel' (song 11), which he had forgotten to perform in 1998. In 2000 a fourth recording was made by Mark Crocombe, again at Ngulkur's initiative, to add another previously omitted song, 'Wulumen Tulh' (song 12). We have also included a performance of a single Ma-yawa *wangga* song performed in Darwin for Marett, Treloyn and Treloyn's students at Charles Darwin University in 2008 as part of a *wangga* documentation session. Somewhat to everyone's surprise, Frank Dumoo and Colin Worumbu Ferguson sang the Ma-yawa song, 'Thalhi-ngatjpirr' (track 24). Ferguson commented afterwards that he had learnt the song by listening to a CD recording given to him by Marett.[4]

The twelve Ma-yawa *wangga* songs are listed in table 9.1. The first, 'Walakandha Ngindji' (track 1), was composed by Maurice Tjakurl Ngulkur (Nyilco) and the remaining songs (2–12) by Charlie Niwilhi Brinken.

---

[3] One additional song composed by Charlie Brinken, 'Malhimanyirr No. 2' (song 13), was still performed at Kununurra in the 1990s, but not at Wadeye. It is not included in our corpus because we do not have permission to reproduce it. A discussion of this song is included in Marett, 2005, pp 219–22.

[4] Performances of 'Thalhi-ngatjpirr' (song 10) and Ngulkur's composition 'Walakandha Ngindji' (song 1) were included amongst Walakandha *wangga* songs performed at a *burnim-rag* ceremony at Batchelor NT in 2009, led by Charles Kungiung and recorded by Barwick and Treloyn, but for reasons explained elsewhere these recordings are not included in the corpus published here.

Track	Song #	Composer	Title	Performers	Recording
Track 01	1	Ngulkur	Walakandha Ngindji	Ngulkur	Mar98-14-s01
Track 02			Walakandha Ngindji	Ngulkur	Mar98-14-s02
Track 03			Walakandha Ngindji	Ngulkur	Mar98-16-s01
Track 04	2	Brinken	Wulumen Kimi-gimi	Ngulkur	Mar98-14-s03
Track 05			Wulumen Kimi-gimi	Ngulkur	Mar98-14-s04
Track 06	3	Brinken	Rtadi-wunbirri	Ngulkur	Mar98-16-s02
Track 07			Rtadi-wunbirri	Ngulkur	Mar98-16-s03
Track 08			Rtadi-wunbirri	Ngulkur	Mar98-16-s04
Track 09			Rtadi-wunbirri	Ngulkur	Mar98-16-s05
Track 10	4	Brinken	Menggani	Ngulkur	Mar98-14-s05
Track 11			Menggani	Ngulkur	Mar98-14-s06
Track 12	5	Brinken	Tjerri	Ngulkur	Mar98-14-s07
Track 13			Tjerri	Ngulkur	Mar98-14-s08
Track 14	6	Brinken	Watjen-danggi	Ngulkur	Mar98-14-s09
Track 15			Watjen-danggi	Ngulkur	Mar98-14-s10
Track 16	7	Brinken	Malhimanyirr	Ngulkur	Mar98-14-s11
Track 17			Malhimanyirr	Ngulkur	Mar98-14-s12
Track 18	8	Brinken	Ma-vindivindi	Ngulkur	Mar98-14-s13
Track 19			Ma-vindivindi	Ngulkur	Mar98-14-s14
Track 20	9	Brinken	Karri-ngindji	Ngulkur	Mar98-14-s15
Track 21			Karri-ngindji	Ngulkur	Mar98-14-s16
Track 22	10	Brinken	Thali-ngatjpirr	Dumoo & Worumbu	Mar98-14-s17
Track 23			Thali-ngatjpirr	Ngulkur	Mar98-14-s18
Track 24			Thali-ngatjpirr	Ngulkur	Tre08-01-s17
Track 25	11	Brinken	Na-Pebel	Ngulkur	Mar99-01-s01
Track 26			Na-Pebel	Ngulkur	Mar99-01-s02
Track 27			Na-Pebel	Ngulkur	Mar99-01-s03
Track 28	12	Brinken	Wulumen Tulh	Ngulkur	Cro00-01-s07
Track 29			Wulumen Tulh	Ngulkur	Cro00-01-s08

Table 9.1 Songs from the Ma-yawa *wangga* repertory discussed in this chapter.

Because Ngulkur's performances of some songs were quite varied and because the recorded repertory is so small, all available recordings have been included here, including one or two of less than ideal quality. Often we need to hear more than one example of a song in order to get a sense of the limits of its form and content. As was pointed out in chapter 2, when songs are not regularly performed in ceremony singers tend to play around more with their texts, introducing interesting variations as they go.

TRACK 1 (Mar98-14-s01)
Song 1: Walakandha Ngindji

Sung text	Free translation
walakandha ngindji kiny warri kurzi	A certain Walakandha is living here for a whole year
ngata devin bugim rtadi-nanga kuwa	All he has is a solitary house with a white roof
(mana walakandha)	(Brother Walakandha)
(repeated)	

This song, whose title translates as 'a certain Walakandha', was composed by Maurice Ngulkur, and is an adaptation of 'Walakandha No. 2' from the Walakandha *wangga* repertory (chapter 8, track 23). The text, originally composed simultaneously by Thomas Kungiung and Terence Dumoo, is about Terence Dumoo living alone at Kubuwemi for a whole year following a move back to his traditional country from Wadeye. Here Ngulkur adapts the Walakandha *wangga* text by singing it to a melody widely used in the Ma-yawa *wangga* repertory, modifying the melody in various ways so as to accommodate structural features typical of Marri Tjavin song (see further details in the music analysis section of this chapter). For a more detailed discussion of the ways that Ngulkur evokes in song the common, yet separate, interests of the Marri Ammu and the Marri Tjavin by balancing different formal elements in this song, see Marett, 2005, pp 137–50.

SONG STRUCTURE SUMMARY

VOCAL SECTION 1

Melodic section 1

Text phrase 1

Rhythmic mode 5c (fast uneven quadruple)

walakandha	**ngindji**	**kiny**	**warri**	**kurzi**		**mm**
walakandha	one	whole	wet season	3MIN.S.R sit		SW

A certain Walakandha is living here for a whole year

Text phrase 2

Rhythmic mode 5c (fast uneven quadruple)

ngata	**devin**	**bugim**	**rtadi**	**-nanga**	**kuwa**
house	solitary	white	roof	3MIN.M.ADVERS	3MIN.S.R stand

All he has is a solitary house with a white roof

INSTRUMENTAL SECTION 1

Rhythmic mode 5a (fast even)

VOCAL SECTION 2

Melodic section 1

Text phrase 1

Rhythmic mode 1 (without clapsticks)

walakandha	**ngindji**	**kiny**	**warri**	**kurzi**
walakandha	one	whole	wet season	3MIN.S.R sit

A certain Walakandha is living here for a whole year

Text phrase 2

Rhythmic mode 1 (without clapsticks)

ngata	**devin**	**bugim**	**rtadi**	**kuwa**	**mana**	**walakandha**
house	alone	white	roof	3MIN.S.R stand	brother	walakandha

A solitary house with a white roof is here Brother! Walakandha!

INSTRUMENTAL SECTION 2

Rhythmic mode 5b (fast doubled)

TRACK 2 (Mar98-14-s02)

Song 1: Walakandha Ngindji

Sung text	Free translation
ngata devin bugim rtadi-nanga kuwa	All he has is a solitary house with a white roof
mana nidin-ngin-a kubuwemi mana	Brother! My dear country! Kubuwemi! Brother!
walakandha ngindji kiny warri kurzi	A certain Walakandha is living here for a whole year.
ngata devin bugim rtadi kuwa	A solitary house with a white roof is here

In his second rendition of 'Walakandha Ngindji', Ngulkur rearranges the text of vocal section 1 from the previous version, adding new material—a series of calls to Walakandha and to country—in text phrase 2. Marett has argued that textual instability of this sort occurs most frequently in songs, such as these, that are not regularly sung in ceremony (Marett, 2005, p 200). Because of the linguistic closeness of Marri Ammu and Marri Tjavin (see chapter 3), and perhaps also because of his long familiarity with the Walakandha *wangga* repertory as a dancer, Ngulkur has no difficulty in improvising on the text. Indeed, the song demonstrates Ngulkur's especially close relationship to Marri Tjavin people and country.

Figure 9.4 Maurice Tjakurl Ngulkur (right) dances to the Walakandha *wangga* at a circumcision ceremony in Wadeye in 1988. Other dancers include Les Kundjil and Ambrose Piarlum (with spear). The singer is Martin Warrigal Kungiung. Photograph by Mark Crocombe, reproduced with the permission of Wadeye community.

SONG STRUCTURE SUMMARY

VOCAL SECTION 1

Melodic section 1

Text phrase 1

Rhythmic mode 5c (fast uneven quadruple)

ngata	**devin**	**bugim**	**rtadi**	**-nanga**	**kuwa**
house	solitary	white	roof	3MIN.M.ADVERS	3MIN.S.R stand

All he has is a solitary house with a white roof

Text phrase 2

Rhythmic mode 5c (fast uneven quadruple)

mana	**nidin**	**-ngin**	**-a**	**kubuwemi**	**mana**
brother	country	1MIN.O	PERF	place name	brother

Brother! My dear country! Kubuwemi! Brother!

INSTRUMENTAL SECTION 1

Rhythmic mode 5a (fast even)

VOCAL SECTION 2

Melodic section 1

Text phrase 1

Rhythmic mode 1 (without clapsticks)

walakandha	ngindji	kiny	warri	kurzi
walakandha	one	whole	wet season	3MIN.S.R sit

A certain Walakandha is living here for a whole year

Text phrase 2

Rhythmic mode 1 (without clapsticks)

ngata	devin	bugim	rtadi	kuwa
house	alone	white	roof	3MIN.S.R stand

A solitary house with a white roof is here

INSTRUMENTAL SECTION 2

Rhythmic mode 5b (fast doubled)

TRACK 3 (Mar98-16-s01)

Song 1: Walakandha Ngindji

Sung text	Free translation
walakandha ngindji kiny warri kurzi	A certain Walakandha is living here for a whole year
ngata devin bugim rtadi-nanga kuwa	All he has is a solitary house with a white roof
mana nadirri na kubuwemi	Brother! Nadirri at Kubuwemi
walakandha ngindji kiny warri kurzi	A certain Walakandha is living here for a whole year
ngata devin bugim rtadi-nanga kuwa	All he has is a solitary house with a white roof
mana vindivindi kavulh	Brother! Old Man! He is always here

In this version of 'Walakandha Ngindji,' recorded at a bravery award ceremony at Peppimenarti the day after tracks 1 and 2 were recorded at Wadeye, Ngulkur further elaborates the text by adding a third text phrase in vocal section 1. During the didjeridu introduction Ngulkur says that he is going to take up the subject of a certain old man or Walakandha.

SONG STRUCTURE SUMMARY

VOCAL SECTION 1

Melodic section 1

Text phrase 1

Rhythmic mode 5c (fast uneven quadruple)

walakandha	**ngindji**	**kiny**	**warri**	**kurzi**
walakandha	one	whole	wet season	3MIN.S.R sit

A certain Walakandha is living here for a whole year

Text phrase 2

Rhythmic mode 5c (fast uneven quadruple)

ngata	**devin**	**bugim**	**rtadi**	**-nanga**	**kuwa**
house	solitary	white	roof	3MINS.M.ADVERS	3MIN.S.R stand

All he has is a solitary house with a white roof

Text phrase 3

Rhythmic mode 5c (fast uneven quadruple)

mana	**nadirri**	**na**	**kubuwemi**
brother	placename	LOC	place name

Brother! Nadirri at Kubuwemi

INSTRUMENTAL SECTION 1

Rhythmic mode 5c (fast uneven quadruple)

VOCAL SECTION 2

Melodic section 1

Text phrase 1

Rhythmic mode 5c (fast uneven quadruple)

walakandha	**ngindji**	**kiny**	**warri**	**kurzi**
walakandha	one	whole	wet season	3MIN.S.R sit

A certain Walakandha is living here for a whole year

Text phrase 2

Rhythmic mode 5c (fast uneven quadruple)

ngata	**devin**	**bugim**	**rtadi**	**-nanga**	**kuwa**
house	solitary	white	roof	3MIN.M.ADVERS	3MIN.S.R stand

All he has is a solitary house with a white roof

Text phrase 3

Rhythmic mode 5c (fast uneven quadruple)

mana	**vindivindi**	**kavulh**
brother	oldman	3MIN.S.R lie

Brother! Old Man! He is always here

INSTRUMENTAL SECTION 2

Rhythmic mode 5c (fast uneven quadruple)

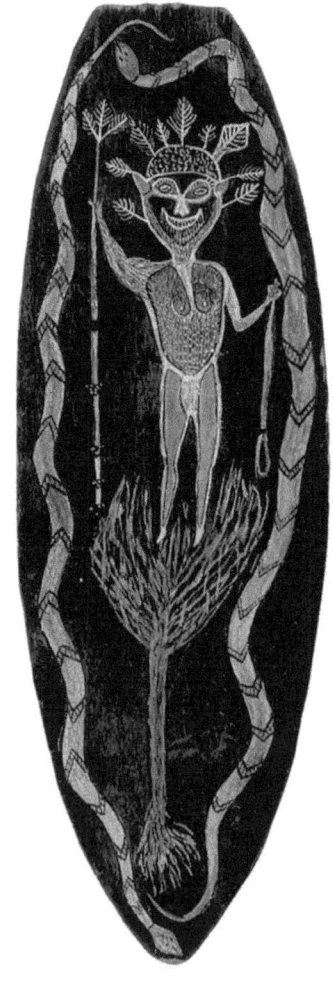

Figure 9.5 A bark painting by Charlie Niwilhi Brinken, depicting a Ma-yawa ancestor. Courtesy of Sotheby's Australia, reproduced with the permission of Wadeye community.

TRACKS 4 and 5 (Mar98-14-s03, s04)

Song 2: Wulumen Kimi-gimi

Sung text	Free translation
wulumen kimi-gimi kavulh-a-gu (repeated)	This is what the Old Man [Ma-yawa] has always done

This song is an assertion that Marri Ammu ceremonial performance rests upon ancestral precedent. The verb *kimi-gimi* has a broad semantic field, which in this case embraces all forms of ceremonial activity—singing, dancing, playing the didjeridu. This is what the Ma-yawa ancestors, referred to here as *wulumen* (Aboriginal English for Old Man), laid down as the foundation of law at the beginning of time.

Various stylistic elements in this song—including the use of a melody that is shared with seven other Ma-yawa *wangga* songs, the uneven quadruple clapstick pattern, and isorhythm (the repetition of the same text with identical rhythm)—are typical of the Ma-yawa *wangga*.

SONG STRUCTURE SUMMARY

VOCAL SECTIONS 1–3

Melodic section 1

Text phrases 1–2

Rhythmic mode 5c (fast uneven quadruple)

wulumen	kimi-gimi	kavulh	-a	-gu
old man	3MIN.A.R.doREDUP	3MIN.S.R.lie	PERF	TOP

This is what the Old Man [Ma-yawa] has always done [i.e., danced, sung, played didjeridu]

INSTRUMENTAL SECTIONS 1–3

Rhythmic mode 5c (fast uneven quadruple)

TRACK 6 (Mar98-16-s02)

Song 3: Rtadi-wunbirri

Sung text	Free translation
wulumen vindivindi kavulh-a-gu	This is what the Old Man [Ma-yawa] has always done
wulumen vindivindi kavulh-a-gu	This is what the Old Man [Ma-yawa] has always done
rtadi-wunbirri-wunbirri kisji	At Rtadi-wunbirri, like this
kisji-gisji kavulh-a-gu	He has always done it like this
wulumen vindivindi kavulh-a-gu (repeated)	This is what the Old Man [Ma-yawa] has always done

Like 'Wulumen Kimi-gimi,' this song asserts that ceremonial performance rests on the precedent laid down by the Ma-yawa ancestors, here referred to by both the Aboriginal English term *wulumen* (old man) and the Marri Ammu word *vindivindi* (old man). The verb *kimi-gimi* (do) is understood but not sung. The place where the ancestors performed, and continue to perform, is at the dance ground at Rtadi-wunbirri, a flat area on the top of the cliffs at Karri-ngindji, near Tjindi in Marri Ammu country.

This song uses a melody that it shares with only one other Ma-yawa *wangga* song, 'Wulumen Tulh' (tracks 28 and 29). Ngulkur performed this song at the Peppimenarti bravery award ceremony.

SONG STRUCTURE SUMMARY

VOCAL SECTION 1

Melodic section 1

Text phrases 1–2

Rhythmic mode 1 (without clapsticks)

wulumen	**vindivindi**	**kavulh**	**-a**	**-gu**
old man	old man	3MIN.S.R.lie	PERF	TOP

This is what the Old Man [Ma-yawa] has always done [i.e., danced, sung, played didjeridu]

Text phrase 3

Rhythmic mode 1 (without clapsticks)

rtadi-wunbirri-wunbirri	**kisji**
place name REDUP	like this

At Rtadi-wunbirri, like this

Text phrase 4

Rhythmic mode 1 (without clapsticks)

kisji-gisji	**kavulh**	**-a**	**-gu**
like this REDUP	3MIN.S.R.lie	PERF	TOP

He has always done it like this

INSTRUMENTAL SECTION 1

Rhythmic mode 5a (fast even)

VOCAL SECTION 2

Melodic section 1

Text phrases 1–3

Rhythmic mode 1 (without clapsticks)

wulumen	**vindivindi**	**kavulh**	**-a**	**-gu**
old man	old man	3MIN.S.R.lie	PERF	TOP

This is what the Old Man [Ma-yawa] has always done [i.e., danced, sung, played didjeridu]

INSTRUMENTAL SECTION 2

Rhythmic mode 5b (fast doubled)

TRACK 7 (Mar98-16-s03)
Song 3: Rtadi-wunbirri

Sung text	Free translation
wulumen vindivindi kavulh-a-gu	This is what the Old Man [Ma-yawa] has always done
wulumen vindivindi kavulh-a-gu	This is what the Old Man [Ma-yawa] has always done
nidin-gu rtadi-wunbirri-wunbirri kisji	Country! Rtadi-wunbirri! Like this!
kisji-gisji kavulh-a-gu	He has always done it like this
wulumen vindivindi kavulh-a-gu	This is what the Old Man [Ma-yawa] has always done
wulumen vindivindi kavulh-a-gu	This is what the Old Man [Ma-yawa] has always done
nidin-gu rtadi-wunbirri-wunbirri kisji	Country! Rtadi-wunbirri! Like this!

SONG STRUCTURE SUMMARY

VOCAL SECTION 1

Melodic section 1

Text phrases 1–2

Rhythmic mode 1 (without clapsticks)

wulumen	**vindivindi**	**kavulh**	**-a**	**-gu**
old man	old man	3MIN.S.R.lie	PERF	TOP

This is what the Old Man [Ma-yawa] has always done [i.e., danced, sung, played didjeridu]

Text phrase 3

Rhythmic mode 1 (without clapsticks)

nidin	**-gu**	**rtadi-wunbirri-wunbirri**	**kisji**
country	TOP	place name REDUP	like this

Country! Rtadi-wunbirri! Like this!

Text phrase 4

Rhythmic mode 1 (without clapsticks)

kisji-gisji	**kavulh**	**-a**	**-gu**
like this	3MIN.S.R.lie	PERF	TOP

He has always done it like this

INSTRUMENTAL SECTION 1

Rhythmic mode 5a (fast even)

VOCAL SECTION 2

Melodic section 1

Text phrases 1–2

Rhythmic mode 1 (without clapsticks)

wulumen	**vindivindi**	**kavulh**	**-a**	**-gu**
old man	old man	3MIN.S.R.lie	PERF	TOP

This is what the Old Man [Ma-yawa] has always done [i.e., danced, sung, played didjeridu]

Text phrase 3

Rhythmic mode 1 (without clapsticks)

nidin	**-gu**	**rtadi-wunbirri-wunbirri**	**kisji**
country	TOP	place name REDUP	like this

Country! Rtadi-wunbirri! Like this!

INSTRUMENTAL SECTION 2

Rhythmic mode 5b (fast doubled)

TRACK 8 (Mar98-16-04)

Song 3: Rtadi-wunbirri

Sung text	Free translation
wulumen vindivindi kavulh-a-gu	This is what the Old Man [Ma-yawa] has always done
wulumen vindivindi kavulh-a-gu	This is what the Old Man [Ma-yawa] has always done
rtadi-wunbirri-wunbirri nidin-gu	At that country which is Rtadi-wunbirri
kisji-gisji kavulh-a-gu	He has always done it like this
(repeated)	

SONG STRUCTURE SUMMARY

VOCAL SECTION 1

Melodic section 1

Text phrases 1–2

Rhythmic mode 1 (without clapsticks)

wulumen	**vindivindi**	**kavulh**	**-a**	**-gu**
old man	old man	3MIN.S.R.lie	PERF	TOP

This is what the Old Man [Ma-yawa] has always done [i.e., danced, sung, played didjeridu]

Text phrase 3

Rhythmic mode 1 (without clapsticks)

rtadi-wunbirri-wunbirri	**nidin**	**-gu**
place name REDUP	country	TOP

At that country which is Rtadi-wunbirri

Text phrase 4

Rhythmic mode 1 (without clapsticks)

kisji-gisji	**kavulh**	**-a**	**-gu**
like this REDUP	3MIN.S.R.lie	PERF	TOP

He has always done it like this

INSTRUMENTAL SECTION 1

Rhythmic mode 5a (fast even)

VOCAL SECTION 2

Melodic section 1

Text phrases 1–2

Rhythmic mode 1 (without clapsticks)

wulumen	**vindivindi**	**kavulh**	**-a**	**-gu**
old man	old man	3MIN.S.R.lie	PERF	TOP

This is what the Old Man [Ma-yawa] has always done [i.e., danced, sung, played didjeridu]

Text phrase 3

Rhythmic mode 1 (without clapsticks)

rtadi-wunbirri-wunbirri	**nidin**	**-gu**
place name REDUP	country	TOP

At that country which is Rtadi-wunbirri

Text phrase 4

Rhythmic mode 1 (without clapsticks)

kisji-gisji	**kavulh**	**-a**	**-gu**
like this REDUP	3MIN.S.R.lie	PERF	TOP

He has always done it like this

INSTRUMENTAL SECTION 2

Rhythmic mode 5b (fast doubled)

TRACK 9 (Mar98-16-05)

Song 3: Rtadi-wunbirri

Sung text	Free translation
wulumen vindivindi kavulh-a-gu	This is what the Old Man [Ma-yawa] has always done
wulumen vindivindi kavulh-a-gu	This is what the Old Man [Ma-yawa] has always done
nidin-gu rtadi-wunbirri-wunbirri kisji	At that country which is Rtadi-wunbirri, like this
wulumen vindivindi kavulh-a-gu	This is what the Old Man [Ma-yawa] has always done
nidin-gu rtadi-wunbirri-wunbirri kisji	At that country which is Rtadi-wunbirri, like this

In this version, Ngulkur employs an old-fashioned style of clapstick beating (rhythmic mode 5*) for instrumental section 1. This pattern, in which a passage of fast doubled beating is followed by a passage of fast even beating, is typical of the early Walakandha *wangga* (see chapter 3, chapter 8). Note that the didjeridu drops out briefly in the final instrumental section.

SONG STRUCTURE SUMMARY

VOCAL SECTION 1

Melodic section 1

Text phrases 1–2

Rhythmic mode 1 (without clapsticks)

wulumen	**vindivindi**	**kavulh**	**-a**	**-gu**
old man	old man	3MIN.S.R.lie	PERF	TOP

This is what the Old Man [Ma-yawa] has always done [i.e., danced, sung, played didjeridu]

Text phrase 3

Rhythmic mode 1 (without clapsticks)

nidin	**-gu**	**rtadi-wunbirri-wunbirri**	**kisji**
country	TOP	Place name REDUP	like this

At that country which is Rtadi-wunbirri, like this

INSTRUMENTAL SECTION 1

Rhythmic mode 5*

VOCAL SECTION 2

Melodic section 1

Text phrase 1

Rhythmic mode 1 (without clapsticks)

wulumen	**vindivindi**	**kavulh**	**-a**	**-gu**
old man	old man	3MIN.S.R.lie	PERF	TOP

This is what the Old Man [Ma-yawa] has always done [i.e., danced, sung, played didjeridu]

Text phrase 2

Rhythmic mode 1 (without clapsticks)

nidin	**-gu**	**rtadi-wunbirri-wunbirri**	**kisji**
country	TOP	Place namerREDUP	like this

At that country which is Rtadi-wunbirri, like this

INSTRUMENTAL SECTION 2

Rhythmic mode 5b (fast doubled)

TRACKS 10 and 11 (Mar98-14-s05 and s06)

Song 4: Menggani

Sung text	Free translation
menggani kimi-gimi kavulh-a-gu (repeated)	This is what Menggani has always done

The Dreaming site (*kigatiya*) for the butterfly, Menggani, lies in the jungle inland from Tjindi. On both tracks 10 and 11, you can hear the sound of the late afternoon wind blowing the leaves of the surrounding trees. As is often the case when there is no dancing, the instrumental sections are very short.

SONG STRUCTURE SUMMARY

VOCAL SECTIONS 1–3

Melodic section 1

Text phrases 1–2

Rhythmic mode 5c (fast uneven quadruple)

menggani	**kimi-gimi**	**kavulh**	**-a**	**-gu**
butterfly site	3MIN.A.R.sayREDUP	3MIN.S.R.lie	PERF	TOP

This is what Menggani has always done [i.e., danced, produced butterflies]

INSTRUMENTAL SECTIONS 1–3

Rhythmic mode 5c (fast uneven quadruple)

TRACK 12 (Mar98-14-s07)

Song 5: Tjerri

Sung text	Free translation
karra mana tjerri	Brother Sea Breeze!
wumburri kin-pa-diyerr	The wave is breaking at the creek
kayirr-a kagan-dja kisji	All along! In this place here! Like this!
karra mana tjerri	Brother Sea Breeze!
kin-pa diyerr kavulh	It is always breaking at the creek
purangang kisji	The sea! Like this!
karra mana tjerri	Brother Sea Breeze!
kagan-(dja) mana tjerri kin-pa diyerr	In this place here, brother! It is breaking at the creek
karra mana tjerri	Brother Sea Breeze!
kin-pa diyerr kavulh	It is always breaking at the creek
purangang kagan-dja kisji	The sea! In this place here! Like this!

'Tjerri' refers both to the Dreaming (*ngirrwat*) for Sea Breeze, which is addressed as 'elder brother' (*mana*), and to its Dreaming site (*kigatiya*), a beach not far from Pumurriyi in the south of Marri Ammu country. During the didjeridu introduction, Ngulkur announces, 'Now I'm going to take up "Sea Breeze." It's our Dreaming.' In this rendition of the song, Ngulkur focuses on the waves that break at the creek mouth as a result of the action of this Dreaming. Notice how the song text emphasises both the immediacy of the Dreaming in the present moment—'All along! In this place here! Just like this'—as well as the aspect of ancestral power deposited in that place at the beginning of time—'It is always breaking right here at the creek' (literally 'it lies here [from the beginning] breaking right along the creek').

Here the dominant Ma-yawa *wangga* melody is rendered in an unmeasured and elaborated, often melismatic, form, which is fitted to the highly variable text in the moment of performance.

SONG STRUCTURE SUMMARY

VOCAL SECTION 1

Melodic section 1

Text phrase 1

Rhythmic mode 1 (without clapsticks)

karra	**mana**	**tjerri**
SW	brother	Sea Breeze

Brother Sea Breeze!

Text phrase 2

Rhythmic mode 1 (without clapsticks)

wumburri	**kin**	**-pa**	**-diyerr**
wave	3MIN.S.R move	breaks	creek

The wave is breaking at the creek

Text phrase 3

Rhythmic mode 1 (without clapsticks)

kayirr	**-a**	**kagan**	**-dja**	**kisji**
3MIN.S.R travel	PERF	ANAPH.DEIC	really	like this

All along! In this place here! Like this!

Melodic section 2

Text phrase 4

Rhythmic mode 1 (without clapsticks)

karra	**mana**	**tjerri**
SW	brother	Sea Breeze

Brother Sea Breeze!

Text phrase 5

Rhythmic mode 1 (without clapsticks)

kin	**-pa**	**diyerr**	**kavulh**
3MIN.S.R.go	breaks	creek	3MIN.S.R.lie

It is always breaking at the creek

Text phrase 6

Rhythmic mode 1 (without clapsticks)

purangang	**kisji**
sea	like this

The sea! Like this!

INSTRUMENTAL SECTION 1

Rhythmic mode 4a (moderate even)

VOCAL SECTION 2

Melodic section 1

Text phrase 1

Rhythmic mode 1 (without clapsticks)

karra	**mana**	**tjerri**
SW	brother	Sea Breeze

Brother Sea Breeze!

Text phrase 2

Rhythmic mode 1 (without clapsticks)

kagan	**-(dja)**	**mana**	**tjerri**	**kin**	**-pa**	**diyerr**
ANAPH.DEIC	really	brother	Sea Breeze	3MIN.S.R.go	breaks	creek

In this place here, brother! It is breaking at the creek

Text phrase 3

Rhythmic mode 1 (without clapsticks)

karra	**mana**	**tjerri**
SW	brother	Sea Breeze

Brother Sea Breeze!

Text phrase 4

Rhythmic mode 1 (without clapsticks)

kin	**-pa**	**diyerr**	**kavulh**
3MIN.S.R.go	breaks	creek	3MIN.S.R.lie

It is always breaking at the creek

Text phrase 5

Rhythmic mode 1 (without clapsticks)

purangang	kagan	-dja	kisji
sea	ANAPH.DEIC	really	like this

The sea! In this place here! Like this!

INSTRUMENTAL SECTION 2

Rhythmic mode 5b (fast doubled)

TRACK 13 (Mar98-14-s08)
Song 5: Tjerri

Sung text	Free translation
karra mana tjerri	Brother Sea Breeze!
(kagan-dja) kinyi-ni kavulh	(Right here and now), he is always manifesting himself
karra mana tjerri	Brother Sea Breeze!
kinyi-ni kavulh (kagan-dja)	He is always manifesting himself (right here and now)
purangang kin-pa-diyerr kavulh kagan-dja kisji	The sea is always breaking at the creek, right here, like this

In the second rendition, Ngulkur shifts the emphasis squarely onto the immanent, self-creating aspect of the Dreaming (*ngirrwat*). TGH Strehlow maintained that the core meaning of *altjira*, the Arrernte term cognate with *ngirrwat*, is 'that which derives from … the eternal, uncreated, springing from itself,' or 'that which has sprung out of its own eternity' (Strehlow, 1971, p 614). The way that the Murriny Patha at Wadeye spoke to Stanner about the Rainbow Serpent Dreaming (Kunmanggurr) resonates with this. Kunmanggurr was said to be a *kardu bangambitj*, a 'self-finding' person (that is, 'self-creating and self-subsistent') (Stanner, 1989 [1963], p 249).

In text phrase 2, vocal section 1 of 'Tjerri' we have an expression that points directly to this self-creating aspect of the Dreaming while at the same time referencing the intersection of the present moment and the eternal, 'Right here and now, he is always manifesting himself.' The idea of self-manifestation is expressed by the verb *kinyi-ni*, which combines the third-person singular form of the intransitive verb 'he moves' or 'he is active' (*kinyi*) with the third-person masculine reflexive suffix (*ni*) to mean 'he makes himself active.' The notion of the Dreaming springing out of the eternal is carried by the auxiliary verb *kavulh*, 'he lies' or 'he has done it forever' and the fact that this happens in the present moment by *kagan-dja*, 'right here and now' (Marett, 2005, pp 27–28). Indeed, the intersection of the eternal and the present is here underscored even more strongly than in the previous item.

This is the item transcribed and discussed as an example of the formal conventions of *wangga* in chapter 2.

SONG STRUCTURE SUMMARY

VOCAL SECTION 1

Melodic section 1

Text phrase 1

Rhythmic mode 1 (without clapsticks)

karra	**mana**	**tjerri**
SW	brother	Sea Breeze

Brother Sea Breeze!

Text phrase 2

Rhythmic mode 1 (without clapsticks)

kagan	**-dja**	**kinyi**	**-ni**	**kavulh**
ANAPH.DEIC	really	3MIN.A.R.make	3MIN.M.REFL	3MIN.S.R.lie

Right here and now, he is always manifesting himself

Text phrase 3

Rhythmic mode 1 (without clapsticks)

karra	**mana**	**tjerri**
SW	brother	Sea Breeze

Brother Sea Breeze!

Text phrase 4

Rhythmic mode 1 (without clapsticks)

kinyi	**-ni**	**kavulh**	**kagan-**	**-dja**
3MIN.A.R.make	3MIN.M.REFL	3MIN.S.R.lie	ANAPH.DEIC	really

He is always manifesting himself right here and now

Text phrase 5

Rhythmic mode 1 (without clapsticks)

purangang	**kin**	**-pa**	**-diyerr**	**kavulh**	**kagan-**	**-dja**	**kisji**
sea	3MIN.S.R.go	breaks	creek	3MIN.S.R.lie	ANAPH.DEIC	really	like this

The sea is always breaking at the creek, right here, like this

INSTRUMENTAL SECTION 1

Rhythmic mode 4a (moderate even)

VOCAL SECTION 2

Melodic section 1

Text phrase 1

Rhythmic mode 1 (without clapsticks)

karra	**mana**	**tjerri**
SW	brother	Sea Breeze

Brother Sea Breeze!

Text phrase 2

Rhythmic mode 1 (without clapsticks)

kinyi	**-ni**	**kavulh**
3MIN.A.R.make	3MIN.M.REFL	3MIN.S.R.lie

He is always manifesting himself

Text phrase 3

Rhythmic mode 1 (without clapsticks)

karra	**mana**	**tjerri**
SW	brother	Sea Breeze

Brother Sea Breeze!

Text phrase 4

Rhythmic mode 1 (without clapsticks)

kinyi	**-ni**	**kavulh**
3MIN.A.R.make	3MIN.M.REFL	3MIN.S.R.lie

He is always manifesting himself

Text phrase 5

Rhythmic mode 1 (without clapsticks)

purangang	**kin**	**-pa**	**diyerr**	**kavulh**	**kagan-**	**-dja**	**kisji**
sea	3MIN.S.R.go	breaks	creek	3MIN.S.R.lie	ANAPH.DEIC	really	like this

The sea is always breaking at the creek, right here, like this

INSTRUMENTAL SECTION 2

Rhythmic mode 5b (fast doubled)

TRACK 14 (Mar98-14-s09)

Song 6: Watjen-danggi

Sung text	Free translation
karra mana kayirr-a kani-tjippi-ya kayirr-a	Brother! He was making footprints as he went
wandhi-wandhi kimi kayirr-a	He looked behind as he went
kani-tjippi-ya watjen-danggi	Dingo was making his prints
karra mana wandhi-wandhi kimi kayirr-a	Brother! He deliberately looked back
watjen-danggi	Dingo!

Although *wangga* songs are sung in circumcision ceremonies as well as for mortuary rites, it is rare for a song to address the theme of circumcision directly. Since circumcision is seen as being analogous to death (the boy dies to childhood and is reborn as a man), the death-related themes are as appropriate in this context as in mortuary rites. This song is an exception in that it seems to refer directly to the initiation process. When a boy is removed from the society of women and taken on a ritual journey and seclusion prior to the circumcision rites, he is referred to as a wild dog (*watjen danggi* in Marri Ammu, *ku were* in Murriny Patha). This song, then, is probably about a boy being taken into seclusion in Marri Ammu country. As he walks up the beach towards from the cliffs at Karri-ngindji to Yilhyilhyen beach (see track 15), the wild dog looks back, just as a boy will look back to the relatives that he has left behind. Ngulkur told Marett that this song is one of the few in the corpus that does not refer to a Dreaming or a Dreaming place, but this statement seems to be contradicted by the announcement that he makes during the didjeridu introduction: 'I'm going to take up "Dingo running across the sand." It's really my Dreaming.' This was perhaps a slip made in the heat of the performance.

The construction of this song, while not unique in the *wangga* genre, is somewhat unusual. It comprises a series of statements about the wild dog, strung together in sequence. The melody and the rhythm are also unusual. No other Ma-yawa *wangga* uses this melody, which is quite distinct from the two associated with Dreamings (perhaps indicating that the song is not about a Dreaming). The use of beating in a moderate tempo is also rare at Wadeye. While it occurs in a number of the early songs of the Walakandha *wangga* repertory—songs that are no longer sung—it has not been used for any other Wadeye *wangga* for several decades (see chapter 8 and Marett, 2007). In Ngulkur's repertory this mode also occurs in the internal instrumental sections of 'Tjerri' (tracks 12–13) and 'Karri ngindji' (tracks 20–21).

SONG STRUCTURE SUMMARY

VOCAL SECTION 1

Melodic section 1

Text phrase 1

Rhythmic mode 4a (moderate even)

karra	**mana**	**kayirr**	**-a**	**kani**	**-tjippi**	**-ya**	**kayirr**	**-a**
SW	brother	3MIN.S.R travel	PERF	3MIN.S.R.walk	print	PERF	3MIN.S.R travel	PERF

Brother! He was making footprints as he went

Melodic section 2

Text phrase 2

Rhythmic mode 4a (moderate even)

wandhi-wandhi	**kimi**	**kayirr**	**-a**
behind REDUP	3MIN.A.R.do	3MIN.S.R travel	PERF

He looked behind as he went

Text phrase 3

Rhythmic mode 4a (moderate even)

kani	**-tjippi**	**-ya**	**watjen-danggi**
3MIN.S.R.walk	print	PERF	dingo

Dingo was making his prints

INSTRUMENTAL SECTION 1

Rhythmic mode 4a (moderate even)

VOCAL SECTION 2

Melodic section 1

Text phrase 1

Rhythmic mode 4a (moderate even)

karra	**mana**	**wandhi-wandhi**	**kimi**	**kayirr**	**-a**
SW	brother	behind REDUP	3MIN.A.R.do	3MIN.S.R travel	PERF

Brother! He deliberately looked back

Text phrase 2

Rhythmic mode 4a (moderate even)

watjen-danggi
dingo

Dingo!

INSTRUMENTAL SECTION 2

Rhythmic mode 4a (moderate even)

TRACK 15 (Mar98-14-s10)

Song 6: Watjen-danggi

Sung text	Free translation
mana watjen kani-tjippi-ya kayirr-a	Brother dog! He was making his prints all along
wandhi-wandhi kimi kayirr-a watjen-danggi	He looked right back all along, dingo
mana kani-tjippi-ya kayirr-a watjen-danggi	Brother! He was making his prints, dingo
yilhyilhyen-gu	Towards Yilhyilhyen
karra mana kani-tjippi-ya kani-tjippi-ya wandhi	Brother! he was making his prints behind
yilhyilhyen-gu	Towards Yilhyilhyen

SONG STRUCTURE SUMMARY

VOCAL SECTION 1

Melodic section 1

Text phrase 1

Rhythmic mode 4a (moderate even)

mana	**watjen**	**kani**	**-tjippi**	**-ya**	**kayirr**	**-a**
brother	dog	3MIN.S.R.walk	print	PERF	3MIN.S.R travel	PERF

Brother dog! He was making his prints all along

Text phrase 2

Rhythmic mode 4a (moderate even)

wandhi-wandhi	**kimi**	**kayirr**	**-a**	**watjen-danggi**
behind REDUP	3MIN.A.R.do	3MIN.S.R travel	PERF	dingo

He looked right back all along, dingo

Melodic section 2

Text phrase 3

Rhythmic mode 4a (moderate even)

mana	**kani**	**-tjippi**	**-ya**	**kayirr**	**-a**	**watjen-danggi**
brother	3MIN.S.R.walk	print	PERF	3MIN.S.R travel	PERF	dingo

Brother! He was making his prints, dingo

Text phrase 4

Rhythmic mode 4a (moderate even)

yilhyilhyen	**-gu**
place name	TOP

Towards Yilhyilhyen

INSTRUMENTAL SECTION 1

Rhythmic mode 4a (moderate even)

VOCAL SECTION 2

Melodic section 1

Text phrase 1

Rhythmic mode 4a (moderate even)

karra	mana	kani	-tjippi	-ya	kani	-tjippi	-ya	wandhi
SW	brother	3MIN.S.R.walk	print	PERF	3MIN.S.R.walk	print	PERF	behind

Brother! he was making his prints behind

Text phrase 2

Rhythmic mode 4a (moderate even)

yilhyilhyen	-gu
place	TOP

Towards Yilhyilhyen

INSTRUMENTAL SECTION 2

Rhythmic mode 4a (moderate even)

TRACK 16 (Mar98-14-s11)

Song 7: Malhimanyirr

Sung text	Free translation
malhimanyirr karri-mi-ga-kap kavulh	Junglefowl is always making her nest and calling out
mungirini kapil karri-gap kavulh	In the dense jungle, she is always piling up and calling out
(repeated)	

Tracks 16 and 17 are about *malhimanyirr*, the junglefowl (*Megapodius freycinet*), a large ground-dwelling bird that creates its nest by piling soil into a mound, continually scratching and turning the material. It is common in coastal areas of the Northern Territory. Its Dreaming site is at Anggaleni in the south of Marri Ammu country. This bird was Maurice Ngulkur's personal totem, a fact that he repeatedly makes explicit in the rendition on track 17. *Kanyi-ngin* is short for *kanyirra-ngin* (literally, 'my Dreaming,' or 'my totem').

SONG STRUCTURE SUMMARY

VOCAL SECTIONS 1–3

Melodic section 1

Text phrase 1

Rhythmic mode 5c (fast uneven quadruple)

malhimanyirr	**karri**	**-mi**	**-ga-kap**	**kavulh**
junglefowl	3MIN.A.R hands	nest	calls out REDUP	3MIN.S.R.lie

Junglefowl is always making her nest and calling out

Melodic section 2

Text phrase 2

Rhythmic mode 5c (fast uneven quadruple)

mungirini	**kapil**	**karri**	**-gap**	**kavulh**
jungle	big	3MIN.A.R use hands	call out	3MIN.S.R lie

In the dense jungle, she is always piling up [earth for her nest] and calling out

INSTRUMENTAL SECTIONS 1–2

Rhythmic mode 5c (fast uneven quadruple)

INSTRUMENTAL SECTION 3

Rhythmic mode 5c (fast uneven quadruple)

TRACK 17 (Mar98-14-s12)

Song 7: Malhimanyirr

Sung text	Free translation
malhimanyirr karri-mi-ga-kap kavulh	Junglefowl is always making her nest and calling out
mungirini kapil kanyi-nigin	In the dense jungle, my totem
malhimanyirr karri-mi-ga-kap kanyi-nigin kavulh	My Dreaming, junglefowl is making her nest, my totem!
mungirini kapil kanyi-nigin	In the dense jungle, my totem
malhimanyirr karri-mi-ga-kap kavulh	Junglefowl is always making her nest and calling out
mungirini kapil malhimanyirr kanyi-nigin	In the dense jungle, junglefowl, my totem

SONG STRUCTURE SUMMARY

VOCAL SECTION 1

Melodic section 1

Text phrase 1

Rhythmic mode 5c (fast uneven quadruple)

malhimanyirr	karri	-mi	-ga-kap	kavulh
junglefowl	3MIN.A.R use hands	nest	calls out REDUP	3MIN.S.R.lie

Junglefowl is always making her nest and calling out

Melodic section 2

Text phrase 2

Rhythmic mode 5c (fast uneven quadruple)

mungirini	kapil	kanyi	-ngin
jungle	big	totem	1MIN..O

In the dense jungle, my totem

Melodic section 3

Text phrase 3

Rhythmic mode 5c (fast uneven quadruple)

malhimanyirr	karri	-mi	-ga-kap	kanyi	-ngin	kavulh
junglefowl	3MIN.A.R hands	nest	calls out REDUP	totem	1MIN.O	3MIN.S.R.lie

My Dreaming, junglefowl is making her nest, my totem!

Melodic section 4

Text phrase 4

Rhythmic mode 5c (fast uneven quadruple)

mungirini	kapil	kanyi	-ngin
jungle	big	totem	1MIN.O

In the dense jungle, my totem

INSTRUMENTAL SECTION 1

Rhythmic mode 5c (fast uneven quadruple)

VOCAL SECTION 2

Melodic section 1

Text phrase 1

Rhythmic mode 5c (fast uneven quadruple)

malhimanyirr	**karri**	**-mi**	**-ga-kap**	**kavulh**
junglefowl	3MIN.A.R hands	nest	calls out REDUP	3MIN.S.R.lie

Junglefowl is always making her nest and calling out

Melodic section 2

Text phrase 2

Rhythmic mode 5c (fast uneven quadruple)

mungirini	**kapil**	**malhimanyirr**	**kanyi**	**-ngin**
jungle	big	junglefowl	totem	1MIN.O

In the dense jungle, junglefowl, my totem

INSTRUMENTAL SECTION 2

Rhythmic mode 5c (fast uneven quadruple)

TRACK 18 (Mar98-14-s13)

Song 8: Ma-vindivindi

Sung text	Free translation
karra mana kani-put-puwa kuwa	Brother is standing up in number four leg
yenmura kani-put-puwa kisji kavulh	On the headland he is always in number four leg like this
karra mana kinyi-ni-venggi-tit kani	Brother keeps making number four leg
karra mungarri kapil kinyi-ni-venggi-tit kavulh	Deep sleep! He makes himself lie in number four leg
karra mana kinyi-ni-venggi-tit kavulh	Brother is making himself lie in number four leg
karra mana kinyi-ni-venggi-tit kavulh	Brother is making himself lie in number four leg

The items on track 18 and 19 describe a Ma-yawa, here referred to simply as 'Old Man,' at his Dreaming site above the cliffs at Karri-ngindji in Marri Ammu country (see also song 9, tracks 20–21). He is depicted both standing up and lying down asleep in the posture known as 'number four leg,' that is with one leg bent with the foot crossing or against the knee of the straight leg. The Marri Tjavin and the Marri Ammu frequently depict their song-giving ancestors (Walakandha or Ma-yawa) in this position; and there is an association of this posture with the giving and receiving of songs.[5]

The melody is the one used for the majority of songs about Marri Ammu Dreamings, and the fast uneven quadruple rhythmic mode is the most commonly used in the Ma-yawa *wangga* corpus.

---

5 The 'number four leg' pose is also mentioned in the repertoires of Muluk (chapter 5), Mandji (chapter 6), Lambudju (chapter 7), and the Walakandha *wangga* (chapter 8).

SONG STRUCTURE SUMMARY

VOCAL SECTION 1

Melodic section 1

Text phrase 1
Rhythmic mode 5c (fast uneven quadruple)

karra	**mana**	**kani**	**-put**	**-puwa**	**kuwa**
SW	brother	3MIN.S.R.walk	walk	leg	3MIN.S.R.stand

Brother is standing up in number four leg

Text phrase 2
Rhythmic mode 5c (fast uneven quadruple)

yenmura	**kani**	**-put**	**-puwa**	**kisji**	**kavulh**
point	3MIN.S.R go	walk	leg	like this	3MIN.S.R.lie

On the headland [at Karri-ngindji], he is always [standing] in number four leg like this

Melodic section 2

Text phrase 3
Rhythmic mode 5c (fast uneven quadruple)

karra	**mana**	**kinyi**	**-ni**	**-venggi**	**-tit**	**kani**
SW	brother	3MIN.A.R.make	3MIN.M.REFL	knee	bend	3MIN.S.R.walk

Brother keeps making number four leg

Text phrase 4
Rhythmic mode 5c (fast uneven quadruple)

karra	**mungarri**	**kapil**	**kinyi**	**-ni**	**-venggi**	**-tit**	**kavulh**
SW	sleep	big	3MIN.A.R.make	3MIN.M.REFL	knee	bend	3MIN.S.R.lie

Deep sleep! He makes himself lie in number four leg

INSTRUMENTAL SECTION 1

Rhythmic mode 5c (fast uneven quadruple)

VOCAL SECTION 2

Melodic section 1

Text phrase 1

Rhythmic mode 5c (fast uneven quadruple)

karra	mana	kinyi	-ni	-venggi	-tit	kavulh
SW	brother	3MIN.A.R.make	3MIN.M.REFL	knee	bend	3MIN.S.R.lie

Brother is making himself lie in number four leg

Text phrase 2

Rhythmic mode 5c (fast uneven quadruple)

karra	mana	kinyi	-ni	-venggi	-tit	kavulh
SW	brother	3MIN.A.R.make	3MIN.M.REFL	knee	bend	3MIN.S.R.lie

Brother is making himself lie in number four leg

INSTRUMENTAL SECTION 2

Rhythmic mode 5c (fast uneven quadruple)

TRACK 19 (Mar98-14-s14)

Song 8: Ma-vindivindi

Sung text	Free translation
karra mana kinyi-ni-venggi-tit kavulh	Brother is making himself lie in number four leg
karra mungarri kapil kinyi-ni-venggi-tit kavulh mungarri	Deep sleep! He makes himself lie asleep in number four leg sleep
karra mana kinyi-ni-venggi-tit kavulh	Brother is making himself lie in number four leg
karra mungarri kapil kinyi-ni-venggi-tit kavulh	Deep sleep! He makes himself lie asleep in number four leg
karra mana kinyi-ni-venggi-tit kavulh	Brother is making himself lie in number four leg
karra mungarri kapil kinyi-ni-venggi-tit kavulh	Deep sleep! He makes himself lie in number four leg

There is some digital noise on this track, but we have included it for comparison with the previous track.

SONG STRUCTURE SUMMARY

VOCAL SECTION 1

Melodic section 1

Text phrase 1

Rhythmic mode 5c (fast uneven quadruple)

karra	**mana**	**kinyi**	**-ni**	**-venggi**	**-tit**	**kavulh**
SW	brother	3MIN.A.R.make	3MIN.M.REFL	knee	bend	3MIN.S.R.lie

Brother is making himself lie in number four leg

Text phrase 2

Rhythmic mode 5c (fast uneven quadruple)

karra	**mungarri**	**kapil**	**kinyi**	**-ni**	**-venggi**	**-tit**	**kavulh**	**mungarri**
SW	sleep	big	3MIN.A.R.make	3MIN.M.REFL	knee	bend	3MIN.S.R.lie	sleep

Deep sleep! He makes himself lie asleep in number four leg, sleep

Melodic section 2

Text phrase 3

Rhythmic mode 5c (fast uneven quadruple)

karra	**mana**	**kinyi**	**-ni**	**-venggi**	**-tit**	**kavulh**
SW	brother	3MIN.A.R.make	3MIN.M.REFL	knee	bend	3MIN.S.R.lie

Brother is making himself lie in number four leg

Text phrase 4

Rhythmic mode 5c (fast uneven quadruple)

karra	**mungarri**	**kapil**	**kinyi**	**-ni**	**-venggi**	**-tit**	**kavulh**
SW	sleep	big	3MIN.A.R.make	3MIN.M.REFL	knee	bend	3MIN.S.R.lie

Deep sleep! He makes himself lie in number four leg

INSTRUMENTAL SECTION 1

Rhythmic mode 5c (fast uneven quadruple)

VOCAL SECTION 2

Melodic section 1

Text phrase 1

Rhythmic mode 5c (fast uneven quadruple)

karra	mana	kinyi	-ni	-venggi	-tit	kavulh
SW	brother	3MIN.A.R.make	3MIN.M.REFL	knee	bend	3MIN.S.R.lie

Brother is making himself lie in number four leg

Text phrase 2

Rhythmic mode 5c (fast uneven quadruple)

karra	mungarri	kapil	kinyi	-ni	-venggi	-tit	kavulh
SW	sleep	big	3MIN.A.R.make	3MIN.M.REFL	knee	bend	3MIN.S.R.lie

Deep sleep! He makes himself lie in number four leg

INSTRUMENTAL SECTION 2

Rhythmic mode 5c (fast uneven quadruple)

TRACK 20 (Mar98-14-s15)
Song 9: Karri-ngindji

Sung text	Free translation
karra mana meri nganggi kani-djet diyerr kuwa	Brother! Our man is sitting at the foot of the cliff
ma yawa kani-djet na wudi-pumininy-pumininy	The Ma-yawa is sitting at the freshwater spring
karra mana meri kani-djet kuwa kagan-dja kisji	Brother is sitting right here where the cliff stands up, like this
meri-gu mana kagan-dja kisji	It's brother in human form who is right here like this
mana ma yawa wudi-pumininy-pumininy	Brother Ma-yawa! Freshwater spring
karra mana purangang kagan-dja-nginanga-kuwa	Brother! The tide is coming in on me right here
mana nganggi diyerr meri ngalvu wudi-pumininy-pumininy	Our Brother is at the cliff! Many people! Freshwater spring

Karri-ngindji, the line of cliffs just south of Tjindi Creek in the north of Marri Ammu country, is the Dreaming site (*kigatiya*) for the Ma-yawa ancestors. They are referred to in a number of Ma-yawa *wangga* songs. A Ma-yawa ancestor is described in this song (tracks 20 and 21) as 'a brother [that is, a Dreaming] in human form' (*meri-gu mana*).

At the foot of the cliff is a freshwater spring (*wudi-pumininy*) that flows into the sea at high tide, but is exposed at low tide. This is where the Ma-yawa like to sit. Marett has written extensively about two important contexts in which the world of the living and the world of the dead interpenetrate: one is when deceased ancestors appear in the dreams of the living to give them songs; the other is when humans perform the songs, dances and ceremonies given to them by the dead. In Marri Ammu songs and paintings, fresh water represents the living; salt water the dead. The flowing of the freshwater spring into the saltwater ocean therefore symbolises these processes and the liminal space (whether that be dream or ceremony) in which they occur (see further Marett, 2005, p 17).

Because the text phrases of this song are rather long, it is sometimes difficult to distinguish words that occur at the end of the phrase, when the singer's breath is at its weakest. This situation is not helped by the fact that the two singers do not always agree. This is inevitable when song texts are as unstable as they are here.

Figure 9.6 The cliffs at Karri-ngindji. Photograph by Allan Marett, reproduced with the permission of Wadeye community.

SONG STRUCTURE SUMMARY

VOCAL SECTION 1

Melodic section 1

Text phrase 1

Rhythmic mode 1 (without clapsticks)

karra	**mana**	**meri**	**nganggi**	**kani**	**-djet**	**diyerr**	**kuwa**
SW	brother	man	1/2MIN..PRO	3MIN.S.R go	sit	cliff	3MIN.S.R.stand

Brother! Our man [Ma-yawa] is sitting at the foot of the cliff

Text phrase 2

Rhythmic mode 1 (without clapsticks)

ma	**yawa**	**kani**	**-djet**	**na**	**wudi**	**-pumininy-pumininy**
male human class	yawa	3MIN.S.R.go	sit	LOC	water	spring REDUP

The Ma-yawa is sitting at the freshwater spring

The Ma-yawa *wangga* repertory • 389

INSTRUMENTAL SECTION 1

Rhythmic mode 4a (moderate even)

VOCAL SECTION 2

Melodic section 1

Text phrase 1

Rhythmic mode 1 (without clapsticks)

karra	mana	meri	kani -djet	kuwa	kagan	-dja	kisji
SW	brother	man	3MIN.S.R.go sit	3MIN.S.R stand	ANAPH.DEIC	really	like that

Brother is sitting right here where it [the cliff] stands up, like this

Text phrase 2

Rhythmic mode 1 (without clapsticks)

meri	-gu	mana	kagan	-dja	kisji
man	TOP	brother	ANAPH.DEIC	really	like this

It's brother in human form who is right here like this

mana	ma	yawa	wudi	-pumininy-pumininy
brother	human class	yawa	water	spring REDUP

Brother Ma-yawa! Freshwater spring

INSTRUMENTAL SECTION 2

Rhythmic mode 4a (moderate even)

VOCAL SECTION 3

Melodic section 1

Text phrase 1

Rhythmic mode 1 (without clapsticks)

karra	mana	purangang	kagan	-dja	-nginanga	-kuwa
SW	brother	sea	ANAPH.DEIC	really	1MIN.ADVERS	3MIN.S.R stand

Brother! The tide is coming in on me right here

Text phrase 2

Rhythmic mode 1 (without clapsticks)

mana	nganggi	diyerr	meri	ngalvu	wudi	-pumininy-pumininy
brother	1/2MIN.S.PRO	cliff	human	many	water	spring REDUP

Our Brother is at the cliff! Many people! Freshwater spring

INSTRUMENTAL SECTION 3

Rhythmic mode 5b (fast doubled)

TRACK 21 (Mar98-14-s16)

Song 9: Karri-ngindji

Sung text	Free translation
karra mana wudi-pumininy kagan-dja kurzi	Brother is right here at the spring
karra mana wudi-pumininy kagan-dja kurzi	Brother is right here at the spring
karra mana wudi-pumininy kurzi	Brother is at the spring
karra mana wudi purangang kisji	Brother! Fresh water and salt water! Like this!
karra mana wudi-pumininy-pumininy	Brother is at the spring

SONG STRUCTURE SUMMARY

VOCAL SECTION 1

Melodic section 1

Text phrase 1

Rhythmic mode 1 (without clapsticks)

karra	mana	wudi	-pumininy	kagan	-dja	kurzi
SW	brother	water	spring	ANAPH.DEIC	really	3MIN.S.R.sit

Brother [i.e., Ma-yawa] is right here at the spring

Text phrase 2

Rhythmic mode 1 (without clapsticks)

karra	mana	wudi	-pumininy	kagan	-dja	kurzi
SW	brother	waterhole	spring	ANAPH.DEICre	really	3MIN.S.R.sit

Brother [i.e., Ma-yawa] is right here at the spring

Text phrase 3

Rhythmic mode 1 (without clapsticks)

karra	mana	wudi	-pumininy	kurzi
SW	brother	water	spring	3MIN.S.R.sit

Brother [i.e., Ma-yawa] is at the spring

INSTRUMENTAL SECTION 1

Rhythmic mode 4a (moderate even)

VOCAL SECTION 2

Melodic section 1

Text phrase 1

Rhythmic mode 1 (without clapsticks)

karra	mana	wudi	purangang	kisji
SW	brother	water	salt water	like this

Brother! Fresh water and salt water! Like this!

Text phrase 2

Rhythmic mode 1 (without clapsticks)

karra	mana	wudi	-pumininy- pumininy
SW	brother	water	spring REDUP

Brother is at the spring

INSTRUMENTAL SECTION 2

Rhythmic mode 5b (fast doubled)

TRACKS 22–23 (Mar98-14-s17, s18)

Song 10: Thalhi-ngatjpirr

Sung text	Free translation
meri ngalvu-kinyil kani nidin na kaddi devin kurzi kaddi-gu kirriminggi thalhi ngatjpirr kirriminggi (repeated)	Lots of people like to go to country that is just for us As for us, we say, only we fish at Thalhi-ngatjpirr

Thalhi-ngatjpirr is a fish Dreaming site near Tjindi in the north of Marri Ammu country. Senior Marri Ammu frequently complain about the non-Aboriginal fishermen, both recreational and commercial, who fish there, and this is the interpretation that Ngulkur offered. It should be noted that the wide semantic field of the verb *kirrimi* leaves the song open to other interpretations with regard to what it is that is done at Thali-ngatjpirr.

SONG STRUCTURE SUMMARY

VOCAL SECTIONS 1–3

Melodic section 1

Text phrase 1

Rhythmic mode 5c (fast uneven quadruple)

meri	ngalvu	-kinyil	kani	nidin	na	kaddi	devin	kurzi
human	many	3MIN.A.R.want	3MIN.S.R.go	country	LOC	1AUG.EXCL.PRO	alone	3MIN.S.R.sit

Lots of people like to go to country that is just for us

Text phrase 2

Rhythmic mode 5c (fast uneven quadruple)

kaddi	-gu	kirriminggi	thalhi ngatjpirr	kirriminggi
1AUG.EXCL.PRO	DTOP	1.EXCL.AUG.A.R.do	Dreaming place	1.EXCL.AUG.A.R.do

As for us, we say, only we do it [i.e., fish] at Thalhi-ngatjpirr

INSTRUMENTAL SECTIONS 1–3

Rhythmic mode 5c (fast uneven quadruple)

TRACK 24 (Tre08-01-s17)

Song 10: Thalhi-ngatjpirr

Sung text	Free translation
meri ngalvu-kinyil kani na nidin kaddi devin kisji	Lots of people like to go to our country which is just for us, like this
meri ngalvu-kinyil kani na nidin kaddi devin kisji	Lots of people like to go to our country, which is just for us, like this
kaddi-gu kirriminggi thalhi ngatjpirr kirriminggi	As for us, we say, only we do it [i.e., fish] at Thalhi-ngatjpirr
(repeated)	

In 2008, Sally Treloyn recorded Frank Dumoo, backed up by Colin Worumbu Ferguson, singing a version of 'Thali-ngatjpirr.' Dumoo slightly alters the word order in the first text phrase of each vocal section, as well as the form of the song, replacing the couplet form of the original with the AAB text form most characteristic of the Walakandha *wangga*. There are a number of other alterations, including a change of melody (which probably simply results from the didjeridu being too high).

SONG STRUCTURE SUMMARY

VOCAL SECTION 1

Melodic section 1

Text phrases 1–2

Rhythmic mode 5c (fast uneven quadruple)

meri	**ngalvu**	**-kinyil**	**kani**	**na**	**nidin**	**kaddi**	**devin**	**kisji**
human	many	3MIN.A.R.want	3MIN.S.R.go	LOC	country	1AUG.EXCL.PRO	alone	like this

Lots of people like to go to our country, which is just for us, like this

Text phrase 3

Rhythmic mode 5c (fast uneven quadruple)

kaddi	**-gu**	**kirriminggi**	**thalhi ngatjpirr**	**kirriminggi**
1AUG.EXCL.PRO	DTOP	1.EXCL.AUG.A.R.say	Dreaming place	1.EXCL.AUG.A.R.do

As for us, we say, only we do it [i.e., fish] at Thalhi-ngatjpirr

INSTRUMENTAL SECTION 1

Rhythmic mode 5c

VOCAL SECTION 2

Melodic section 1

Text phrases 1–2

Rhythmic mode 5c (fast uneven quadruple)

meri	**ngalvu**	**-kinyil**	**kani**	**na**	**nidin**	**kaddi**	**devin**	**kisji**
human	many	3MIN.A.R.want	3MIN.S.R.go	LOC	country	1AUG.EXCL.PRO	alone	like this

Lots of people like to go to our country, which is just for us, like this

Text phrase 3

Rhythmic mode 5c (fast uneven quadruple)

kaddi	**-gu**	**kirriminggi**	**thalhi ngatjpirr**	**kirriminggi**
1AUG.EXCL.PRO	DTOP	1.EXCL.AUG.A.R.say	Dreaming place	1.EXCL.AUG.A.R.do

As for us, we say, only we do it [i.e., fish] at Thalhi-ngatjpirr

INSTRUMENTAL SECTION 2

Rhythmic mode 5c

TRACKS 25–27 A General Introduction

Song 11: Na-Pebel

Sung text	Free translation
mana na pebel nidin vali-ngin-sjit ngunda (repeated)	Brother, stand up and show me the country at Pebel

Na-Pebel is a sandbar in the shape of a dilly bag (*pebel*) near the mouth of Tjindi Creek. In the first two items (tracks 25 and 26), the singer asks his brother—perhaps a Dreaming, since the term 'brother' is often used to address Dreamings—to point out Na-Pebel to him, as indeed Ngulkur did for me, the first time I visited his country (figure 9.7). In the third item (track 27) the singer asks to be shown the thing that is like Na-Pebel. By this he probably means the dilly bag from which the place derives its name and thus underscores the co-referential relationship between place and object. Like 'Watjen-danggi' this song has its own individual melody, which is distinct from the two melodies used elsewhere in the Ma-yawa *wangga* repertory for songs about Dreamings.

SONG STRUCTURE SUMMARY

TRACK 25 (Mar99-01-s01)

VOCAL SECTIONS 1–3

Melodic section 1

Text phrase 1

Rhythmic mode 5c (fast uneven quadruple)

mana	na	pebel	nidin	vali	-ngin	-sjit	ngunda
brother	LOC	place name	country	2MIN.A.IR.fingers	1MIN.O	show	2MIN.S.IR.stand

Brother, stand up and show me the country at Pebel

INSTRUMENTAL SECTIONS 1–3

Rhythmic mode 5c (fast uneven quadruple)

TRACK 26 (Mar99-01-s02)

Song 11: Na-Pebel

Sung text	Free translation
mana na pebel nidin vali-ngin-sjit ngunda (repeated)	Brother, stand up and show me the country at Pebel

SONG STRUCTURE SUMMARY

VOCAL SECTIONS 1–2

Melodic section 1

Text phrase 1

Rhythmic mode 5c (fast uneven quadruple)

mana	na	pebel	nidin	vali	-ngin	-sjit	ngunda
brother	LOC	place name	country	2MIN.A.IR.fingers	1MIN.O	show	2MIN.S.IR.stand

Brother, stand up and show me the country at Pebel

INSTRUMENTAL SECTIONS 1–2

Rhythmic mode 5c (fast uneven quadruple)

Figure 9.7 Maurice Ngulkur points out Na-Pebel to Allan Marett, 1999. Photograph by Allan Marett, reproduced with the permission of Wadeye community.

TRACK 27 (Mar99-01-s03)

Song 11: Na-Pebel

Sung text	Free translation
mana thawurr gimin vali-ngin-sjit na pebel	Brother, show me the thing that is like Pebel
mana thawurr gimin vali-ngin-sjit na pebel	Brother, show me the thing that is like Pebel
mana thawurr pebel	Brother, the thing that belongs to Pebel

SONG STRUCTURE SUMMARY

VOCAL SECTIONS 1–2

Melodic section 1

Text phrase 1

Rhythmic mode 5c (fast uneven quadruple)

mana	**thawurr**	**gimin**	**vali**	**-ngin**	**-sjit**	**na**	**pebel**
brother	thing NC	like	2MIN.A.IR fingers	1MIN.O	show	LOC	place name

Brother, show me the thing that is like Pebel

INSTRUMENTAL SECTIONS 1–2

Rhythmic mode 5c (fast uneven quadruple)

VOCAL SECTION 3

Melodic section 1

Text phrase 1

Rhythmic mode 5c (fast uneven quadruple)

mana	**thawurr**	**pebel**
brother	thing NC	place name

Brother, the thing that belongs to Pebel

INSTRUMENTAL SECTION 3

Rhythmic mode 5c (fast uneven quadruple)

Figure 9.8 Maurice Ngulkur shows Allan Marett a dilly bag, *pebel*. Photograph by Allan Marett, reproduced with the permission of Wadeye community.

TRACK 28 (Cro00-01-s07)

Song 12: Wulumen Tulh

Sung text	Free translation
wulumen kidin-mitit-a-gu wulu tulh	This is what made the old man angry, Old Man Tulh
wulumen kidin-mitit-a tulh	It made Old Man Tulh angry
miyi-gu kidin-mitit-a-gu	It was the tucker [Hairy Cheeky Yam] that made him angry
miyi-gu kidin tulh kisji	It was the tucker that made Tulh [angry] like this
wulumen tulh kidin-mitit-a kisji	It made old man Tulh angry, like this
wulumen tulh kidin-mitit-a kisji	It made old man Tulh angry, like this
miyi-gu kidin nal kisji	It was the tucker [that made him angry] just like this
kidin-mitit-a-gu	This is what made him angry
wulumen tulh kidin-mitit-a-gu kisji	Old Man Tulh, it made him angry like this
wulumen tulh kidin-mitit-a kisji	Old Man Tulh, it made him angry like this
miyi-gu kidin nal kisji	It was the tucker that did it, just like this

The song on tracks 28 and 29 relates to the story of the Ma-yawa ancestor known as Wulumen Tulh ('Old Man Tulh') and the Dreaming Tjiwilirr 'Hairy Cheeky Yam'. This song, together with its associated myths and paintings, is discussed in detail in Marett, 2005, pp 15–23 (see also Ford & Nemarluk, 2003).

In brief, the story relates how Old Man Tulh came back from hunting to his camp at Pumurriyi to find that his wives had not prepared any food. He therefore ate some raw hairy cheeky yam (tjiwilirr), which is toxic when uncooked. He was so angry that he threw it everywhere, which is why it now grows prolifically at Pumurriyi.

The quality of the original recording of this song was poor. Nonetheless, because the song is so important, we have included it here.

SONG STRUCTURE SUMMARY

VOCAL SECTION 1

Melodic section 1

Text phrase 1

Rhythmic mode 5c (fast uneven quadruple)

wulumen	**kidin**	**-mitit**	**-a**	**-gu**	**wulu**	**tulh**
old man	3MIN.A.R.see	be angry	PERF	TOP	old man	name

This is what made the old man angry, Old Man Tulh

Text phrase 2

Rhythmic mode 5c (fast uneven quadruple)

wulumen	**kidin**	**-mitit**	**-a**	**tulh**
old man	3MIN.A.R.see	be angry	PERF	name

It made Old Man Tulh angry

Text phrase 3

Rhythmic mode 5c (fast uneven quadruple)

miyi	**-gu**	**kidin**	**-mitit**	**-a**	**-gu**
plant	TOP	3MIN.A.R.see	be angry	PERF	TOP

It was the tucker [Hairy Cheeky Yam] that made him angry

Text phrase 4

Rhythmic mode 5c (fast uneven quadruple)

miyi	**-gu**	**kidin**	**tulh**	**kisji**
plant	TOP	3MIN.A.R.see	name	like this

It was the tucker that made Tulh [angry] like this

INSTRUMENTAL SECTION 1

Rhythmic mode 5c (fast uneven quadruple)

VOCAL SECTION 2

Melodic section 1

Text phrase 1

Rhythmic mode 5c (fast uneven quadruple)

wulumen	**tulh**	**kidin**	**-mitit**	**-a**	**kisji**
old man	name	3MIN.A.R.see	be angry	PERF	like this

It made old man Tulh angry, like this

Text phrase 2

Rhythmic mode 5c (fast uneven quadruple)

wulumen	**tulh**	**kidin**	**-mitit**	**-a**	**kisji**
old man	name	3MIN.A.R.see	be angry	PERF	like this

It made Old Man Tulh angry, like this

Text phrase 3

Rhythmic mode 5c (fast uneven quadruple)

miyi	**-gu**	**kidin**	**nal**	**kisji**
plant	TOP	3MIN.A.R.see	just	like this

It was the tucker [that made him angry] just like this

Text phrase 4

Rhythmic mode 5c (fast uneven quadruple)

kidin	**-mitit**	**-a**	**-gu**
3MIN.A.R.see	be angry	PERF	TOP

This is what made him angry

INSTRUMENTAL SECTION 2

Rhythmic mode 5c (fast uneven quadruple)

VOCAL SECTION 3

Melodic section 1

Text phrase 1

Rhythmic mode 5c (fast uneven quadruple)

wulumen	**tulh**	**kidin**	**-mitit**	**-a**	**-gu**	**kisji**
old man	name	3MIN.A.R.see	be angry	PERF	TOP	like this

Old Man Tulh, it made him angry like this

Text phrase 2

Rhythmic mode 5c (fast uneven quadruple)

wulumen	tulh	kidin	-mitit	-a	kisji
old man	name	3MIN.A.R.see	be angry	PERF	like this

Old Man Tulh, it made him angry like this

Text phrase 3

Rhythmic mode 5c (fast uneven quadruple)

miyi	-gu	kidin	nal	kisji	
plant	TOP	3MIN.A.R.see	just	3MIN.S.R	be like

It was the tucker that did it, just like this

INSTRUMENTAL SECTION 3

Rhythmic mode 5c (fast uneven quadruple)

TRACK 29 (Cro00-01-s08)

Song 12: Wulumen Tulh

Sung text	Free translation
wulumen tulh kidin-mitit-a-gu	This is what made Old Man Tulh angry
wulumen tulh kidin-mitit-a-gu	This is what made Old Man Tulh angry
miyi-gu tjiwilirr nal kisji	It was the Hairy Cheeky Yam, just like this
kuwa-butj kani-ya	He kept throwing it away
kuwa-rrin kisji	It grows everywhere like this
wulumen tulh kidin-mitit-a	It made Old Man Tulh angry
miyi-gu tjiwilirr nal kisji	It was Hairy Cheeky Yam just like this
wulumen tulh kidin-mitit-a	It made Old Man Tulh angry
miyi-gu tjiwilirr nal kisji	It was Hairy Cheeky Yam just like this
kuwa-butj kani-ya	He kept throwing it away
kuwa-rrin kisji	It grows everywhere like this
kuwa-butj kani-ya	He kept throwing it away
kuwa-rrin kisji	It grows everywhere like this

SONG STRUCTURE SUMMARY

VOCAL SECTION 1

Melodic section 1

Text phrases 1–2

Rhythmic mode 1 (without clapsticks)

wulumen	**tulh**	**kidin**	**-mitit**	**-a**	**-gu**
old man	name	3MIN.A.R.see	be angry	PERF	TOP

This is what made Old Man Tulh angry

Text phrase 3

Rhythmic mode 1 (without clapsticks)

miyi	**-gu**	**tjiwilirr**	**nal**	**kisji**
plant	TOP	Hairy Cheeky Yam	just	3MINS.R be like

It was the Hairy Cheeky Yam, just like this

Text phrase 4

Rhythmic mode 1 (without clapsticks)

kuwa	**-butj**	**kani**	**-ya**
3MINS.R.stand	throw away	3MINS.R.go	PERF

He kept throwing it away

Figure 9.9 A bark painting by Charlie Niwilhi Brinken, showing Wulumen Tulh on the left, and the singer himself on the right (for further information see discussion in Marett, 2005, p 17). Courtesy of Sotheby's Australia, reproduced with the permission of Wadeye community.

Text phrase 5

Rhythmic mode 1 (without clapsticks)

kuwa	**-rrin**	**kisji**
3MINS.R.stand	be everywhere	like this

It grows everywhere like this

INSTRUMENTAL SECTION 1

Rhythmic mode 5a (fast even)

VOCAL SECTION 2

Melodic section 1

Text phrase 1

Rhythmic mode 1 (without clapsticks)

wulumen	**tulh**	**kidin**	**-mitit**	**-a**
old man	name	3MIN.A.R.see	be angry	-PERF

It made Old Man Tulh angry

Text phrase 2

Rhythmic mode 1 (without clapsticks)

miyi	**-gu**	**tjiwilirr**	**nal**	**kisji**
plant	TOP	Hairy Cheeky Yam	just	like this

It was Hairy Cheeky Yam just like this

Text phrase 3

Rhythmic mode 1 (without clapsticks)

wulumen	**tulh**	**kidin**	**-mitit**	**-a**
old man	name	3MIN.A.R.see	be angry	-PERF

It made Old Man Tulh angry

Text phrase 4

Rhythmic mode 1 (without clapsticks)

miyi	**-gu**	**tjiwilirr**	**nal**	**kisji**
Plant	TOP	Hairy Cheeky Yam	just	like this

It was Hairy Cheeky Yam like this

Melodic section 2

Text phrase 5

Rhythmic mode 1 (without clapsticks)

kuwa	-butj	kani	-ya
3MINS.R.stand	throw away	3MINS.R.walk	PERF

He kept throwing it away

Text phrase 6

Rhythmic mode 1 (without clapsticks)

kuwa	-rrin	kisji
3MINS.R.stand	be everywhere	like this

It grows everywhere like this

Text phrase 7

Rhythmic mode 1 (without clapsticks)

kuwa	-butj	kani	-ya
3MINS.R.stand	throw away	3MINS.R.walk	PERF

He kept throwing it away

Text phrase 8

Rhythmic mode 1 (without clapsticks)

kuwa	-rrin	kisji
3MINS.R.stand	be everywhere	like this

It grows everywhere like this

INSTRUMENTAL SECTION 2

Rhythmic mode 5b (fast doubled)

MUSICAL ANALYSIS OF MA-YAWA REPERTORY

Song structure overview

Perhaps because every track in the chapter is from an elicited recording, all items have either two or three vocal and instrumental sections in roughly equal numbers (greater numbers of vocal and instrumental sections tend to appear in ceremonial or tourist performances).

Text structure overview

The repertory exhibits a much larger proportion of textual instability than any other. In five songs ('Wulumen Kimi-gimi' (tracks 4–5), 'Menggani' (tracks 10–11), 'Malhimanyirr' (tracks 16–17), 'Thalhi-ngatjpirr' (tracks 22–24) and 'Na-Pebel' (tracks 25–27), the texts, usually consisting of a couplet or a repeated single text phrase, tend to stay relatively stable from one vocal section to another within an item (though it may vary from one item to another, as it does in the third item of both 'Malhimanyirr' and 'Na-Pebel'). It is these more stable texts that tend to have three vocal sections per item. In the other seven songs, texts vary considerably from one vocal section to another, and from one item to another.

The Ma-yawa *wangga* repertory is also remarkable for using no ghost language in its texts.

Rhythmic mode overview

It can be seen immediately from table 9.2 that vocal sections of most Ma-yawa *wangga* songs are in one of two rhythmic modes: either rhythmic mode 1 (unmeasured) or, if the song is measured, rhythmic mode 5c (fast uneven quadruple). The exception is 'Watjen-danggi', which uses rhythmic mode 4a throughout.[6] Ngulkur never uses the slow measured tempo band.

Tempo band of vocal section	#	Song title	Rhythmic mode of VS	Rhythmic mode of IIS	Rhythmic mode of FIS
Unmeasured					
Without clapsticks	5	'Tjerri' (tracks 12–13)	1	4a	**5b**
	9	'Karri-ngindji' (tracks 20–21)	1	4a	**5b**
	12	'Wulumen Tulh' (track 29)	1	5a	**5b**
	3	'Rtadi-wunbirri', (tracks 6–8)	1	5a	**5b**
	3	'Rtadi-wunbirri' (track 9)	1	5*	**5b**
Unmeasured/Measured					
	1	'Walakandha Ngindji' (tracks 1–2)	5c, 1	5a	**5b**
Measured					
Moderate (117bpm)	6	'Watjen-danggi' (tracks 14–15)	4a	4a	4a
Fast (134–46bpm)	1	'Walakandha Ngindji' (track 3)	5c	5c	5c
	2	'Wulumen Kimi-gimi', (tracks 4–5)	5c	5c	5c
	4	'Menggani', (tracks 10–11)	5c	5c	5c
	7	'Malhimanyirr', (tracks 16–17)	5c	5c	5c
	8	'Ma-vindivindi', (tracks 18–19)	5c	5c	5c
	10	'Thalhi-ngatjpirr' (tracks 22–24)	5c	5c	5c
	11	'Na-Pebel' (tracks 25–27)	5c	5c	5c
	12	'Wulumen Tulh' (track 28)	5c	5c	5c

Table 9.2 Rhythmic modes used in the Ma-yawa *wangga* (track reference to chapter 9). VS= vocal section, IIS= internal instrumental section, FIS= final instrumental section. FIS is bold when different.

---

6   Marett has pointed out a number of structural similarities between 'Watjen-danggi' and 'Yenmilhi No. 1' from the Walakandha *wangga* repertory, each of which is unique within its respective repertory with regard to text structure, melody and rhythmic mode (Marett, 2005, pp 128-29).

Presenting the same text in different rhythmic modes in successive items

One song, 'Wulumen Tulh' is performed first in a measured (rhythmic mode 5c) version (track 28) and then in an unmeasured (rhythmic mode 1) version (track 29). This may point back to the days when the Ma-yawa *wangga* probably coexisted alongside the early Walakandha *wangga* of Stan Mullumbuk.

Presenting the same text in different rhythmic modes in different vocal sections within an item

In two items of 'Walakandha Ngindji' (tracks 1-2), a vocal section in rhythmic mode 5c is followed by one in rhythmic mode 1. Marett has argued elsewhere (Marett, 2005, p 141) that this is a matter of balancing the dominant rhythmic mode of the later Walakandha *wangga* (rhythmic mode 1) with the dominant rhythmic mode of the Ma-yawa *wangga* (rhythmic mode 5c).

Distribution of rhythmic mode between vocal sections and instrumental sections

Songs in rhythmic mode 1 use either 4a (moderate even) or 5a (fast even) for non-final instrumental sections, and rhythmic mode 5b (fast doubled) for final instrumental sections. These patterns are also found in the repertories of Jimmy Muluk and the Walakandha *wangga*. It may be significant that the two songs that use rhythmic mode 4a for internal instrumental sections ('Karri-ngindji' and 'Tjerri') share a dorian mode melody, while the two songs using 5a in this position ('Rtadi-wunbirri' and 'Wulumen Tulh') share a major mode melody (see discussion of melody below). As is almost always the case across all *wangga* repertories, songs that use rhythmic modes 4a and 5c in their vocal sections use the same mode throughout all vocal and instrumental sections.

Distribution of rhythmic mode between internal and final instrumental sections

Songs in rhythmic mode 1 use several different rhythmic modes in their internal instrumental sections, which can be in 4a (moderate even), 5a (fast even) or 5* (mixed doubled and even beating), but they all use rhythmic mode 5b (fast doubled) for their final instrumental section.[7] Songs in rhythmic modes 4a and 5c use the same rhythmic mode in both internal and final instrumental sections.

Mixing of rhythmic modes within an instrumental section

In one and only one internal instrumental section of 'Rtadi-wunbirri' (track 9) Ngulkur uses the complex 5* pattern found in some of Stan Mullumbuk's early Walakandha *wangga* (see chapter 8), which consists of a stretch of fast doubled beating (rhythmic mode 5b), followed by a stretch of fast even beating (rhythmic mode 5a), followed by the 'Walakandha *wangga* cueing pattern' (♫ ♩ ♫ ♩ ♩ 𝄽).

Cueing patterns in instrumental sections

Ngulkur uses the Walakandha *wangga* cueing pattern in the instrumental sections in rhythmic mode 5a and 5b, but his usage is slightly different from that found in the Walakandha *wangga*. For example, whereas the Walakanda *wangga* non-final instrumental sections always have two sequences of beating in rhythmic mode 5a, each followed by the Walakandha *wangga* cueing pattern, in 'Rtadi-wunbirri' there is only one sequence of beating in rhythmic mode 5a followed by the Walakandha *wangga* cueing pattern. In all the other non-final instrumental sections that follow vocal sections in rhythmic mode 1, the double sequence used in the later Walakandha *wangga* is followed, but the cueing pattern at the end of each phase of beating is truncated to simply ♫ ♩ ♩. It is as if Ngulkur is in effect using the same form of non-final instrumental section as the Walakandha *wangga*, but finding ways to make it

---

7 Note that this pattern also prevails in the versions of 'Walakandha Ngindji' (tracks 1–2) that use rhythmic mode 1 in the second (final) vocal section.

individually his. The final instrumental sections are, however, performed just as they are in the later Walakandha *wangga*.

Melody overview

As table 9.3 shows, only four melodies are used in the repertory. Eight songs share a single melody in the dorian modal series, while two share a melody in the major modal series. All songs that share a melody, except 'Walakandha Ngindji' (song 1, which uses the dorian series) concern Marri Ammu Dreamings or Dreaming sites. We cannot know now what the significance was of using the major (rather than the dorian) mode melody for the Dreaming sites and Dreamings mentioned in 'Rtadi-wunbirri' and 'Wulumen Tulh'. We may speculate that since in other *wangga* repertories melodies are associated with lineages or families, and one of the inherent features of families is shared relationships to Dreamings, this melodic difference may once have reflected different family interests in these two Dreamings. As Marett has pointed out in *Songs, dreamings and ghosts* (Marett, 2005, pp 79–80) in much of Aboriginal Australia there is a strong association between melody and ancestral Dreamings. In some places, melodies are even referred to as the 'taste' or 'scent' of a Dreaming (C Ellis, 1984, p 171; C Ellis, et al., 1978, p 74; RM Moyle, 1979, p 71).

	Song title(s)	Number of items
Melodies using the dorian series		
1	'Walakandha Ngindji', 'Wulumen Kimi-gimi', 'Menggani', 'Thalhi-ngatjpirr', 'Tjerri', 'Malhimanyirr No. 1', 'Ma-vindivindi', 'Karri-ngindji'	8
2	'Watjen-danggi'	1
Melodies using the major series		
3	'Rtadi-wunbirri', 'Wulumen Tulh'	2
4	'Na-Pebel'	1

Table 9.3 The melodies of the Ma-yawa *wangga*.

We regard it as significant that two of the songs that are not about Dreamings and Dreaming sites ('Watjen-danggi' and 'Na-Pebel') each have their own unique melody, and these melodies are quite different from the two used for songs about Dreamings and Dreaming places.

The third song that is not about Dreamings, 'Walakandha Ngindji', shares the dorian mode melody (numbered 1 in table 9.3) that is otherwise used for most of the Marri Ammu Dreamings and Dreaming sites mentioned in the Ma-yawa *wangga*. Marett has argued that this is a deliberate gesture by its composer Ngulkur, who, in adapting this song from 'Walakandha No. 2' (chapter 8, track 23), balanced elements of form signifying Marri Ammu and Marri Tjavin interests. Thus, while the text remains essentially the same as in the Walakandha *wangga* and the principles for rhythmicising its text are also essentially Marri Tjavin, Ngulkur uses the most characteristic melody (and the most common rhythmic mode) of the Ma-yawa *wangga* to mark the song as his own composition.

Notes on selected tracks

'Walakandha Ngindji' (tracks 1–2)

The rhythmic mode used in vocal section 1 of track 1, rhythmic mode 5c (fast uneven quadruple), is the mode most commonly used in the Ma-yawa *wangga*. In vocal section 2 Ngulkur presents the song text in rhythmic mode 1, the most common rhythmic mode of the Walakandha *wangga*. Marett argues that this is a gesture to acknowledge the derivation of the song from that repertory (2007, p 141).

In track 2 Ngulkur rearranges the text of vocal section 1 so that the second text phrase of item 1 becomes text phrase 1 of item 2, but he maintains the rhythmic modal characteristics of each vocal section, using fast uneven quadruple beating (rhythmic mode 5c) for the first vocal section, and the unaccompanied rhythmic mode 1 for the second vocal section.

'Tjerri' (track 12)

The first vocal section is performed over two melodic sections, whereas the second vocal section covers a single melodic section, as do both vocal sections of the following item (track 13). In both items, the first instrumental section is in rhythmic mode 4a (moderate even), while the final instrumental section, performed in rhythmic mode 5b (fast doubled), is performed significantly more slowly than usual in Ngulkur's repertory, at about crotchet = 130bpm.

'Wulumen Tulh' (tracks 28–29)

In the first rendition (track 28), Ngulkur presents the song in rhythmic mode 5c (fast uneven quadruple), the most common rhythmic mode used in the Ma-yawa *wangga*. In the second (track 29) he sings the vocal sections in rhythmic mode 1 (without clapsticks).

REFERENCES

Anderson GDS (1992). *Murlarra: a clan song series from central Arnhem Land*. Unpublished thesis (PhD). University of Sydney, Sydney.

Anonymous (1951, 16 February). Native leader shanghaied. *Northern Standard (1921-1955)*, p. 1. Retrieved 4 April 2011, from nla.gov.au/nla.news-article49482563.

Anonymous (1948, April 20). A royal tour disappointment. *The West Australian (1879-1954)*, p. 6. Retrieved 5 April 2011, from nla.gov.au/nla.news-article46904700.

Anonymous (1882, 7 January). News and notes. *Northern Territory Times and Gazette (1873-1927)*, p. 2. Retrieved 26 November 2010, from nla.gov.au/nla.news-article3151789.

Anonymous (1879, 3 May). News and notes. *Northern Territory Times and Gazette (1873-1927)*, p. 2. Retrieved 13 December 2010, from nla.gov.au/nla.news-article3148254.

Australian Broadcasting Corporation (1942). Songs by Australian Aborigines, with commentary by Peter Hemery. ABC archives tape number 72/10/543, 16-inch disc (33rpm). Sydney: Australian Broadcasting Commission.

Barwick L (2011). Musical form and style in Murriny Patha djanba songs at Wadeye (Northwest Australia). In M Tenzer & J Roeder (eds), *Analytical and cross-cultural studies in world music*. Oxford and New York: Oxford University Press.

Barwick L (2006). Marri Ngarr lirrga songs: a musicological analysis of song pairs in performance. *Musicology Australia*, 28 (2005-2006): 1-25.

Barwick L (2005). Performance, aesthetics, experience: thoughts on Yawulyu mungamunga songs. In E Mackinlay, S Owens & D Collins (eds), *Aesthetics and experience in music performance* (pp 1-18). Amersham, Bucks: Cambridge Scholars Press.

Barwick L (2003). Tempo bands, metre and rhythmic mode in Marri Ngarr 'Church Lirrga' songs. *Australasian Music Research*, 7: 67-83.

Barwick L, Blythe J, Ford L, Reid N, Walsh M & Wadeye Aboriginal Languages Centre (2010). Wadeye Song Database. Retrieved 17 January 2011, from sydney.edu.au/wadeyesong/.

Barwick L & Marett A (2011). Aural snapshots of musical life: Simpson's 1948 recordings. In M Thomas & M Neale (eds), *Exploring the legacy of the Arnhem Land expedition in 1948: science, diplomacy and Aboriginal studies in a trans-national context* (pp 355-91). Canberra: ANU E Press.

Barwick L, Marett A, Blythe J & Walsh M (2007). Arriving, digging, performing, returning: an exercise in rich interpretation of a *djanba* song text in the sound archive of the Wadeye Knowledge Centre, Northern Territory of Australia. In RM Moyle (ed), *Oceanic music encounters—the print resource and the human resource: essays in honour of Mervyn McLean* (pp 13-24). Auckland: University of Auckland.

Barwick L, Marett A, Walsh M, Reid N & Ford L (2005). Communities of interest: issues in establishing a digital resource on Murrinh-patha song at Wadeye (Port Keats), NT. *Literary and Linguistic Computing*, 20(4): 383-397.

Basedow H (1907). *Anthropological notes on the western coastal tribes of the Northern Territory of South Australia*. Adelaide: Royal Society of South Australia.

Brandl M, Walsh M, Haritos A & Northern Land Council (1979). *Kenbi land claim : to vacant crown land in the Cox Peninsula, Bynoe Harbour and Port Patterson areas of the Northern Territory of Australia / by the Northern Land Council on behalf of the traditional owners. Prepared by Maria Brandl, Adrienne Haritos, Michael Walsh*. Darwin: The Northern Land Council.

Coppinger RW (1883). *Cruise of the 'Alert': four years in Patagonian, Polynesian, and Mascarene waters (1878-82)*. London [England]: W Swann Sonnenschein.

Dixon RMW (2002). *Australian languages*. Cambridge: Cambridge University Press.

Dixon RMW (1980). *The languages of Australia*. Cambridge: Cambridge University Press.

Dixon RMW & Koch G (1996). *Dyirbal song poetry*. St Lucia, Queensland: University of Queensland Press.

Elkin AP & Jones T (1958). *Arnhem Land music (north Australia)*. Sydney: University of Sydney.

Ellis C (1984). Time consciousness of Aboriginal performers *Problems and solutions: Occasional essays in musicology presented to Alice M. Moyle* (pp 149–85). Sydney: Hale & Iremonger.

Ellis C, Ellis AM, Tur M & McCardell A (1978). Classification of sounds in Pitjantjatjara-speaking areas. In L Hiatt (ed.), *Australian Aboriginal concepts* (pp 68–80). Canberra: Australian Institute of Aboriginal Studies.

Ellis CJ (1985). *Aboriginal Music: Education for Living*. St. Lucia, Australia: University of Queensland Press.

Etheridge R (1894). An Australian Aboriginal musical instrument. *Journal of the Anthropological Institute of Great Britain and Ireland*, 23: 320–24

Evans N (1989). Linguistic convergence in the Wogait: the case of Wadyiginy, Pungupungu and Kungarrakany. Unpublished manuscript PMS4779. Canberra: Australian Institute of Aboriginal and Torres Strait Islander Studies.

Ewers JK (1954). *With the sun on my back*. 2nd edn. Sydney: Angus and Robertson.

Falkenberg J (1962). *Kin and totem: Group relations of Australian Aborigines in the Port Keats district*. Oslo: Oslo University Press.

Ford L (2007). 'Too long, that *wangga*': analysing *wangga* texts over time. *Australian Aboriginal Studies*, 2007(2): 76–89.

Ford L (2006). Marri Ngarr lirrga songs: a linguistic analysis. *Musicology Australia,* 28 (2005–2006): 26–58.

Ford L (1997). *Batjamalh dictionary and texts*. Canberra: Panther Press.

Ford L (1990). *The phonology and morphology of Bachamal (Wogait)*. Australian National University, Canberra.

Ford L & Klesch M (2003). 'It won't matter soon, we'll all be dead': endangered languages and action research. *Ngoonjook: Journal of Australian Indigenous Issues*, 23: 27–43.

Ford L, Kungul A & Jongmin J (2000). A sociolinguistic survey of Wadeye: linguistic behaviour of the Marri Ngarr, Magati Ke, Marri Amu and Marri Tjebin. Paper presented at the Top End Linguistic Society meeting, Darwin.

Ford L & Nemarluk E (2003). *Mi-Tjiwilirr i Wulumen Tulh (Hairy cheeky Yam and Old Man Tulh): ancestral knowledge of the Marri Amu Rak Tjindi Malimanhdhi people*. Batchelor, NT: Batchelor Press.

Furlan A (2005). *Songs of continuity and change: the reproduction of Aboriginal culture through traditional and popular music*. Unpublished thesis (PhD). University of Sydney, Sydney.

Green I (1994). The Daly language family: a reassessment, Proto western Daly. Unpublished manuscript prepared for the Comparative Australian Project. Canberra: Australian National University.

Jebb MA (2002). *Blood, sweat and welfare: a history of white bosses and Aboriginal pastoral workers*. Nedlands WA: University of Western Australia Press.

Keen I (1994). *Knowledge and secrecy in Aboriginal religion*. Oxford, UK: Clarendon Press.

Knopoff S (1992). Yuta manikay: juxtaposition of ancestral and contemporary elements in the performances of Yolngu clan songs. *Yearbook for Traditional Music*, 24: 138–53.

Manmurulu D, Apted M & Barwick L (2008, 16 August). Songs from the Inyjalarrku: the use of non-decipherable, non-translatable, non-interpretable language in a set of spirit songs from North-West Arnhem Land. Paper presented at the 2008 Symposium on Indigenous Music and Dance. Charles Darwin University, Darwin.

Marett A (2010). Vanishing songs: how musical extinctions threaten the planet. *Ethnomusicology Forum*, 19(2): 249–62.

Marett A (2007). Simplifying musical practice in order to enhance local identity: The case of rhythmic modes in the Walakandha *wangga* (Wadeye, Northern Territory). *Australian Aboriginal Studies*, 2007(2): 63–75.

Marett A (2005). *Songs, dreamings and ghosts: the wangga of North Australia*. Middletown, CT: Wesleyan University Press.

Marett A (2003). Sound recordings as maruy among the Aborigines of the Daly region of north-west Australia. In L Barwick, A Marett, J Simpson & A Harris (eds). *Researchers, communities, institutions and sound recordings*. Sydney: University of Sydney. Retrieved from hdl.handle.net/2123/1511.

Marett A (2000). Ghostly voices: Some observations on song-creation, ceremony and being in northwest Australia. *Oceania*, 71(1): 18–29.

Marett A & Barwick L (2003). Endangered songs and endangered languages. In J Blythe & RM Brown (eds), *Maintaining the Links: Language Identity and the Land. Seventh conference of the Foundation for Endangered Languages, Broome W.A.* (pp 144–51). Bath, UK: Foundation for Endangered Languages.

Marett A & Barwick L (1993). *Bunggridj-bunggridj: wangga songs by Alan Maralung, northern Australia*. Washington DC: Smithsonian Folkways CD SF40430.

Marett A, Barwick L & Ford L (2001). Rak Badjalarr: *wangga* songs by Bobby Lane, Northern Australia. Audio compact disc of research recordings with accompanying scholarly booklet. Canberra: Aboriginal Studies Press.

Marett A, Yunupiŋu M, Langton M, Gumbula N, Barwick L & Corn A (2006). The National Recording Project for Indigenous Performance in Australia: year one in review. *Backing Our Creativity: the National Education and the Arts Symposium, 12–14 September 2005* (pp 84–90). Surry Hills, NSW: Australia Council for the Arts.

Mountford CP (1948). Expedition to Arnhem Land, 1948. Volume 1, personal journal. Unpublished manuscript. Adelaide, SA.

Moyle AM (1992 [1977]). Australia: Aboriginal Music/Australia: Musique Aborigene. On *UNESCO collection: Music and Musicians of the World/Musiques et Musiciens du Monde* [audio compact disc]. Ivry-sur-Seine: AUVIDIS-UNESCO-IICMSD D8040. Released as an LP in 1977. Released as a CD in 1992.

Moyle AM (1967a). Songs from the Northern Territory. Volume 1 [LP disc recording re-released on audio compact disc 1997]. Canberra: Australian Institute of Aboriginal and Torres Strait Islander Studies.

Moyle AM (1967b). *Songs from the Northern Territory: companion booklet for five 12 inch LP discs (Cat No. I.A.S. M-001/5)*. Canberra: Australian Institute of Aboriginal Studies.

Moyle AM (1966). *A handlist of field collections of recorded music in Australia and Torres Strait*. Canberra: Australian Institute of Aboriginal Studies.

Moyle RM (1979). *Songs of the Pintupi: music in a Central Australian society*. Canberra: Australian Institute of Aboriginal Studies.

Northern Territory of Australia (1957). Register of wards, *Northern Territory Government Gazette No. 19B*, 13 May. Darwin: Northern Territory Government.

Povinelli E (1993). *Labor's lot: the power, history, and culture of aboriginal action*. Chicago: University of Chicago Press.

Sandefur JR (1991). A sketch of the structure of Kriol. In S Romaine (ed.), *Language in Australia* (pp 204–12). Cambridge & Melbourne: Cambridge University Press.

Sansom B (1980). *The camp at Wallaby Cross: Aboriginal fringe dwellers in Darwin*. Canberra: Australian Institute of Aboriginal Studies.

Sharifian F (2006). A cultural-conceptual approach and world Englishes: the case of Aboriginal English. *World Englishes*, 25(1): 11–22.

Sharifian F (2005). Cultural conceptualisations in English words: A study of Aboriginal children in Perth. *Language and Education*, 19(1): 74–88.

Simpson C (1951). *Adam in ochre: inside Aboriginal Australia*. Sydney: Angus & Robertson.

Simpson C (writer) (1948). Delissaville: death rite for Mabalung. Radio feature, 15 March. Sydney: Australian Broadcasting Commission.

Spencer B (1914). *Native tribes of the Northern Territory of Australia*. London: Macmillan.

Stanner WEH (1992). Notebooks c. 1932–1970. Unpublished manuscript, Canberra.

Stanner WEH (1989 [1963]). *On Aboriginal religion*. Sydney: University of Sydney.

Strehlow TGH (1971). *Songs of Central Australia*. Sydney: Angus & Robertson.

Toner P (2003). Melody and the musical articulation of Yolngu identities. *Yearbook for Traditional Music*, 35: 69–95.

Toner P (2001). *When the echos are gone: a Yolngu musical anthropology*. Unpublished PhD thesis. Canberra, Australian National University.

Tryon D (1974). *The Daly family languages*. Canberra: Pacific Linguistics.

Various artists (1991). *Bushfire: traditional Aboriginal music*. Compact disc. Sydney: Larrikin TCLRF-247.

Wildey WB (1876). *Australasia and the Oceanic region, with some notices of New Guinea: from Adelaide—via Torres Straits—to Port Darwin thence round West Australia*. Adelaide: G Robertson.

APPENDIX 1

Characteristics of the rhythmic modes

In this appendix we give more detail on the conventions surrounding each group of rhythmic modes, in particular as regards the accompanying dance. Because of tempo variability between repertoires we first discuss the rhythmic modes in relative terms, without ascribing specific tempi (see discussion of tempo below).

Rhythmic mode 1

In Marri Tjavin this rhythmic mode is termed *ambi tittel* 'without clapsticks', while in Mendhe the equivalent term is *piya-therr nangga* 'without clapsticks'. We first encountered an example of rhythmic mode 1 in our analysis of 'Tjerri' in chapter 2. Songs in this rhythmic mode occur in all repertoires (see cross-repertory analysis below), but are particularly prominent in the Walakandha *wangga* repertory (chapter 8). Together with the absence of stick beating, a key feature of rhythmic mode 1 is the delivery of the text in somewhat metrically irregular speech rhythm. The rhythm of the didjeridu is similarly irregular. Indeed the absence of a regular didjeridu pulse is one of the strongest features of rhythmic mode 1. The degree of coordination between the metrically irregular delivery of the singer and of the didjeridu varies from performer to performer. In cases where the didjeridu player knows the songs well, the rhythm of the didjeridu part may closely follow that of the song; in other cases, there is little coordination. As mentioned above, the dancing executed during vocal sections in rhythmic mode 1 is also metrically unstructured.

Slow rhythmic modes

The majority of slow tempo songs (rhythmic mode 2, known as *derela* 'slow' in Mendhe) use the same clapstick beating pattern throughout. From time to time, it may also occur within an item in two contrasting forms: the usual slow even stick beating (in this case designated rhythmic mode 2a) and a rarer form (rhythmic mode 2b), in which the stick beating is suspended while the slow even pulse is maintained by the didjeridu and voice.[1] The maintenance of a regular coordinated slow pulse by the didjeridu and voice clearly distinguishes rhythmic mode 2b from the other mode that lacks clapstick beating, namely the unmeasured rhythmic mode 1. Sometimes the audience will reinforce the beat by continuing hand clapping even after the stick beating has stopped. For example, in Jimmy Muluk's 'Puliki' (chapter 5, track 1) the first six vocal sections are sung with slow even beating (rhythmic mode 2a) in melodic section 1 of each vocal section, while in melodic section 2 the beating is suspended (rhythmic mode 2b). Another example of suspended slow even beating occurs in Barrtjap's 'Yagarra Delhi Nyebindja-ng Barra Ngarrka' (chapter 4, track 24). In both these cases, the didjeridu pulse continues to clearly articulate a regular duple subdivision of the beat during the suspension of the clapstick beating.

At Belyuen, dancing to rhythmic mode 2a is slow, with regular foot movements cued to the slow clapstick beat. Only one or two dancers perform, representing the ancestral ghosts *wunymalang*. The effect can be eerie and almost menacing. Since clapstick beating refers to the movements of the ancestral beings the songs celebrate, songs with regular slow beating indicate a slow gait, such as the ancestral buffalo swimming (as in Billy Mandji's performance of Muluk's song 'Puliki', chapter 5, track 2). At

---

[1] In the song structure summaries in chapters 4–9, we use the unmarked term 'rhythmic mode 2' for passages of slow even stick beating in songs in which there is no contrast with the suspended form, reserving the use of the 'a' and 'b' terms for songs in which a contrast exists.

Wadeye, where only a few older men remember how to dance rhythmically and slowly to rhythmic mode 2, most dancers nowadays simply perform for rhythmic mode 2 as they would for the unmeasured rhythmic mode 1, that is, with unstructured and unmeasured movements.

Moderate rhythmic modes (tempo bands 3 and 4)

Moderate rhythmic modes are used relatively infrequently, and are found in two tempo bands: slow moderate (rhythmic modes 3a and 3b) and moderate (rhythmic modes 4a, b, c, d, e).

The slow moderate tempo band occurs only in the repertory of Bobby Lambudju Lane, and comprises two rhythmic modes, each used in only one song.

- Rhythmic mode 3a (slow moderate even) is used for 'Tjerrendet' (chapter 7, track 15).

- Rhythmic mode 3b (slow moderate uneven triple) (♩ ♩ 𝄾) is used for 'Walingave' (chapter 7, track 18).

We have never seen dancing for these slow moderate songs, so are unable to comment on any distinguishing characteristics.

There are four rhythmic modes in the moderate tempo band.

- Rhythmic mode 4a (moderate even). For an example, see the Ma-yawa *wangga* song 'Watjendanggi' (chapter 9, tracks 14 and 15). While all repertories use this mode sparingly, if at all, for vocal sections, it is used quite extensively by Jimmy Muluk (chapter 5) in his instrumental sections. In the performance of 'Tjerri' discussed in chapter 9 (track 13) it is used for the first instrumental section.

- Rhythmic mode 4b (moderate uneven quadruple) (♩ ♩ ♩ 𝄾) is used in only two songs: Lambudju's 'Bangany-nyung Nye-bindja-ng' (chapter 7, track 17) and Billy Mandji's 'Song from Anson Bay' (chapter 6, tracks 9 and 10).

- Rhythmic mode 4c (moderate uneven triple) (♩ ♩ 𝄾) is also used in only two songs: Lambudju's 'Karra ve Kan-ya Verver' (chapter 7, tracks 11–12), and Billy Mandji's 'Happy Song No. 4' (chapter 6, track 12) (vocal and instrumental section 1 only).

- Rhythmic mode 4d (moderate uneven quintuple) (♩ ♩ 𝄾 ♩ 𝄾) is used only by Barrtjap and for only three of his songs, 'Yagarra Nga-bindja-ng Nga-mi Ngayi' (chapter 4, track 2), 'Yagarra Tjüt Balk-nga-me Ngami' (chapter 4, track 22) and, 'Ya Rembe Ngaya Lima Ngaya' (chapter 4, track 21), where it is used only in the coda.

- Rhythmic mode 4e (moderate doubled) is used in the final instrumental sections of a number of Jimmy Muluk songs (see table 5.2).

- Rhythmic mode 4*, used only in some internal instrumental sections of the slow versions of Muluk's songs 'Lame Fella' and 'Lerri' (chapter 5, tracks 13 and 19), consists of a sequence of doubled beating followed by even beating in the moderate tempo band (rhythmic mode 4e followed by rhythmic mode 4a). It is comparable in morphology and use to rhythmic mode 5* in the fast tempo band (see further below).

Rhythmic mode 4a also occurs in a variant form, written 'rhythmic mode 4a (var)', which is analogous to rhythmic mode 2b (suspended slow beating). In rhythmic mode 4a (var), which is only used to accompany vocal sections, the beating is very quiet or even absent for most of a text phrase or melodic section, and typically gradually increases in volume. Examples of this occur in Muluk's 'Piyamen.ga' (chapter 5, tracks 10–12) as well as in the early Walakandha *wangga*, in 'Walakandha No. 9a' (chapter 8, track 8). In the latter case, the reintroduction of the beating is done partway through a line without any gradation of volume. Rhythmic mode 4b is given similar treatment in the first vocal section of Mandji's 'Song for Anson Bay' (chapter 6, track 9), where the variant form is designated as rhythmic mode 4b (var).

The dancing used for the moderate tempo band is cued to the clapstick beating and includes similar movements and organisation of the dance space as found for fast rhythmic modes. Moderate tempo songs may indicate a walking motion of the relevant ancestral being.

Fast rhythmic modes (tempo band 5)

Four rhythmic modes (5a–5d) may be distinguished in the fast tempo band, the first three of which are widely used, particularly in instrumental sections, where the most vigorous dancing occurs. In Marri Tjavin these modes are known as *tarsi verri* (literally, 'quick foot').

- Rhythmic mode 5a (fast even). In Mendhe this type of clapstick beating is called *merrguda*. This rhythmic mode is used far more frequently in instrumental sections than in vocal sections. Most singers have only one or two songs that use it for the vocal section—the exception is Billy Mandji, five of whose six fast songs use this mode—and in such cases, the fast even beating is sustained throughout both the vocal and instrumental sections. In two songs Mandji also performs a suspended version of this rhythmic mode (5a [var]) for the first text phrase or two of a vocal section (the pulse being maintained by the didjeridu). This variant form also occurs in Rusty Benmele Moreen's performance of 'Rak Badjalarr' (chapter 7, track 4, vocal section 1). A further variant occurs in Philip Mullumbuk's 'Wedjiwurang' (track 38), where the volume of the clapsticks gradually decreases. Male dancers typically perform stamping movements on alternate legs, synchronising their footsteps with the clapstick beats.[2] This marking of the beat is typically less emphatic in the vocal sections than in instrumental sections, where male dancers perform a highly structured sequence of approaches and stamping movements, with final flourishes performed to synchronise with the clapstick patterns that signal the end of the instrumental section.

- Rhythmic mode 5b (fast doubled) is beating at twice the rate of rhythmic mode 5a. It often includes further interlocking beats inserted by the second singer (as seen, for example, in the version of 'Tjerri' discussed in chapter 2). The steps of the dancers follow the crotchet beat, so that they effectively perform the same movements for this mode as for rhythmic mode 5a. This mode is used extensively for vocal sections by only one songman, Tommy Barrtjap, who uses it for six songs, in five of which vocal sections in rhythmic mode 5b are followed by vocal sections in rhythmic mode 5c (fast uneven quadruple),[3] and in another by rhythmic mode 5a (fast even) (see further below). By far the most extensive use of rhythmic mode 5b is in the final instrumental sections of songs that have vocal sections in rhythmic modes 1 or 2.

- Rhythmic mode 5c (fast uneven quadruple) (♩ ♩ ♩ 𝄽). This rhythmic mode is used extensively in the Ma-yawa *wangga* repertory, where nine of the twelve songs are in this mode, and by Barrtjap, four of whose songs are entirely in this rhythmic mode while a further five have some vocal sections in rhythmic mode 5c and others in 5b. The use of this rhythmic mode by other singers during vocal sections is more limited, though all repertories except the later Walakandha *wangga* have examples of songs in rhythmic mode 5c. With the exception of the examples by Barrtjap just cited (and one song where Billy Mandji uses rhythmic mode 5c only for the first vocal and instrumental section), songs in rhythmic mode 5c are usually sung in this mode throughout.

---

2   As previously mentioned, women mark the beat of the clapsticks by arm movements rather than leg movements.

3   See for example 'Naya Rradja Bangany Nye-ve' (chapter 4, tracks 16–19), a longer analysis of which is contained in *Songs, dreamings and ghosts* (Marett, 2005, pp 174–79).

For this mode dancers typically perform stamping on alternate legs with the three clapstick beats, marking time in the air for the fourth beat (a rest by the sticks). For the next cycle they commence on the opposite leg, giving the pattern [LRL, RLR] over two cycles of the uneven (gapped) clapstick pattern (♩♩♩ 𝄽 ♩♩♩ 𝄽).

- Rhythmic mode 5d (fast uneven triple) (♩♩ 𝄽). This occurs in vocal sections in one song only, Lambudju's 'Rak Badjalarr' (chapter 7, track 1). It is, however, used in instrumental sections and codas by Barrtjap (see table 4.2). As for rhythmic mode 5c, dancers synchronise their footfalls with the clapstick beats, marking time with a kick in the air for the clapstick rest, giving the repeated pattern [RL,RL,RL] (or [LR,LR,LR]). This produces a marked impression of limping or lameness, which is frequently cited as an attribute of *wunymalang* ghosts. As mentioned in chapter 7, this song is regarded as particularly powerful in calling up these ancestral ghosts.

- Rhythmic mode 5e (fast uneven sextuple) (♩♩♩♩♩ 𝄽) is used only in Benmele's performance of 'Rak Badjalarr' (chapter 7, track 4). Presumably this would be danced in a similar style to the other uneven rhythmic modes, that is, with alternate leg stamping followed by a kick in the air on the clapstick rest, giving the pattern [RLRLR,LRLRL].

- There is also a mixed fast rhythmic mode, designated as 5*, which is used only in instrumental sections in some songs in the Walakandha *wangga* and Ma-yawa *wangga* repertories.[4] It consists of a sequence of fast doubled beating (rhythmic mode 5b) followed by fast even beating (rhythmic mode 5a) followed by the 'Walakandha *wangga* cueing pattern'. It is comparable to Jimmy Muluk's use of a similar sequence in the moderate tempo band (rhythmic mode 4*). Both 4* and 5* constitute cases of mixed rhythmic mode.

---

4   For the Walakandha *wangga*, it is used in 'Walakandha No. 6', 'Ngiimb-andja', 'Walakandha No. 9b', and 'Yenmilhi No. 2' (chapter 8, tracks 2, 4, 9 and 11), and in the Ma-yawa *wangga* repertory in 'Rtadi-wunbirri', where it is used in one internal instrumental section (chapter 9, track 9).

APPENDIX 2

List of recordings

Code	AIATSIS	Details
?Hodd82	-	Recording of Thomas Kungiung singing Walakandha *wangga*, possibly recording by Bill Hoddinott c. 1982. Location of original recording unknown. This copy lodged at the Wadeye Aboriginal Languages Centre.
AF2002-03	-	Kenny Burrenjuck singing at a ceremony for the launch of 'Rak Badjalarr' CD, Belyuen, 2002, recorded by Alberto Furlan, DAT tape.
Cro00-01	-	Elicited recording of Maurice Ngulkur singing Ma-yawa *wangga* made by Mark Crocombe at Wadeye in May 2000. Cassette recording. Original lodged at Wadeye Language Centre.
Croc04	-	Elicited recording of Philip Mullumbuk singing 'Wedjiwurang'. Recorded at Wadeye by Mark Crocombe, 2004
Elk52-19B	A4691A	Jimmy Bandak singing *wangga*, recorded at Delissaville (Belyuen) by AP Elkin on 9 June 1952. 'University of Sydney, Arnhem Land Expedition 1952.' 17x16 (13–29) RPX6817–6833. Columbia Gramophone Company (Aust), Sydney. AIATSIS: A4691a.
Eni92	-	Circumcision ceremony at Wadeye, recorded by Michael Enilane, 1992 (precise date unknown). Recording lodged at the Wadeye Aboriginal Languages Centre.
Kof86-01_4	-	Thomas Kungiung and others singing Walakandha *wangga*, recorded by Frances Kofod at Wadeye, 16 and 17 June 1986. Original recording held by the recordist.
Mad64-02	A1131	Lawrence Wurrpen singing Barrtjap *wangga*. Recorded at Beswick Creek (Bamyili/Barunga) by Ken Maddock. 15 November 1964.
Mar86-03	A16734–5	Tommy Barrtjap singing his *wangga*. Recorded at Belyuen by Allan Marett on 24 June 1986. Nagra reel to reel.
Mar86-04	A16736–7	Lambudju (Bobby Lane) singing his *wangga*. Recorded at Belyuen by Allan Marett on 24 June 1986. Nagra reel to reel.
Mar88-04_05	A16792–3	Tommy Barrtjap singing his *wangga*. Recorded at Belyuen by Allan Marett on 22 March 1988. Nagra reel to reel.
Mar88-23_24	A16812–14	Recording of a circumcision ceremony made by Allan Marett at Wadeye on 17 May 1988. Nagra reel to reel.
Mar88-30	A16820	Elicited recording made by Allan Marett at Peppimenarti on 6 June 1988. Nagra reel to reel.
Mar88-39	A16829	Recording of a *burn-im-rag* ceremony made by Allan Marett at Nadirri on 19 June 1988. Nagra reel to reel.
Mar88-40_42	A16830–32	Recording of a *burn-im-rag* ceremony made by Allan Marett at Batchelor on 11 September 1988. Nagra reel to reel.
Mar88-54	A16930	Elicited recording made by Allan Marett at Peppimenarti on 20 November 1988. Nagra reel to reel.
Mar91-04	A16938	Elicited performance recorded at Belyuen by Allan Marett on 15 November 1991. Nagra reel to reel.
Mar97-04	A16963–64	Informal performance recorded at Belyuen by Allan Marett on 31 July 1997. DAT tape.
Mar97-05	A16966–67	Elicited performance recorded by Allan Marett and Linda Barwick at Belyuen on 1 August 1997. DAT recording.

Code	AIATSIS	Details
Mar97-13-14	A16974–75	Informal performance recorded at Mandorah by Allan Marett on 8 November 1997. Cassette tape. (Mar97:14 is not catalogued by AIATSIS).
Mar98-07	A17050–51	Elicited recording by Allan Marett made at Wadeye on 23 September 1998. DAT recording.
Mar98-14	A17069	Elicited recording by Allan Marett made at Wadeye on 6 October 1998. DAT recording.
Mar98-15	A17070–72	Elicited recording made by Allan Marett at Wadeye on 15 October 1998. DAT recording.
Mar98-16	A17073	Recording of singing before a bravery award ceremony made by Allan Marett at Peppimenarti on 7 October 1998. DAT recording.
Mar99-01	A17080–82	Elicited recording made by Allan Marett at Wadeye on 6 July 1999. DAT recording.
Mar99-02	A17083–84	Recording of a funeral made by Allan Marett at Wadeye on 9 July 1999. DAT recording.
Mar99-04	A17087–88	Elicited recording made by Allan Marett at Wadeye on 21 July 1999. DAT recording.
Moy59-03	A1243	Elicited performance recorded by Alice Moyle in 1959 (precise date unknown).
Moy62-01	A1370	Elicited performance recorded by Alice Moyle at Bagot on 21 May 1962.
Moy62-26	A1379	Recorded by Alice Moyle at a *burn-im-rag* ceremony at Bagot 12 July 1962.
Moy62-27	A1379	Recorded by Alice Moyle at the Darwin Eisteddfod, 13 July 1962.
Moy68-01_2	A1143a	Tourist corroboree recorded by Alice Moyle at Mandorah, 2 June 1968.
Moy68-02_4	A1143a–b	Elicited performance recorded by Alice Moyle at Delissaville (Belyuen) 3 June 1968.
Moy68-05	A1144a	Elicited performance recorded at Delissaville (Belyuen) by Alice Moyle on 3 June 1968.
Rei74-01	-	Recording of a circumcision ceremony made by Lesley Reilly (nee Rourke) at Wadeye in 1974. Cassette recording. AIATSIS: as yet uncatalogued.
Tre08-01	-	Elicited recording made by Sally Treloyn at Lee Point (Darwin) in 2008. Flash-RAM recording.
WASA23	-	Recording dated 1992 held by Wadeye Language Centre at DO23. Recordist and precise date unknown. Location of original unknown.
Wes61	LA399B	Recorded at Beswick Creek (Barunga) by LaMont West on 24 October and 7 November 1961.

ABOUT THE AUTHORS

Allan Marett

Allan Marett is emeritus professor of musicology at the University of Sydney, where he was professor and head of department until 2007. He was a founding director of the National Recording Project for Indigenous Performance in Australia—an initiative that aims to record and document the highly endangered traditions of Australian Indigenous music and dance. His book *Songs, dreamings and ghosts: the wangga of north Australia* won the 2006 Stanner Award, and the CD *Rak badjalarr: wangga songs by Bobby Lane, northern Australia*, which he co-authored with Linda Barwick and Lysbeth Ford, won a Northern Territory Indigenous Music award. Together with Linda Barwick and others, he has edited a number of anthologies of writing on Australian Indigenous music and endangered cultures. His current research focuses on the classical song traditions of Western Arnhem Land as well as the music and culture of the Daly region, where he has worked for more than twenty-five years. Marett is also active in the field of Sino–Japanese music history. He is a past president of the Musicological Society of Australia and past vice-president of the International Council for Traditional Music.

Linda Barwick

Linda Barwick is an associate professor (research only) at the University of Sydney and Director of the Pacific and Regional Archive for Digital Sources in Endangered Cultures (PARADISEC), an internationally acclaimed research facility established in 2003 by a number of Australian universities, led by the University of Sydney with support from the Australian Research Council (ARC). She is an ethnomusicologist who has undertaken fieldwork in Australia, Italy and the Philippines, and is particularly interested in the uses of digital technologies for extending access to research results by cultural-heritage communities. Recent song documentation projects include the ARC-funded Murriny Patha song project, the Western Arnhem Land song project, funded by the Hans Rausing Endangered Languages Program (School of Oriental and African Studies, University of London), and the Iwaidja Documentation Project, funded by the Volkswagen Stiftung (based in the Max Planck Institute, Nijmegen). Her many publications include multimedia CDs accompanied by extensive scholarly notes, produced in collaboration with Indigenous singers and their communities. She has contributed to a number of initiatives to develop awareness and capacity in the digital humanities, including the Australian e-Humanities Network and several projects funded under the ARC's e-research special research initiatives program.

Lysbeth Ford

Dr Lysbeth Julie Ford, research associate of the University of Sydney, is a linguist who has spent thirty years working with the last fluent speakers of four endangered Aboriginal languages from the Daly River region of Australia's Northern Territory to document these morphologically complex languages. She has published grammars and dictionaries of these languages and, since 1994, collaborated with the University of Sydney's ethnomusicologists Allan Marett and Linda Barwick to document the extensive song repertories of the song men from these language groups. She is currently collaborating with a Yolngu woman elder from Elcho Island in the north-east of the NT to document *milkarri*, the women's keening songs unique to this region.

While working for the Batchelor Institute of Indigenous Tertiary Education, Lysbeth Ford trained many Indigenous linguists and taught semi-speakers of Indigenous languages literacy in these languages. In 1997, she co-authored a book about PhD education for mature-age students, and has contributed to recent ARC reports on Aboriginal English, and Indigenous secondary and post-secondary education in the Northern Territory. Since 2006, she has been based in Tasmania, but continues to undertake short-term consultancies in the field of language maintenance.

LIST OF CD TRACKS
CD 1: Barrtjap repertory (chapter 4)

These tracks are available online at wangga.library.usyd.edu.au as well as in a separetely issued set of CDs available from Sydney University Press.

Track	Song Number	Title	Recording
Track 01	1	Ya Bangany-nyung Nga-bindja Yagarra	Moy68-05-s02
Track 02	2	Yagarra Nga-bindja-ng Nga-mi Ngayi	Moy68-05-s03
Track 03	3	Bangany-nyung Ngaya	Moy68-05-s04
Track 04		Bangany-nyung Ngaya	Moy68-05-s05
Track 05	4	Kanga Rinyala Nga-ve Bangany-nyung	Moy68-05-s06
Track 06		Kanga Rinyala Nga-ve Bangany-nyung	Moy68-05-s07
Track 07	5	Ya[garra] Nga-bindja-ng Nga-mi	Moy68-05-s08
Track 08		Ya[garra] Nga-bindja-ng Nga-mi	Moy68-05-s09
Track 09	6	Yagarra Bangany Nye-ngwe	Moy68-05-s10
Track 10	7	Be Bangany-nyaya	Moy68-05-s11
Track 11	8	Nyere-nyere Lima Kaldja	Mar88-04-s02
Track 12	9	Nyere-nye Bangany Nyaye	Mar88-04-s03
Track 13	10	Karra Ngadja-maka Nga-bindja-ng Ngami	Mar88-04-s07
Track 14	11	Yerre Ka-bindja-maka Ka-mi	Mar88-05-s11
Track 15	12	Yagarra Ye-yenenaya	Mar88-05-s02
Track 16	13	Naya Rradja Bangany Nye-ve	Elk52-19B-s04
Track 17		Naya Rradja Bangany Nye-ve	Mar97-04-s16
Track 18		Naya Rradja Bangany Nye-ve	Mad64-02-s15
Track 19		Naya Rradja Bangany Nye-ve	Mar88-05-s03
Track 20	14	Yagarra Nedja Tjine Rak-pe	Mar88-05-s06
Track 21	15	Ya Rembe Ngaya Lima Ngaya	Mar88-05-s13
Track 22	16	Yagarra Tjüt Balk-nga-me Nga-mi	Mar86-03-s04
Track 23	17	Yagarra Tjine Rak-pe	Mar86-03-s06
Track 24	18	Yagarra Delhi Nya-ngadja-barra-ngarrka	Mar86-03-s05
Track 25	19	Nga-ngat-pat-pa Mangalimba	Mar97-04-s07
Track 26	22	Anadadada Bangany-nyaya	Mar97-04-s04

CD2: Muluk repertory (chapter 5)

Track	Song Number	Title	Recording
Track 01	1	Puliki (Buffalo)	Moy68-02-s05
Track 02		Puliki (Buffalo)	Moy68-01-s04
Track 03		Puliki (Buffalo)	Moy62-27-s05
Track 04		Puliki (Buffalo)	Mar97-13A-s05
Track 05	2	Tjinbarambara (Seagull)	Moy68-02-s02
Track 06		Tjinbarambara (Seagull)	Mar97-13A-s04
Track 07	3	Wak (Crow)	Moy68-02-s03
Track 08	4	Wörörö (Crab)	Moy68-02-s04
Track 09	5	Pumandjin (Place name: a hill)	Moy62-26-s21
Track 10	6	Piyamen.ga (Shady Tree) Two items	Moy62-26-s15_16
Track 11		Piyamen.ga (Shady Tree)	Moy62-26-s17
Track 12		Piyamen.ga (Shady Tree) Two items	Moy62-26-s18_19
Track 13	7	Lame Fella	Moy62-26-s06
Track 14		Lame Fella	Moy62-26-s09
Track 15	8	Rtadi-thawara (Walking on the Mangroves)	Moy62-26-s10
Track 16		Rtadi-thawara (Walking on the Mangroves)	Moy62-26-s11_12
Track 17		Rtadi-thawara (Walking on the Mangroves)	Moy62-26-s13_14
Track 18		Rtadi-thawara (Walking on the Mangroves)	AF2002-03-s03
Track 19	9	Lerri (Happy Dance)	Moy62-26-s22_23
Track 20		Lerri (Happy Dance)	Moy62-26-s24

CD3: Mandji repertory (chapter 6)

Track	Song Number	Title	Recording
Track 01	1	Duwun	Moy62-27-s09
Track 02		Duwun	Mar88-40-s12
Track 03	2	Happy (lerri) Song No.1	Moy68-01-s01
Track 04		Happy (lerri) Song No.1	Mar88-41-s04
Track 05	3	Happy (lerri) Song No.2	Moy68-01-s02
Track 06	4	Happy Song No. 3	Moy62-27-s10
Track 07	5	Duwun crab song	Moy68-01-s03
Track 08	6	Karra Mele Ngany-endheni-nö	Mar88-40-s13
Track 09	7	Song from Anson Bay	Moy59-03-s03
Track 10		Song from Anson Bay	Moy59-03-s04
Track 11	8	Robert Man.guna's Song	Moy62-27-s08
Track 12	9	Happy (lerri) Song No. 4	Mar88-40-s09
Track 13	10	Happy (lerri) Song No. 5	Mar88-42-s04
Track 14	11	Happy (lerri) Song No. 6	Mar88-42-s05

CD4: Lambudju repertory (chapter 7)

Track	Song Number	Title	Recording
Track 01	1	Rak Badjalarr	Mar86-04-s07
Track 02		Rak Badjalarr	Moy62-01-s01
Track 03		Rak Badjalarr	Wes61-s15
Track 04		Rak Badjalarr	Wes61-s25
Track 05		Rak Badjalarr	Mar97-13-s13
Track 06		Rak Badjalarr	Tre08-01-s26
Track 07	2	Bandawarra-ngalgin	Mar86-04-s02
Track 08		Bandawarra-ngalgin	Mar86-04-s03
Track 09		Bandawarra-ngalgin	Mar86-04-s04
Track 10	3	Karra Balhak Malvak	Mar86-04-s09
Track 11	4	Karra-ve kanya-verver	Mar86-04-s01
Track 12		Karra-ve kanya-verver	Moy62-01-s02
Track 13	5	Benmele	Mar86-04-s10
Track 14	6	Winmedje	Mar86-04-s06
Track 15	7	Tjerrendet	Mar86-04-s05
Track 16	8	Tjendabalhatj	Mar86-04-s11
Track 17	9	Bangany Nye-bindja-ng	Mar91-04-s04
Track 18	10	Walingave	Mar91-04-s05
Track 19	11	Djappana	Mar91-05-s04
Track 20		Djappana	Mar91-05-s05
Track 21		Djappana	Mar91-05-s06
Track 22		Djappana	Mar91-05-s07
Track 23	12	Karra Balhak-ve	Moy59-03-s01_02
Track 24	13	Lima Rak-pe	Moy62-01-s03
Track 25	14	Mubagandi	Mar97-05-s01
Track 26		Mubagandi	Mar97-05-s02
Track 27		Mubagandi	Mar97-05-s03
Track 28	15	Bende Ribene	Tre08-01-s08
Track 29	16	Limila Karrawala	Tre08-01-s14

CD5: Walakandha *wangga* repertory (chapter 8)

Track	Song Number	Title	Recording
Track 01	(i-a)	Walakandha No. 8	Kof86-03-s07
Track 02	ii	Walakandha No. 6	Rei74-01-s15
Track 03	iii	Wutjelli No. 2	Rei74-01-s16
Track 04	iv	Nginimb-andja (2 items)	Rei74-01-s19
Track 05	v	Walakandha No. 7	Mar99-04-s18
Track 06	i-a	Walakandha No. 8a (RM 5c)	?Hodd82-s01
Track 07	i-b	Walakandha No. 8b (RM 4a)	?Hodd82-s04
Track 08	vi-a	Walakandha No. 9a (RM 1+4a)	?Hodd82-s02
Track 09	vi-b	Walakandha No. 9b (RM1)	?Hodd82-s03
Track 10	vii	Yendili No. 6	?Hodd82-s06
Track 11	viii	Yenmilhi No. 2	?Hodd82-s08
Track 12	1	Kubuwemi	Mar88-23-s02
Track 13	2	Yendili No. 1	Mar88-23-s03
Track 14	3	Yendili No. 2	Mar88-23-s08
Track 15	4	Walakandha No. 1	Mar88-24-s02
Track 16	5a	Truwu [Truwu A melody]	Mar88-39-s02
Track 17	5b	Truwu [Truwu B melody]	Mar99-02-s14
Track 18	5c	Truwu [Truwu A/B melody]	Eni92-s08
Track 19	6	Nadirri	Mar88-30-s15
Track 20	7	Yenmilhi No. 1	Mar88-54-s03
Track 21	8	Mirrwana	Mar88-40-s11
Track 22	9	Wutjelli No. 1	Eni92-s11
Track 23	10	Walakandha No. 2	Eni92-s06
Track 24	11	Pumurriyi (2 items)	Kof86-01/2-s15
Track 25	12	Thidha ngany (2 items)	Kof86-01/2-s11
Track 26	13	Dhembedi–ndjen	Kof86-01/2-s12
Track 27	14	Tjagawala	Kof86-03/4-s10
Track 28	15	Karra	Kof86-03/4-s09
Track 29	16	Yendili No. 5	WASA23-s06
Track 30	17	Yendili No. 3	Mar98-15-s06
Track 31	18	Lhambumen	Mar99-04-s16
Track 32	19	Yendili No. 4	Eni92-s24
Track 33	20	Walakandha No. 3	Mar99-04-s07
Track 34	21	Karra yeri-ngina	Mar99-04-s08
Track 35	22	Walakandha No. 4	Mar99-04-s10

Track	Song Number	Title	Recording
Track 36	23	Walakandha No. 5	Mar98-15-s21
Track 37	24	Kinyirr	Mar99-04-s21
Track 38	25	Wedjiwurang	Croc04-01-s01
Track 39	26	Tjinmel	Mar98-07-s11

CD6: Ma-yawa *wangga* repertory (chapter 9)

Track	Song Number	Title	Recording
Track 01	1	Walakandha Ngindji	Mar98-14-s01
Track 02		Walakandha Ngindji	Mar98-14-s02
Track 03		Walakandha Ngindji	Mar98-16-s01
Track 04	2	Wulumen Kimigimi	Mar98-14-s03
Track 05		Wulumen Kimigimi	Mar98-14-s04
Track 06	3	Rtadi-wunbirri	Mar98-16-s02
Track 07		Rtadi-wunbirri	Mar98-16-s03
Track 08		Rtadi-wunbirri	Mar98-16-s04
Track 09		Rtadi-wunbirri	Mar98-16-s05
Track 10	4	Menggani	Mar98-14-s05
Track 11		Menggani	Mar98-14-s06
Track 12	5	Tjerri	Mar98-14-s07
Track 13		Tjerri	Mar98-14-s08
Track 14	6	Watjen Danggi	Mar98-14-s09
Track 15		Watjen Danggi	Mar98-14-s10
Track 16	7	Malhimanyirr	Mar98-14-s11
Track 17		Malhimanyirr	Mar98-14-s12
Track 18	8	Ma-vindivindi	Mar98-14-s13
Track 19		Ma-vindivindi	Mar98-14-s14
Track 20	9	Karri-ngindji	Mar98-14-s15
Track 21		Karri-ngindji	Mar98-14-s16
Track 22	10	Thali-ngatjpirr	Mar98-14-s17
Track 23		Thali-ngatjpirr	Mar98-14-s18
Track 24		Thali-ngatjpirr	Tre08-01-s17
Track 25	11	Na-Pebel	Mar99-01-s01
Track 26		Na-Pebel	Mar99-01-s02
Track 27		Na-Pebel	Mar99-01-s03
Track 28	12	Wulumen Tulh	Cro00-01-s07
Track 29		Wulumen Tulh	Cro00-01-s08

INDEX

A

Aboriginal languages
  Aboriginal English 25–26, 38, 86, 193, 365
  Batjamalh 23, 25–26, 30–32, 35–36, 49, 65–89, 93, 96, 105, 118, 125, 129, 135, 145–146, 149, 159, 239, 255, 260, 263, 272. *See also* Wadjiginy people
  Daly languages 23, 75
  Emmi 23, 26, 30, 32–33, 65–70, 76–88, 159, 165, 219, 222, 226–227, 234, 236–237, 239, 255, 268, 272. *See also* Emmiyangal people
  Marri Ammu 23, 26, 36, 38, 41, 56, 65–70, 72, 76–78, 83–89, 167, 282, 302, 318, 355–356, 359–360, 365–366, 372, 378, 381, 384, 388, 392, 407. *See also* Marri Ammu language group
  Marri Tjavin 23, 25–26, 32–33, 35–36, 38–39, 41, 56, 62, 65–70, 72, 76–78, 83–90, 165, 167, 219, 228–230, 234, 237, 247, 281–282, 297, 302, 304–305, 307–309, 313, 334, 337, 346, 355–356, 359–360, 384, 407. *See also* Marri Tjavin language group
  Mendhe 23, 26, 30, 32, 65–70, 77–90, 155, 159, 164–165, 172, 178, 193, 195, 197, 210, 215–218, 219, 221, 223, 228–230, 234, 236–237. *See also* Mendheyangal people
  Murriny Patha 23, 36–39, 66, 83, 172, 281, 329, 375, 378. *See also* Murriny Patha language group
Ahmat, George 33, 219
Alalk 239, 253, 269
'Anadadada Bangany-nyaya' 94, 147–150
Anson Bay 30, 32, 36, 149, 213, 221, 226, 231–232
Arnhem Land 23, 36, 41, 49, 234, 356

B

Badjalarr (North Peron Island). *See* North Peron Island (Badjalarr)
Banakula (Red Cliff) 118
Bandak, Jimmy 26, 32, 56–57, 93, 130–131, 140, 253
Bandawarra Ngalgin [place] 249, 253

'Bandawarra-ngalgin' [song] 214, 240, 249–252, 276–280
'Bangany Nye-bindja-ng' 240, 263, 276, 278
'Bangany-nyung Ngaya' 49, 53, 94, 101–103, 150
Barakbana (South Peron Island). *See* South Peron Island (Barakbana)
Barradjap, Tommy. *See* Barrtjap (Barandjak, Burrenjuck, Barradjap), Tommy
Barrtjap (Barandjak, Burrenjuck, Barradjap), Tommy 26, 31, 32, 35, 38, 46, 56, 68, 92, 95, 144, 218, 240, 245, 352. *See also* Barrtjap's *wangga*
Barrtjap's *wangga* 93–154
Barunga (Beswick Creek, Old Beswick) 23, 40, 42, 132, 242, 245
Barwick, Linda 27, 28, 66, 145, 179, 205, 218, 220
Batjamalh. *See* Aboriginal languages: Batjamalh
'Be Bangany-nyaya' 94, 114–118, 150–154
Belyuen (Delissaville). *See also* Wadjiginy people
  ceremonies 27–30, 35, 93, 130, 144–145, 155–156, 159, 205, 240, 262
  community 23, 25, 30–31, 76, 135, 219
  dance 27, 31, 35, 47, 93, 95, 158, 175, 179, 192, 218, 223, 237, 265, 273
  language 65–66, 77, 234
  lineages 30, 32–33, 36, 56, 132, 155, 234, 247
  song dreaming 32–33, 143, 147, 242, 260
  wangga 23, 25, 26, 29–30, 32, 34–36, 38, 42, 45, 49–50, 57, 59, 69, 93, 140, 151, 164, 218, 220, 224, 239, 242, 245, 247–248, 275, 278, 285–286, 292, 352
'Bende Ribene' 77, 240–241, 274, 278, 280
Benmele. *See* Moreen, Rusty Benmele
'Benmele' [song] 240–241, 245, 259–260, 262, 276, 278
Berrida [ancestor] 281, 332
Berrida family 85, 307, 332–333
Beswick Creek 33, 132, 242, 245
Bickford, Boy. *See* Bigfoot, Roy Mardi
Bigfoot, Roy Mardi 218, 261
Bilbil, Ian 34, 224
Bilbil, Marjorie 32, 218
Birrarri, Joe Malakunda 37, 40–41
body painting 25, 43, 53
Brinken, Charlie Niwilhi ('Charlie Port Keats') 26, 41, 355–358, 364, 402

burnim-rag ceremonies 13, 25–27, 27–30, 33, 35, 38–40, 42, 100, 105, 130–131, 156, 164, 178, 223, 225, 228, 233, 237, 262, 307, 313, 329, 355–357, 378. *See also* funeral ceremonies
Burrenjuck, Esther 135
Burrenjuck family 93, 147, 152
Burrenjuck, Kenny 13, 26, 32, 34–35, 66, 93–94, 102, 105, 130, 135, 144–145, 147, 156, 205, 219, 224
Burrenjuck, Timothy 32, 34–35, 93
Burrenjuck, Tommy. *See* Barrtjap (Barandjak, Burrenjuck, Barradjap), Tommy

C

Central Australia 31, 356
ceremonial leaders. *See* ritual leaders and specialists
ceremonial reciprocity 29, 37–39, 281, 355
Christianity, influence of 25, 39, 42, 284. *See also* Roman Catholic missions
Chula, John 288, 302
circumcision ceremonies 25, 48, 378
    Belyuen 29
    Wadeye 24, 28–29, 37, 37–39, 50–51, 212, 286, 302–303, 309, 315, 317, 328, 355, 361
clapstick beating
    and dance phrases 49
    and rhythmic modes 47, 52, 58, 60
    Barrtjap's *wangga* 135, 217
    conventions of 48, 59–62
    Lambudju's *wangga* 280
    Manji's *wangga* 231, 234, 237
    Ma-yawa *wangga* 370
    Muluk's *wangga* 213, 215–216
    Walakandha *wangga* 293, 338, 352
Cleverly, John 33, 219, 221
codas, conventions of 45–46, 60–62
composition. *See* song creation (dreaming songs)
conventions of *wangga* 45–64
corroborees 31, 33, 35, 47, 155–156, 158–159, 167, 172, 175, 192, 193, 209, 218, 233, 240
    corroborees for tourists 30–31, 33–35, 47, 93, 155–156, 159, 165, 172, 174, 227
country, attachment and ties to 29–30, 36–38, 39, 77, 83, 118, 120, 135, 141, 149, 152, 155, 159, 174, 226, 242–247, 249, 260, 267, 279–280, 282, 289, 303, 309, 317, 323, 326, 359, 378. *See also* Dreaming sites (*kigatiya*)

Cox Peninsula 30–31, 35, 77, 93, 135, 152, 155–156, 221, 243, 260. *See also* Belyuen (Delissaville); Larrakiya people
Crocombe, Mark 24, 28, 41, 50–51, 281, 288, 302–303, 355, 357, 361

D

Daly region 23, 25, 30, 33, 36–39, 49, 56, 93, 223, 226, 242
dance. *See also* number four leg; women: women's dance
    and clapstick beating 48
    artistic representations of 250, 356, 402
    Barrtjap's *wangga* 96
    circumcision ceremonies 37
    conventions of 23, 25, 36–38, 45, 49, 82, 219
    Lambudju's *wangga* 249–252, 263–265
    Mandji's *wangga* 223, 225, 227
    Ma-yawa *wangga* 366
    Muluk's *wangga* 155–156, 158–163, 165, 192
    performed during ceremonies 27, 30, 35, 47, 50–51
    rhythmic modes 49, 54, 212
    Walakandha *wangga* 281–282, 311
Darwin eisteddfod 33, 156, 159, 164
Darwin region 23, 30–31, 33–34, 36, 40, 65–66, 77, 93, 155–157, 159, 164, 219, 221, 226–227, 357
death 26–27, 29, 39, 165, 172, 240, 259, 281, 309, 318, 321–322, 331, 332, 378. *See also* burnim-rag ceremonies; funeral ceremonies
Delissaville. *See* Belyuen (Delissaville)
'Dhembedi-ndjen' 283, 302, 320–321, 353
didjeridu 24–26, 30–31, 35, 41, 45, 48–49, 52–55, 96, 100, 105, 132, 149, 152–153, 178, 213–216, 218, 224, 236, 263, 274, 278, 280, 289, 302, 310, 324, 349, 355–356, 362, 365–372, 378, 393
    kanbi (didjeridu in Marri Tjavin) 355
    kenbi (didjeridu in Batjamalh) 25, 224, 355
didjeridu mouth sounds 52, 100, 105, 132, 149
dingo 356, 378–380. *See also* 'Watjen-danggi'
djanba genre 23, 27, 29, 33, 37–39, 41, 56, 219, 281, 329
'Djappana' 241, 268–269, 277
Docherty, Richard (Father) 36–37
Doyle, John 240
Dreaming (*altjira*, *durlk*, *ngirrwat*) 49, 57, 90, 356, 372, 375. *See also* song creation

428 • For the sake of a song

(dreaming songs); totems and totemic sites

Dreaming sites (*kigatiya*) 49, 57, 86, 89–90. *See also* totems and totemic sites
  Barrtjap's *wangga* 143, 152
  Ma-yawa *wangga* 356, 371–372, 378, 381, 384, 388, 389, 392, 407
  Walakandha *wangga* 282, 304, 336, 343
Dumoo, Basil 41
Dumoo, Claver 323
Dumoo family 42, 57, 331
Dumoo, Frank 37–38, 40–42, 51, 85, 90, 281, 285, 291, 298, 302, 323, 355, 357, 393
Dumoo, John 283, 292, 302, 311, 323, 324, 350, 355
Dumoo, Maudie Attaying 89, 283, 305, 325, 328, 351–352
Dumoo, Terence 283, 317, 323, 350–351, 359
Dumoo, Wagon 26, 40, 42, 283, 298–299, 302–303, 304–305, 321–322, 324, 326, 329, 331, 349–351
'Duwun Crab Song' 221, 226, 233–236, 286
Duwun (Indian Island) 80, 143, 221–223, 234, 239. *See also* 'Duwun' [song]
'Duwun' [song] 221–223, 233–237

E

Elkin, AP 29–30, 33–34, 56, 93–94, 130
Ellis, Catherine 356, 407
Emmiyangal people 23, 30, 32–33, 35, 65–66, 77–78, 219, 221, 226, 233–234, 239, 272
Enda, Brian 266–267
endangered languages 26, 65–66. *See also* language of *wangga*

F

Ferguson, Colin Worumbu 26, 31–33, 35–36, 40–42, 56–57, 90, 156, 159, 164–166, 212, 219, 221, 242–243, 247, 267, 274, 276, 355, 357, 393
Ferguson, Harry 32
Ford, Lysbeth 26, 66, 105, 145–146, 156, 159, 218
fresh water 29, 391–392. *See also* wudi-pumin-iny (spring); salt water
funeral ceremonies 13, 25, 41, 309
Furlan, Alberto 29, 34–35, 39, 156, 205, 219

G

Garinyi, Dolly 130
ghost language 27, 29, 40
ghosts 29–30, 56–57, 147, 233, 248. *See also* song-giving ghosts
  ancestral 27, 49–50, 355–356
  cosmology and ceremony 69
  ghost language 93, 105, 113, 118, 149, 151, 159, 164, 178, 193, 195, 197, 206, 210, 214–217, 219, 222, 225–227, 231, 233–234, 236, 240, 276, 346, 405
  ngutj (ghosts in Emmi-Mendhe) 159, 178–180, 183–185, 216, 231
  song-giving ghosts 23, 25–27, 36, 56, 96, 100–101, 105, 108, 121, 123, 125, 135, 140, 149, 172, 178–179, 193, 222, 228, 234, 260, 263, 279, 281, 287, 309, 313, 317, 384
  totemic 155, 228
  wunymalang (ghosts in Batjamalh) 32, 68, 93, 96, 100–101, 105, 123, 141–142, 242, 255
Gordon, Robert 26, 155–156, 159, 164–165
Gordon, Thomas 33, 156, 164
Gumbuduk, James 164

H

Hairy Cheeky Yam Dreaming (*tjiwilirr*) 90, 398–399, 401–402. *See also* 'Wulumen Tulh'
Hairy Cheeky Yam Dreaming (Wilha) 143, 152. *See also* 'Yagarra Delhi Nye-bindja-ng Barra Ngarrka'
'Happy (*lerri*) Song No. 1' 221, 223–225, 234–237
'Happy (*lerri*) Song No. 2' 221, 225–226, 233–237
'Happy (*lerri*) Song No. 3' 221, 226, 235, 237–238
'Happy (*lerri*) Song No. 4' 221, 233, 235–238
'Happy (*lerri*) Song No. 5' 221, 233–235
'Happy (*lerri*) Song No. 6' 221, 233, 235
happy (*lerri*) songs 118, 120, 125, 129, 136, 138, 151, 153, 157, 206, 233. *See also* 'Lerri'
Haritos, Adrienne 239, 275
Havelock, Jimmy 95, 140
Headache Dreaming (Pumut) 88, 281–282, 331–332. *See also* 'Karra Yeri-ngina'
health 30, 37
Hoddinott, Bill 292

I

imitation 56, 164
Indian Island. *See* Duwun (Indian Island)
instrumental introductions, conventions of 45, 52–53
instrumental sections, conventions of 25–26, 45–46, 49, 52, 54–55, 58, 60–62

J

Jongmin, Bob Wak 66
Jorrock, Alice 159
Jorrock, Henry 179, 218
Jorrock, Nicky 280
Junglefowl Dreaming (Malhimanyirr) 90, 381–382, 384

K

Kanamgek. *See* Rainbow Serpent Dreaming (Kanamgek, Kunmanggurr)
'Kanga Rinyala Nga-ve Bangany-nyung' 69, 94, 105–107, 150, 213
kapuk. *See* burnim-rag ceremonies; *See* ritual washing (*kapuk*)
karra. *See* vocables (untranslatable)
'Karra' 283, 306, 322, 347, 350
'Karra Balhak Malvak' 240–241, 253–255, 267, 272, 277–279
'Karra Balhak-ve' 241, 269–271, 277, 278, 280
'Karra Bangany-nyaya Nga-p-pindja' 93
'Karra Mele Ngany-endheni-nö' 221, 228–231, 234–238
'Karra Ngadja-maka Nga-bindja-ng Ngami' 94, 121–122, 153
'Karra-ve Kanya-verver' 240–241, 255–258, 276–280
'Karra Yeri-ngina' 91, 281, 283, 347, 350–351. *See also* Headache Dreaming (Pumut)
Karri-ngindji [Ma-yawa Dreaming site] 356, 366, 378, 384, 389
'Karri-ngindji' [song] 358, 388–392, 405–407
Katherine region 31, 33–34, 36
Kenbi Dancers 31, 35, 93
kigatiya. *See* Dreaming sites (*kigatiya*)
Kimberley region 23, 33, 36, 38, 157
King, George 31, 33
Kinyirr [Dreaming site] 282
'Kinyirr' [song] 85, 283, 335–336, 347
Kiyuk people 23, 32
Kofod, Frances 40, 284–285, 302, 318

Kriol 66, 77
Kubuwemi [place] 282, 317, 329–331, 362
'Kubuwemi' [song] 85, 213, 283, 298, 302–304, 326–327, 349–350, 351
Kundjil family 57
Kundjil, Les 24, 26, 32, 34, 40–42, 219–221, 242, 272, 274–275, 281–284, 298–299, 302, 305, 309–310, 315, 324, 326–329, 350–352, 353–354, 361
Kungiung, Charles 26, 28, 40–42, 356–357
Kungiung family 57, 284
Kungiung, Martin Warrigal 26, 28, 283, 302, 310, 311, 313, 320, 324, 350, 361–362
Kungiung, Maurice Ngulkur Warrigal 281
Kungiung, Ned Narjic 351
Kungiung, Thomas 26, 40, 42, 282–285, 292–295, 297–298, 300, 302, 307, 309, 315, 317, 319, 324, 350–354, 359
Kunmanggurr. *See* Rainbow Serpent Dreaming (Kanamgek, Kunmanggurr)
Kununurra 23, 33, 34, 40, 219, 357
Kuy 23

L

Lambudju (Bobby Lane). *See* Lane, Bobby Lambudju
Lambudju, Jack 239
Lambudju's *wangga* 239–280
'Lame Fella' 49, 61–62, 157, 192–197, 211–214, 217, 236
land claims 31–32, 140
Lane, Bobby Lambudju 26, 32, 35, 218, 238, 242, 244, 248, 266, 269, 275, 279. *See also* Lambudju's *wangga*
language of *wangga* 65–90
Larrakiya people 30–33, 36, 152
Laurence, Allan 47, 158, 175, 192
'Lerri' 206–209, 211–214, 217
lerri songs. *See* happy (*lerri*) songs
Lhambumen [place] 282, 326
'Lhambumen' [song] 85, 213, 283, 326–328, 347, 350–351, 353
'Lima Rak-pe' 240–241, 270–271, 276, 278
'Limila Karrawala' 240–241, 275, 278, 280
liminality 27, 39, 56, 100, 272, 388
Lippo, Agnes 27
Lippo, Audrey 260, 278
Lippo, Tommy 95, 218
lirrga genre 23, 27, 29, 36–39, 41, 48, 56, 65, 89, 212, 281
Lyons, Tommy Imabulk 31

M

Maddock, Ken 33
Malak Malak people 23
Malakunda. *See* Birrarri, Joe Malakunda
malh. See ritual cries (*mahl*)
Malhimanyirr. *See* Junglefowl Dreaming (Malhimanyirr)
'Malhimanyirr No. 1' 407
'Malhimanyirr No. 2' 357
'Malhimanyirr' [song] 55, 90, 358, 381–384, 404–405, 426
Malvak, Aguk 239, 253, 269, 278
Manbi, George 95
Mandji, Billy. *See also* Mandji's *wangga*
   lineage 26, 32, 218, 247, 279
   repertory and performances 35, 45, 49, 56, 69, 156, 159, 164, 213, 216, 221–222, 233–235, 237, 253, 286, 413–415
   song dreaming 195
   transmission of songs 218, 224–226
Mandji's *wangga* 219–237
Mandorah 31, 34–35, 66, 93, 155–156, 159, 164, 172, 218, 223, 225, 227, 240, 247–248, 261, 418
Man.guna, Robert 219, 221, 233–235, 237–238. *See also* 'Robert Man.guna's Song'
Manpurr, Mosek 32–33, 95
Maralung, Alan 23
Marett, Allan 43, 50, 52–53, 218, 220, 248, 265, 267, 273, 327–328, 327–329, 331, 343, 357, 389, 396, 398
Marranunggu people 23, 77–78, 83
Marri Ammu language group
   ceremonies and performances 38–39, 83, 282, 302, 365, 378
   country 23, 56–57, 65, 77, 83, 318, 356, 366, 372, 381, 384, 388, 392
   dance 83, 282
   Dreaming and Dreaming sites 56–57, 356, 366, 384, 388, 392, 407–408
   history 66
   language 26, 36, 41, 65–70, 72, 77–78, 83–88
   lineages 355
   song-giving ghosts 23, 355, 384
   songmen 26, 41, 69, 355
   wangga 38, 57, 69, 76, 83, 85, 167, 318, 359–360
Marri Dan language group 23
Marri Ngarr language group 23, 36, 38–39, 65–66, 77–78, 83, 89, 281, 302, 305

Marrithiyel language group 23, 40, 77, 83
Marri Tjavin language group
   ceremonies and performances 38, 41, 219, 282
   country 23, 39, 65, 66, 83, 234, 282, 307
   dance 62, 282, 302
   Dreaming and Dreaming sites 304, 337, 355
   history 66
   language 25–26, 33, 35–36, 38, 65, 67–70, 72, 77–78, 83–90, 165, 219, 228, 234, 247, 297, 305, 313, 346, 360
   lineage 247, 281, 356
   song-giving ghosts 23, 384
   songmen 25–26, 32, 41, 83, 281, 355
   wangga 26, 32, 56, 76, 83, 167, 234, 237, 281, 309–310, 334, 359–360, 407
maruy 36, 255. *See also* meri-men.gu; sweat
Matige langauge group 23, 38–39, 302, 343
'Ma-vindivindi' 358, 384–388, 405, 407
Ma-yawa (Old Man) Dreaming 318, 362, 365–371, 398–403
Ma-yawa *wangga* 355–408
Melpi, Leo 15, 24
Melville Island 147
Mendhe 77–83
Mendheyangal people 23, 30, 32–33, 65–66, 69, 77–78, 83, 155, 226
Menggani (Butterfly Dreaming) 90, 371. *See also* 'Menggani' [song]
'Menggani' [song] 371–372, 404–405, 407
meri-men.gu 36. *See also* sweat
metre 49, 54, 65
   Barrtjap's *wangga* 100, 151–153
   Mandji's *wangga* 236
   Muluk's *wangga* 213
Mica Beach 35, 47, 49, 79–80, 93, 155–163, 174–175, 192, 195
Mileru, Philip 33, 219
Milik Beach 135
Miller, Gretchen 50, 224, 265, 273
'Mirrwana' 57, 283, 313–316, 318, 347, 350–351
missions. *See* Roman Catholic missions
modality (melodic) 56–58, 67–68, 73–75, 79, 81–82, 86, 88–89
   Barrtjap's *wangga* 152
   Lambudju's *wangga* 277–278
   Mandji's *wangga* 237
   Ma-yawa *wangga* 407–408
   Muluk's *wangga* 214
   Walakandha *wangga* 349–351
Moreen, Ginger 95

Moreen, Rusty Benmele 26, 33, 239–243, 245, 247, 259, 269–270, 275–279
Mosek. *See* Manpurr, Mosek
Moyle, Alice 32–33, 52, 81, 92, 94, 155–157, 159, 164–166, 172, 174, 178, 193, 209, 218, 221–223, 225–227, 231, 233, 242, 244, 257, 261, 269–270
Moyle River 83, 282, 331, 334–335
Moyle, Tommy 288
'Mubagandi' 25, 35, 56, 77, 241, 271–273, 274, 278, 280
Mullumbuk family 42
Mullumbuk, Marlip Philip 24, 26, 40, 42, 46, 85–86, 88–89, 237, 281, 283–284, 328
Mullumbuk, Stan 26, 40, 42, 45, 57, 85, 91, 214, 281–282, 282–291
Muluk, Jimmy
   ceremonies and performances 31, 33, 35, 38, 46, 155–156, 159, 164, 167, 218, 227, 352
   country 155, 174
   dance 253, 286
   family 175
   song creation 46, 57, 66, 209–211, 214–215, 236–237, 238, 286, 292, 294, 338, 346, 348
   song transmission 156, 159, 165–166, 205, 219, 247
Muluk's *wangga* 26, 32–33, 35, 45, 49, 69, 155–218, 212, 352, 406
Munggulu, George 95, 130
Munggum 281, 307–308, 332
Munggumurri 85, 281, 332–333
Mun.gi, Nym 239, 245, 255
Murgenella 140
Murriny Patha language group
   ceremonies 36
   ceremonies and performances 38–39, 329
   country 38–39
   Dreaming and Dreaming sites 172, 375
   history 38
   language 36–37, 66, 83, 378
   wangga 23, 38, 281
musical analysis
   Barrtjap's *wangga* 149–153
   Lambudju's *wangga* 276–280
   Mandji's *wangga* 233–238
   Ma-yawa *wangga* 404–408
   Muluk's *wangga* 209–218
   Walakandha *wangga* 346
musical traditions 26. *See also* conventions of *wangga*

mythology. *See* Dreaming (*altjira, durlk, ngirrwat*); *See* Dreaming sites (*kigatiya*)

N

Nadirri [place] 29, 83, 85, 282, 286, 305, 307, 331, 336. *See also* Kubuwemi [place]
'Nadirri' [song] 40, 283, 302, 306, 309–310, 322, 347, 350
Nama, Alan 218
Na-Pebel [place] 395–396
'Na-Pebel' [song] 356–358, 395–399, 404–405, 407
'Naya Rradja Bangany Nye-ve' 93–94, 129–135, 150, 153
Nemarluk, Edward 288, 302
'Nga-ngat-pat-pa Mangalimba' 94, 144–147
Ngan'gikurunggurr people 23
Ngan'gityemerri language group 41
'Ngaya Lima Bangany-nyaya' 93–94
Ngenawurda, Honorata 85, 323
Ngen'giwumirri language group 23
'Nginimb-andja' 281–282, 289–292
ngirrwat. *See* Dreaming (*altjira, durlk, ngirrwat*)
Ngulkur, Maurice Tjakurl
   ceremonies and performances 28, 52, 53–57, 62, 302, 361, 366, 370, 372, 375
   country and Dreamings 378, 381–382, 392, 395, 398
   dance 62, 281, 302
   song creation 26, 41, 46, 57, 91, 317, 359–360, 362, 405–408
   song transmission 355
   wangga 40, 45, 49, 356–362
Ngumali 85, 282, 334–335
Ngunbe, Gemma 292
Ngurndul family. *See* Kundjil family
ngutj. *See* ghosts: *ngutj* (ghosts in Emmi-Mendhe)
Ninnal, Cyril 41
Niwilhi. *See* Brinken, Charlie Niwilhi ('Charlie Port Keats')
northern Australia and Northern Territory 25–26, 30–31, 35–36, 42, 45, 93, 155–157, 205, 219, 226, 253, 355, 357, 381
North Peron Island (Badjalarr) 54, 72, 77, 205, 240–245, 247–248, 253–257, 260, 269–270, 275–280. *See also* Peron Islands; 'Rak Badjalarr' [song]
number four leg 86, 178–180, 183–185, 228, 253, 286–287, 315, 384–388

'Nyala Nga-ve Bangany' 93, 94
'Nyere-nye Bangany Nyaye' 94, 120–121, 150–151, 153, 270
'Nyere-nyere Lima Kaldja' 94, 118–119, 149–151

O

Old Man Dreaming. *See* Ma-yawa (Old Man) Dreaming
'Old Man Tulh' [song]. *See* 'Wulumen Tulh'
orthography 37, 70–71
oysters 72, 243–244, 246–247, 260

P

painting 356, 364, 402
painting up. *See* body painting
pastoral industry 33
Pelhi [place] 85, 282, 311–312. *See also* 'Yen-milhi No. 1'
Peppimenarti 40, 42–43, 53, 223, 237, 310, 311, 355, 357, 362, 366
performance conventions 45–63
Peron Islands 65, 261. *See also* North Peron Island (Badjalarr); South Peron Island (Barakbana)
Perrederr 65, 83, 282, 331
Piarlum, Ambrose 28, 40–41, 51, 54–55, 284–285, 291, 302, 336, 343, 361
'Piyamen.ga' 46, 55, 62, 157, 178–192, 197, 210–217, 228, 237, 348, 352
Point Charles 30, 66
Port Keats. *See* Wadeye
Pott, Brucie 95
Prince of Wales (son of George King) 31, 95
'Puliki' 47, 49, 55–56, 62, 79, 157–165, 167
'Pumandjin' 157, 174–177, 210–212, 214, 223
Pumurriyi [place] 282, 318, 372, 399
'Pumurriyi' [song] 85, 283, 302, 318, 321, 346, 350
Pumut (Headache Dreaming). *See* Headache Dreaming (Pumut)

R

Rainbow Serpent Dreaming (Kanamgek, Kun-manggurr) 375
Rak Badjalarr [CD] 205, 242, 248, 269
'Rak Badjalarr' [song] 54, 72, 240–248, 270, 275–280. *See also* Peron Islands
Rankin, Douglas 241, 257

Rankin, Nipper 95
reciprocity. *See* ceremonial reciprocity
recordings 23, 25–26, 32–36, 40–41, 45, 56
    Barrtjap's *wangga* 93–94, 102, 108, 129, 152
    Lambudju's *wangga* 239, 241, 248–249
    Mandji's *wangga* 219
    Ma-yawa *wangga* 355, 357–358
    Muluk's *wangga* 155–157, 205, 221, 237
    Walakandha *wangga* 282, 284–285, 292, 300, 302–303, 325, 338, 348
Red Cliff. *See* Banakula (Red Cliff)
Reilly, Lesley 284, 286
repertories of *wangga*. *See wangga* repertories
repetition and truncation of text 53, 108, 153, 216, 223, 259, 263, 346, 365
rhyme 76, 114
rhythmic modes
    Barrtjap's *wangga* 150–152
    conventions of 26, 45–49, 58–60
    Lambudju's *wangga* 276–277
    Mandji's *wangga* 234–237
    Ma-yawa *wangga* 405–407
    Muluk's *wangga* 210–214
    Walakandha *wangga* 347–350
ritual cries (*mahl*)
    Barrtjap's *wangga* 96, 135
    Lambudju's *wangga* 247, 274
    Mandji's *wangga* 233
ritual leaders and specialists 37, 41, 46, 93, 281, 324
ritual washing (*kapuk*) 13, 27–30, 100, 105, 130, 262
'Robert Man.guna's Song' 221, 233, 235, 237–238. *See also* Man.guna, Robert
Roman Catholic missions 36–38, 66
'Rtadi-thawara' 61–62, 157, 197–205, 210–214, 217
Rtadi-wunbirri [place] 343–345, 356
'Rtadi-wunbirri' [song] 85, 358, 365–371, 406–408
Rtidim 282, 315

S

salt water 29, 87, 356, 388, 391–392. *See also* wudi-puminiry (spring); fresh water
Sea Breeze Dreaming. *See* Tjerri
Simpson, Colin 29, 262
Singh, Johnny 156
smoke, purification by 25, 27
social change and *wangga* 23, 29–43, 135. *See also* endangered languages

social relationships. *See* ceremonial reciprocity
song creation (dreaming songs) 23, 25, 27, 32, 36, 68, 83. *See also* song-giving ghosts; transmission of *wangga*
    Barrtjap's *wangga* 93, 96, 105, 108, 121, 147, 149
    Lambudju's *wangga* 255, 260, 263, 272
    Mandji's *wangga* 222, 234, 237
    Ma-yawa *wangga* 281
    Walakandha *wangga* 285–286, 317, 323–324, 328, 331, 343
'Song from Anson Bay' 221, 231–232, 234–236, 238
song-giving ghosts. *See* ghosts: song-giving ghosts
songmen (*medjakarr, ngalinangga*) 23, 25–26, 29, 31–32, 34–35, 40–42, 46–47, 52, 56, 63, 65–66, 68–69, 75–76, 80, 83, 88, 90
    Barrtjap's *wangga* 93, 96, 100–102, 125, 135, 149, 153
    Lambudju's *wangga* 242–243, 253, 261, 267
    Mandji's *wangga* 221, 233–234, 237, 239
    Ma-yawa *wangga* 355
    Muluk's *wangga* 155, 178, 193, 205, 219
    Walakandha *wangga* 285, 286, 292, 302, 324
songs, inherited 25, 26–27, 32, 35, 57, 93, 219, 221, 226, 234, 239, 242–243, 253, 278, 355. *See also* transmission of *wangga*
song structure
    Barrtjap's *wangga* 149
    Mandji's *wangga* 233
    Ma-yawa *wangga* 404
    Muluk's *wangga* 209
    Walakandha *wangga* 346
songs with hidden meanings 135–136, 155–156, 159, 165, 172, 193, 197, 242, 259, 261–262, 266–267, 270–271, 281, 305, 307, 356, 392
song texts 49, 55, 65–92
sorcery 259, 262
southern Daly region 32–33
South Peron Island (Barakbana) 135, 249. *See also* Peron Islands
spelling. *See* orthography
spirit language. *See* ghost language
Stanner, WEH 29, 36–40, 375
Strehlow, TGH 375
sweat 26, 56. *See also* meri-men.gu; *maruy*

T

taboos 27
Talc Head 34, 93, 174
teaching songs. *See* transmission of *wangga*
tempo 26, 47–49, 52, 54–55, 58–60, 62
    Barrtjap's *wangga* 100, 106, 132, 138, 151–152
    Lambudju's *wangga* 276, 279–280
    Mandji's *wangga* 223, 225, 233, 235–236, 238
    Ma-yawa *wangga* 378, 405
    Muluk's *wangga* 195, 212–214, 216
    Walakandha *wangga* 293, 347–349, 352–353
terminating patterns 45
text structure
    Barrtjap's *wangga* 149
    Mandji's *wangga* 234
    Ma-yawa *wangga* 346
    Muluk's *wangga* 209–210
    Walakandha *wangga* 276
Thalhi-ngatjpirr (Fish Dreaming site) 392–394
'Thalhi-ngatjpirr' [song] 357–358, 392–394, 404–405, 407
Thardim, Raphael 310
'Thidha nany' 283, 302, 319–320, 347, 350
Tiwi Islands 143
'Tjagawala' 281, 283, 298, 302, 321–322, 347, 350, 353
'Tjendabalhatj' 241, 262, 277, 278, 280
'Tjerrendet' 240–241, 261, 276–278, 277
Tjerri (Sea Breeze Dreaming) 49, 372–377
'Tjerri' [song] 45, 356, 358, 372–378, 405–407
'Tjinbarambara' 57, 157, 164–167, 209, 211–212
Tjindi 366, 371, 388, 392, 395
'Tjinmel' 336
tjiwilirr. *See* Hairy Cheeky Yam Dreaming (*tjiwilirr*)
Tjulatji 239, 253, 269
totems and totemic sites 27, 29, 39, 56–57, 80, 85, 155, 165, 167, 195, 197, 228, 281, 337–338, 356, 381–384. *See also* Dreaming (*altjira, durlk, ngirrwat*); Dreaming sites (*kigatiya*)
tourist coroborees. *See* coroborees: coroborees for tourists
trade songs 36, 38
transcriptions 40–41, 52, 54, 68, 70–71, 106, 111, 129, 143, 152, 226, 231, 233
transmission of *wangga* 25, 31–32, 35–36, 42, 57, 86. *See also* song-giving ghosts; songs, inherited
    Barrtjap's *wangga* 93, 129–130

Lambudju's *wangga* 243, 248, 255, 267, 269, 272, 277–278
Mandji's *wangga* 220, 239
Ma-yawa *wangga* 355, 357
Muluk's *wangga* 164, 220
Treloyn, Sally 34–35, 40–41, 242, 248, 356–357, 393
truncation of text. *See* repetition and truncation of text
'Truwu' [A/B melody] 57, 283, 309, 332, 350–352
'Truwu' [A melody] 57, 283, 307–308, 332, 350–352
Truwu beach 282, 286, 307, 315–316, 319
'Truwu' [B melody] 57, 283, 302, 309–310, 332, 350–352
Tulh. *See* 'Wulumen Tulh'
Two Fella Creek 260

V

vocables 25, 41, 54, 68–69, 71, 76. *See also* ghost language
　Barrtjap's *wangga* 100, 105, 114, 129, 135, 138, 144, 149, 151
　Lambudju's *wangga* 239–240, 244, 272, 276, 279
　Mandji's *wangga* 219, 223, 225–226, 228, 231, 233–234, 236, 238
　Muluk's *wangga* 197, 205–206, 209–210
　Walakandha *wangga* 286–287, 297
vocal sections, conventions of 25–26, 45–47, 55
vocal timbre. *See* voice quality
vocatives 89, 306
voice quality 56, 63, 164, 236

W

Wadeye 23, 27, 34, 69, 219, 266, 292, 305, 317, 318, 323, 359, 361, 364, 375, 398, 402
　ceremonies 24, 28–29, 36–37, 39, 41, 43, 50–51, 53, 56, 212, 214, 237, 281, 286, 288, 309, 311, 315, 355–357, 361–362. *See also* ceremonial reciprocity
　country 38, 83, 234, 247, 284, 389, 396
　history 36–40
　language 65–66, 83
　songmen 26, 38, 56, 220, 272, 327, 343
　wangga 25–26, 27, 29, 32, 33, 39–43, 45, 59, 155, 247, 281–282, 302–303, 327–329, 331, 343, 352, 357, 378. *See also* Ma-yawa *wangga*; Walakandha *wangga*

Wadeye Aboriginal Language Centre 302
Wadeye Aboriginal Sound Archive 219, 302, 323
Wadjiginy people. *See also* Belyuen (Delissaville)
　country 30, 32, 66, 77, 140–141, 152, 242–243, 253, 255
　language 23, 26, 65, 77
　songmen 31–33, 69, 76, 93, 193, 219
　wangga 33, 36, 239
'Wak' 57, 157, 167–172, 210–212, 214
Wak, Bob. *See* Jongmin, Bob Wak
Walakandha ancestors 281–282, 300, 307, 326, 332
Walakandha ceremonies 281–286, 293, 303, 306, 309, 311, 313, 315, 317, 320, 324, 328–329, 334
'Walakandha Ngindji' 356–360, 405–407
'Walakandha No. 1' 283, 302, 306, 310
'Walakandha No. 2' 283, 317
'Walakandha No. 3' 283
'Walakandha No. 4' 283, 307
'Walakandha No. 5' 283, 353
'Walakandha No. 6' 282, 286–287, 287, 289, 352
'Walakandha No. 7' 282, 291–293, 295
'Walakandha No. 8' 282–283, 286, 292–294, 302, 348
'Walakandha No. 8a' 283, 285–286, 293–294, 352
'Walakandha No. 8b' 283, 294–295, 352
'Walakandha No. 9' 292, 295, 348
'Walakandha No. 9a' 283, 295–297, 298, 348–349, 352
'Walakandha No. 9b' 283, 296–297, 352
Walakandha *wangga* 281–318
'Walingave' 241, 266–267, 277–278
Walsh, Michael 284, 348
wangga conventions. *See* conventions of *wangga*
wangga, history of 29–43
wangga repertories. *See* Barrtjap's *wangga*; *See* Lambudju's *wangga*; *See* Mandji's *wangga*; *See* Ma-yawa *wangga*; *See* Muluk's *wangga*
Warrigal. *See* Kungiung, Martin Warrigal
'Watjen-danggi' 356, 358, 378–381, 395, 405–406, 407
'Wedjiwurang' 46, 85–86, 89, 91, 284, 337–344, 348
Wilha. *See* Hairy Cheeky Yam Dreaming (Wilha)
'Winmedje' 74, 241, 260, 277, 278, 280

women
  society of 378
  song creation and transmission 25, 89, 305
  women's dance 49–50, 75, 174–175, 178, 223, 249, 263, 265, 356
Woodie, David 95
Woodie, Harold 95
Woodie, Maggie 130
Woody, Jacky 218
'Wörörö' 157, 172–174, 209, 211–212, 214, 294
Worumbu, Colin. *See* Ferguson, Colin Worumbu
wudi-pumininy (spring) 90–91, 343, 356, 388, 391
'Wulumen Kimi-gimi' 358, 365–366, 404–405, 407
'Wulumen Tulh' 318, 356–357, 398–404
wunymalang (ghosts in Batjamalh). *See* ghosts: *wunymalang* (ghosts in Batjamalh)
Wurrpen, Lawrence 33–34, 93–94, 132, 153, 241, 243, 245, 248, 276, 278–280
Wutjelli (ancestor) 281, 287–288, 300–301, 315–316
'Wutjelli No. 1' [song] 283, 315–316, 347, 350, 353
'Wutjelli No. 2' [song] 282, 287–288, 315, 347–348, 350

Y

'Ya Bangany-nyung Nga-bindja Yagarra' 94, 96–100, 150–152
'Yagarra Bangany Nye-ngwe' 94, 113–114, 150
'Yagarra Delhi Nya-ngadja-barra-ngarrka' 75, 94, 142–144, 150, 152–153, 213
'Yagarra Delhi Nye-bindja-ng Barra Ngarrka' 151
'Yagarra Nedja Tjine Rak-pe' 94, 135–137, 140, 149–151, 270
'Ya[garra] Nga-bindja-ng Nga-mi' 75, 94, 108–112, 114, 149–152
'Yagarra Nga-bindja-ng Nga-mi Ngayi' 94, 100–101, 140, 150–151
'Yagarra Tjine Rak-pe' 94, 141–142, 150–151
'Yagarra Tjüt Balk-nga-me Nga-mi' 75, 94, 100, 140–141, 150–151
'Yagarra Ye-yenenaya' 94, 125–129, 151
'Ya Rembe Ngaya Lima Ngaya' 94, 138–140, 150, 153
Yarrowin, Roger (Rossie) 25–26, 31–32, 34–35, 56–57, 77, 108, 115, 241–242, 268, 272–274, 277, 280

Yederr 23, 326, 343
Yendili Hill 83, 87, 282, 304–305, 323–324, 326, 332–334
'Yendili No. 1' 213, 283, 298, 302–305, 326
'Yendili No. 2' 89, 283, 305–306
'Yendili No. 3' 283, 298, 305, 325–326
'Yendili No. 4' 283, 298, 305, 328–329
'Yendili No. 5' 85–86, 281, 283, 323–325
'Yendili No. 6' 283, 292, 295, 297–300, 352
'Yene yene' 284, 348
Yenmilhi Hill 83, 282, 311–312
'Yenmilhi No. 1' 281–282, 311–312, 347, 349–350, 405
'Yenmilhi No. 2' 283, 292, 300–302, 347–348, 350, 352–353
Yenmungirini (Headache Dreaming site) 85, 88, 282, 331–332
'Yerre Ka-bindja-maka Ka-mi' 94, 123–125, 150